GOOD

WIFE

WISE

MOTHER

TAIWAN

AND THE WORLD

William Lavely,

Madeleine Yue Dong,

James Lin

SERIES EDITORS

Fang Yu Hu

GOOD WIFE

WIFE

✳

WISE

MOTHER

Educating

Han Taiwanese

under

Japanese Rule

UNIVERSITY OF WASHINGTON PRESS   SEATTLE

Good Wife, Wise Mother was made possible in part by funding from the Taiwan Studies Program, a division of the Henry M. Jackson School of International Studies at the University of Washington.

Additional support for this publication was provided by the Chiang Ching-kuo Foundation for International Scholarly Exchange and by the Department of History and College of Arts and Sciences at the University of Tennessee at Chattanooga.

Copyright © 2024 by the University of Washington Press

Design by Mindy Basinger Hill / Composed in FreightText Pro

This book will be made open access within three years of publication thanks to Path to Open, a program developed to bring about equitable access and impact for the entire scholarly community, including authors, researchers, libraries, and university presses around the world. Learn more at https://about.jstor.org/path-to-open/.

UNIVERSITY OF WASHINGTON PRESS *uwapress.uw.edu*

LIBRARY OF CONGRESS CATALOGING-IN-PUBLICATION DATA

Names: Hu, Fang Yu, author.

Title: Good wife, wise mother : educating Han Taiwanese girls under Japanese rule / Fang Yu Hu.

Description: Seattle : University of Washington Press, [2024] | Series: Taiwan and the world | Includes bibliographical references and index.

Identifiers: LCCN 2023050770 | ISBN 9780295752631 (hardcover ; acid-free paper) | ISBN 9780295752648 (paperback ; acid-free paper) | ISBN 9780295752655 (ebook)

Subjects: LCSH: Education—Taiwan—History—To 1945. | Education—Japan—Colonies—History. | Women—Taiwan—Effect of education on. | Women—Taiwan—Social conditions—History. | Taiwan—Civilization—Japanese influences. | Japan—Taiwan—Colonies. | Sex differences in education—Japan. | Feminism—Japan—History. | Women's rights—Japan—History. | Sex role—Japan—History.

Classification: LCC LA1136.H836 2024 | DDC 371.8220951249/09041—dc23/eng/20240531

LC record available at https://lccn.loc.gov/2023050770

This paper meets the requirements of ANSI/NISO Z39.48-1992 (Permanence of Paper).

❋

FOR MY

SOLE LIVING

GRANDMOTHER,

Hsing,

AND

ALL MY

grandparents

WHO HAVE

PASSED

CONTENTS

ACKNOWLEDGMENTS   ix

NOTES ON TERMINOLOGY AND TRANSLATION   xiii

INTRODUCTION   Contextualizing Taiwan   1

1   Institutionalizing Girls' Education   21

2   Embracing Educated Girls and Women   60

3   Mobilizing for the War   91

4   Remaking the Home   132

5   Colonial Nostalgia   170

GLOSSARY   211

NOTES   213

BIBLIOGRAPHY   253

INDEX   273

ACKNOWLEDGMENTS

This book is a culmination of a personal and intellectual journey that traces its roots to my undergraduate studies and takes shape in graduate school. Intrigued by the ubiquitous use of Japanese words and consumption of Japanese food in my family while growing up first in Taiwan and then in the United States, as an undergraduate I researched Japanese colonial education to understand my grandparents' childhood and young adulthood. After completing a master's thesis on the "modern woman" concept in colonial Taiwan, I began a doctoral dissertation on colonial education and gender at the University of California, Santa Cruz. Research trips to Taiwan after completing my dissertation led to the creation of this book, which remains Taiwan-centric but with more nuanced and fascinating perspectives.

Starting with Gail Hershatter, people at the University of California, Santa Cruz, have made this book possible. Gail's dedication to and support for my Taiwan-centric project means much beyond words. In addition to her groundbreaking and phenomenal scholarship that has inspired the approaches I have taken in this book, Gail's teaching and mentorship have trained me to be a conscientious and compassionate teacher and mentor, which informed my scholarship. I am also deeply indebted to Alan Christy, Noriko Aso, and the late Emily Honig for their mentorship and pedagogy. I thank Alice Yang and Minghui Hu for shaping the inception of this book. The intellectual and collegial community that started with Jeremy Tai, Dustin Wright, Michael Jin, Carla Takaki-Richardson, Amanda Shuman, Shelly Chan, Stephanie Chan, Yajun Mo, and Nellie Chu at UC Santa Cruz has provided invaluable support and care. This UC Santa Cruz community grew to include Angelina Chin, Alexander "Sasha" Day, Xiaoping Sun, Ana Maria Candela, Wenqing Kang, Xiaofei Gao, Stephanie Montgomery, and Melissa Brzycki.

I am indebted to many in Taiwan. Dr. Jungwon Jin's guidance provided much comfort during my first research residency in Taiwan. Dr. Yu Chienming's research and advice have been crucial to my research questions and to the methods used in this book. Besides her research advice, I thank Professor Hsu Pei-hsien for letting me audit her graduate seminar at the National Taiwan Normal University, where I learned much about the field and networked with young scholars from Taiwan and Japan. Many thanks to the Institute of Taiwan History at Academia Sinica and the Research Association of the Educational History of Taiwan (Taiwan jiaoyu shi yanjiu hui) for inviting me to present my work. Although they were brief exchanges, Dr. Hsu Hsueh-chi, Professor Wan-yao Chou, Dr. Chen Peifeng, and Dr. Lung-chih Chang have provided encouragement for my project. I am grateful to the Institute of Taiwan History for expanding my network with young and seasoned scholars of Taiwan history, whose kindness and assistance have helped make my research go smoothly in Taiwan. It is impossible to name all of them, but I hope you know who you are. Many thanks to librarians at the National Taiwan Library and Academia Sinica.

This book could not have been completed without help from those in Japan. Dr. Hong Yuru (Ko Ikujo) has been and continues to be an incredible mentor and scholar. Professor Go Komei gracefully gifted a valuable source for my book after a brief meeting. I am truly grateful to the Taiwan Association (Taiwan kyōkai) for granting me access to their archive. I sincerely thank the countless public libraries across Japan. Young scholars in Kyushu and Okinawa also provided inspiration for rethinking the Taiwan–Japan connections during and after Japanese colonialism.

As a Taiwan specialist based in the United States, I experience more academic loneliness than other specialists who might find more colleagues in this country. Fortunately, I have received support from colleagues who are not familiar with Taiwan. My colleagues at the Department of History at the University of Tennessee at Chattanooga have been absolutely phenomenal—the works-in-progress workshops and writing retreats have strengthened this project. Mike Thompson always made sure I had the funding needed to conduct research and give presentations as well as the time to write; Will Kuby's advice on my book proposal was invaluable, and his excitement about my project is always encouraging; Kira Robison reviewed the introduction of this book and has provided welcome reassurances throughout; and Susan Eckelmann has commented helpfully on part of a chapter. Shannon McCarragher, Jeremy Strickler, Shawn Trivette, and Ryan Edwards provided encouragement and support for this book at the University of Tennessee at Chattanooga. Big thanks to Jeremy Strickler for suggesting the title of my book. Meetings with old and new acquaintances at various conferences have often highlighted academic interests of this book project, and thus its significance. I also feel fortunate to join a growing community of Taiwan specialists based in the United States.

This project would not be possible without the generous funding from the Fulbright Program, Academia Sinica, University of California Pacific Rim Research Program, Chiang Ching-kuo Foundation, American Association of University Women, and the University of Tennessee at Chattanooga. I am thankful to the Japan Foundation and Critical Language Scholarship for proving the language training and research funding necessary to complete this book project during its early stage.

I am truly indebted to Lorri Hagman, the recently retired executive editor at the University of Washington Press, for expressing a strong interest in my book early on and encouraging me throughout the writing process. I am thankful for the care and energy that the Taiwan and the World series editors and the staff at the University of Washington Press have shown in publishing my book. I am most grateful to the three anonymous reviewers of my manuscript. I was overjoyed to receive comments and suggestions from experts on Taiwan history and Japanese empire who read my book manuscript so closely. Each reviewer provided a different angle that complemented those from other reviewers, which strengthened the book overall. I again thank the anonymous readers of my article published in *Twentieth-Century China*, which forms most of chapter 3 in this book.

I am completely beholden to all the interviewees for this project, many of whom are no longer with us in this world. Regardless of whether I cited their narratives, I was inspired and moved by every interviewee's experience. The tenacity and energy of my grandmother, who represents this generation of Japanese-educated Taiwanese, are limitless. I have dedicated this book to her, my only living grandmother, who has been an inspiration and instrumental in my project since its inception. Without her personal network and accompaniment on some interviews, this book would have

ACKNOWLEDGMENTS

a very limited selection of women's voices and experiences. I thank all of my family members, relatives, friends, acquaintances, and colleagues for introducing me to their grandparents, classmates, neighbors, clients, and informants. I won't acknowledge everyone by name because nearly all of my interviewees wished to be anonymous, likely because they fear political retaliation. Still, I must thank Tseng Ling-yi and Yang Chao-chieh for introducing me to some informants.

Finally, I want to thank my families and friends. My spouse, Jason, has supported this project since its inception while enduring months and years apart at various times. My children, Fred, Eric, and Roselyn, have provided necessary laughter and comfort. My parents, siblings, in-laws, and friends across continents have provided unwavering support, care, and encouragement. While it takes a village to raise a child, it took several communities across states, countries, and continents to finish this work. I am forever grateful to everyone and every institution involved in completing and publishing this book.

NOTES ON TERMINOLOGY
AND TRANSLATION

This book uses the term *Han Taiwanese* to refer to the ethnic Han residents of Taiwan whose ancestors came from Fujian and Guangdong in China before 1945. Regional variations existed in mainland China, and I do not presume that there is one unified set of Han customs and practices. Taiwan's frontier status under the Manchu Qing rule may also have shaped the Han culture in Taiwan differently from that in mainland China. Therefore, I only use the term *Han Chinese* when it applies to mainland China.

To make this work more accessible to modern-day readers, I have translated the following terminologies differently from Patricia Tsurumi, who wrote the first major study on Japanese colonial education in Taiwan: I translate the primary-level school for Japanese children as "Japanese elementary school" (Jp. *shōgakkō*), compared with Tsurumi's "primary school." I translate a school for Han Taiwanese children as "Taiwanese primary school" (Jp. *kōgakkō*), compared with Tsurumi's "common school," which is a literal translation. I translate the girls' secondary education institute as "girls' middle school" (Jp. *jogakkō*), compared with Tsurumi's "girls' higher school," which is a literal translation. However, I translate the "ethics" course (Jp. *shūshin*) the same way as Tsurumi, whereas others might translate it as a "morals" or "civics" course. I sometimes use "imperial ethics" to emphasize the infusion of Japanese history and culture in this course.

Taiwan continues to be a multilingual society, and the romanization of place-names and people's names in this book seeks to reflect historic authenticity and common usage. For major cities in Taiwan, I adopt the common romanization used in Taiwan today. For names of Taiwanese people (except famous people or scholars who have published in English), I adopt the Pinyin system for consistency, which means Mandarin Chinese pronunciation, even though people in Taiwan today do not use it. Also note, I adopt the Pinyin system even though Taiwanese people living under Japanese rule pronounced their names in Japanese or their native language, such as Taiwanese Hoklo, and never Mandarin Chinese. I use the Taiwanese Hoklo *pe̍h-ōe-jī* romanization to write certain key terms said by my interviewees because most interviews were conducted in Taiwanese Hoklo. I use the Japanese romanization system for school lessons, school names, concepts, and administrative counties that existed during the Japanese period because many of them were renamed or no longer exist.

GOOD

WIFE

WISE

MOTHER

INTRODUCTION

Contextualizing Taiwan

Born in 1930 in Yilan City in eastern Taiwan, Li Que'niang worked as a nurse for forty-four years before her retirement. Her experience was not atypical in Taiwan under Japanese rule (1895–1945), where old Han Taiwanese practices persisted even as new opportunities became available to girls and women:

> My mom gave birth to six children, three boys and three girls; I was the fourth child. . . . my [two] older brothers passed away when I was young. . . . Because of family financial difficulties, both of my younger sisters were given away at a young age. . . . So our household only had three children: my older sister, myself, and my younger brother. . . . My sisters' adopted families didn't send them to school because they . . . were needed to help with chores and babysitting. . . .
> My dad graduated from the National Language School [Jp. Kokugo Gakkō] and worked as a teacher at Karyō [Guoling] Primary School . . . [but later] he also quit [his job]. . . . He started many different business ventures . . . but failed every time. . . . Our livelihood thus depended on my mom making clothes for other people. . . . Mother was very clever. Although she never attended Japanese school, she understood the Japanese language. . . .
> My older sister graduated from the advanced course program [Jp. *kōtōka*] at the primary school [Jp. *kōgakkō kōtōka*] . . . and wanted to take the entrance exam to get into Ranyō [Lanyang] Girls' Middle School [Jp. Ranyō Kōtō Jogakkō] when it first opened, but our

family finances couldn't afford it. . . . After I [also] graduated from the advanced course program at the primary school, I had to work to support my family. Those who graduated in the top five of the class had the opportunity to work at the City Municipal Office. Including me, three of us were assigned to work at the Food Bureau. . . . But we later passed the exam to Yilan Provincial Hospital [in 1946 with Japan-trained Taiwanese physicians and the same Japanese curriculum] and received the training of assistant nurse, and then worked at Yilan Hospital.[1]

Taiwan under Japanese rule was a period of transition and change during which old ideas and practices clashed and blended with new ones under the new regime. The old practice of giving daughters away to reduce parents' financial burden and using girls as babysitters to their younger siblings instead of sending them to school remained dominant in patrilineal Han Taiwanese society, which valued boys more than girls. Some lucky girls attended primary school, but they had to continue to perform household labor and contribute to the family income after graduation. Although limited to those from elite and upper-middle-class families, more educational opportunities became available to girls than under Manchu Qing rule (1683–1895), and educated girls became more visible in public in schools, offices, and other settings. Japanese education had a lasting impact on postwar Taiwanese society, and Li's experiences illustrate the opportunities and limitations that Han Taiwanese customs and Japanese colonialism involved for girls and women.

This book investigates the creation, implementation, and impact of Japanese colonial education in Taiwan by examining gender, ethnicity, and socioeconomic status. Focusing on the Han population, the ethnic majority in Taiwan, and viewing it through the lens of girls' education, this book highlights Taiwan's uniqueness as a colonial crossroads between Han Taiwanese customs and Japanese ideas and practices. An examination of "good wife, wise mother" (Jp. *ryōsai kenbo*), a gender-specific ideal propagated by the Japanese reformers at the turn of the twentieth century, shows that some Han Taiwanese embraced *dōka*, the Japanese assimilation project, by navigating through old Han Taiwanese and new Japanese ideas and practices as well as ideas from the New Culture Movement in China.[2] The various interpretations of *dōka* and the instability of the "good wife, wise mother" ideal reveal the inherent contradictions in colonial discourses like *dōka*, which simultaneously promoted inclusion and exclusion. By focusing on the experiences of Taiwanese schoolgirls and Taiwanese responses to Japanese educational policies and gender ideals, this book argues that *dōka* reinforced gender division and ethnic hierarchy, with uneven effects on women of different backgrounds. This continued from the onset of colonization until the wartime period, when ethnic hierarchy became blurry even while gender division remained. It shows that education was not an elite privilege. Even though it reinforced elite privilege over the lower classes, education offered more work opportunities for the lower classes. Although the Japanese colonizers succeeded in persuading many Taiwanese to educate their daughters, such education took place under a political system that presupposed a colonial hierarchy based on ethnic divisions in a society already permeated by Han Taiwanese customs characterized by a hierarchical gender sphere ideology. *Dōka* was always gendered, as gender expectations were fundamental to its foundation and success. In short, both top-down and bottom-up factors limited the growth and influence of girls' education in Taiwan and in Taiwanese women's lives. Nonetheless, the hybrid "good wife, wise mother" ideal of the Japanese educational system helped develop Taiwan's postwar economy and form a distinct identity.

Although colonial officials seemed to have complete control over the educational system, the divergent interpretations of the "good wife, wise mother" ideal in official and nonofficial sources and the uneven effects on educated girls and women revealed in oral histories and interviews suggest that, as old practices persisted, the colonial state was less powerful and absolute than some might have presumed. Moreover, although the colonial state sought to assimilate as many Taiwanese as possible of all socioeconomic backgrounds through *dōka*, only 10 percent of all students completed their primary education in the forty years following the establishment of Taiwanese primary schools.[3] Instead of explaining factors that contributed to the low number of educated girls and women under the Japanese system, this book focuses on the impact this education had on Taiwanese women and society. Even though only a minority of women were educated by the end of Japanese rule, Japanese education reached girls and women of all socioeconomic backgrounds, and this book examines the significance of girls' education for several groups in Taiwan. It is without question that this gendered, colonial education produced a lasting legacy on many Han Taiwanese women and their households into the postwar, (post)colonial period under the authoritarian Chinese Nationalist one-party rule (1945–89/91) and since democratization to this day.

GENDERED ASSIMILATION IN THE AGE OF NEW IMPERIALISM

Although colonial officials used race and ethnicity as the main markers of political and socioeconomic hierarchy, this book argues that gender remained the most powerful and persistent defining marker of sociopolitical hierarchy in Taiwan. The guiding principle of Japanese colonial education sought to make everyone in the empire "Japanese" by teaching Japanese as the "national language" (Jp. *kokugo*) and inculcating imperial ethics (Jp. *shūshin*).[4] In essence, to become Japanese meant speaking Japanese, being ready to contribute to industrialization, and for male subjects, to be prepared to serve in the military.[5] Becoming a loyal Japanese subject willing to die for the state was the goal of public education in both the metropole and the colonies. Women were integral to *dōka* as "good wives, wise mothers." That meant that a woman should support her husband and educate her children at home with knowledge and skills she had obtained in school. In Japanese colonial thinking the home was important because it was the basis of the nation, and a "good wife, wise mother" was responsible for improving the quality of the home.[6]

Existing studies on *dōka* focus on assimilation based on race, ethnicity, or nationality, erasing the difference that gender creates in shaping the lives of the colonized population. In the nineteenth century, assimilation implemented by colonial officials in many empires presupposed their superiority to the colonized yet promised equality between all races/ ethnicities once assimilation was complete. However, as Homi Bhabha asserts, colonial mimicry, which is an assimilationist behavior, reveals the "desire for a reformed, recognizable Other, as a subject of a difference that is almost the same, but not quite" the same as the colonizers.[7] At the same time, Bhabha observes, "The menace of mimicry is its double vision which in disclosing the ambivalence of colonial discourse also disrupts its authority."[8] This is the inherent contradiction of assimilation—colonizers encouraged it, and many colonized elites desired it so they could be seen and treated as equals; however, as Bhabha asserts, fulfilling this desire meant the destruction of the colonial state by questioning its superiority over the colonized.[9]

Dōka in Taiwan reveals the contradiction in the Japanese implementation of assimilation, which resulted in a dichotomy of inclusion (universal culture, impartiality) and exclusion (legal segregation, discrimination) of the colonial subjects in the "Japanese national family."[10] In his study of Japanese imperialism and nationalism, Komagome Takeshi argues that Japanese leaders ruled the empire through two sets of inherently contradictory policies to implement *dōka*: the "national integration" (Jp. *kokumin tōgō*) that justified discrimination (Jp. *sabetsuka*) based on "consanguineal nationalism" (Jp. *ketsuzoku nashonarizumu*) and the "cultural integration" (Jp. *bunka tōgō*) that proclaimed equality (Jp. *dōitsuka*) based on "linguistic nationalism" (Jp. *gengo nashonarizumu*).[11] He explains that in national integration, Japanese leaders codified everyone's ethnicity through the household registration system, and it could not be changed.[12] In cultural integration, anyone could use *kokugo* (Japanese as the "national language") education to become "civilized" and bond with Japanese people by embracing Japanese modernization, such as cutting the Qing-period Manchu queue hairstyle (i.e., shaving half of one's head and braiding the rest) and popularizing hygienic practices.[13]

Similarly, in her study of *kokugo* education, Eika Tai views legal integration and cultural assimilation as interlocking concepts in governing Taiwan and concludes that this cultural assimilation through the instruction of *kokugo* failed in the end because of the discriminatory legal system.[14] The main legal barrier separating residents of Taiwan from those in the metropole was Law 63. Passed by the Japanese national legislature, the Imperial Diet, in 1896, the law gave the governor-general of Taiwan the sole power to pass laws, which meant that no laws from the metropole were effective without the governor-general's approval.[15] The dichotomy of inclusion and exclusion in *dōka* documented by Komagome and Tai was created by Japan's simultaneous embarkment in nation building and empire building, what Sayaka Chatani calls "nation-empire" building, where *dōka* was essential to the success of building the nation-empire.[16]

Dōka was crucial to building this nation-empire, and colonial officials and settlers blended the concept of modernization and civilization in Taiwan and Korea. Hara Takashi (1856–1921), an advocate of *dōka* in Taiwan in the 1890s who served as Japan's prime minister after World War I, viewed it as "the political, legal, economic, and educational integration of the colony into the metropole" under the *naichi enchō* (extending the mainland) campaign in Korea.[17] In the case of colonial Korea (1910–45), Jun Uchida explains that *dōka* implies "civilization (*bunmeika*), Japanization (*Nihonka* or *Nihonjinka*), imperialization (*shinminka*), and nationalization (*kokuminka*)" where the ultimate goal of *dōka* was the "exportati[on of] Japan's modernizing reforms" by imposing Japanese versions of hygiene, scrupulousness, and civility depending on "Korea's evolving 'cultural level' (*mindo*)."[18] Uchida observes that the education bureau chief in colonial Korea viewed *dōka* as a "civilizing mission" to produce Japanese-proficient, loyal imperial subjects, while the vice governor-general, Yamagata Isaburo (1858–1927), emphasized the making of "industrious and hard-working people."[19] Similar programs were implemented in Taiwan. As Evan Dawley notes, modernization (Jp. *kindaika*) in colonial Taiwan refers to "urbanization, hygiene, scientific methods and rationality, and the ideal of mass participation in politics."[20] Moreover, Chen Peifeng emphasizes that Japanese-language instruction was the driving force behind modernization in Taiwan as Taiwanese confronted cultural domination and grappled with the concepts of civilization imposed by the colonial authority.[21] By examining the discourse around and implementation of the "good wife, wise mother" ideal in Taiwan, this book shows that *dōka* was not only about becoming Japanese but also about becoming modern and "civilized" in the Japanese model.

Japan was a latecomer and the only non-Western empire in the age of imperialism at the turn of the twentieth century. Therefore, to cast itself as a benevolent colonizer to other imperialists and to the colonized population, Japanese leaders showcased modernization efforts in Taiwan—including an island-wide railway system, a hygiene and public health campaign, and mass education. In contrast to most European colonies in Africa and Asia, where only elites received education, Japan's educational programs in Taiwan targeted the entire population, including girls. However, the premise of Japan's "civilizing mission" was similar to that of European colonizers who considered themselves to be the "harbingers of progress and improvement" in modernity.[22] Japanese leaders shared the European belief that the "colonizing power symbolize[s] modernity" to justify further developments in the colonies.[23] They "studied the British and French imperial models and implemented what they saw as an improved version of the French civilizing mission."[24] In other words, Japanese leaders during the Meiji period (1868–1912) did not simply mimic what Europeans did in their colonies; they implemented what they believed would be most beneficial for the nation-empire.

As part of this effort, the gendered, colonial education in Taiwan incorporated the foundational ideas of the recently established Japanese school system. The Meiji school system, which "preserv[ed] cultural traits" while borrowing some foreign ideas, was created when Japanese leaders combined the instructions of morals and Confucianism from old Tokugawa schooling with observations they made during the Iwakura Mission (1871–73) in Europe and the United States.[25] Japanese leaders used this educational system along with compulsory military service and the construction of state Shinto shrines to "inculcat[e] patriotism, loyalty to the emperor, and the virtues of diligence and thrift."[26] Although a national educational system was implemented with the Educational System Order (Jp. Gakusei) in the metropole in 1872 and "a national, standard school language was necessary to effectuate teaching," a standard Japanese language was not created until 1900 with regulations that "establish[ed] a standard script and to condone a standard for readings."[27] Meiji intellectuals connected the Japanese language with "a national past and the identity of the Japanese."[28] If one's proficiency in standard Japanese determined their Japaneseness, then everyone, including Japanese in the metropole, had to attend school to become Japanese. It was in the schools where Meiji reformers sought to "inculcate morality, especially those civic virtues that would mobilize support for the new government in its efforts to save the nation from decline and perhaps conquest."[29]

Guided by the Imperial Rescript on Education (Jp. Kyōiku Chokugo) of 1890 with virtues written in Confucian language, children of all socioeconomic status and gender were required to receive primary education in mainland Japan.[30] However, the multitrack system in secondary and tertiary levels for vocational and technical training and academic schools embodied the existing socioeconomic hierarchy, which "was neither egalitarian nor meritocratic" for many boys and men, and excluded all girls and women.[31] The Education Ministry maintained that gender co-education should end after primary education and that girls and women should have access to different educational opportunities from boys and men in separate public and private secondary and tertiary schools in the metropole. Even after an extension of compulsory education and an expansion of postprimary education in the first three decades of the twentieth century, education remained "elitist" and gender inequality persisted in the metropole.[32] Although Japanese leaders did not call this educational effort *dōka,* the mission of the national education in the metropole resembled that of *dōka* in non-Japanese areas like Taiwan. Therefore, it makes sense that Japanese leaders would continue the classist and gendered education model in colonial Taiwan, except that, in Taiwan, ethnicity was an additional discriminatory factor that intersected with socioeconomic status and gender.

Although Japanese leaders sought to distinguish Japan from other imperial powers by providing similar educational opportunities in the colonies as in the metropole, how the attempt to reinforce racial, ethnic hierarchy by Japanese officials in Taiwan mirrored European colonial officials in Africa speaks to the age of New Imperialism. New Imperialism began in the late nineteenth century, when European powers expanded their empires after industrialization. Japanese leaders believed that imperial expansion would safeguard Japan from Western encroachment. Racial and ethnic segregation was implemented to define roles for different groups in these empires. European colonizers segregated Africans from whites and imposed different policies, including training Africans to be farmers and industrial laborers and mandating that whites receive education.[33] Similarly, the Japanese colonial authority established a segregated educational system in Taiwan to create loyal, Japanese-speaking colonial subjects from the local populations who would become low-level government clerks and Japanese-language teachers while ethnic Japanese would hold higher positions in Taiwan's government and industry.[34] Although education was not compulsory until the wartime period, Japanese residents in Taiwan behaved as if they were in the metropole, where education was compulsory, and had over 90 percent school enrollment rates in 1908, over 93 percent after 1913, and over 98 percent after 1924.[35] With higher enrollment rates, more educational opportunities, and better resources and quality of instruction, educated Japanese occupied higher positions in government bureaucracy, "managerial or other skilled professions" with higher pay in Taiwan.[36]

Japanese leaders began claiming Japanese superiority in civilizing other Asian countries between 1894 and 1905 after several diplomatic and military victories such as the treaty revision with the British (1902) and Japan's victories in the First Sino-Japanese War (1894–95) and the Russo-Japanese War (1904–5).[37] With the decline of China as the center of civilization in East Asia following China's defeat by Great Britain in the Opium War (1839–42) and Japan's self-proclaimed identity as the "possessor of the best of Asia" with a destiny to "revive Asia," as Stefan Tanaka argues, some Japanese intellectuals claimed that Japan was "the most-advanced nation of Asia," with "cultural, intellectual, and structural superiority over China," and hence the rest of Asia.[38]

In Taiwan, primary education was segregated into three tiers based on ethnicity: Japanese elementary schools (Jp. *shōgakkō*) for Japanese (Jp. *naichijin*); Taiwanese primary schools (Jp. *kōgakkō*) for Han Taiwanese (Jp. *hontōjin*); and indigene primary schools (Jp. *banjin kōgakkō*) and indigene children's education centers (Jp. *bantō kyōikusho*) for Taiwanese indigenes.[39] This school segregation suggests that Japanese colonial officials might have established educational programs depending on their perceived level of civilization: Japanese as the most civilized, Han Taiwanese as the less civilized who can be transformed to become "an integral part of modern Japan," and Taiwanese indigenes as the least civilized, who needed to be "tamed" to become obedient subjects.[40] Note here that ethnic segregation was not new to Japanese or Han Taiwanese, both of whom had othered indigenous minorities before Japan's colonization of Taiwan in 1895.[41] What was new was that *dōka* included the ideas of "*dōbun dōshu* (same script, same race) and *isshi dōjin* (impartiality and equal favor)," referring to the shared Chinese written script and Asian race among Japanese and non-Japanese East Asians that would let them be treated equally in the nation-empire.[42] Therefore, this eth-

CONTEXTUALIZING TAIWAN

nic segregation in educational opportunities contradicted the supposed sameness and equality embedded in *dōka*, which Japan's nation-empire building relied on as Japan "engaged in a process of national extension (Jp. *naichi enchō*) to new lands with which Japan shared certain cultural and even racial affinities."[43] Hence, ethnic segregation (discrimination) coexisted with cultural affinity (impartiality) in Taiwan under Japanese rule. By examining the educational system in Taiwan, the contradiction between words (promises) and actions (implementation) inherent in *dōka* becomes obvious.

School segregation by ethnicity in Taiwan, where ethnic Japanese children were motivated to pursue a purely academic education while Han Taiwanese children were encouraged to seek vocational training as they learned about the virtue of "diligence" in the ethics course, suggests that Japanese colonial officials might have anticipated the racial stereotype of the "lazy, idle colonized" Africans that European colonizers had created to also be a problem in Taiwan. Creating a skilled, hardworking labor force was a priority of Japanese officials to govern the colony and enrich the nation-empire. In Africa, the propagation of white superiority and black inferiority helps explain why European colonial authorities focused on industrial education that linked labor with Christianity in Africa, where Europeans presumed Christianity to be superior to native religions.[44] Diligent laborers were often linked to building strong nation-states that depended on industrialization and capitalism during the age of New Imperialism. Protestant asceticism, Max Weber argues, shaped capitalistic developments by linking capitalism with Christianity, where the "waste of time" was the "deadliest of sins" because "every hour lost is lost to labour for the glory of God."[45] This critique against idleness echoed Tokugawa society's disapproval of "idleness in women of all ages," except in elite women.[46] Thus, even without converting to Christianity, Japanese officials found European critiques against idleness compatible with the Tokugawa value of diligence and advocated hard work as key to building the nation-empire. In fact, Meiji Japan did not need to adopt Christianity because it had the emperor system (Jp. *tennosei*). As historian Komagome notes, school grounds in the Japanese empire functioned like a "state church" (Jp. *kokkyōkai*) that taught imperial morals based on the Imperial Rescript on Education, which were treated like rituals for the religion-like emperor system.[47] Although Japanese officials and educators did not depict Taiwanese as lazy like what the Europeans did in Africa, they were concerned about this potential issue and sought to train diligent workers through vocational training and diligent housewives through homemaking lessons in the *kokugo* education to achieve *dōka*.

By linking industriousness and idleness to levels of civilization, the self-proclaimed civilized colonizers positioned themselves as reformers of the uncivilized or less civilized colonized society. This civilizing mission was incorporated into the assimilation project. In French colonies, schools began emphasizing the French language as part of its civilizing mission starting in the mid-nineteenth century.[48] French colonizers believed in the educational focus of assimilating the Africans into modernity and "a higher level of civilisation."[49] In contrast, the British colonial government in Kenya sought literacy and technical education as the educational focus.[50] Meanwhile, colonial educational efforts in Taiwan suggest that Japanese officials were ambitious and sought to achieve the civilizing mission as well as to create a skilled labor force. Chatani has pointed out that Japanese *dōka* differs from French assimilation in that Japanese policymakers focused on trying to "mak[e] the colonized similar to the colonizer rather than making the colonized better in the universal scale of civilization," which was how French policymakers implemented their self-proclaimed universal French republicanism.[51] She emphasizes the difference between Japanese and European imperialism during the interwar years, when European powers were trending toward indirect rule whereas Japanese leaders persisted in their assimilationist approach to prepare Japanese subjects for total war.[52] In other words, Japanese modernization and colonization as implemented in *dōka* was a conscious selection of ideas used in mainland Japan and other colonial societies that Japanese officials believed would expand and maintain the nation-empire.

"GOOD WIFE, WISE MOTHER"
AS A REGIONAL AND GLOBAL DISCOURSE

In addition to race or ethnicity, which many scholars of colonial studies have discussed, this book shows that the Japanese colonial authority used gender to increase the supposed distance of civilizational levels between the colonizer and the colonized. Mainly, gendered assimilation intensified colonial mimicry because it reinforced existing Han Taiwanese gender roles while incorporating the colonized into the nation-empire, making assimilation appear attainable among the colonized Taiwanese. As part of this Taiwanese initiative to embrace "civilization," progressive elites selectively adapted and, at times, rejected Japanese educational policies for girls. Gendered assimilation thus emphasized the supposed unassimilable "backwardness" of Han Taiwanese who continued to hold on to old practices that treated girls like undesirable objects to be sold through marriage such as arranged marriage and early marriage with bride price. By introducing gender into the discussion on *dōka* in Japan's first overseas colony, this book shows that the promise of inclusion became even less attainable and thus slowed assimilation to the supposedly superior Japanese civilization when colonial officials and educators characterized the colonized as feminine, depicting colonized women as the symbol of Taiwan's "backwardness."

The centrality of gender in *dōka* is clear in the implementation of "good wife, wise mother" around the world at the turn of the twentieth century. This ideal of womanhood was crucial to the civilizing mission of the colonizers. Providing homemaking training in schools was a global concept that began in the nineteenth century and was popularized by the mid-twentieth century. The cult of domesticity was created in the nineteenth century, when some Europeans and Americans began to envision the home as a private space as it became "separated from the workplace," and they assigned women to serve the nation from the home while men focused on the public sphere.[53] Education was essential in creating republican womanhood in the early nineteenth-century United States as intellectuals delegated to women the role of teaching their sons to be patriots who would perform civic duties, including making sacrifices for the state, while ensuring that their husbands continued to fulfill their civic duty.[54] Similarly, an ideal English woman in the nineteenth century was a literate housewife who read magazines to gain new knowledge on household management while overseeing bookkeeping and managing servants.[55]

"Good wife, wise mother" was a new formulation of ideal womanhood introduced to Taiwan in the 1890s after it first emerged in Japan in the same decade. Constructed by engaging with the cult of domesticity in the West, it was part of a Japanese national, imperial, and colonial project that the Japanese imperialists brought with them to East Asia. The Meiji state proclaimed the role of "good wife, wise mother" as the way for women to become ideal subjects of the nation-state.[56] This concept spread to China around 1903 and Korea in 1906 as East Asians faced Western encroachment, and intellectuals in these countries became deeply concerned with the survival of their nations in the late nineteenth and early twentieth centuries.[57] East Asian leaders and intellectuals found the creation of "good wives, wise mothers" through education an essential means to strengthen their nation.[58] This modern womanhood symbolized national strength in East Asia at the turn of the twentieth century. While there were anti-Japanese and non-Japanese pan-Asianists, this ideal was, nonetheless, taken up seriously in China, Korea, and Taiwan, and welcomed by many reformers who believed it was necessary to educate girls and women to strengthen their resistance to Euro-American imperialists. Although variations of "good wife, wise mother" emerged over time, the essential role of girls' education in producing these ideal women remained and spread with the increased desire to build and strengthen one's nation.

Just as Euro-American societies created different models of modern womanhood, the Japanese version was not fixed. Historian Kathleen Uno asserts that the "good wife, wise mother" ideal garnered the support of liberal and conservative nationalists in Japan because it was a vague concept. She observes that liberal nationalists who were "more open to Western models could support" educated motherhood, while conservative nationalists would rally behind the "good wife" role as "a frugal manager and hard worker in the enterprise household (*ie*)."[59] The inherent ambiguity of this ideal allowed anyone to interpret it to best suit their own agendas. Japanese leaders considered the home to be the "root of the state" that determined national strength, thus the quality of the housewife determined the quality of the home.[60] By connecting the home and the nation in this way, women's work in the home sphere "had public implications."[61] Perhaps it was no coincidence that the link between the home and the nation-empire was established by the "good wife, wise mother" ideal. *Kokka*, the Japanese term for the "nation," is a two-character term in which its first character (Jp. *kuni*) means "country" or "state," while its second character (Jp. *ie*) means "family" or "home." It was impossible to construct the nation-empire without the home and impossible to create the ideal home without the ideal woman.

Not only did the "good wife, wise mother" ideal change and continue to change in Japan, China, and Korea, the discussions continued after its importation to Taiwan. Adopting Michel Foucault's conception of discourse, this book examines the "good wife, wise mother" ideal to "bring out the 'will to knowledge'" in Japan's nation-empire-building project.[62] To discuss the "good wife, wise mother" ideal is to acknowledge that a discussion took place, to identify all speakers' perspectives, to understand "the institutions which prompt people to speak about it and which store and distribute the things that are said . . . [and] to locate the forms of power, the channels it takes, and the discourses it permeates in order to reach the most tenuous and individual modes of behavior."[63] An analysis of this discourse and its educational curriculum suggests that Japanese colonial officials and educators did not always agree on the "good wife, wise mother" ideal, nor did Taiwanese elites and intellectuals. To colonial officials and educators, the goal of the "good wife, wise mother" was to penetrate and assimilate individual Taiwanese homes and children with educated girls and women as its agents. This book identifies "instances of discursive production . . . of the production of power . . . of the propagation of knowledge . . . to write the history of these instances and their transformations."[64] Following Edward Said's application of Foucault's idea when he argues that Orientalism is "a system of knowledge about the Orient" well supported by European "socio-economic and political institutions" that led to how "European culture gained in strength and identity by setting itself off against the Orient,"[65] this book shows that "good wife, wise mother" was supported by official and nonofficial knowledge production and made possible by colonial and educational institutions to help Japanese leaders to assimilate Taiwan into the nation-empire based on ethnic and gender divisions.

By discussing the discourse of the "good wife, wise mother" ideal and showing that divergent views among Han Taiwanese elite and intellectuals existed, this book joins other studies that have moved away from the colonizer-colonized binary to focus on the complex relationships on the ground, which revealed the colonial state to be less dominating than previously presumed. For example, Evan Dawley shows that in colonial Taiwan, Taiwanese elites occupied a liminal space in which they "frequently and directly engaged with foreign regimes and settlers" as a survival technique while Japan built its nation-empire.[66] In her study of Japanese settlers in Korea, Jun Uchida argues that some Japanese settlers, whom she calls "brokers of the empire," opposed *dōka* because they wanted to maintain higher status over Koreans. She emphasizes that the resistance and opposition of Japanese settlers to some colonial policies in Korea revealed that the colonial state was "less unitary and autocratic in practice."[67] In her study of youth groups in Japan, Taiwan, and Korea, Chatani argues that although the Japanese system of youth groups was created across the empire as part of *dōka*, "the social mechanism of rural youth mobilization was more multidimensional, more diverse, and more locally grounded than anything that state policies could possibly produce on their own."[68] She emphasizes that the Japanese empire was actually an "unorganized, haphazard, and fragile state that depended heavily on a variety of social forces to create and maintain its nation-like hegemony."[69] These studies show that various historical actors' self-interests obstructed the implementation of *dōka* in the nation-empire-building project, rendering the colonial state less powerful and effective in controlling the colonized and the settler population.

Often the colonized population, ranging from collaborators to rebels, made decisions based on their economic interests instead of political ideologies. Although the educational system embodied *dōka* and represented the colonial state, this book shows that not all Japanese educators agreed on what made up an ideal woman (chapter 1), and while some Han Taiwanese seemed to align with the colonial authority in their support of girls' education while retaining certain old ideas, some intellectuals criticized the colonial state by pointing out how education had failed schoolgirls but inadvertently reinforced colonial hierarchy by accepting the premise of educating girls (chapters 1 and 2).

Although the discourses on ideal womanhood revealed different voices within a society and around the world, each ideal revealed how a modern nation-state sought to rebuild, strengthen, or expand its power in the world. The link between education and women's responsibility at

CONTEXTUALIZING TAIWAN

home was a common thread in different ideals as well. In addition to scientific household management and child-rearing skills, housewives were expected to practice modern hygiene to produce and to preserve a healthy family. This was also the training that schoolgirls received in African colonies and colonial Taiwan in the twentieth century.[70] The meaning of "good wife, wise mother" changed over time and adopted local characteristics to suit local needs. What remained the same was the perceived purpose of "good wife, wise mother": the role of educated women in the home sphere was connected to national strength. Hence, the story of girls' education in Taiwan under Japanese colonial rule is not only important in understanding Taiwanese and regional history; it is also important when examining the discourse on "good wife, wise mother" to understand the global history of girls' education in the age of New Imperialism.

OUTLINE OF THE BOOK

This book seeks to highlight the discrepancy between what government policy intended and how the policies actually played out while detailing how the local population responded to, adapted to, and was transformed by Japanese education. To capture this discrepancy, the first part of the book (chapters 1–3) relies on textual sources and includes periodicals, textbooks, and fictions to understand the discourse on the ideal womanhood and educational programs. The second part of the book (chapters 4–5) incorporates oral histories and interviews to capture the lived experiences of these educated women, including those from the lower echelon of society, to draw attention to the impact of socioeconomic status on the educational and professional opportunities of girls and women as well as on their marriage. Throughout the book, I intentionally note the ethnicity, gender, and language used by each writer, whenever available, to illustrate the diverse views held by Taiwanese and Japanese people.

Published oral histories and interviews I conducted figure prominently in the last two chapters of the book. The incorporation and selection of interviews and oral histories seeks to let women speak for themselves, to give them voice, and to illustrate noticeable changes in Taiwanese homes and society. They do not represent or speak for the majority or all women. Most interviews were conducted using Taiwanese Hoklo (Ch. Taiyu, Minnanhua) with some Japanese and Mandarin Chinese. The language choice serves several practical purposes: First, it seeks to capture interviewees from the lower socioeconomic backgrounds because they are less likely to have received enough schooling to retain Japanese proficiency and to have learned Mandarin Chinese during the postwar period. Second, I hoped that they would feel comfortable speaking with me because they would feel a sense of familiarity speaking in their native language. Introduced by family, friends, and colleagues from the United States, Taiwan, and Japan, interviewees consisted of thirty-nine women and fourteen men, born between 1915 and 1933, in Los Angeles and various locations throughout Taiwan between 2010 and 2013. Not every interviewee appears in the book. With a tacit understanding that these interviewees might be concerned about political retributions because they lived through the forty years of martial law in Taiwan from 1947 to 1987, I use pseudonyms for all interviewees except a few who preferred to use their real names. To further protect their identity, I have removed each interviewee's birth year from the book.

The book moves in chronological order starting with chapter 1 examining the discourse on "good wife, wise mother" and its implementation in the educational curriculum, showing how it changed from the 1900s to the 1930s. It traces the importation of "good wife, wise mother" from Japan to Taiwan by Japanese officials and educators as well as Han Taiwanese elites in periodicals at the turn of the twentieth century to the 1930s by analyzing government-approved periodicals. Some Taiwanese elites embraced this new ideal womanhood by incorporating Confucian ideas, which represented the old. The coexistence of modern womanhood and old classical Chinese and Confucian texts reveals the complexity of living in colonial Taiwan. Chapter 1 also discusses gendered curriculum in school and argues that the *kokugo* education reveals that *dōka* was always gendered. By focusing on government-issued Japanese-language textbook lessons and their accompanying illustrations, chapter 1 demonstrates how the colonial authority applied gender to its modernizing project and civilizing mission to maintain ethnic and gender hierarchy in Taiwan. The promise of "impartiality and equal favor" in *dōka* was never going to be fulfilled.

CONTEXTUALIZING TAIWAN

Chapter 2 examines how Han Taiwanese intellectuals viewed girls' education from the 1920s to the 1940s. It discusses how these intellectuals expressed their doubts about the modernizing impact of girls' education in periodicals and fictions between the 1920s and the 1940s. This book treats Taiwan as a hybrid of Chinese and Japanese cultures as it transitioned from a periphery of the Qing empire to a model colony in the Japanese empire in the first half of the twentieth century. Caught between two empires and always in flux, new ideas and policies in both China and Japan influenced Han Taiwanese thinking. At the same time that the Japanese colonial authority imposed its version of modernity on the people of Taiwan, chapter 2 reveals, Taiwanese elites and intellectuals sought to create their own version of modernity by incorporating existing Han Taiwanese ideas on gender roles with new ideas introduced by Japanese colonial educators and Chinese intellectuals in mainland China. In their move to embrace modernization without becoming Japanese, Han Taiwanese elites and intellectuals nonetheless ended up reinforcing the gender hierarchy embedded in *dōka*. Chapter 2 shows that by arguing against Japanization, Taiwanese intellectuals scrutinized (male) teacher–(female) student interactions to criticize the unequal colonial hierarchy built into the educational system, in essence using one version of assimilationist rhetoric to counteract another version. Gendered assimilation thus exposed the inherent unequal colonial relations, where sexual and labor exploitation of Han Taiwanese schoolgirls by their Japanese teachers became the top concern among Taiwanese and symbolized colonial hierarchy in the eyes of Taiwanese intellectuals.

Chapter 3 describes the pinnacle of Japanese colonial rule in Taiwan—wartime mobilization of schoolgirls from 1937 to 1945. It surveys the practice of gendered education in wartime Taiwan by examining how the colonial government expanded the responsibilities of schoolgirls, thus blurring the distinction between Taiwanese and Japanese schoolgirls of all class backgrounds by the end of the war. By looking at school as a site of mobilization, the chapter argues that wartime labor was gendered and reinforced women's roles in the Japanese empire. The seeming disappearance of ethnic and class divisions while gender division remained strong speaks to the quick and unsustainable expansion of the Japanese empire. In fact, conscription of Taiwanese men into the military on the front line and hiring them as the labor force on the home front was the only way to keep the empire operational. Despite that, life became increasingly difficult during the wartime mobilization. Yet oral interviews in chapter 3 show that, ironically, schoolgirls remembered the war with some fondness.

Chapter 4 evaluates the impact of colonial education on the marriage practices and domestic lives of educated girls and women toward the end of Japanese rule and the early postwar years, roughly from the 1940s to the 1950s. It argues that while Japanese education brought more profound changes to women of lower socioeconomic backgrounds than to those of higher socioeconomic standing, home training with Han Taiwanese customs continued to shape the life of an educated woman before and after marriage in colonial and postwar Taiwan. Thus, Japanese education created an uneven impact on Han Taiwanese women and households. When examining the impact of girls' and women's education, many studies have focused primarily on elite women feminists or political activists. This focus on elites inadvertently highlights the positive modernizing effects of education, specifically how it produced a group of educated women who became feminists fighting for women's political, economic, and social rights.[71] By focusing on the educated elites, these studies tell the story of a few lucky, mostly elite, women who inevitably challenged authorities. Along with chapter 3, chapter 4 seeks to complicate the story by including the experiences of Han Taiwanese girls from various socioeconomic backgrounds in the Japanese empire. These women's life stories reveal that home training remained important, often complementing school training. Han Taiwanese girls and women who received Japanese education thus became a hybrid of "good wives, wise mothers" with Taiwanese and Japanese influences at home, at work, and in public during and after Japanese colonial rule.

Chapter 5 examines recollections of colonial education from former Taiwanese students in the 2010s and Japanese teachers in the 1970s. It was impossible to ignore the strong nostalgia that permeated most of the interviews I conducted in the 2010s, so I decided to discuss colonial nostalgia in the book's final chapter. The chapter shows that the way in which the colonizers and colonized populations embraced colonial nostalgia reveals the gendered and colonial nature of the educational system under

CONTEXTUALIZING TAIWAN

Japanese rule. The chapter illustrates that their personal interactions with Japanese teachers and others proved to be a more powerful factor than institutional discriminatory practices in their memory of Japanese rule. Their nostalgic narratives often contradict their claim of Japanese fairness and equality. It is clear that their colonial nostalgia often serves to criticize the Chinese Nationalist government corruption in postwar Taiwan. This chapter also shows how the teacher-student interactions disrupted the colonizer-colonized binary because teachers were colonial agents who sometimes acted on behalf of their colonized students.

This book demonstrates that Han Taiwanese schoolgirls, a product of the *kokugo* education to achieve *dōka*, found themselves at the bottom of the state-prescribed ethnic hierarchy and at the bottom of a gender hierarchy inscribed by prevailing Han Taiwanese gender norms (chapters 1–2). Even when ethnic and socioeconomic divisions blurred during wartime mobilization, gender division remained intact (chapter 3). Although gender hierarchy was reinforced, as this book demonstrates, girls' education in Taiwan nonetheless changed the lives of tens of thousands of Han Taiwanese who attended colonial schools (chapter 4). Just as importantly, framed as a project to create "good wives, wise mothers," girls' colonial education in Taiwan also provided an important site for ideological contestations about modernity, civilization, and identity (chapters 2 and 5). Lastly, girls' education during the Japanese period bequeathed a lasting legacy in postwar Taiwan itself (chapters 4 and 5).

1

❀

INSTITUTIONALIZING GIRLS'
EDUCATION

On January 23, 1910, *Taiwan nichinichi shimpō* (Taiwan daily news), the main government-approved newspaper published in both Japanese and classical Chinese in Taiwan from 1898 to 1941, provided a brief history and update of Mōkō (Mengjia) Primary School with an interview with its principal, Mr. Katō Tadatarō. Mr. Katō emphasized the importance of girls' education:[1]

> Mr. Katō suddenly shifted to girls' education. He asked, "Where does a 'good wife, wise mother' come from? If girls' education does not flourish, then there will be no 'good wives, wise mothers.' Our school focuses on girls' education.... In addition to providing handicraft training, such as sewing, embroidery, artificial flower-making, and knitting, our school also teaches imperial ethics [Jp. *shūshin*], *kokugo* [Japanese language], arithmetic, singing, games, classical Chinese, drawing, and other subjects.... Instructors must teach all that is necessary for a 'good wife, wise mother' [to know]. Heavy makeup is forbidden. Gold rings and other expensive accessories and clothing are not allowed. Simplicity and cleanliness are the best." Concerning the matters on foot-binding and unbinding feet, the principal frowned suddenly, "Taiwan has many harmful customs, with foot-binding being the worst. It is torture. Although one's natural body came from her parents, yet it was made to shrink, limiting a girl's mobility. It is heartless. Thus, the Fujian area [in mainland

China] went on a decline.[2] This is because women bound their feet and could not assist with their husbands' agricultural production. Therefore, we cannot delay unbinding these feet. Out of 82 students enrolled in girls' school here, 26 bound their feet, 36 unbound their feet, and 20 have natural feet. . . . Unbinding feet is a more urgent matter than cutting [a boy's] queue hair."[3]

The publication of this article marked the first time the Japanese-run newspaper directly linked the ideal "good wife, wise mother" to Han Taiwanese girls. It describes the production of ideal wives and mothers as taking place on school grounds, where girls would not only receive homemaking training but would also acquire literacy and basic knowledge of a wide range of subjects. The school policy on their students' outward appearance suggests the importance of two feminine virtues—thrift and simplicity—regardless of one's socioeconomic background. Katō's criticism of foot-binding reveals his view of the practice as uncivilized since it damaged girls and women emotionally and physically. His criticism also linked a girl's physical mobility to the economic production of her husband and, consequently, her community. Principal Katō's remarks illustrate how colonial officials and ideologues believed that girls' education, the production of ideal wives and mothers, the civilizing process, and the abandonment of old customs had been closely interconnected since the early colonial period.

This chapter discusses the "good wife, wise mother" discourse and its implementation in the educational system in Taiwan under Japanese rule. It examines views held by Japanese officials and educators and those Han Taiwanese elites who embraced official views on girls' education, demonstrating that the implementation of "good wife, wise mother" in Taiwan was crucial to *dōka* in the eyes of both the colonial authority and some Taiwanese elites. The focus of the ideal womanhood changed over time, but educational officials did not always implement curriculum according to the contemporary discourse. This discrepancy suggests that colonial officials and educators had different interpretations of this ideal womanhood and did not always coordinate because the ultimate goal of *dōka* was general enough to allow officials and educators to implement the educational programs and the training of "good wives, wise mothers" differently.

CHAPTER 1

Although divergent views existed, colonial officials and educators agreed that educated women would form the foundation of a Japanese-speaking Taiwanese population who would reform Han Taiwanese society from within the home. In implementing *dōka*, colonial officials incorporated the responsibilities of a "good wife, wise mother" and prescriptions about normative gender roles into the school curriculum to impart their versions of modernization and civilization to Taiwanese children.

On its face, the concept *dōka*, often translated as "assimilation," implies the processes of inclusion, integration, or even leveling. This chapter argues that, in fact, *dōka* created and maintained gender and ethnic hierarchies in colonial Taiwan. The chapter first discusses how the discourses on "good wife, wise mother" in the metropole from the late nineteenth century to the 1920s coincided with the early colonial rule of Taiwan. It reveals that the discourse and the educational curricula sometimes aligned contemporaneously, but sometimes school programs were implemented before the discourse. By analyzing lessons and accompanying illustrations in language textbooks, the chapter engages with how colonial officials created and maintained ethnic and gender hierarchies through education in its "civilizing mission" in Taiwan. The chapter then focuses on concerns from officials and educators regarding external factors that could corrupt or destroy the "good wife, wise mother" ideal that were similar to those expressed in the metropole in the 1920s. Finally, an examination of discussions on Japanese dialects in the 1930s reveals Taiwan's colonial status in the discourse of "good wife, wise mother."

THE "GOOD WIFE, WISE MOTHER" DISCOURSE IN THE METROPOLE, 1890S–1920S

Before examining the official and nonofficial discourses on "good wife, wise mother" in Taiwan, it is essential to understand how this ideal womanhood was first formulated in the metropole because Japanese colonial educators imported this ideal and elements of the Japanese educational system to Taiwan. Japanese leaders attempted to transform everyone under Japanese control into loyal subjects of Japan through *dōka*, in which the promotion of "good wife, wise mother" as the modern ideal of womanhood targeted girls and women in the nation-empire. The two-character terms

INSTITUTIONALIZING GIRLS' EDUCATION

23

of "wise wife" (Jp. *ryōsai*, Ch. *xianqi*) and "good mother" (Jp. *kenbo*, Ch. *liangmu*) existed in Confucian texts, but not together.[4] However, Nakamura Masanao (1832–1891), principal of Tokyo Women's Higher Normal School in 1875, believed that a good wife and wise mother was essential to the education of young children.[5] After observing the effect of education for girls and women in England, Nakamura created "good wife, wise mother" as the ideal for women in a new, modern Japan.[6]

 In building the nation-empire with new roles for women, this Meiji model differed from the ideal womanhood of the Tokugawa period (1603–1867), when the main responsibility of women from the elite class of the samurai and wealthy merchants was to obey one's husband and parents-in-law.[7] Influenced by Neo-Confucianism, popular instructional texts such as Kaibara Ekken's *Onna daigaku* (Greater learning for women) promoted women's responsibility in the household during the Tokugawa period. The Tokugawa model's emphasis on the married woman's frugality and modesty while managing her household resembled some of the expectations from the "good wife, wise mother" ideal. However, the Tokugawa model differed from the Meiji model in that it operated in the big, multigenerational, extended family household with in-laws, and the education of children, sometimes even the caring of children in rural areas, was the father's responsibility in Tokugawa Japan. A woman's role as the wife and daughter-in-law was more important in that period than that of the mother as shown in elite samurai households, where women could have servants care for their children.[8] In contrast, the concept of "good wife, wise mother" was centered on nuclear families in a modern industrial society.[9] Because of their new role in the nuclear family structure, education became key to training girls to become mothers who would transmit knowledge to their children at home in Meiji Japan.

Beginning in the Meiji period, "good wife, wise mother" became the official ideal that formed the foundation of girls' education in Japan. With the onset of the Meiji Restoration in 1868, Japanese leaders became concerned with building a strong nation-state and school, and the home quickly became the site of *dōka* to transform everyone into Japanese citizens, defined by their loyalty to the emperor. *Dōka* of girls and women was defined as the ability to speak (standard) Japanese and manage the household as good wives and mothers. As historian Koyama Shizuko emphasizes, Japanese leaders recognized the importance of educating girls to prepare them to be mothers who would teach children at home to become *kokumin* (modern national subjects) and thus ensure Japan's independence from Western powers. The Meiji state called on women to contribute as modern nationals whose duties were to manage the household and raise and educate children, which reflected a gender division of labor in a modern home. The responsibility of educating children shifted from the father to the mother during the Meiji period, and the training of "good wife, wise mother" took place in the school instead of the home. After the First Sino-Japanese War, the "good wife, wise mother" concept became the official principle of girls' education as the central government promulgated the Educational Ordinance Concerning Girls' Middle Schools (Jp. Kōtō Jogakkō Rei) in 1899 in the metropole.[10] This ideal womanhood was new in Japan. It was institutionalized only four years after Japan's colonization of Taiwan.

Girls' school enrollment rates in Japan increased after the First Sino-Japanese War, when Japanese policymakers and educators began discussing the importance of producing "good wives, wise mothers" in schools to strengthen Japanese war efforts on the home front. Koyama observes that they believed this was key to winning wars in the future, as the government would be able to mobilize women to contribute indirectly to the war effort as supportive wives of soldiers and mothers whose children would be part of the military and labor force in the future. The elementary school enrollment rate of girls was low in Japan during the first half of the Meiji period: 37 percent of girls compared to 72 percent of boys were enrolled in school in 1892, and 16,000 boys attended middle school (Jp. *chūgakkō*) while only 2,800 girls attended girls' middle schools (Jp. *kōtō jogakkō*). Elementary school enrollment rates for girls increased quickly in the late 1890s: more than 50 percent of school-age girls in 1897, and more than 70 percent in 1900 as the result of an aggressive educational recruitment campaign, the inclusion of a sewing curriculum, and the training of women teachers.[11]

As Koyama Shizuko contends, some Japanese leaders and educators came to believe that Japan's victory in the First Sino-Japanese War occurred because of Japan's widespread public education, where girls received the homemaking training to help strengthen Japan's wars from the home.[12] Girls' middle schools became the fertile grounds for training ideal women. Unlike boys' middle schools, girls' middle schools did not offer courses in "Chinese, natural history, science, chemistry, law and institutions, or economics," and schoolgirls only received "less than half the instructional hours in courses such as mathematics and the foreign language than middle school boys."[13] Instead, girls' middle schools required students to take ethics, sewing, home economics (Jp. *kaji*), and music, while handicrafts (Jp. *shugei*), education, and foreign language were electives. Some educators proposed courses such as psychology, education, and physiology to prepare schoolgirls for the home education of their children. Other educators also advocated that women gain some formal teaching experiences in kindergarten or elementary school before marriage.[14] The modern housewife training in girls' middle school, with its emphasis on developing schoolgirls' character and household skills, stood in contrast to the emphasis on science and abstract knowledge in boys' secondary education. Secondary education thus ensured greater gender divergence than primary education in constructing national subjects of Japan. The goal of and the courses in this gendered curriculum appeared similar to those in colonial Taiwan, except there the curriculum started in primary education, which suggests that the colonial authority might have valued women's potential contribution more than men's work for keeping Taiwan under Japanese control.

World War I changed the official discourse on "good wife, wise mother" again when the state deemed women's more visible and public participation in the modernizing project necessary to national strength. As noted by Koyama, more women had become working professionals earning a salary in the post–World War I era. Moreover, Japanese educators discussed the need for Japanese women to achieve fitness and health through physical education to produce healthy babies. They also emphasized the need for women to learn how to be scientific, rational, and efficient in household management. In short, the revised conceptualization of "good wife, wise mother" sought to train women to take care of household matters and child-rearing, to become part of the labor supply, to participate in social work, and to improve society by receiving higher levels of education and more physical education, obtaining scientific knowledge, and participating in wartime mobilization efforts.[15]

GENDERING MODERNIZATION IN THE *KOKUGO* EDUCATION (1898–MID-1930S)

Gender-segregation policies for Han Taiwanese women made teaching the Japanese language, *kokugo*, into a means of producing "good wives, wise mothers" since the start of Japanese colonial rule. In 1897, the Japanese colonial government set up the Girls' Department in the First Attached School of the National Language School (Jp. Taiwan Sōtokufu Kokugo Gakkō Dai Ichi Fuzoku Gakkō Joshi Bunkyōjō) for Han Taiwanese girls and women in Taipei, funded by the Japanese national treasury. Although the government had also set up language institutes (Jp. *kokugo denshūsho*) and attached schools to the National Language School (Jp. Taiwan Sōtokufu Kokugo Gakkō) to teach Japanese language to Han Taiwanese girls and boys as part of *dōka*, the Girls' Department segregated Taiwanese girls and women from Japanese students and Taiwanese boys and men.[16] The physical segregation was created because of gendered training where girls and women were trained to be "good wives, wise mothers" whereas boys and men received training to become government clerks and teachers.[17] The Girls' Department had two programs: girls ages eight to fifteen were enrolled in the primary educational program, and girls and women ages fifteen to thirty were enrolled in the handicrafts program. When primary schools (Jp. *kōgakkō*) were established for Han Taiwanese children in 1898, the colonial authority elevated the status of the Girls' Department to an attached school of the National Language School. This girls' attached school continued its two programs until 1906, when its students in the primary educational program were transferred to a local primary school. The handicrafts program at the school remained as a secondary educational program. The attached school eventually became Taihoku (Taipei) Girls' No. 3 Middle School (Jp. Taihoku Daisan Jogakkō) in 1922.[18] The number of schools increased with the number of students. There were 796 primary schools for Taiwanese children and 146 elementary schools for Japanese children in 1938, and 1,099 national schools (Jp. *kokumin gakkō*), which referred to all primary-level schools, at the end of 1944.[19] A total of 22 girls' middle schools (Jp. *jogakkō*), including three private ones, and 22 home economics schools (Jp. *kasei gakkō*), were established in Taiwan at the end of World War II.[20]

The establishment of educational opportunities for girls and women soon after colonization suggests that the colonial government recognized the importance of girls' education in making *dōka* a success. With the promulgation of the Primary School Ordinance of Taiwan (Jp. Taiwan Kōgakkō Rei) in 1898, the colonial government designed a school curriculum to implement *dōka*. According to the 1898 ordinance, all students, boys and girls, were required to take six years of Japanese language, imperial ethics, essay writing, reading, calligraphy, arithmetic, singing, and exercise lessons. The curriculum changed with the Revised Primary School Regulation of 1907, which recognized that primary education might be four, six, or eight years depending on local circumstances. After 1907, essay writing, reading, and calligraphy lessons were removed, and classical Chinese was added; sewing for girls was added for four-year and six-year primary schools. For six-year primary schools, handiwork (Jp. *shukō*), agriculture, and commerce were added to the fifth- and sixth-grade curricula. An eight-year school included handiwork, agriculture, and commerce courses for boys and science and drawing for all students.[21] With Japanese language and imperial ethics as core courses and classical Chinese as a motivation for Taiwanese families to send their children to schools, the clearly gendered curriculum in the 1907 regulation coincided with the development of the discourses on "good wife, wise mother" for Han Taiwanese girls and women.

The discourse in the metropole influenced the discourse in Japanese- and Chinese-language periodicals and girls' education in Taiwan concurrently as colonial officials implemented educational programs.[22] Resonating with the metropole, the discourse on "good wife, wise mother" in the early years of the publication of *Taiwan nichinichi shimpō* was always linked to girls' middle school education.[23] However, the lack of middle schools for Han Taiwanese girls before 1919 meant that Taiwanese girls were trained to become "good wives, wise mothers" starting in primary schools since there was only one secondary educational program for Taiwanese girls and women. Independent and separate secondary schools were only available to Japanese girls until 1919, when a separate girls' middle school was established for Taiwanese girls.[24] This focus on home-making in primary school training differed from the curriculum in the metropole. Tanahashi Gentarō, the director of the Imperial Educational

Museum, lamented that Japanese girls, unlike those in Germany and England, did not receive home economics lessons or practice chores in elementary schools.[25] The absence of a discussion of Taiwanese girls' education in Tanahashi's article suggests that it targeted Japanese settlers and might have been a reprint. The "good wife, wise mother" training was eventually implemented in elementary school in the metropole as well.[26] But before this change, Japanese schoolgirls in Taiwan and the metropole would not receive the "good wife, wise mother" training until they attended girls' middle schools, in contrast to Taiwanese girls, who started in primary schools. This early start in Taiwan suggests that Japanese officials and educators viewed gender training to be essential in controlling a colony, hence the early importation of the "good wife, wise mother" ideal to Taiwan.It also shows that Taiwanese girls and women had limited educational opportunities.

Early on, both Japanese and Han Taiwanese educators linked motherhood and the nation to Han Taiwanese girls' primary education in their discourse on the ideal woman, in contrast to initially linking it to secondary education in the metropole. For instance, presuming that women were *kokumin* (modern national subjects), a September 1901 article in *Taiwan kyōikukai zasshi* (Journal of the Educational Association of Taiwan, 1901–43; renamed *Taiwan kyōiku* in December 1912), the most prominent educational journal written by officials and educators in Taiwan, concluded that women's household training was a necessary part of Taiwanese girls' education.[27] Elaborating on the connection between *kokumin* and girls' education, Zhou Dengxin, a Taiwanese primary school teacher who wrote a Japanese article in *Taiwan kyōiku* in 1915, emphasized that women held the destiny of *kokumin* in their hands because their most important mission in life was that of the mother. Zhou remarked that the mother was responsible for "creating beautiful national subjects and courageous soldiers."[28] He explained the need to educate women to become mothers who could do chores and teach their children.[29] Zhou's Han Taiwanese ethnicity suggests that he was speaking to Taiwanese. The emphasis on household training in the September 1901 article and Zhou Dengxin's article suggests that some colonial officials and educators seemed to be more concerned with producing a generation of patriotic schoolgirls skillful in raising children, specifically boys, than women patriots who could support their husbands. This indicates a shift to a modern conception of the gendered division of household labor—away from the woman's focus on parents and husbands and toward a focus on nurturing children. This echoes the official shift in the metropole from a multigenerational household of the Tokugawa period to a nuclear family during the Meiji period.

Kokugo remained the most important course primary schoolchildren of all grade levels had to take because practically it functioned as a tool of communication and ideologically it contained Japanese spirit, in which "good wives, wise mothers" were expected to be proficient at raising and educating their children as loyal subjects. Starting in 1898, out of twenty-eight hours of lessons every week, language and essay writing, reading, and calligraphy lessons together constituted twenty-one hours for first- and second-graders, twenty-two hours for third- and fourth-graders, and twenty-three hours for fifth- and sixth-graders.[30] According to the 1898 Primary School Ordinance of Taiwan, primary schools would train Taiwanese children to "express themselves and understand others in conversation and writing," and the Japanese-language lesson also acted as a medium for students to learn other lessons such as history, geography, and science.[31] By the wartime period (1937–45), students were taught that they owed their knowledge to the "blessing of *kokugo*" and that *kokugo* embodied Japanese feeling and spirit while connecting all Japanese people together, near and far, ready to sacrifice their lives for the emperor.[32] Many Japanese educators believed that the mastery of *kokugo* would produce *kokumin*, loyal to the emperor and patriotic to Japan.[33] This *kokugo* education aimed to Japanize Taiwanese children, with girls and women playing an essential role at home to achieve *dōka*.

The "good wife, wise mother" ideal appeared to be compatible with a modernist forward-looking, industrializing-age ideology in building a strong nation-empire. The emphasis on the modernizing effects of an educated girl on her home was illustrated by the Japanese-language textbooks (Jp. kokugo yomihon) assigned in Taiwanese primary schools, with five editions total published approximately every decade until the wartime period: 1901–3, 1913–14, 1923–26, 1937–42, and 1943–44.[34] Educated girls were expected to teach their family members about the convenience of modern infrastructure. An example of this expectation can be seen in a description of the postal service in a third-grade language lesson titled

CHAPTER 1

FIG. 1 "Postal Service." Courtesy of the National Taiwan Library.

"Postal Service." A-gyoku, a literate girl, comes home just in time to help her illiterate mother, who needs to contact someone with an urgent matter.[35] The accompanying illustration shows A-gyoku writing the letter and a postal service worker picking up mail from the collection box (fig. 1). The last line in the lesson states, "Since then, the mother understood the convenience of the postal service."[36] The name A-gyoku and the mother and daughter's clothing reveal that this is a Han Taiwanese household that has learned how the postal service works.[37] Furthermore, the lesson reveals that colonial officials expected educated girls to facilitate communication by using modern services. Another example is a fourth-grade lesson titled "Steam," which shows how an educated girl teaches her brother about steam. The text narrates how steam can be created in a pot and concludes by stating that steam cars and steamboats rely on steam to move. The text itself is gender-neutral, but the illustration depicts an older sister giving her younger brother a lesson on science and technology at home (fig. 2). The accompanying illustration shows her explaining while pointing at

INSTITUTIONALIZING GIRLS' EDUCATION

the steam coming out of a boiling teapot. Both children wear traditional Han clothes, thus indicating they are Taiwanese.[38] Steam was an essential part of industrialization and was ubiquitous with the operation of trains at the time. The presumption is that the sister receives this knowledge at school and links her observation from a chore (boiling water) at home to major modern forms of transportation that defined the modern age. The illustration in this case thus conveys a message not explicit in the text of the lesson—transmission of modern knowledge at home. The implicit and the more explicit message common to the lessons is that the benefit of girls' education is that it produces educated girls who spread modern knowledge in their homes, practicing how a future "good wife, wise mother" will transmit an understanding of modern knowledge (steam) into Taiwanese homes and how to act modern (using the postal service).

One major responsibility of a "good wife, wise mother" was caring for the sick using Western medicine, a gendered message that was repeated in several lessons in primary school language textbooks. For example, a second-grade lesson titled "Taking Medicine" from the 1913–14 edition shows a mother-daughter conversation about medicine. After school,

FIG. 2 "Steam." Courtesy of the National Taiwan Library.

A-kō checks on her mother, makes sure she has been taking medicine, and then obtains a prescription refill from the doctor.[39] The same lesson and illustration are replicated with a few more details in the 1923–26 edition: the mother has a cold, but she tells her daughter to rest a while after returning home from school and before going to get medicine for her (fig. 3).[40] The explicit message from the text is that it is important to see a doctor and take medicine to recover one's health. There is also an implicit element of filial piety, a core principle of Confucianism, where the child expresses concern for her parents. Another implicit message is that it is a girl's responsibility to care for the sick and the elderly. Speaking more directly to a girl's responsibility to care for the sick, two other lessons, both titled "Doll's Illness," from the 1913–14 and 1923–26 editions center around role playing. In these lessons, A-bun, the younger sister, invites her older brother, A-gi, to play "doctor." A-bun welcomes A-gi into her house to examine a sick child, which is a doll.[41] The illustrations show that the doctor practices Western medicine, as indicated by his bowler hat, coat, watch, glasses, and black bag (fig. 4).[42] The presentation of the lesson as a dialogue between siblings shows Taiwanese students how to speak politely using correct grammar when inviting a guest into one's house. The pretend play demonstrates for Taiwanese children several good behaviors. One model behavior is that the older sibling takes care of the younger sibling by playing gendered games together, with the girls playing as caregiver of a child, the doll. The other model behavior focuses on gender roles where medical doctors were almost exclusively men and caregivers were mostly women in early twentieth-century Taiwan. These lessons also show that Western medicine was part of modernization as the Western doctor represents modernity. Thus, colonial educators used illustrations to reinforce expected gender roles while teaching children the effectiveness of Western medicine, a marker of modernity.

Through language lessons, colonial educators promoted Western medicine while reinforcing existing gender roles. For example, a fourth-grade lesson titled "Doctor" discusses modern medicine as beneficial compared with harmful superstitions that delay treatment. It details a story of two boys getting sick after playing by the river and returning home late. The lesson states that one boy recovers quickly after a doctor's visit, whereas the other boy remains sick because he relies on praying to deities and

FIG. 3 "Taking Medicine." Courtesy of the National Taiwan Library.

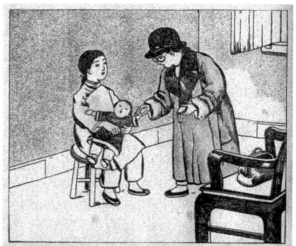

FIG. 4 "Doll's Illness." Courtesy of the National Taiwan Library.

FIG. 5 "Doctor." Courtesy of the National Taiwan Library.

Buddha to heal him. Seeing that his friend is weak and can barely speak a word, the boy who recovered recommends that his sick friend see a doctor right away. The doctor comes and says that the boy will not heal quickly because he did not take medicine immediately after getting sick. Although the text of the lesson does not mention any women, the illustration shows a woman, likely the boy's mother, with hair pinned up in a bun that indicates her married status in Han Taiwanese society. She stands by the sick boy while a doctor diagnoses and treats him (fig. 5). The male doctor practices Western medicine, as indicated by a Western-style bag and a stethoscope as well as his appearance: short hair, a Western-style bowtie, a button-up shirt, and pants.[43] This lesson explicitly criticizes Taiwanese reliance on the divine to cure one's illness and advocates for Western medicine, which was part of modernization, to treat illness. Soon after colonization began, colonial officials started training medical professionals and promoting Western medicine as part of Japan's "scientific colonialism" that sought to "bring science and civilization to the colonies."[44] The explicit message here is that one could remain sick by following the old ways or recover quickly by trusting modern medicine. The accompanying illustration provides an added gender message that it

INSTITUTIONALIZING GIRLS' EDUCATION

35

was a woman's responsibility to care for her child and the sick. Because the text in many lessons was gender-neutral, illustrations provided insights into how colonial officials and educators sought to impart their views on gender roles and modernization efforts to Taiwanese children.

Besides Western medicine, lessons on cleanliness from the early editions of language textbooks also show that colonial officials recognized that promoting hygiene and public health was a major part of governing Taiwan while linking hygiene to the level of civilization. This conveyed the colonial hierarchy of superior Japanese and inferior Taiwanese. Japanese officials had to deal with "fatal epidemics and lethal miasmas" such as malaria, plague, and cholera, so they framed them as part of Japan's civilizing mission to "persuade indigenous societies to accept colonization."[45] Targeting second-graders, "Be Clean," a lesson from the first edition of textbooks (1901–3), emphasizes the importance of maintaining one's cleanliness to remain healthy. The lesson begins by speaking directly to the reader, "Everyone, please keep your body clean." It continues by stating that should one get sick, others would not like to be near them. Although the content does not specify ethnicity, the accompanying illustration reveals that a Han Taiwanese is the unclean one (fig. 6). The image shows two Taiwanese boys in traditional Han Taiwanese clothes and queue hairstyle (that is, shaving half of one's head and braiding the rest). One wears a traditional Han Taiwanese hat and a pair of shoes while the other one is barefoot in knee-length shorts. In the back, one boy wears a school uniform, and another is shown wearing traditional Japanese clothes. Both boys standing in the back wear Western hats. The Taiwanese boy in the hat is walking away from the barefoot Taiwanese boy. Both Japanese boys and the Taiwanese boy in the hat are looking at the barefoot Taiwanese boy as if to scold him. The barefoot Taiwanese boy is also the largest figure in the illustration, as if to enhance the process of native identification.[46] Through the textbook illustration, colonial officials might be implying that the barefoot Taiwanese boy, likely of a lower socioeconomic background since he could not afford shoes, is the unclean target of the language lesson. Japanese educators saw uncleanliness as one of the "bad habits" of the Taiwanese.[47] Modern nation-states and empires, including Japan, campaigned on cleanliness and hygiene as markers of modernity and civilization.[48] By connecting

FIG. 6 "Be Clean." Courtesy of the National Taiwan Library.

one's hairstyle and clothing to cleanliness, the message conveyed by the illustration is that not all Han Taiwanese have modernized or become civilized like the Japanese. The illustration also suggests that changes had taken place under Japanese control, and Taiwan could be, and was, on its path to modernization and civilization thanks to Japanese guidance.

Although to deal with the reality of epidemics and lethal diseases language textbooks included lessons on hygiene and modern medicine starting with the first edition (1901–3), the "good wife, wise mother" discourse did not focus on hygiene and public health in Taiwan until after World War I, which coincided with when it became important to the discourse in the metropole. In 1919, Akiyoshi Otoji, the principal at Government-General of Taiwan Taihoku (Taipei) Girls' Middle School (Jp. Taiwan Sōtokufu Taihoku Kōtō Jogakkō), a school for Japanese girls only, emphasized the importance of hygiene, economization, and virtue for Japanese nationals in a Japanese article that recognized the

INSTITUTIONALIZING GIRLS' EDUCATION

difficulty of reforming old customs and declared that women residing in Taiwan had to fulfill their duties as women and national subjects.[49] While discussing the necessity of changing Taiwanese customs and spreading the Japanese language, Tanaka Yujirō, a Government-General of Taiwan school inspector, wrote a 1920 article that affirmed that women were expected to manage the household and educate their children while practicing good morals, hygiene, and spending habits.[50] The influence from the metropole was clear as both Akiyoshi and Tanaka stressed hygiene and economization, which echoed the movement in the metropole during the interwar period to apply science, rationality, and efficiency to homemaking.

On the one hand, ideal womanhood is a modern construct, but on the other hand, colonial officials and educators often presented this modern ideal as a continuation of an ancient and timeless gender system. This more conservative gloss was presumably formulated to encourage Taiwanese families to enroll their girls in school. Taking into consideration the low number of Taiwanese schoolgirls in the early colonial period—only 1 percent of school-age Han Taiwanese girls were enrolled in school in 1908 and 7.36 percent in 1919[51]—colonial officials and educators presented the "good wife, wise mother" training as timeless to encourage enrollment in Taiwanese primary schools to achieve *dōka*.[51] A certified educator, Cai Shitian incorporated Confucian ideals and phrases into his 1917 article, written in classical Chinese and published in *Taiwan kyōiku*, to make girls' education appealing to Taiwanese elites, who were well-versed in classical Chinese, and to persuade them to send their daughters to school.[52] Cai began with core principles from the Imperial Rescript on Education, followed by several Confucian texts—the *Great Learning* (Ch. Daxue), the *Classic of Filial Piety* (Ch. Xiaojing), and, most extensively, the *Family Instructions of Zhu Xi* (Ch. Zhuzi jiaxun). He linked the nation with the home, which was based on filial piety, while connecting it to the Rescript, the most important government proclamation on loyalty and filial piety, which were Confucian core values. Cai urged Han Taiwanese to practice values advocated by these Confucian classics and the Rescript by implementing a type of home education where women would care for their children in a household based on women's "natural gentility" and obedience. He argued that the "good wife, wise mother" training in home education would prepare women to be responsible for children's education and home management.[53] Similar to other journal articles that discussed this ideal womanhood, Cai emphasized motherhood and not wifehood in discussing how girls' education would improve the home. By citing filial piety, a theme common in Confucian texts and the Imperial Rescript on Education, Cai integrated Japanese loyalty (the nation-empire) with individual household responsibilities (the home).

Although the "good wife, wise mother" ideal functioned similarly in both the metropole and Taiwan as an attempt to strengthen the nation-empire, its discourse and implementation revealed Taiwan's distinct colonial status. The discourse in Taiwan included presenting this modern womanhood as an ancient Confucian ideal to convince Taiwanese who followed Han Taiwanese ideas and customs to send their daughters to school. Given that limited girls' middle school opportunities existed for the Taiwanese in the first half of Japanese rule, the implementation of "good wife, wise mother" in Taiwanese primary schools concurrently with its implementation in girls' middle schools in the metropole demonstrates that gender training was an essential part of the *kokugo* education that sought to achieve *dōka* among as many Taiwanese as possible. Although the discourse on the ideal womanhood did not address hygiene and public health until after World War I in both the metropole and Taiwan, the incorporation of gendered lessons on hygiene and Western medicine into the early editions of the language lessons reflects the urgency of transforming Taiwan into a colony of healthy labor for the colonial regime and a healthy environment for Japanese settlers. The *kokugo* education emphasized modernization, which required everyone, men and women, boys and girls, to acquire scientific knowledge. However, knowledge was gendered, as women were expected to care for the sick, the young, and the elderly while transmitting modern knowledge. Colonial educators introduced these gendered lessons early in children's education, before the fifth grade, by embedding them in the text and illustrations of textbook lessons that contained modern knowledge and life lessons. The discourse and implementation of this modern womanhood illustrate the importance that colonial officials placed on girls' education as key to modernizing and civilizing Taiwan to produce loyal, healthy, and Japanese-speaking subjects to expand the nation-empire.

GENDERING LEVELS OF CIVILIZATION

During the age of New Imperialism, both colonizers and the colonized applied gender to the idea of "civilization," which was linked to modernization. Partha Chatterjee argues that in the case of British colonial India, Indian modernity was marked by the male intellectual effort to westernize men but maintain their national identity through women who came to embody traditions in their effort to differentiate themselves from the British colonizers in creating anticolonial nationalism. Men occupied "the world" of modern economy, science, and technology, which was "the material" realm, whereas women should receive formal indigenous education to shoulder the "responsibility for protecting and nurturing [the] quality" of "the home," which symbolized "one's true identity" and was "the spiritual" realm.[54] In essence, men could become westernized and modern, but women embodied the sacred identity of the nation-state. As Japan emerged as a nation-empire in the second half of the nineteenth century, Japanese leaders sought to distinguish Japan from Euro-American imperialism by injecting Japanese essence into their nation-empire-building project and emphasizing the supposed lower level of civilization of their colonized subjects to highlight their own success at modernization. Japanese officials promoted their views of Japanese superiority and Taiwanese inferiority by using women as the embodiment of national essence. Japanese women symbolized the modern, indicating Japanese superiority over Taiwan, whereas Han Taiwanese women represented the backwardness of the old.

The importation of "good wife, wise mother" from the metropole reveals that colonial officials feared possible transgressions by uneducated Han Taiwanese girls and women who would block progress and modernization in Taiwan, thus hurting the nation-empire by slowing down or destroying the Japanese empire. Girls and women were perceived to be the protector, but also potentially the destroyer, of civilization. As early as 1908, Takagi Heitarō, a teacher and principal at Shinchiku (Hsinchu) Primary School, warned that Taiwanese women could be the "destroyer of civilization" in Taiwan. He also suggested that girls' education was a fundamental tool to managing a new colony.[55] He believed that Han girls' education must and would prepare these future housewives to be the "protector of civilization."[56] Interestingly, Takagi's claim that uneducated women could destroy a civilization echoed the prominent view in late nineteenth-century China, when reformers such as Liang Qichao (1873–1929) criticized illiterate women as detrimental to China and advocated for girls' education to produce "mothers of citizens" to save the nation.[57] This similarity might have resonated with Han Taiwanese who were familiar with Chinese affairs. Also published in 1908, the article "On the Necessity of Female Learning," by Seosan Gyodō, linked gendered roles with a strong nation, which included a wise woman who would create a harmonious and clean household while teaching proper manners and etiquette to her children. He concluded that societies with good home education could advance to a higher level of civilization.[58] Hence, women bore the responsibility of civilizing the nation.

Some Taiwanese elites and educators came to share this concern about the danger posed by uneducated women. In his 1919 article published in the classical Chinese section of *Taiwan kyōiku*, Dai Liang linked educated girls with civilization and civilization with power. A teacher at Shinchiku Primary School, Dai believed that uneducated women would prevent their society from becoming civilized because they resisted progress by holding onto superstitions and old practices.[59] He noted that China was weak because it had not changed since antiquity while the two island nations—Great Britain as a global power and Japan as a regional power in East Asia—rose to dominance during Dai's lifetime. Dai identified uneducated women as the reason Taiwan, also an island, remained weak.[60] Similarly, Yang Jiyin, a primary school teacher, wrote an article in 1919 that advocated for girls' education to create "good wives" and "wise mothers" who would then bring happiness to the home and the nation as well as make Taiwan a member of the "civilized world" alongside Euro-American societies.[61] Similar to Dai's belief that Japan was civilized, Ke Yuancheng published "Persuading Girls to Attend School" in 1914 to compare uneducated Han Taiwanese women with educated Japanese women by their manners of speaking and dealing with guests, which depicted Japanese women as the role model for Taiwanese women.[62] Both Dai and Yang sought girls' education as a key to elevate Taiwan's status to be comparable to two imperial powers. Viewing Euro-American societies and Japan as civilized, their perspectives suggest that civilization was equated with a country's power in the world in the twentieth century.

The fear of the potential damage that uneducated Taiwanese girls and women could do to make *dōka* a failure coincided with the depiction in language textbooks of Han Taiwanese girls and women as the embodiment of the supposedly inherent backwardness of the Taiwanese. The accompanying illustrations in these textbooks depict Taiwanese men and boys in increasingly modern appearance, which meant Western clothing and hairstyles, while Taiwanese women and girls remain in traditional Han hairstyle and clothes until the wartime period. For example, illustrations in the second edition of language textbooks (1913–14) suggest that, by the 1910s, Han Taiwanese men and boys had begun to westernize and integrate into the empire by adopting Western looks and coexisting with the Japanese. In this edition of textbooks, all Taiwanese boys have the same short haircut as Japanese boys, and some Taiwanese boys also wear Western hats. In a first-grade lesson about counting, the illustration shows one boy wearing traditional Han Taiwanese clothes and shoes while the other one wears *yukata* and *geta*, Japanese clothes and shoes. Both boys have short haircuts and wear Western-style hats (fig. 7).[63] These boys mix a distinctively Western item with traditional Han Taiwanese and Japanese items. In contrast, girls and women in the illustrations in this edition remain in traditional Han clothing (fig. 3). These illustrations suggest that Taiwanese boys had moved closer to modernization.

Male figures dominate illustrations in school language textbooks, but the number of illustrations of and lessons on girls increased between the first edition (1901–3) and the third edition (1923–26), which correlates to increasing number of Han Taiwanese girls in schools. The number of illustrations that include girls is few and sparse, and girls' appearances do not change between the first two editions of textbooks: girls continue to wear traditional clothing. Most illustrations with girls and women show them in traditional Han clothes, shoes, and hairstyles (figs. 1–5) with a few illustrations of Japanese girls in kimonos (figs. 8–10).[64] Girls become more visible in the 1923–26 textbooks but continue to wear traditional Han clothes, shoes, and hairstyles. Girls' hair in the 1901–3 textbooks tends to be pinned up by hair accessories (fig. 1). The next two editions include some girls in braids and fewer hair accessories (figs. 3 and 4).[65]

FIG. 7 "Counting." Courtesy of the National Taiwan Library.

The illustrations in these textbooks suggest that although Taiwanese men had begun modernizing in the early colonial period, Taiwanese women remained "backward" and unchanged, perhaps resistant to change. An implicit message might be that having more educated boys meant that modernization was more widespread among boys and men in contrast to a greater number of illiterate girls, who were ignorant of modernization since school was the main site of becoming modern in the nation-empire.

To link girls' education with Japan's civilizing mission in Taiwan, Japanese-run periodicals highlighted old customs from Han Taiwanese society, targeting bodily health and foot-binding as major obstacles to progress that were in desperate need of remediation from a civilized country such as Japan. In a 1917 article in *Taiwan kyōiku*, Honda Mokichi, principal of Daitōtei (Dadaocheng) Girls' Primary School (Jp. Daitōtei Joshi Kōgakkō) for Taiwanese children and Taihoku Higher Elementary School (Jp. Taihoku Kōtō Shōgakkō) for Japanese children, pointed out that girls' education was key to eradicating superstitions and harmful customs in Taiwan.[66] Three years later in 1920, in *Fujin to katei* (Women and family; 1919–20), Hiromatsu Yoshiomi criticized foot-binding as restricting Taiwanese women's movements.[67] A teacher at Taihoku Girls' Common Middle School (Jp. Taihoku Joshi Kōtō Futsū Gakkō), Hiromatsu argued that strong and healthy mothers were essential in producing Japanese nationals with strong and healthy bodies. He emphasized the importance of reforming Taiwanese people's physical bodies.[68] Focusing on the importance of bodily appearance and movement, Tanaka Yujirō argued in his January 1920 article in *Fujin to katei* that colonial education had "liberated" Taiwanese women in three ways: the liberation of their bodies because their feet were free and not bound after the eradication of foot-binding, the liberation of their mobility as women's public appearances became socially acceptable, and the liberation of their spirit and mind by obtaining new knowledge in school.[69] This glowing declaration was likely intended to distinguish the colonial state from the Qing state by emphasizing how Taiwanese women's lives had improved after women gained access to education and physical mobility. Concerned with how housewives could improve the bodily health of their households, in his 1920 Chinese article titled "Daily Hygiene at Home" published in *Fujin to katei*, Mishima Namaroku identified seven areas that housewives needed to pay attention to at home: sleep, diet, air, clothing, exercises, cleanup, and bowel movement. He criticized foot-binding as harmful to the body in his discussion of clothing. He emphasized the importance of indoor ventilation. Mishima also highlighted the health benefits of exercise and good posture and discussed disease prevention through hygienic practices.[70] His focus on hygiene was not new to residents of Taiwan who had had contact with sanitation police and the campaigns for social hygiene that had been implemented in Taiwan by 1902 because of its warmer and more humid climate, which made people more susceptible to diseases.[71] Hence, in addition to foot-binding, a housewife in Taiwan needed to pay more attention to the health and cleanliness of her family members in a warmer area with higher humidity than Japan. Colonial officials viewed Taiwanese women as important players in changing Taiwanese customs and teaching the Japanese language because their household duties would enable women to exert influences on the future generation. To ensure that Taiwanese elites and intellectuals fully understood the official effort in educating girls, a Chinese translation of Tanaka's January 1920 article on the "liberation" of Han Taiwanese women was published in the April 1920 issue of *Fujin to katei*, when the journal first included Chinese-language articles.[72]

Even though the practice had become uncommon by the 1920s, foot-binding came to symbolize the danger Taiwanese girls and women posed as destroyers of civilization in colonial Taiwan. Historian Wu Wenxing argues that the colonial government saw the eradication of foot-binding for Han girls and women and the Manchu Qing queue hairstyle for boys and men as part of the assimilation and the modernization projects—with more emphasis on assimilation. Although colonial officials regarded foot-binding as a backward practice among Taiwanese girls and women, it did not ban girls with bound feet from attending school, as is clear from the newspaper interview that began this chapter. Concurrently, the colonial authority supported a Taiwanese-led anti-foot-binding movement from 1900 to the mid-1910s. The movement advocated for those with bound feet to free their feet and for those with natural feet not to begin the practice. The movement eradicated foot-binding among children within one generation, so, by the mid-1910s, few school-age girls bound their feet.[73] Nevertheless, colonial officials and educators continued to use foot-binding to emphasize their civilizing mission. Foot-binding came to symbolize Taiwanese women's problems in the period before Japanese colonization. The focus on foot-binding suggests that colonial officials and educators created what Homi Bhabha calls "racial and sexual" "forms of difference" in colonial discourse to demonstrate their power as "modes of differentiation, defence, fixation, hierarchization."[74] This stereotype that most, if not all, Taiwanese practiced foot-binding "inscribes a form of governmentality that is informed by a productive splitting in its constitution of knowledge and exercise of power" and "institutionalize[s] a range of political and cultural ideologies that are prejudicial, discriminatory, vestigial, archaic" to justify colonialism.[75] The attack on foot-binding by colonial officials and educators was unique in the implementation of *dōka* in Taiwan and also created and maintained ethnic and gender hierarchy because Japanese and Korean women did not bind their feet. Therefore, while the "good wife, wise mother" ideal might have been universal within the Japanese empire as one receiving a modern education, then becoming a nurse assistant, a modern midwife, or a teacher before marriage and finally creating a happy family to benefit society and the nation after marriage, the ideal woman of Taiwanese heritage was also defined by not having bound feet.[76]

In the nation-empire, a "good wife, wise mother" was marked by her Japanese appearance in name, clothing, and housing. Hence, although colonial educators often depicted Taiwanese mothers and sisters performing various household chores to fulfill their gender roles, it was the Japanese mother who imparted life lessons to children in the language textbooks. In two consecutive lessons titled "Delicious Meal I" and "Delicious Meal II," second-grade Taiwanese students read about a nameless child refusing to eat lunch after complaining that it was not tasty. His mother promised that dinner would be delicious. She then took him (the illustration shows a boy) to work in the farm field. Dinner was the same as lunch, but the boy ate plenty after complimenting its deliciousness. In the accompanying illustrations, the mother and the son wore kimonos while eating on the floor in a Japanese-style room and later working in the field wearing Japanese clothes, which indicates their Japanese ethnicity (figs. 8 and 9).[77] The text conveys that a mother was in charge of teaching about gratitude and hard work. But the message conveyed by the illustration is that an ideal mother was a Japanese mother in charge of teaching such lessons to her children at home.

Another example of a mother teaching about virtues appears in a third-grade lesson titled "Compassionate Daughter." The lesson talks about Suzuki Uemon, who sells farmland and clothes to help starving people. It then discusses how Uemon's daughter models her behavior. A preteen girl comes to Uemon's house one winter to ask for some food, and Uemon's daughter takes pity on the girl and asks if she can give her kimono to the girl. Uemon praises her daughter for her deed. The illustration shows a girl in ragged clothing bowing to another young girl in a nice kimono while holding a piece of clothing; a woman dressed in a kimono watches from the side (fig. 10).[78] Reading the text alone, Taiwanese children would learn that kindness is about giving to those in need. They would recognize role models in their parents. In contrast to the text in the "Delicious Meal" lessons where the ethnicity of the mother and the son is unclear, this lesson on compassion and kindness features explicitly Japanese and female names. In both lessons, colonial educators utilized illustrations

FIG. 8 "Delicious Meal I." Courtesy of the National Taiwan Library.

FIG. 9 "Delicious Meal II." Courtesy of the National Taiwan Library.

FIG. 10 "Compassionate Daughter." Courtesy of the National Taiwan Library.

to reinforce the main ideas already in the text with the intersection of ethnicity and gender: a Japanese woman was the "good wife, wise mother" model who embodied and taught virtues of gratitude, kindness, and compassion. In practice, Taiwanese girls and women could dress and live like Japanese while adopting Japanese names, which was part of the *kōminka* (imperial subjectification) movement during the wartime period. But the strong link between outward appearance and ethnicity in the early colonial period meant that the main message the colonial officials wished to impart was that a "good wife, wise mother" was Japanese. Hence, to become a "good wife, wise mother" meant becoming Japanese.

To colonial officials and educators, Japaneseness represented modernity, as "good wives, wise mothers" who embodied Japanese essence without challenging modernization efforts in colonial Taiwan. Hence, colonial educators did not hesitate to include images of women dressed in kimonos in all editions of school language textbooks into the wartime period. There were no concerns about whether such traditional clothing would lower Japan's level of civilization because women in kimonos represented Japaneseness, marking Japan as visibly different from Western powers. In contrast to depicting Japanese women in kimonos as the embodiment of civilized national essence, Taiwanese women shown in traditional Han Taiwanese clothing embodied "backwardness." The persistent depiction of Taiwanese girls and women in traditional Han Taiwanese clothing in the accompanying illustrations in school language textbooks reinforced colonial hierarchy by linking a society's level of civilization with ethnicity, which was represented by one's outward appearance. Additionally, foot-binding became the focus of criticism against old Han Taiwanese practices and represented Taiwanese women's "backwardness" when bodily health became an important part of the responsibilities of "good wives, wise mothers." To colonial officials, Han Taiwanese women in traditional clothing represented Taiwan's inferiority. This focus on outward appearance to compare the civilized and the barbaric was not uncommon as Japanese leadership consistently showcased the presumed higher level of civilization of the Japanese by highlighting the so-called barbarianism of Taiwanese indigenes and other colonized people in the nation-empire.[79] Textbook lessons depicted the Japanese woman as the ideal who would teach her children virtues, whereas the Taiwanese woman behaved like a mindless manual laborer when performing chores and was slow to embrace modernization when compared to her male counterparts. If Han Taiwanese girls and women represented old Taiwan, their becoming modernized and Japanized would mark Taiwan's transformation into a civilized part of the nation-empire. Therefore, for *dōka* to succeed in Taiwan, Taiwanese girls and women had to become "good wives, wise mothers." However, the seeming contradiction of depicting Han Taiwanese girls and women as "backward" and in need of civilizing while simultaneously promoting education that claimed to liberate girls and women so they would transmit modern knowledge to their homes reveals the inherent contradiction in *dōka*—a seemingly attainable but never-achievable goal.

INSTITUTIONALIZING GIRLS' EDUCATION

49

CONCERNS OVER THE IDEAL WOMANHOOD
DURING THE INTERWAR PERIOD

With an increased number of girls enrolled in primary and secondary schools from the late 1910s to the 1930s, attention shifted from convincing Han Taiwanese of the modernizing and civilizing effects of girls' education to identifying corrupting forces that deviated from the fundamental mission of "good wives, wise mothers." Japanese and Taiwanese officials and educators expressed concerns over the negative effects of girls' education, parents' guidance, and heavy household burdens on women. Although they had different motivations for promoting this ideal womanhood, they shared the same concern about educated girls and women having deviated from the ideal when women made individual choices that would not necessarily modernize or civilize Taiwan toward stabilizing colonial rule over Taiwan and expanding the nation-empire.

Some Taiwanese identified greed and materialism as the main problem among educated girls and women, with concerns that the individual interests of these women would not help with modernizing or civilizing Taiwan, which was what had motivated some elites to support girls' education since the early colonial period. For example, although he accepted girls' education as part of a global trend and the importance of girls' education in reforming old customs, Dai Liang criticized educated girls on two grounds in a 1919 article published in the classical Chinese section of *Taiwan kyōiku*. First, he complained that these girls had become "not male and not female" because they did not know how to do chores or cook at home since their parents hired servants. Second, Dai criticized these educated women for using their educational degree to scout out husbands and demand a high bride price.[80] Dai seemed to define a woman by her ability to perform household chores and targeted those of upper-class backgrounds. Also concerned about homemaking skills as an educator, Zhang Shuzi (1881–1946) mentioned in his 1924 article that primary education was required while additional advanced education (Jp. *kōtōka*) was recommended if the family could afford it in his discussion on raising a daughter.[81] He also listed the lessons a mother should provide to her daughter at home: needlework, cooking, and hair combing to cultivate feminine virtues, as well as speaking and mannerism. Zhang cautioned parents against spoiling their daughters.[82] Zhang emphasized the skills that a mother should transmit to her daughter at home. Perhaps because Dai and Zhang were Han Taiwanese, none of their criticisms mentioned the nation-empire. Both pointed out the importance of household training for girls and expressed their concerns about materialism, fearing that educated girls would only consider money when choosing their lifestyle and marriage partners. Note here that these concerns presumed that educated girls had the power to make choices in marriage matters, which was not the case for many Han Taiwanese women. Still, their emphasis on household training suggests that the Taiwanese considered homemaking to be an essential part of girls' education.

With overlapping concerns about materialism, the emergence of the "new woman" (Jp. *atarashii onna*) ideal and professional women in the metropole might explain why some prominent Japanese attacked educated women who seemed to have deviated from the "good wife, wise mother" ideal during the interwar period. For example, Arita Otomatsu (b. 1867), an Osaka-based pharmaceutical supplier who had donated enormous amounts of money to schools all over Japan and promoted the emperor system, lamented that "good wife, wise mother" had become an anachronistic concept for the period (Jp. *jidai sakugo*) in his 1925 article "Free Love? Is It for 'Good Wife, Wise Mother'?," published in *Taiwan nichinichi shimpō*.[83] He criticized women who had become "new women," married for love, and disliked living with their in-laws, accusing them of neglecting their household responsibilities and staying out late.[84] Interestingly, although the "good wife, wise mother" ideal was based on a nuclear family, Arita criticized educated women for not wanting to be in the traditional household. An anonymous writer warned of the danger of women's expanding activities in a 1931 article published in *Taiwan nichinichi shimpō*. The author claimed that this ideal womanhood could not exist in an increasingly complex society where women were beginning to participate in the same activities as men. The writer concluded that women's virtue was a casualty of this trend, as women wore "embarrassingly extreme clothes while walking in broad daylight."[85] The author also criticized an increasing number of women who were filing for divorce to get money. Furthermore, the writer claimed that working women were more prone to monetary temptations, had a high level of vanity, and exposed themselves to work environments with many temptations. The author claimed that some women even cheated on their husbands. "Having lost their sense of virtue, whether it's romantic love or marriage, modern women decided everything based on money. It is a shame that they don't base their decisions on virtue," the writer lamented.[86] Arita and the anonymous writer were likely responding to the phenomena of the "new woman," which appeared in 1910s Japanese society, and that of the "modern girl" (Jp. *moga*) and other forms of the "new woman" that emerged in 1920s Japan.[87] Although none of them specified which model they were attacking, their assault on consumption, material goods, and money indicated that they focused on the "modern girl," the ultimate symbol of wasteful consumption and an antithesis to the "good wife, wise mother."

Addressing concerns over educated women who failed to fulfill their household roles in the changing environment of an educated, industrialized, and capitalistic society, a few reformers advocated changes to girls' education as well as including men's household responsibility in school curricula to promote gender equality. In a 1931 article, Kōra Tomiko (1896–1993), a women's activist, reprimanded parents for spoiling their children instead of educating them to be moral, but she differed from other critics by including boys and parents in the conversation.[88] "We are supposed to guide schoolgirls, as human beings, to live with self-awareness and shoulder responsibility as part of our society so that they will not have the leisure time to be involved in romantic games," Kōra emphasized.[89] She proposed changing the main focus of girls' middle school education from creating homemakers to producing useful human beings for society. Kōra also criticized the double standard society held regarding the two genders. She pointed out that society viewed the conduct and romantic relationships of schoolgirls as problematic but never punished men or schoolboys for similar behaviors. She agreed that students should not frequent places such as cafés and dance halls but observed that precisely because schoolboys and schoolgirls frequented these places together, the colonial authority must focus on the conduct of both schoolgirls and schoolboys, instead of targeting girls.[90] She retained the rhetoric of morality and shunned romance and the socialization of girls and boys, in a stance similar to that taken by supporters of "good wife, wise mother" in the 1920s and 1930s. However, instead of placing the responsibility for educating children solely on the mother, Kōra emphasized that both parents shared responsibility for educating their children.

Kōra was not alone in advocating for men's participation in the home as a discussion on training "good husbands, wise fathers" emerged in the 1930s that would have blurred the gender hierarchy. Perhaps it was because the (male) soldier had been the default ideal manhood since the early Meiji period that even when the famous Meiji educator Fukuzawa Yukichi (1835–1901) proposed the ideal "gentleman of civilization," it never gained much traction in the metropole.[91] In addition to emphasizing the importance of girls' secondary education, contributors to *Taiwan fujinkain* (Taiwan women's world; 1934–39) advocated that the training of "good husband, wise father" in boys' middle school was as important as the ideal womanhood.[92] In its inaugural issue in 1934, Suzuki Yuzusaburo—from private missionary school Seishū Girls' Middle School (Jp. Seishū Jogakkō) in Taihoku, which had both Japanese and Taiwanese students—sent four requests to the periodical. His third request was to train "good husband, wise father" in boys' middle school to create good married couples who would help strengthen the home and the nation. His fourth request was to expand girls' secondary education while promoting the coeducation of Japanese and Taiwanese schoolgirls.[93] Three years later, in 1937, Kobayashi Jun'ichi, a police medical officer, summarized the argument in *Mother's Love*, written by Honda of Taihoku Girls' No. 2 Middle School.[94] Kobayashi agreed with Honda's argument that it was important to fully implement the ideals of "good wife, wise mother" and "good husband, wise father" in the educational system. Kobayashi criticized the lack of a "good husband, wise father" training in the current boys' middle school, high school, and college education. He stressed that the training of both genders for their roles at home was necessary to create the "good family, healthy society" required to establish "the foundation of a rich country, strong military."[95] As educators at girls' middle schools, both Suzuki and Honda were concerned that men were not fulfilling their roles at home. Their views reaffirmed the home as an essential part of the nation, which needed men to work with women to make home a strong building block of the nation-empire. Their view also challenged the rigid gendered division of labor in which men were responsible for the public sphere and women for the private sphere. Suzuki's request to train boys for the home revealed that the training of good couples and wise parents through education would not only strengthen the nation but also Japan's control over Taiwan. However, the ideal of "good husband, wise father" never gained traction like "good wife, wise mother" because the role of boys and men was not to be confined within the household. The household remained exclusively under the control of the "good wife, wise mother."

Although these concerns over how educated women and men should strengthen the households for the nation-empire were expressed in periodicals, colonial officials and educators did not intensify gender training through educational policies or school language textbooks during the interwar period in Taiwan. Major educational ordinances were promulgated in 1919 and 1922 in response to the new approach of governing colonies with cultural assimilation, a departure from the previous military rule.[96] The Taiwan Educational Ordinance (Jp. Taiwan Kyōiku Rei) of 1919 was the first major colonial ordinance that laid out the entire educational system in Taiwan. The New Educational Ordinance of Taiwan in 1922 required courses similar to those of the 1907 regulation with the addition of Japanese history and geography courses, and it reduced the importance of classical Chinese lessons by making them an elective. Gendered training remained in place: boys took vocational learning courses, and girls took sewing and home economics.[97] Perhaps the unchanged gendered training signaled that the colonial state believed in its success. Furthermore, historians Chou Wan-yao and Xu Peixian argue that the focus of the *kokugo* education in primary schools was "cultivating national spirit, teaching *kokugo* and practical learning" after the 1919 ordinance.[98] This focus was reflected in the third edition of primary school language textbooks (1923–26), as it includes sixty-eight lessons on practical learning and modernization; fifty-seven lessons on Japanese history, geography, culture, and the emperor; and forty-six lessons on ethics, out of a total of 249 lessons in this edition of textbooks.[99] The addition of history and geography courses might have allowed colonial officials to replace Japanization content with topics on local society and economy. The inclusion of industry and business might also reflect Taiwan's economic development with an emphasis on agriculture and limited industrialization, although "sugar refinery and food-processing industries" grew after the 1910s in a smallholder system at the mercy of the state.[100] These additions suggest that the colonial authority wanted to celebrate its accomplishments in governing Taiwan.

The success of the "good wife, wise mother" education was celebrated through the example of an educated Taiwanese "good wife, wise mother," who was identified in a 1930 article in *Taiwan nichinichi shimpō*, as if to declare victory after thirty-five years of colonization. As part of the series titled "The Colorful Taiwanese Culture: Taiwanese Women," the newspaper celebrated a Han Taiwanese widow with five children who had lost her husband at the age of thirty-five.[101] The article described Zhang Hongchou as a "good wife, wise mother" who "received education in the

TABLE 1. Hours of instruction per week at a six-year primary school according to the New Educational Ordinance of Taiwan (1922)

	FIRST GRADE	SECOND GRADE	THIRD GRADE	FOURTH GRADE	FIFTH GRADE	SIXTH GRADE
Japanese language	12	14	14	14	10	10
Ethics	2	2	2	2	2	2
Arithmetic	5	5	6	6	4	4
Japanese history	Not offered	Not offered	Not offered	Not offered	2	2
Geography	Not offered	Not offered	Not offered	Not offered	2	2
Science	Not offered	Not offered	Not offered	1	2	2
*Drawing**			1	1	1	1
*Singing**			1	1	1	1
*Exercises**			2	2	2	2
Sewing and home economics (girls only)	Not offered	Not offered	Not offered	2	5	5
Practical learning courses (boys only)	Not offered	Not offered	Not offered	Not offered	4	4
Classical Chinese (elective)	2	2	2	2	2	2

* The drawing, singing, and exercises lessons were allocated a total of three hours together.
Source: Taiwan kyōiku enkaku shi, 379–80.

new era, and full of talents, [she] continues to lead a courageous life." Zhang graduated from Girls' Attached School of the National Language School, in a group of seven graduates in 1908. At the age of sixteen, she became a teacher at Hōrai (Penglai) Primary School. Supposedly, Zhang focused on the education of her children and helped with her husband's winery business and its bookkeeping. The article claimed that the education Zhang received gave her the strength and determination to raise five children on her own after her husband's passing. Her oldest son was enrolled in Giran (Yilan) Agriculture Vocational School, her second-oldest son in Taihoku No. 2 Normal School, and her three younger children in Kensei (Jiancheng) Elementary School, a school that was predominantly Japanese.[102] Zhang was an ideal "good wife, wise mother" who taught at a school before marriage and stayed at home to support her husband's business and to educate her children after marriage. Her children's enrollment at a Japanese elementary school implied that her children were proficient enough in Japanese to be admitted to those schools. This suggests that Japanese was spoken regularly, if not always, in their household. Since Japanese proficiency was an important part of *dōka*, Zhang and her family appeared to be a successful *dōka* story.

With the increased tensions that led to Japan's full-scale war against China, colonial educators highlighted the link between the "good wife, wise mother" ideal and *kokugo* as Japanese proficiency became a measurement of the success of *dōka*. Kakinuma Fumiaki, cofounder and coeditor of *Taiwan fujinkai*, sought to "change Taiwanese customs, [promote] Japan-Taiwan integration, [and] spread the Japanese language through a women's magazine."[103] In the July 1937 issue of *Taiwan fujinkai*, Miyazaki Naosuke promoted the standard Japanese language based in Tokyo and degraded those from the Kyushu and the Kansai areas. Miyazaki emphasized that both school and home were crucial to the refinement of the Japanese language in Taiwan. He claimed that various languages and dialects within Taiwan already constituted a major obstacle, but the bigger problem was the "Taiwan dialect" (Jp. *Taiwan namari*) when speaking Japanese. He defined the dialect as "made up of the worst elements from various places in the metropole," most prominently the Kyushu and Kansai dialects, and labeled the "Taiwan dialect" [as] "the most vulgar and offensive local language."[104] Although he had also placed the blame on schoolteachers, his article mainly targeted women readers by providing a list of words for (Japanese) mothers to pay attention to and to correct their children.[105] Miyazaki's article illuminates another important role of the educated mother: to guard against pollutants to *kokugo*. Once again, an educated mother residing in Taiwan had to be more diligent than those living elsewhere (metropole) because of the number and the origin of different languages and dialects—ranging from Han Taiwanese Hoklo and Hakka languages and dialects to more than a dozen Taiwanese aboriginal languages already in Taiwan before Japanese colonization—that coexisted with different dialects of Japanese residents and teachers in Taiwan. Hence, even Japanese mothers living in Taiwan had to work harder than those in the metropole to purify the Japanese language by removing non-standard Japanese elements in the home.

With influences from the metropole during the 1920s and 1930s, Taiwanese and Japanese educators expressed their anxiety over educated girls and women without full household training or with materialistic tendencies that would prevent them from becoming true "good wives, wise mothers," but the educational policies and curricula did not always reflect this influence. By the end of World War I, many officials and educators were concerned about educated women who had become professionals, as products of Japan's nation-empire building, industrializing, and capitalistic developments, making individual choices without adhering to the official ideal womanhood. Among the criticisms of educated women's behaviors and actions, some educators advocated for including men in creating patriotic households for the nation-empire, but that would surely blur the gender hierarchy, which the "good wife, wise mother" ideal created and reinforced. The "good wife, wise mother" ideal was fundamental to *dōka* as the sole homemaker who created Japanese-proficient, healthy, and modern households at the root of the nation-empire.

Soon after colonization began, colonial officials used girls' education as one important tool to Japanize the colonized population because they believed that Japanese-speaking and Japanese-educated Taiwanese women would spread *dōka* to their home, targeting children. As part of *dōka*, Han

Taiwanese schoolgirls and schoolboys received a gendered and colonial primary education under Japanese rule. It was a gendered curriculum in the sense that Han Taiwanese girls began receiving homemaking training in primary school to prepare them for their future roles as wives and mothers. In contrast, boys received training in agriculture, commerce, or industry, classified as vocational courses, to prepare their future roles as skilled workers who would be responsible for bringing income to the family and helping Taiwan's economy progress, which ultimately benefited the nation-empire. It was a colonial education in the sense that the focus was to produce efficient and loyal workers in the nation-empire who spoke Japanese, while reserving many opportunities for more education that would yield more academic or professional achievements for Japanese residents of Taiwan. School curricula also reveal that the concept of the level of civilization and modernization was gendered to convey Japanese superiority as the colonizing power and Taiwanese inferiority as the colonized people.

While the goal of *dōka* through girls' education might have been clear in that it aimed to produce the ideal woman, the discourse on the "good wife, wise mother" ideal reveals the instability of this concept of modern womanhood. The instability of this ideal was created by the diverse views of it held by Japanese and Taiwanese participants, officials and elites, and mostly men, with few women who were deeply concerned with the implications of trained "good wives, wise mothers" for the nation-empire. Embracing Japan's "civilizing mission," Taiwanese elites incorporated Confucian ideas into this Japanese ideal womanhood in the first half of Japanese colonial rule. By the 1920s, after colonial officials had established the educational system and more women became educated, some Japanese educators and Taiwanese elites shared the same concerns as their counterparts in the metropole about educated girls and women not fulfilling their housewife obligations. They refined the ideal womanhood, and some even proposed the training of "good husband, wise father" to include men in creating strong households. Colonial educators increased their expectations from the "good wife, wise mother" in colonial Taiwan, where the ideal woman needed to put in more effort than her counterparts in the metropole to keep her family healthy and teach the standard Japanese to her children. The discourse on this modern womanhood suggests that this ideal was never fixed but changed depending on the needs of the nation-empire and the interests of officials, elites, and educators.

The *kokugo* education was the core of *dōka* in colonial Taiwan. The illustrations that accompanied the language lessons targeted Taiwanese children who were learning to read and write a non-native language. The illustrations not only helped Han Taiwanese children learn content, but they also conveyed the official colonial perception of ethnic hierarchy using the idea of civilization: Japan as modern and civilized and Taiwan as uncivilized. However, the inherent contradiction of *dōka* was revealed by the inclusion of illustrations that depicted Han Taiwanese girls and women as symbols of a "backward" Taiwan and bearers of modern knowledge to "civilize" Taiwan through the home. Although some Han Taiwanese desired or were made to desire the changes that *dōka* would bring, the underlying principles of gendered assimilation foreshadowed its doom. The next chapter discusses how the first generation of Japanese-educated Taiwanese elites and intellectuals sought to use girls' education and the concept of ideal womanhood to change Taiwan on their own terms under colonial rule, yet ended up reinforcing gender hierarchy as the colonial regime had intended.

2

✲

EMBRACING EDUCATED

GIRLS AND WOMEN

Written during the wartime period by a Taiwanese woman and man, respectively, Yang Qianhe's "The Season When Flowers Blossom" (1942) and Wu Zhuoliu's *Orphan of Asia* (Jp. *Ajia no koji*) (1945) capture the contrast between a "good wife, wise mother" and a "new woman." A journalist for *Taiwan nichinichi shimpō* and a prolific writer who wrote exclusively in Japanese, Yang Qianhe (1921–2011) writes a story lamenting a (Taiwanese) woman's life cycle, in which education has become normalized, but marriage and children still define and confine her:[1]

> This was likely how my classmates got engaged. They agreed to the marriage proposal after hearing about how perfect the marriage candidate is, and then got married. A woman's life, from her innocent infant stage, [she] then passes childhood, and she then attends [girls' middle] school after [primary] school. Just when she has a moment to breathe, she is rushed to get married. Then in the midst of childbirth and child-rearing, she has quickly become weak and old, then dies. . . . Is it really true that every classmate who is married did so whole-heartedly and agreed to get married?[2]

In contrast, Shuchun, the wife of Hu Taiming, the Taiwanese protagonist of Wu Zhuoliu's (1900–1976) famous semi-autobiographical novel, embodies more of a "new woman" rather than a "good wife, wise mother":[3]

After Shuchun graduated [from Jinling University], the couple discovered that they held contradictory views regarding her future.[4] The man wanted his wife to settle down and become a good housewife, whereas the woman insisted on pursuing a career. . . . Unyielding, Shuchun ignored all his suggestions, decided to go into politics, and landed a job in the Diplomatic Bureau with the help of her university.[5]

As a "new woman," Shuchun has a career and engages in political activism even after having a child.[6] As someone who earned a degree from Taihoku Women's Higher Academy (Jp. Taihoku Joshi Kōtō Gakuin), the highest level of education possible for women living in Taiwan, Yang shares her thoughts about education and marriage by centering the story on young women with a girls' middle school degree who initially resisted marriage but ultimately become "good wives, wise mothers."[7] Although a Han Taiwanese woman might become a "good wife, wise mother," Wu's novel suggests that an educated Taiwanese woman was not who Han Taiwanese men desired, as the ideal companion of the protagonist, Taiming, was always Japanese, although he ultimately marries a Chinese woman.[8] Taiming's preference for Japanese and then a Chinese woman over an educated Taiwanese woman suggests Taiwan's complex relationships with Japan and China, as Taiwan had been at the crossroads between the two civilizations. These two fictions suggest that Han Taiwanese female and male intellectuals had expected educated girls to become "good wives, wise mothers" by the end of Japanese rule.

Moving from the previous chapter's discussion of the development of the official discourse and the institutionalization of "good wife, wise mother" from the 1890s to the 1930s, this chapter turns to the Taiwanese discourse on girls' education and their responses to the Japanese ideal of womanhood from the 1920s to the 1940s. It covers the time after the first generation of Japanese-educated Taiwanese elites and intellectuals emerged to voice their views independently from the official discourses.[9] After a brief overview of official campaigns and Taiwanese responses to educating girls before the 1920s, this chapter examines intellectual responses to girls' education from the 1920s to the 1940s to understand how the Taiwanese viewed the "good wife, wise mother" ideal. The chapter shows that by the 1920s, the first generation of Taiwanese who had been fully educated under the Japanese educational system advocated for girls' education wholeheartedly but also used girls' education to criticize the political and economic oppression of the Taiwanese by Japanese colonialism as well as the economic and social oppression of Taiwanese women by old Han Taiwanese values. Their discussions and criticisms incorporated ideas from alternative models of women that emerged in Japan and China during the first feminist movement and the rise of urban cosmopolitanism in the 1910s and the 1920s. Similar to their Japanese counterparts, the educated Taiwanese "new woman" in the 1920s and the urban "black cat" model in the 1930s illustrate the increasing acceptance of girls' education in Taiwan. As official censorship increased starting in the late 1920s and into the 1930s, Taiwanese intellectuals turned to fiction and literature to continue to voice their criticisms. Ultimately, this chapter finds that although Taiwanese men believed girls' education would improve women's status and advance Taiwan, their acceptance of girls' education aimed at producing "good wives, wise mothers" helped them maintain a higher position in the gender hierarchy in colonial Taiwan, leaving women to bear the brunt of colonial and patriarchal oppression.

GRADUAL ACCEPTANCE OF GIRLS' EDUCATION AS A MEANS TO MODERNIZE TAIWAN INTO THE 1920S

The educational level of female characters in Yang's story and Taiming's love interests in Wu Zhuoliu's novel suggest that many Taiwanese had embraced girls' education by the end of the colonial period, and enrollment numbers had increased over time. The primary school enrollment rate was at 1 percent for school-age Taiwanese girls and 8 percent for school-age Taiwanese boys in 1908. It was not until 1932 that the primary school enrollment rate for school-age boys rose past 50 percent, and it took another decade for that of school-age girls to surpass 50 percent.[10] Before 1915, there were fewer than 3,000 girls newly enrolled in school each year. However, the number of new enrollees increased dramatically beginning in 1916.[11] In 1920, over 28,800 girls were attending primary school; this number more than doubled to over 56,400 girls in 1930 and quadrupled to exceeding 226,800 girls in 1940. School enrollment rates increased from 9 percent in 1920 to 43 percent for all school-age girls in 1940, with nearly 61 percent of school-age girls enrolled in 1943, the year compulsory education was implemented.[12]

Although Han Taiwanese practices continued to keep girls at home, school enrollment rates gradually increased over time partly because colonial officials successfully developed some strategies to accommodate such customs. Japanese educators attributed the initial low enrollment rates to traditional Taiwanese society not valuing girls' education. They also documented the discouraging attitudes that schoolgirls in the early colonial period encountered: "Although we saw twelve [girl] enrollees during the time when language training centers were in operation, many were ridiculed by people around them. Some quit school after a few days. Although it was a difficult situation, some continued schooling by dressing up as boys."[13] Taiwanese people were not accustomed to seeing schoolgirls in public in the early colonial period because few girls had studied during

TABLE 2. Number of Taiwanese primary schools and schoolchildren enrolled

YEAR	PRIMARY SCHOOLS	TOTAL SCHOOL-CHILDREN ENROLLED	SCHOOLGIRLS ENROLLED	SCHOOLBOYS ENROLLED	PERCENTAGE OF SCHOOL-AGE GIRLS ENROLLED	PERCENTAGE OF SCHOOL-AGE BOYS ENROLLED
1898	74	7,838	290	7,548	n/a	n/a
1908	203	35,898	3,350	32,641	1.02	8.15
1919	438	125,135	21,961	109,865	7.36	32.42
1933	769	309,768	79,864	215,197	20.61	52.55
1937	n/a	450,032	134,651	297,946	29.83	61.84
1941	n/a	680,577	259,295	421,282	48.70	73.59
1943	n/a	707,352	289,810	417,542	60.95	80.86

Source: The data for the number of primary schools and schoolchildren from 1908 to 1933 came from *Taiwan kyōiku enkaku shi*, 408–10. Other numbers and the percentages of schoolchildren came from Yu, *Ri jü shiqi Taiwan de nüzi jiaoyü*, 286, except for 1898, where the numbers came from Tsurumi, *Japanese Colonial Education in Taiwan*, 19. A discrepancy exists between *Taiwan kyōiku enkaku shi* (1937) and Tsurumi (1977) concerning the total number of schools and students: *Taiwan kyōiku enkaku shi* states there were 76 schools and 6,136 students, but my table is based on Tsurumi's table because it included the gender breakdown.

the Qing period. Public shaming was likely not something that secluded Han Taiwanese girls were accustomed to or could handle in the early twentieth century. Han Taiwanese families resisted sending their daughters to school because families chose to allocate more educational resources and opportunities to their sons, who would continue the patrilineal family line whereas their daughters would marry out of the family.[14] A 1928 article in *Taiwan minbao* (Taiwan people's news) identified a few reasons for the low number of graduates at Shinchiku (Hsinchu) Girls' Primary School: students quitting school to help out with home chores, families' financial burdens, and families valuing boys over girls.[15] This list suggests that domestic tasks and economic concerns combined with patrilineal ideas to produce a gendered allocation of family resources, which limited the enrollment numbers of schoolgirls compared to schoolboys. In a sense, the childcare and household chores expected of girls were more valuable than boys' labor at home, but the costs of schooling boys were more likely to be viewed as worthwhile because sons would remain at home to support and continue the family line after marriage.

Colonial officials tried the following strategies to increase girls' school enrollment rates with success: handicraft exhibits, gender segregation, home visits with girls' mothers as they usually made school decisions, and an increase in children's maximum age of initial enrollment, and in the number of women teachers. Interestingly, girls' enrollment rates in private Chinese academies (Jp. *shobō*) increased concurrently with girls' enrollment in Taiwanese primary schools under Japanese rule, suggesting a general increasing acceptance of educating girls.[16] Despite old Han Taiwanese customs that continued to keep many girls at home, more and more girls began attending school, especially those living in cities and towns.[17] By the 1920s, the first generation of Taiwanese who had been fully educated under the Japanese system, including women, came of age and began to voice their views on various topics, including education.

Although old Han ideas and practices continued to produce more educated boys than educated girls, many Taiwanese elites and intellectuals embraced girls' education as a way to modernize Taiwan as colonial officials imported the "good wife, wise mother" ideal into Taiwanese schools to create loyal Japanese subjects. Colonial officials viewed girls' education as a major colonial project in "modernizing" and "civilizing"

CHAPTER 2

the "backward" colony of Taiwan to achieve *dōka*. Historian Ko Ikujo (Hong Yuru) argues that Han Taiwanese elites embraced "good wife, wise mother" by focusing on its positive effect in modernizing homes and deemphasizing its public goal of producing loyal Japanese subjects. Ko contends that the home was the main focus of this ideal; and the beneficiary of girls' education was the home, not the girls themselves. The educated woman was crucial to a harmonious marriage, in-law relations, household management, and children's education.[18] The focus on the home was similar to how this ideal womanhood functioned in Japan, and it sought to modernize the household through the educated woman. The concept of the nation (Ch. *kuo*, Jp. *kuni*) was ambiguous in "good wife, wise mother," at least in the colonial government mouthpiece, *Taiwan nichinichi shimpō*, according to Ko. Ko explains that sometimes the term "our nation" could be interpreted as Japan and sometimes as China because the writers intentionally avoided being specific about which country they were referring to. Ko argues that this emphasis on girls' education, while being ambiguous about which nation girls' education would benefit, revealed the colonial status of Taiwan because the colonial administration wanted to transform the Taiwanese into loyal Japanese subjects but did not want to explicitly dictate loyalty to Japan because it feared resistance from Taiwanese elites.[19] Ko's finding shows that the focus on the educated women's role in the home appealed to the Han Taiwanese elite tradition of limiting women's role to the domestic sphere. The ambiguity regarding the nation-state in the promotion of ideal womanhood hints at the uneasy relationship between the Japanese rulers and the Taiwanese elites. Colonial officials did not want to risk inciting Han Chinese nationalism among the colonized elites who could potentially be leaders of a colonial resistance. By appealing to Han Taiwanese customs without pressing for national loyalty, colonial officials emphasized modernization and downplayed Japanization to spread their notion of the ideal womanhood to Taiwanese elites in the early colonial period.

Taiwanese elites and intellectuals attempted to break the link between modernization and Japanization in the *kokugo* education to achieve *dōka* by focusing on modernization and avoiding Japanization. According to Chen Peifeng's research, Taiwanese elites simultaneously embraced and rejected this "education to be civilized" (Jp. *bunmei teki na kyōiku*) project in *dōka*.[20] Chen explains that this seeming contradiction only makes sense if one understands that two types of assimilation existed: first, "civilizational assimilation" (Jp. *bunmei e no dōka*), which was often linked to modernization, and second, "national assimilation" (Jp. *minzoku e no dōka*), where the nation refers to Japan and meant becoming Japanese in the Japanization process. According to Chen, the early Meiji nation-state formation was influenced by the idea of (Western) civilization (Jp. *bunmeika*), which was tied to the nation-state-building (Jp. *kokka*) project based on the concept of "rich country, strong military" and industrialization. Meiji's nation-building project thus led Japanese officials to view Japan as superior to the "barbaric" Taiwan and created what Chen calls the "duality of impartiality and discrimination," implemented when governing Taiwan through *dōka*. *Dōka* was dependent on the Japanese national language, which was linked to citizenship (Jp. *kokumin*) and nationality (Jp. *minzoku*), to connect the spirits of all subjects in the nation-empire together. Therefore, Chen emphasizes, colonial officials implemented two types of assimilation as two sides of the same coin when they established the *kokugo* education to bring universal civilization (through modernization) and particular Japanization to the supposedly inferior colonized, maintaining the unequal hierarchy. Chen argues that Han Taiwanese decided to embrace "civilizational assimilation" and rejected "(Japanese) national assimilation" as a path to modernization under Japanese colonial rule.[21] This decision made sense to Han Taiwanese elites and intellectuals who viewed "civilizational assimilation" (modernization) as universal and "national assimilation" (Japanization) as specific to Japan. Although Taiwanese intellectuals suffered from systematic discrimination under colonial rule, as the disadvantaged majority living under their minority foreign rulers, they were proactive in cherry-picking the type of assimilation they desired to establish a civilized, modern society. Both Chen and Ko found that Han Taiwanese elites and intellectuals sought to modernize and "civilize" Taiwan by advocating for (girls') education without becoming Japanese.

By the 1920s, girls' and women's education became a point on which to criticize colonial officials as more Taiwanese elites and intellectuals became influenced by Japanese and Chinese progressive ideas and major anticolonial movements in the region in the 1910s and 1920s. These Taiwanese were exposed to the ideas of liberalism, democracy, and socialism that were widespread among Japanese liberals and radicals in the 1920s. Moreover, along with Japanese liberals and social reformers, Taiwanese intellectuals sympathized with recent Korean and Chinese movements against Japanese imperialism. The March First Movement for Korean independence in 1919 and the May Fourth Movement in 1919 were part of a global anticolonial, anti-imperialist independence movement, inspired by the self-determination clause from Woodrow Wilson's "Fourteen Points" speech in 1918. In contrast, although most Taiwanese intellectuals did not organize anti-imperialist or independence movements, those who received a full Japanese education in Taiwan and then studied in the metropole nevertheless demanded to have the same rights as the Japanese, including educational opportunities and political representation. These movements pushed Japanese colonial governments in Korea and Taiwan to replace military rule with civilian rule in order to pacify the local populations and to prevent anticolonial resistance.[22] The greater political tolerance from colonial officials under civilian leadership allowed Taiwanese to anchor their critique of colonial rule in the purpose and the success of girls' and women's education.

It was in this climate of international and regional political, social, and cultural developments that Taiwanese intellectuals—who studied in Japan, the metropole, and mainland China—became politically and socially active and participated in the discourse on ideal womanhood with influences from Japanese and Chinese thinkers. Made up of older conservative and younger liberal activists who shared the same desire to be treated equally to the Japanese, these intellectuals formed the Taiwan Cultural Association (Jp. Taiwan Bunka Yōkai) in 1921 "to improv[e] the cultural level of the Taiwanese people."[23] In 1927, the conservative faction split to form the Taiwan Popular Party (Jp. Taiwan Minshūtō) after the liberal faction took control of the organization. Some members of Taiwan Cultural Association founded the first independent Taiwanese journal to criticize colonial policies and traditional problems in Taiwan.[24] They established *Taiwan seinen* (Taiwan youth), a Japanese-language journal, in Tokyo in 1920 and renamed it *Taiwan minbao* (Taiwan people's news) in 1923, which then published both Japanese- and Chinese-language articles. It was then renamed *Taiwan xin minbao* (Taiwan new people's news) in

1929. *Taiwan minbao* discussed political, economic, social, and cultural issues of Taiwan to criticize Japanese colonial rule.[25] Regarding women's issues, women's liberation was most contributors' focus.[26] In addition to "Japanese left-wing ideologies of socioeconomic egalitarianism," contributors to *Taiwan minbao* were influenced by ideas on women's liberation from the New Culture Movement in China (mid-1910s–1920s).[27] Also, *Taiwan minbao*'s inaugural title of *Taiwan seinen* (Taiwan youth) resembled *Xin qingnian* (New youth), the title of the journal that began the New Culture Movement in China. As early as 1920, some Taiwanese intellectuals embraced the vernacular language movement (Ch. *baihuawen*) in China and advocated the same in Taiwan.[28] Although there were strong Chinese progressive influences, the conservative faction remained present and vocal in *Taiwan minbao*.[29]

Progressive ideas from China's New Culture Movement that challenged Japan's "good wife, wise mother" ideal influenced how Taiwanese elites and intellectuals viewed women's role and their education in the 1920s. After losing in the First Sino-Japanese War, Chinese intellectuals such as Liang Qichao advocated women's education as essential to strengthening the nation and people.[30] From the late Qing period (1890s–1912) to the early Republican period in the 1910s, the "wise wife, good mother" ideal (Ch. *xianqi liangmu*), which is the Chinese phrase for "good wife, wise mother," became popular as Chinese intellectuals embraced girls' education. However, the New Culture Movement replaced this ideal with one exemplified by the character Nora from Henrik Ibsen's play *A Doll's House*. A middle-class housewife, Nora leaves her household to face an unknown future. Chinese intellectuals who advocated for the liberation of women viewed "wise wives, good mothers" as "traditional" and the opposite of their new ideas of coeducation, jobs for women, love marriage, a limitation on the number of children, and free divorce. They remade the "good wife, wise mother" image into that of an evil, ignorant, and wasteful stay-at-home housewife who was addicted to consumerism, didn't do any household chores, and played all day long.[31] This Chinese remake clearly contradicted two defining markers of a "good wife, wise mother" in the Japanese version—thrift and diligent household management. But this remake allowed Chinese intellectuals of the New Culture Movement to reject the "good wife, wise mother" ideal as a Confucian-inspired model

CHAPTER 2

to advocate for a free, liberated Nora of New China who would help strengthen the Chinese nation-state, something that the "good wife, wise mother" ideal failed to accomplish previously in China.

Clearly influenced by the New Culture Movement as were some who had or still lived in China, male and female writers for *Taiwan minbao*, likely the liberal faction, focused on advocating for women's liberation from the oppressive force of the traditional family system and marriage practices. As part of their advocacy for the liberation of women, they covered topics such as education for girls and women, economic independence, political participation, and free marriage[32]—all themes the New Culture Movement activists advocated in mainland China. *Taiwan minbao* advocated education for girls and women as well as other issues in a campaign to elevate the status of Taiwan into the ranks of civilized societies.[33] Most contributors to *Taiwan seinen* and *Taiwan minbao* were men, but twenty-eight women intellectuals living in Japan, Taiwan, and China between 1920 and 1929 contributed to thirty-nine articles on women's issues in *Taiwan minbao*.[34] Many of these women studied in mainland China after having received at least primary education in Taiwan. One example was Lü Jinwu, who studied at Hunan Women's No. 1 Normal School in China. Lü advocated education for girls and women, free choice in marriage, economic independence, and the right to political participation.[35]

Although the New Culture Movement influenced some Taiwanese, many Taiwanese intellectuals in the 1920s, likely the conservative faction, used the same talking points as colonial officials and educators from the "good wife, wise mother" ideal. As discussed in chapter 1, the discourses on "good wife, wise mother" in Japanese-run periodicals such as *Taiwan nichinichi shimpō* and *Taiwan kyōiku* all linked girls' education to home education, society, and the nation. Some articles in *Taiwan seinen* and *Taiwan minbao* used the same concepts to promote girls' education. For example, a Chinese-language article in the August 1920 issue of *Taiwan seinen* linked the home with society and civilization while equating national education (Ch. *guojia jiaoyu*) and social education (Ch. *shehui jiaoyu*) with home education (Ch. *jiating jiaoyu*). The article stressed that the home was the foundation of humanity and should provide spiritual and bodily practice that was useful for the nation and society. Women were the core of home education, the writer argued, because they shoulder great responsibility as wives and mothers who would affect the future generations. The article concluded that girls' education was thus an urgent matter in Taiwan.[36] The cover of the October 1924 issue of *Taiwan minbao* is another example of a Taiwanese intellectual following the colonial official line. Titled "The Hope for the Spread of Girls' Education: The Need to Establish Women's Normal Education," the article emphasized that Taiwanese intellectuals viewed girls' education as important and identified a way to increase girls' enrollment rates by training more women teachers in formal teacher-training programs. The article asserted that education was key to remaking the home and society as well as women's character.[37] Although these Taiwanese intellectuals criticized Japanese colonialism, they viewed the education of girls and women set up by the colonial state as important for Taiwan's development.

As Taiwanese support for girls' education spread, alternative models of the educated woman emerged to reflect the cultural, social, and economic changes of the 1920s and the 1930s. The first model was the Taiwanese "new woman" (Jp. *atarashii josei, atarashii onna, shinfujin*), a product of the anti-foot-binding movement and girls' education that emerged in the 1920s. This "new woman" was usually a girls' middle school graduate, although the group sometimes included Taiwanese primary and Japanese elementary school graduates. She was from an elite or middle-class background and enjoyed a new "life course" by delaying her marriage and possibly pursuing more education.[38] Then, in the 1930s, another model emerged because of a more developed market economy and urban culture mainly in Taipei. This was called "black cat" (Tw. Hoklo *o'niau*), which was the Taiwanese Hoklo term for "modern girl." The "black cat" was defined by an aura of charisma, coolness, wildness, mystery, and danger. She symbolized consumerism in Taiwan and was characterized by luxury and enjoyment. Dressed in "Western dresses and high heels with her hair permed," a "black cat" enjoyed dancing and drinking.[39] The Taiwanese "new woman" was likely less threatening to the official ideal than the "black cat" because the educational and socioeconomic background of the "new woman" resembled that of the "good wife, wise mother." Although the "new woman" might delay her marriage, her additional educational training and premarital employment reveals more of her upper-middle socioeconomic status and higher marriage marketability rather than her status as a liberated woman. In contrast, the "black cat" was a wasteful, fun individual, the opposite of the frugal "good wife, wise mother" who focused on household management and children. Although the "black cat" might have been seen as a threat, its emergence in the 1930s coincided with tightened political control and wartime mobilization and was limited by the low number of urbanized areas for women to consume urban goods and services. The "new woman" seemed to be limited to the upper classes and was defined by her education, whereas the "black cat" was more inclusive across socioeconomic status and defined by her consumption. Although the class differences suggest that these models opposed each other, they shared a common trait—they were educated girls and women—and this education had become widespread because of the official promotion of the "good wife, wise mother" ideal. Nevertheless, neither model posed a serious threat to the official ideal because the "new woman" could become a "good wife, wise mother" upon marriage, and the potential growth of "black cats" was hindered by political suppression and low urbanization rates. These two alternative models illustrate the success of the official campaign of girls' education.

The Taiwanese "new woman" shared its name with the new models in the metropole, demonstrating the impact of the "good wife, wise mother" ideal as more and more educated women evaluated and questioned the official ideal that led to the emergence of several versions of the "new woman" (Jp. *atarashii onna*) by the 1910s. One model was a woman professional who advocated for gender equality with equal educational, social, and legal responsibilities and rights for women themselves and not for someone else. Another model was a state-protected mother who would manage her home with privileges and state welfare for the social good. The other ideal viewed women as having been subjugated by capitalism and advocated for socialist reforms to improve women's situation. In other words, some educated women promoted gender equality among working professionals as individuals, some advocated for state-supported motherhood instead of expecting "good wives, wise mothers" to be responsible for their individual households, and others wanted new economic reforms to advocate girls' education for women's sake.[40] In effect, the gender equality model focused on women's individuality and not the nation-empire. The state-funded motherhood model, for example, called for the state to do more to fully support "good wives, wise mothers," with the implication that these mothers could better support the nation-empire in return. The socialist model criticized existing economic problems caused by capitalism and industrialization, which were started by the Meiji state to build the nation-empire. With girls' school enrollment rates at over 90 percent, the increasing number of educated women since the Russo-Japanese War had produced a group of women activists who spoke publicly on behalf of women—as individuals and as a collective group—where economy and livelihood seemed to be key issues. Many in the metropole viewed these models as threatening to the "good wife, wise mother" ideal, but none of them actually opposed their role in the home. Also, all of these models, the official ideal included, presumed that girls and women would be educated. Thus, marking a "new woman" as educated in 1910s Japanese society was similar to the Taiwanese "new woman" ideal of the 1920s.

While the "new woman" ideals in Taiwan and Japan were only similar in presuming these women as educated, the Taiwanese "black cat" of the 1930s shared greater resemblance with the (in)famous "modern girl" (Jp. *modan gaaru* or *moga* for short) in Japan than with the "new woman" ideals. Having emerged in mass media in 1920s Japan, as historian Miriam Silverberg finds, the "modern girl" was a "glittering, decadent, middle-class consumer who, through her clothing, smoking, and drinking, fl[ou]ts tradition in the urban playgrounds of the late 1920s."[41] The "modern girl" was no political activist. She was sexually promiscuous and remained independent of men and family. But, as Silverberg argues, ultimately "the discourse on the Modern Girl was more about imagining a new Japanese woman than about documenting social change," and the public attention to her body was connected to the material culture of the 1920s.[42] Silverberg asserts that the "Modern Girl's notoriety thus corresponded historically with the transition in state policy toward women's position within the family."[43] The "modern girl" reflects the reality of 1920s Japan as educated women had more work options and engaged in more political activities. Silverberg argues that the "modern girl" "inverted the role of the Good Wife and Wise Mother" as she symbolized the "overwhelming 'modern' or non-Japanese change instigated by both women and men during an era of economic crisis and social unrest."[44]

CHAPTER 2

The Japanese "modern girl" was "part of a global phenomenon" where "modern girls" were characterized by "their use of specific commodities and their explicit eroticism. . . . Adorned in provocative fashions, in pursuit of romantic love, Modern Girls appeared to disregard roles of dutiful daughter, wife, and mother" with "various colonial and national incarnations" around the world during the interwar years of the 1920s and 1930s.[45] The "modern girl" of the 1920s and the 1930s can be seen as an antithesis to the cult of domesticity of the nineteenth and twentieth centuries around the globe. In this sense, both the Japanese model and the Taiwanese "black cat" were created by urban consumerism that reflected a global trend during the interwar years.

The Korean "new woman" transformed over time to encompass different versions in contrast to various versions of womanhood that emerged in colonial Taiwan, semi-colonial China, and imperial Japan. First characterized by a Western-style education to bring forth "civilization and enlightenment" from the mid-1800s to the early 1900s, Jiyoung Suh finds, the "new woman" received the same education as the "wise wife, good mother," which was linked to Japan's "good wife, wise mother" ideal, women's liberation, and Korean nationalism. In the 1920s, Korean intellectuals recognized the conflict between the Japanese ideal womanhood and women's liberation. By the mid-1920s, the "new woman" in Korea came to embody "extravagance," "frivolity," and "consumption and sexual promiscuity" that resembled the "modern girl."[46] As a result, Korean media conflated the "new woman" and "modern girl" in the 1930s. Suh argues that the "new woman" has "a clear social feminist consciousness" that marks her as different from the "modern girl."[47] Regardless of the transformation, Suh maintains that the "new woman" had always been characterized as one who had completed more than secondary education, which had stood in contrast to the backward "old-fashioned woman" since the turn of the twentieth century.[48]

The necessity and urgency of educating girls to develop one's society motivated many colonized elites to advocate for girls' education. One such example is Lin Shuangsui, daughter of the famous Lin family from Wufeng, Taichung, who received all of her education in Tokyo after the age of seven.[49] She expressed her concern over the state of Taiwanese girls' education and its connection to Taiwan's development and women's activism in a Japanese article she wrote in 1920. Her family background supported her studies at the prestigious Aoyama Women's Academy (Jp. Aoyama Jogakuin) in Japan, which explains her fluency in Japanese.[50] Published in *Taiwan seinen*, Lin lamented that Taiwanese women were not politically active like Japanese women in the metropole. She also criticized those Taiwanese who focused on boys' education while ignoring girls' education at a time when both women and men were responsible for creating the new family in society. She believed that the lack of educated women was a hindrance to Taiwan's development.[51] Perhaps because she feared the colonial state or had embraced the idea that Taiwanese were inferior to Japanese, Lin seemed to blame Taiwanese, not the colonial state, for slowing down development in Taiwan by criticizing Taiwanese women for their political inactivism and Taiwanese families for favoring boys over girls. Her view stood in contrast to the cover article of the October 1924 issue of *Taiwan minbao*, which criticized the colonial government for failing to provide enough instructors in schools.[52] Lin linked the number of educated girls and women to the level of women's activism, regardless of whether it was the colonial state or the Taiwanese who were responsible. In other words, fewer educated women meant there were fewer women activists who might engage in discussing political, social, and economic changes that would produce alternative models to the official womanhood.

By linking educated women with women's activism, Lin provided a possible explanation for why no alternative model of womanhood posed a serious threat to the official ideal of womanhood in Taiwan in contrast to the more competitive models in China, Japan, and Korea. Scholars have documented the vibrant women's movement in China during the New Culture Movement, the strong feminism in Japan in the first half of the twentieth century, and the prominent women leaders in colonial Korea. In contrast, scholars debate the existence of women's movements in Taiwan under Japanese rule. Presuming that highly educated women were needed to start and run women's movements, Yu Chien-ming argues that no women's movement existed because the few women's groups formed under Japanese rule, such as women's youth groups (Jp. *joshi seinendan*) and maiden associations (Jp. *shojokai*), organized activities closely aligned with *dōka*. Yu also explains that the independent women's mutual encouragement associations (Ch. *gonglihui*) and women's cooperative advancement associations (Ch. *xiejinhui*) were more about networking than political activism against the colonial authority.[53] In contrast, Yang Cui argues that the women's movement began in the 1920s to fight against problems caused by capitalism, patriarchy, and colonialism.[54] Doris Chang argues in agreement that women's movements emerged as "integral parts of colonial Taiwan's social and political movements" as "Taiwanese feminist discourse emerged" in the 1920s.[55] These three scholars agree that some educated women formed groups, but they disagree on the nature of their activities—working with colonial officials versus fighting against colonial policies and Han Taiwanese customs. One important player in the women's movement was the Christian and mission schools, which produced some educated women who engaged in activism. Many studies have shown that Christian schools were successful in producing women activists after providing opportunities for women, including education.[56] In contrast to widespread Christian and mission schools for girls and women in Japan, China, and Korea, a tighter control of private schools by the colonial state, targeting Christian schools, allowed only three Christian girls' middle schools and two Christian boys' middle schools to operate in Taiwan.[57] The low number of Christian schools caused them to produce only a few students, which reduced their influence in Taiwan. Thus, these factors contributed to a short-lived or nonexistent women's movement in Taiwan compared to major anticolonial political independence movements in Korea and China and strong women's movements across other East Asian societies.

Similar to their Chinese and Korean counterparts who turned away from the official Japanese ideal in the 1920s, some Taiwanese intellectuals criticized the "good wife, wise mother" ideal but continued to champion girls' education. In 1923, one writer described girls' education in Japan as one with the goal of producing "good wives, wise mothers" who would obey their husbands without question. This education thus produced the "gentlest women in the world."[58] The article then praised Chinese women for their independence and political activism, while criticizing some Japanese and all Taiwanese women for not expressing their own thoughts. Its anonymous author concluded with the hope that men would let women be free and that women would wake up and participate in

EMBRACING EDUCATED GIRLS AND WOMEN

the liberation movement.[59] Another article, titled "Better Wife, Wiser Mother," published in 1926, criticized the purpose of the "good wife, wise mother" education at the girls' middle school. The writer lamented that such secondary education did not aim to produce talented people for society and the nation. The piece ended by expressing pity for young women in Taiwan who believed in this ideal at a time when the women's liberation movement was widespread globally.[60] Although both articles criticized those women with homemaking training and remained silent in the first wave of feminism, girls' and women's education was presumed necessary. In other words, various people agreed that educating girls and women was good but disagreed on the content of the education and how educated women should behave.

Both *Taiwan minbao* articles took a similar position to Japanese and Chinese feminists in the 1910s and the 1920s who denounced the ideal of "good wife, wise mother" and instead advocated for women's liberation. Their critique differed from those who promoted this ideal womanhood to modernize one's society. As discussed in chapter 1, the Japanese colonizers attacked foot-binding and the Manchu queue hairstyle to portray the Han Chinese culture of the Han Taiwanese as inferior while depicting the "good wife, wise mother" ideal from Japan as modern. By looking to the discussions on a modern ideal woman among Chinese intellectuals in the 1920s, some Han Taiwanese came to view China as the model for Taiwanese and Japanese women. To them, Japan no longer had a monopoly on defining Asian modernity. From their perspective, China had emerged as the more modern society. Regardless of where Han Taiwanese placed China in relation to Japan, educated Taiwanese seemed to view Taiwan as falling behind both Japan and China in promoting women's rights and activism, which seemed to mark a society's modernity and thus level of civilization. This mentality might help explain the ranking of the ideal companion by Hu Taiming, protagonist of *Orphan of Asia*: Japanese first, Chinese second, Taiwanese last.

Often, instead of directly criticizing the "good wife, wise mother" ideal or offering a competitive model to challenge this official ideal as a way to criticize the gendered, segregated educational system in Taiwan, some Taiwanese intellectuals, to criticize the colonial state, denounced the improper behavior of teachers, who were colonial agents. For example, the November 1923 issue of *Taiwan minbao* reported that a male teacher at a girls' middle school in Shōka (Changhua) had coerced a schoolgirl into a sexual relationship with him in exchange for financing her education after her father's business failed. The article cited the teacher's talk about prostitutes and virgins during class to show his unhinged sexual desire. Reportedly, the male teacher, likely Japanese because of his Japanese-sounding nickname, was not satisfied with one partner and later also persuaded a woman teacher to join him in a three-person relationship. The anonymous reporter criticized the inaction of the principal at the school. The scandal only became public after a parent complained that this male teacher had hit one of the schoolgirls who witnessed this relationship when they happened to visit the dormitory where the coerced schoolgirl and the woman teacher lived.[61] This teacher was part of a privileged group in the colony due to his Japanese ethnicity. As a man in a highly gendered society and a highly respected career professional with the status of a government official and a good salary in Taiwan, he could pay for the schoolgirl's education when her family could no longer fulfill their obligations. In Taiwanese eyes, his power allowed him to coerce an underage child and an adult woman colleague to fulfill his sexual desires and physically abuse a child witness without any accountability. The physical violence and sexual assault that he carried out as a schoolteacher, protected by school authorities through negligence, accentuated the dangers that colonial schools posed to children. The emphasis on school officials' negligence and the absence of any disciplinary actions in the report revealed an abuse of power, something that Taiwanese intellectuals would not fail to recognize and criticize as schools represented an extension of the colonial authority.

By reporting on the sexual exploitations of schoolgirls, writers of *Taiwan minbao* undoubtedly saw a parallel between teacher-student relations and the colonial hierarchy that harmed the less powerful, which contradicted the impartial and equal treatments from the colonial state guaranteed by *dōka* and the goal of liberating girls and women from Han customs that some Taiwanese sought to accomplish. Coverage from August 1924 on the same middle school in Shōka reported on a Japanese male teacher, who had divorced two to three times, holding schoolgirls in his arms under the pretense of a game while on a field trip. The writer criticized the teacher for treating these students like prostitutes. The report stated that no student complained because some students were pure and naive and did not know the seriousness of the matter, while others feared that reporting would negatively impact their grades.[62] A 1930 article reported on a teacher forcing three schoolgirls in the advanced course of a primary school to take nude pictures.[63] Another article from 1930 reported on a male teacher who sexually harassed a sixteen-year-old fifth-grader. That teacher was married with children. The article concluded by questioning the inaction of education officials. It also stated, "No wonder some parents don't feel safe sending their daughters to school."[64]

Often, the ethnicity of the teachers was not explicitly identified, but readers could infer their ethnicity based on the higher percentage of Japanese to Taiwanese teachers and from their surname as the name-changing campaign did not begin until the wartime period of the mid- to late 1930s. These reports contrasted the sexual immorality of male teachers with the purity and innocence of schoolgirls, whose main concern remained following teachers' orders to earn good grades. The comment on the school as an unsafe place suggests that some saw that schoolgirls needed protection, as the vulnerable and weaker gender, and were not in a position of power to challenge their teachers. Although this coverage ranged from primary to secondary school students, the underlying message of sexual exploitation and the violation of female chastity remained the same. Through these reports, *Taiwan minbao* portrayed schoolgirls in their early to mid-teens as vulnerable to their teachers, who embodied sexual predators in a heterosexual framing that excluded schoolboys. These Japanese male teachers represented the colonial authority while schoolgirls symbolized the Taiwanese people exploited by the Japanese. Applying the gender analysis to the power dynamic, these reports seem to reinforce the idea of male domination and power, embodied by the colonizer, over the presumed weak girls and women, embodied by the colonized.

This power relations metaphor is also implicit in the complaints that Taiwanese parents filed against teachers for exploiting their daughters as a critique of the colonial state for supporting acts that hindered the goal of educating girls and women to modernize Taiwanese homes. In a 1924 article in *Taiwan minbao* titled "Girls' Middle School Students? Maids?," a father argued that students at a girls' middle school in Changhua behaved like servants. He described in detail that schoolgirls purchased groceries using their own money and cooked for their teachers every Saturday in the name of receiving practical training. He noted that students either hired servants or themselves cleaned the teachers' dormitory and the school. The writer criticized the teachers and their associates for calling on schoolgirls to make and serve tea. He concluded by saying that these teachers should have hired women as interns using their own salary instead of using students' pocket money, which came from students' guardians.[65] Families were upset with the labor and the economic exploitation of schoolgirls because they certainly did not send their daughters to school to be unpaid servants. Girls were to be educated to become ideal women for modern homes, not to work in someone else's homes or pay for their teachers' expenses. These tasks were performed mostly by schoolgirls, not schoolboys, because such tasks were considered domestic and thus allocated to girls and women. Teachers, mostly Japanese men, who took advantage of schoolgirls' labor and financial status, came to symbolize the greed and exploitation of Japanese colonialism. However, although educated Taiwanese and guardians of schoolgirls were critical of labor exploitation, Taiwanese schoolgirls did not necessarily remember manual labor as exploitation. As will be discussed in chapter 5, some former schoolgirls fondly remembered performing these manual labor tasks.

Anticolonial progressive Taiwanese intellectuals in the 1920s focused on the liberation of Taiwanese women from constraints placed by old Han Taiwanese customs while criticizing the colonial authority by reporting incidents of schoolgirl exploitation. They were concerned with women's well-being and the positive impact of education on women's status in society. The sexual exploitation of schoolgirls by their teachers symbolized the two main manifestations of inequality in colonial Taiwan: colonialism and gender. Their families and Taiwanese intellectuals were concerned about sexual and labor exploitation perpetrated by teachers, who represented the colonial authority. Taiwanese wanted the benefits of modern schooling—modernization and civilization—without the exploitation and inequality embedded in the system. However, even as they embraced the modernization aspect of *dōka*, Taiwanese male intellectuals also embraced the inherent gendered dimension of *dōka*, which reinforced gender hierarchy in the nation-empire. Thus, colonialism

EMBRACING EDUCATED GIRLS AND WOMEN

79

combined with patriarchy limited opportunities for girls and women. Therefore, although Taiwanese intellectuals believed they could support girls' education to benefit from Japanese modernization without assimilating to become Japanese, they could be seen as complicit in the colonial project of producing "good wives, wise mothers" to make *dōka* a success. This was an inherent dilemma for the colonized population, where their acceptance of modernization through girls' education to advance their society and become equal with the colonizers reinforced colonial and gender hierarchy: Taiwanese performed manual labor in lower-paying jobs and women focused on domestic tasks, whereas Japanese dominated managerial and higher positions and men were the sole income earners. Because assimilation was inherently gendered, it was difficult, if not impossible, for Taiwanese to cherry-pick *dōka* without reinforcing its embedded gender hierarchy.

GENDERING IDEAL WOMANHOOD IN TAIWANESE FICTION IN THE 1930S AND THE 1940S

Under tightened media control in the 1930s and the 1940s, Taiwanese writers turned to fiction to illustrate the double burden—ethnicity and gender—that gendered assimilation placed on Taiwanese girls and women. Their lives did not improve because the colonial state and Han customs dictated the value of their education. The Great Depression of 1929 and the tightened control of the colonial authority in the 1930s led to a great reduction in the number of journals that could openly discuss women's liberation or criticize colonial policies. Taiwanese intellectuals turned to fiction to offer their political, economic, and social critiques. Fiction is not intended to be read literally, but the lack of direct critiques in journals meant that fiction became the main site of unraveling Taiwanese views on politically and socially sensitive topics. Alongside the police and sugar association, writer Ou Zongzhi observes, women's issues comprised the other main topic Taiwanese writers focused on in the 1930s to offer political and social criticisms. Through their works, writers criticized the treatment of girls and women as goods to be sold and bought. They depicted female protagonists as victims of arranged marriage without autonomy or as enjoying a love-based marriage but failing in other aspects of life. Reflecting reality, many stories discussed the suffering of girls and women as adopted daughters, child-brides, and concubines. In other words, women were powerless victims of a patriarchal society.[66] Although there were many male writers and very few women writers in Taiwan under Japanese rule, works written by two women and two men will be discussed here to illustrate their concerns and gender differences.

To show how the colonial state and the patriarchy created unhappy homes, the writer-political activist Ye Tao (1905–70) incorporated her personal experiences with the challenges that educated women faced in 1930s Taiwan into her short fiction "Beloved Child" (1935). Ye was born into a middle-class household, received a classical Chinese education, and then attended primary school. After completing three years of training, she became a teacher at her alma mater at the age of fifteen. She eventually quit her teaching job to head the Women's Section of the Taiwan Farmers' Association in 1928. She met her husband, Yang Kui, also a writer, through their political activism in 1927. Both were arrested, and they were jailed together by Japanese authorities. Ye had been in Japanese prison twelve times. After their marriage, Yang focused on writing while Ye focused on giving speeches as an activist. She was seen as the "face" of her household while her husband stayed at home to focus on writing and tending to the family, an arrangement that their friends considered to be reversed gender roles. Life was difficult, and they tried several things to make a living—Yang did logging while Ye designed and made children's clothes to be sold on the street. The couple also founded the literary magazine *Taiwan New Literature* before the war began and made a living by growing flowers on rented land and selling them at the market. Ye managed her household finances and, after her husband contracted tuberculosis in the 1930s, borrowed money to fully support her family.[67] Ye's challenges resembled those of the main character, Suying, in her fiction "Beloved Child." In the story, because of their constant imprisonment for political activism and consequent poverty, Suying and her husband's oldest son developed night blindness from the lack of vitamin A, which suggests malnutrition.[68]

Written from the perspectives of female characters, Ye Tao's "Beloved Child" hints at the impossibility of a financially independent household born out of romantic love under Japanese colonialism. The story centers on an encounter between two former girls' middle school classmates, Suying and Baozhu. Currently looking for employment, Suying is a former Taiwanese primary school teacher who has postponed her marriage to support her parents. She has been forced to leave her job because of her relationship with her now husband, a political activist. Faced with financial pressure and stress, she has developed some kind of nervous system disorder. Suying's husband's political activism has led to his confinement, either incarceration or house arrest. The confinement then leads to him contracting tuberculosis. He does not eat much food or take medicine because they cannot afford them. Their only child has become blind because of malnutrition, also caused by poverty. Because of her financial challenges, Suying envies her friend Baozhu, who came from a rich capitalist family and has married a local official. However, Baozhu envies Suying's marriage based on love because she married to fulfill her father's wishes. She presumes that Suying's child is perfect and healthy because he was born out of love. Baozhu has chosen not to have any children because she believes that her children would be born with mental illnesses or syphilis because of her husband's repeated infidelity.[69]

Ye Tao's fiction suggests that the ideal womanhood continued to be defined by a woman's ability to produce healthy children, yet colonialism and patriarchy hindered the actual creation of ideal women and households. Ye and her character Suying fulfilled an ideal that many educated Taiwanese progressives from the 1920s envisioned—a marriage based on love and a child born out of love. However, the 1930s was a period of tightened colonial control and was unfriendly to idealistic Taiwanese intellectuals. Romantic love between couples, where one person was politically active, would ultimately lead to unemployment and then to poverty, which would then lead to hunger and might cause illness, as shown in Ye's life and Suying's storyline. In contrast to Suying, Baozhu is a wealthy woman in a loveless marriage. The story implies that Baozhu likely contracted syphilis from her husband, who probably contracted the disease from prostitutes. Baozhu is financially well-off, but her loveless marriage, plagued by infidelity, disease, and lack of children, does not resemble the ideal nuclear family that the colonial government likely envisioned with the "good wife, wise mother" training. Except for the lack of children, Baozhu's marriage seems to resemble premodern-era arranged marriages characterized by infidelity. Both characters received the highest education possible for women living in Taiwan. Although both women have some power in making some life decisions and continue to lead a life, through Suying's ability to search for employment because of her education and Baozhu's decision not to have children, readers see that the larger external forces prevent them from creating and maintaining happy homes. Colonial oppression thus negates the positive impact of education by forcing Suying to quit her job, while patriarchy treats Baozhu's education as a tool in marriage politics. Overall, "Beloved Child" can be read as a critique of the colonial government through Suying's life and the patriarchal system through Baozhu's experience. "Beloved Child" suggests that, even with modern education, women's lives remained largely unchanged and powerless, as both the government and the family acted in their own interests at the expense of educated women.

In contrast to Ye Tao's protagonists, who speak in women's voices to offer implicit critiques of the colonial state and the patriarchal family, male writers such as Long Yingzong explicitly criticize old Han Taiwanese practices, through female supporting characters, without leveling an explicit attack against the colonial state. Through "The Town with Papaya Trees" (1937), a story about a male protagonist's future plans for his career and marriage, Long criticizes the practices of bride price and early marriage as the main reasons why debt was common in Taiwan. His story includes several female supporting characters who, despite having girls' middle school degrees, are haunted by illness and/or debt. In the story, an educated wife looks pale and is sick but has to take care of five children while dealing with high debt. Another female character contracted a sexually transmitted disease from her husband, a wealthy debaucher and wife abuser. This character has contracted tuberculosis and attempted suicide after her mother-in-law refused to spend money on her treatments. She was also forced to marry by her brother, who only cared about her husband's socioeconomic status and wealth.[70] A graduate of the Taiwan Business School (Jp. Taiwan Shōkō Gakkō) who was privileged with steady employment in financial and literary sectors during and after Japanese rule, Long criticized bride price, medical debt, and the emotional and physical abuse of women. Long is also known

EMBRACING EDUCATED GIRLS AND WOMEN

for exploring the inner world of intellectuals, commoners, and women by incorporating the challenges posed by the wartime imperialization program into his stories.[71]

Long's story and other fictions reveal that status, wealth, and old practices overpowered the transformative power of girls' education. The fate of many female characters in "The Town with Papaya Trees" resembles that of many other fictional characters from the colonial period: women end up dead by suicide or become crazy as a result of loveless engagement or marriage, the sale of their children because of poverty, or rape, with patriarchy as the root of women's suffering.[72] These stories often describe women being left to their suffering without others to care for or support them. Long emphasizes the persistence of old customs and human greed as motivating people to embrace education to further their personal goals. Although some have names, many female characters are nameless and identified only as the wife or sister of a male character. The nameless characters suggest that women are dependent on men in a patriarchal society, and Long likely seeks to demonstrate women's lack of control over their lives as they are treated as goods to be traded and used by men. In this sense, colonial education failed Taiwanese girls and women because it did not change their lives compared to before Japanese colonization. If Japanese colonial officials seemed to promise modernization and civilization through *dōka*, Long, Ye, and other writers did not seem to think education "modernized" or "civilized" Taiwan to make positive changes to girls' and women's lives when old Han Taiwanese customs persisted and seemed to have become empowered by a colonial state that reinforced women's role at home.

By the wartime period, when the colonial authority demanded loyalty and labor from the Taiwanese without criticism of the colonial state, Yang Qianhe published "The Season When Flowers Blossom" to express the helplessness felt by educated girls and women without criticizing the colonial state. In "The Season When Flowers Blossom," readers learn that four out of eleven schoolgirls were already engaged before graduation. The narrator, Huiying, laments that a woman's life moves from being an innocent infant to an adult who produces and raises children before finally dying of old age, as quoted at the beginning of this chapter. Huiying believes that graduates have no goals in life and thus settle for marriage. Although Huiying resists getting married young, all characters, both reluctant and willing, view marriage as inevitable. Huiying applies to and accepts a job without informing her family beforehand because her neighbors would talk, but she quits her job after six months.[73] Her action reveals that girls' middle school graduates were not expected to work, especially those from an upper-class background. One of Huiying's classmates, the wife of a physician, declares that one's life is incomplete without marriage because marriage will bring about every emotion and experience, happy and bitter ones, and more importantly, it marks one's transition into adulthood. The story ends with Huiying happily visiting her best friend and the friend's newborn son at the hospital.[74]

Yang Qianhe's short story does not explicitly criticize the purpose of girls' education or old customs, but it highlights the anxiety felt by some of the most highly educated young women, who had limited, if any, choices in life. Education was part of an upper-middle-class girl's experience but would not revolutionize her life course. It did not inspire these women to set personal goals, other than marriage. These young women were not expected to work permanently, if at all, after completing their education. Their existence was defined by arranged marriage and, as the ending of the story suggests, having their own children after marriage. "The Season When Flowers Blossom" suggests that education did not have any life-changing effects for girls and women, except expanding their social network of friends. Also worthy of note, it was unlikely for highly educated women to lead peaceful lives during wartime mobilization because of anxiety, as depicted in Yang's fiction. However, considering the year the story was published, either Yang sought to narrate a fantasy life before the war or to emphasize the impossibility of such lifestyle during the war.

As literary critic Xu Junya pointed out, women writers depicted their female characters differently from their male counterparts even though they shared similar critiques against patriarchy. Xu emphasizes that women writers depicted traditional female characters as worthy of respect because these "women writers had to resist capitalist, colonial, and patriarchal control to crack open the illusion of colonized women being liberated."[75] In contrast, as Xu observes, male writers, who were no longer bound by traditions and had become critical of these old traditions, wrote from the view that they pitied these female characters for the suffering caused by their own foolishness and ignorance, while placing these characters within the often traditional social confines in Taiwan.[76] Xu notes that women writers tended to create female characters with individual personalities without reliance on men, whereas male writers often created female characters who lacked confidence and were desperately trapped. The gendered depiction of female characters reveals that male writers saw "the liberation of women as part of social reform" rather than being genuinely concerned about women's welfare.[77] In contrast, the characters of women writers often embodied part of their own experiences or observations. Ultimately, Xu asserts, male writers addressed women's issues as a means to an end by depicting women as a symbol of oppression, whereas women writers actually cared about women's issues, engaging in constant self-reflection and seeking to use their education and skills to draw attention to those issues.[78]

Written during the war but published after Japanese colonial rule had ended, Wu Zhuoliu incorporates his life experiences into *Orphan of Asia* and offers many critiques against Han Taiwanese customs and the institutionalized discrimination of the colonial state but suggests that Taiwanese had embraced the "good wife, wise mother" ideal. Wu graduated from Taihoku Normal School (Jp. Taihoku Shihan Gakkō) and worked as a primary school teacher before quitting his profession in 1940 to protest the abusive treatment of Taiwanese teachers by Japanese educational inspectors. He worked as a reporter in China in 1941 and then in Taiwan after 1942.[79] Although similar to other male writers in sympathizing with female characters who are victims of patriarchal practices, Wu differs from other male writers in that he sets up different ideals of educated women as the love interests for the male protagonist, Hu Taiming. Like Wu, Taiming graduated from a teacher-training program and became a primary school teacher before he quit his job after witnessing several discriminatory practices against Taiwanese teachers and students and after experiencing a big heartbreak.[80]

As discussed in the introductory section, although Taiming ends up marrying a "new woman," his ideal woman resembles the "good wife, wise mother" ideal. Taiming's first love interest is a fellow teacher who is Japanese named Naito Hisako. She will not accept his love because of their different ethnicities, and she views Taiwanese as barbaric and unhygienic. Although he struggles between loving Hisako and disapproving of her prejudice against Taiwanese, Taiming has been annoyed with Ruie, a fellow Taiwanese, who shows much affection and kindness toward him. He later appreciates her kindness but, nevertheless, leaves Taiwan for Japan, the metropole. He considers Taiwanese women to be "boorish."[81] After marriage, Taiming becomes unhappy with Shuchun because she does not perform the tasks expected of a wife or mother. She spends her time outside the household, enjoying her professional, social, and political life, which is almost antithetical to the "good wife, wise mother" model. His hope that her pregnancy will bring out the so-called innate call of a mother is dashed when Shuchun "fully recovered her old self as a new woman" after childbirth and assigns the household servant to tend to their child.[82] Taiming believes that he would enjoy his life if his wife were a Japanese woman whom he met in the metropole. Interestingly, it is not Ruie, the kind and affectionate Taiwanese teacher, whom he recalls but Tsuruko, a Japanese woman in the metropole, that he wishes had become his wife instead of a Chinese "new woman."[83] Taiming's preference likely reflects the more open atmosphere in the metropole, where Taiwanese men experienced less discrimination than at home in Taiwan and could have a relationship with Japanese women. The novel also does not describe any of Tsuruko's actions as discriminatory, in contrast to Hisako.

Taiming's choice of the ideal marriage partner suggests that many educated Taiwanese men had embraced the ideal of "good wife, wise mother" that pointed to an educated Japanese woman as the ideal combination of womanhood, education, and ethnicity. Ultimately, Taiming desires someone who conforms to the colonial official ideal rather than any alternative models from Japan, China, or Taiwan. Although competing models existed in the metropole, Japanese women seem to represent the official ideal and Taiming's dream companion in *Orphan of Asia*. Taiming's wife represents the "new woman" ideal popular among progressive intellectuals from mainland China, a product of the New Culture Movement, whom Taiming seems to regret marrying. Through Hisako, Tsuruko, Ruie, and Shuchun, the novel suggests that women represented levels of desired civilization—Japanese ranked the highest, followed by Chinese, and Taiwanese ranked the lowest in the eyes of educated Taiwanese. Taiming's choice to teach in mainland China and marry a Chinese woman, which ends with his sudden and forced departure from mainland China and leaving behind Shuchun and his child, suggests that a Taiwanese attempting to escape Japanese influence and assimilate into Chinese society would be an utter failure because a Taiwanese would never be trusted by either group. Feeling frustrated at home in Taiwan, alienated in Japan, and rejected in China, Taiming represents Taiwanese living at the crossroads of Japan and China. Additionally, a Taiwanese woman could never become a "good wife, wise mother" because of her ethnicity, which suggests that *dōka* would ultimately fail in Taiwan.

Although Taiwanese fictions in the 1930s criticized girls' education for not improving women's lives, Wu Zhuoliu's novel and Yang Qianhe's short fiction seem to suggest that the "good wife, wise mother" ideal triumphed during the wartime period. In work colored by the economic and wartime plight of the 1930s and the 1940s, these writers used the sufferings of the female characters in the stories to question the modernizing impact of girls' and women's education. Their writings suggest that not only did colonial education fail but society as a whole also failed girls and women. Through their fiction, Ye Tao and Long Yingzong expose the economic hardship that even educated Taiwanese faced in the 1930s because political oppression limited their economic opportunities. However, after the onset of Japan's full-scale war against China, colonial authorities sought to use "good wives, wise mothers" to rally the colonized population to support the war in spirit and in practice. The absence of an alternative to the "good wife, wise mother" ideal in Yang's fiction "When Flowers Blossom" coincides with the early wartime period, when the colonial government intensified its gendered mobilization efforts. This mobilization will be discussed in more detail in chapter 3. Written in the late wartime period, Wu Zhuoliu's novel presents several models with the official ideal of "good wife, wise mother" as the most desirable but also unattainable one. Hence, gendered assimilation was highly desirable but never attainable for the Taiwanese.

Educated Taiwanese, conservatives and liberals alike and mostly men because of the large gap between school enrollment rates for boys compared to those of girls, accepted the basic premise of the ideal of "good wife, wise mother"—that educated women were key to creating a modern and civilized society. However, many also criticized the colonial state and the patriarchal system for hindering women's status and thus slowing down Taiwan's path to becoming modern and civilized. Some Taiwanese criticized the sexual and labor exploitation of schoolgirls by male teachers in order to critique the unequal colonial hierarchy inherent in the educational system. They also denounced the cruelty of older Han Taiwanese customs and practices in a patriarchal system that maintained an unequal gender hierarchy. As both male and female writers criticized patriarchy and colonialism for causing and perpetuating women's suffering, their writings revealed a gender difference: male writers' depiction of hopeless women served as one issue in the greater social movement to advance Taiwan, whereas women writers' depiction of strong-willed female characters sought to focus on women's rights and issues.

Whether or not it was invoked explicitly, the "good wife, wise mother" ideal, whose existence was to build and strengthen the nation-empire, remained the dominant figure in contradistinction to other models of womanhood that were not seen as likely to increase the power of the nation-empire in Taiwan. In a sense, it was in Taiwan that the "good wife, wise mother" campaign in East Asia was the most successful because no competitive alternative threatened the official ideal in Taiwan. The emergence of several "new woman" models and the "modern girl" as competitors to the "good wife, wise mother" in Japan, the call for women's liberation against the "good wife, wise mother" model during the New Culture Movement in China, and the explicitly anticolonial stance of the Korean "new woman" reveal that "good wife, wise mother" encouraged the production of competing ideals in East Asian societies. Taiwan seemed to be an anomaly in that its "new woman" and "black cat" developed later than in other East Asian societies and posed no serious threat to the official ideal. The low schoolgirl enrollment rates before the 1930s and strict control of Christian schools likely hindered the development of a mature women's movement to effectively challenge the official ideal. Taiwan's colonial status and its delayed women's activism when compared to Japan, China, and Korea might help explain why some intellectuals such as Wu Zhuoliu would rank Taiwan behind Japan and China, where Japan or China was the model for Taiwan to follow to become modern. Because *dōka* was always gendered, Taiwanese could never became "true" Japanese in the nation-empire.

Although Taiwanese intellectuals embraced girls' education as part of their effort to accept the modernization part of *dōka* while rejecting its embedded Japanization, girls' education was tied to the "good wife, wise mother" ideal. This official ideal ended up reinforcing the existing patriarchal system based on Han Taiwanese customs by defining a woman's role as being in the home, which perpetuated patriarchy. The discourses on the "good wife, wise mother" ideal and girls' education among Taiwanese intellectuals show that these intellectuals could not embrace modernization without also accepting the embedded gender hierarchy. Thus, Taiwanese men might benefit from modernization but much less so for women. Even though Han Taiwanese schoolgirls no longer bound their feet and were allowed to receive education under Japanese rule, the persistence of a gender hierarchy, supported by patriarchy and the colonial state, hindered the improvement of the status and life cycle of girls and women from the old to a modern society.

3

✽

MOBILIZING

FOR THE WAR

Xu Xianxian was in her early twenties when the American bombing began in 1943. She lived in Taipei, the capital of Taiwan under Japanese rule. At the time, she had already graduated from home economics school and was working in the banking industry. She rushed home after work because air raids had become regular occurrences, and everyone expected them at certain hours:

> We all ate and showered quickly [after work]. At around 9:00 p.m., we all went to hide [in the bomb shelters]. . . . It was when the moon was out. American planes flew over our heads. The planes looked beautiful, but we were also very scared. The planes flew over our heads. If they had dropped the bombs then, you know [we would have died]. But we were also curious, [we wondered] what American planes looked like. It was very bright. They dropped fluorescent light, and all of Taipei City became very bright. It was prettier than the night lit up by the moonlight. We were curious and wanted to see, but we were also scared.[1]

Xu's complex response to the bombing—terror mixed with curiosity and a certain appreciation—was typical of how many Taiwanese girls and women responded to the wartime period. They recalled the war and air raids as a scary time. Yet they also found some pleasure in the disruption of their daily routine. Looking back nearly seven decades later, virtually everyone remembered the air raids and evacuations. But what they also recalled were the small pleasures of daily routines—farming, putting things together for soldiers, and practicing the virtues of thrift and simplicity on and outside of school grounds.

This chapter explores how the colonial government mobilized Han Taiwanese schoolgirls as a major source of labor on the home front during World War II. It examines the intersection between war and education and the gendered dimensions of wartime labor. As the war intensified and Han Taiwanese schoolboys trained for military service, the colonial government mobilized female labor, especially unmarried young women and schoolgirls, to ensure continuous wartime production and daily operations in Taiwan. In addition to receiving wartime training on school grounds, schoolgirls were mobilized to contribute to agricultural production and to cheer on soldiers. However, with intensive air raids in the final year of the war, schoolgirls' wartime school routine was disrupted, and students either stopped attending school or had to evacuate to the hills. Wartime mobilization illustrates how the state reinforced gender roles and expanded the role of women through gender-specific activities to maintain its control over the colonized population in the midst of a war. Ultimately, the colonial state was successful at coercing cooperation from colonized peoples of all ages, genders, and classes, regardless of whether they were loyal to the Japanese state. In contrast to the gendered assimilation of the prewar period, the war expanded the space of the ideal woman from the home setting to the public setting as schoolgirls and "good wives, wise mothers" often had to perform their caring and supportive role outside of their households for soldiers, people who were not family members or were complete strangers.

As seen in Taiwan, the young, educated female population in a colony played an important role on the home front as the colonial government differentially mobilized the colonial population depending on age, gender, and region. Even colonized children and youths were not exempt from participating in this total war as part of a "total empire."[2] According to Joshua S. Goldstein, "the socialization of children into gender roles helps reproduce the war system."[3] Boys were socialized to be masculine, which was connected to their aggressive killing on the front line.[4] In the case of Japan, Sabine Frühstück argues that twentieth-century Japanese militarism successfully positioned children as innocent, vulnerable, and

CHAPTER 3

in need of maternal nurturing but who simultaneously received gendered training through "playful, enjoyable," and "physical" war games: boys as soldiers and girls as nurses.[5] In other words, the war reinforced gender roles, and gender roles also strengthened the war system. This total war operated within Japan's "total empire," which Louise Young argues was created by nineteenth-century imperialism and modernization where the empire's military conquest would not be successful without "cultural, military, political, and economic" mobilization in the metropole, from businesses, the media, and intellectuals to organized "war support associations, business unions, colonization committees," "chambers of commerce, political parties, and women's groups."[6]

Age and gender were important factors shaping one's role during wartime mobilization. The war destabilized the categories of class and ethnicity, but gender norms remained within colonial Taiwan. Yoshiko Miyake's study found that the Japanese state was reluctant to mobilize women's labor in the industrial sector. When it finally did, it targeted unmarried women because the state wished to propagate the domestic role of married women, specifically women's reproductive roles.[7] Unlike Great Britain and the United States, the Japanese state valued women's reproductive labor more than their industrial labor. In addition to official policies, Japanese authorities continued to promote the idea of "good wife, wise mother" through wartime films that championed traditional family values and women's supportive roles during wartime.[8] Mobilization policies in Japan were exported to Taiwan. Yang Yahui's study on the wartime training of women of different ages in various regions in Taiwan argues that, as the colonial education policy and wartime mobilization reinforced the women-home relationship and gender roles, the government emphasized that female labor served the nation and was an important part of wifely and motherly virtues.[9] Unmarried women, including schoolgirls, were an important source of labor mobilization during World War II. This chapter argues that the making of imperial subjects was gendered during wartime mobilization. Gendered assimilation became almost attainable for the Taiwanese toward the end of the war compared to the prewar *dōka* efforts. The labor and resources necessary to sustain the war led to the increasing incorporation of Taiwan into the nation-empire.

THE ROLE OF TAIWAN IN JAPANESE
EXPANSION AND *KŌMINKA*

From the mid-1930s to 1945, the mobilization of women and children was crucial to the Japanese effort to establish Taiwan as an important base for the expansion of Japanese imperial ambitions. The appointment in September 1936 of Kobayashi Seizō, the first governor-general of Taiwan with a military background after eighteen years of civilian rule, signaled Japan's ambitions in Southeast Asia and the Pacific.[10] Kobayashi set three goals for Taiwan: *kōminka* (imperial subjectification), *kōgyōka* (industrialization), and *nanshinka* (southern expansion).[11] The goal of *kōminka* was to turn the Taiwanese into loyal Japanese imperial subjects, and the purpose of *kōgyōka* was to transform Taiwan into an important agricultural-processing site with links to South China and Southeast Asia.[12] The mission of *nanshinka* was to make Taiwan into the core base for Japan's expansion into Southeast Asia and the Pacific.[13] These three goals foreshadowed the role that the Taiwanese, including children and young women, would play on the front line and the home front in Japan's full-scale war in China and the Pacific.

The *kōminka* movement was the single most important effort by the colonial government to transform the thinking of the colonized population during wartime mobilization. According to Leo Ching, *kōminka* was a disruptive change from the assimilation policy that had preceded it because it shifted the responsibility of becoming Japanese "from the colonial state to the colonized subjects," each member of which was asked to transform from being a person "living as Japanese to being an imperial subject willing to die" for the empire.[14] The concept of *kōminka* appeared in official documents in 1936 and was implemented after Japan's full-scale invasion of China (July 1937) as colonial officials became increasingly concerned about the loyalty of the Han Taiwanese population, whose ancestors came from mainland China.[15] Through *kōminka*, Japanese leaders sought to increase Japaneseness and reduce Chineseness among the Han Taiwanese population through campaigns to spread the Japanese language; name changes from Taiwanese to Japanese; teaching of the Japanese anthem; Shintō shrine worship; bans on Taiwanese operas and puppet shows; and critiques of superstitions, traditional marriage,

CHAPTER 3

and funeral practices.[16] These policies show the colonial effort to Japanize the lifestyle of every Taiwanese. Although school administrators and teachers, with the backing of the state, designed activities to coerce patriotic behaviors, it is unclear whether these behaviors reflected their thinking. Nevertheless, Ching asserts that cultural assimilation during *kōminka* freed the Taiwanese from the political and economic inequality inherent in *dōka* as they adopted Japanese names and spoke only Japanese to show their loyalty to Japan.[17] Similarly, Takashi Fujitani argues that wartime mobilization led Japanese leaders to shift from "treating colonial subjects simply as objects of rule to considering them active subjects of self-knowledge and reflection" in Japan's quest to form a "postcolonial, multiethnic nation-state and empire."[18] Fujitani observes that the volunteer military programs and other patriotic acts in Japanese colonies can be seen as the product of this shift from "vulgar" (exclusionary) racism to "polite" (inclusionary) racism. The shift in official policy helps explain why some Taiwanese might have contributed to the war effort because they felt that they belonged in the nation-empire or were even true Japanese.[19] Although these studies argue that ethnic divisions were blurred because the colonized population had choices in performing patriotic acts, this chapter suggests that individual choices were limited by one's gender, and thus the war reinforced gender divisions.

The colonial government's increasing demand for Taiwanese men to provide military service foreshadowed the need to mobilize female and child labor on the home front. The colonial government solicited and drafted Taiwanese men for military service as military porters (Jp. *gunfu*) and military civilian employees (Jp. *gunsoku*) around 1937, as volunteer soldiers (Jp. *shiganhei*) in 1942, and as conscripted soldiers in 1945.[20] As military porters, Taiwanese recruits transported food supplies, luggage, and ammunition; worked as military farmers who grew vegetables for military consumption in mainland China and Southeast Asia; and were responsible for construction work.[21] The civilian employees performed technical, legal, prison guard, and translation work as well as other miscellaneous tasks.[22] As casualties increased and the supply of Japanese draftees failed to meet the demand of Japan's expansion into Southeast Asia and the Pacific after 1941, Japanese leadership turned to Taiwanese men as a source of combat forces. A special army volunteer system went into effect in Taiwan in February 1942, a special navy volunteer system became effective in both Taiwan and Korea in August 1943, and a military draft was implemented in Taiwan in January 1945.[23] By offering their services and their lives on the front line, what Leo Ching called "the materialization of assimilatory practices," Taiwanese men thus became imperial Japanese subjects, comparable to their Japanese counterparts in practice.[24]

When mobilizing the home front, the colonial government targeted Taiwanese male and female youths under the age of twenty-five who were not enrolled in school by organizing them into youth groups. These youths were important as agricultural and military laborers on the home front and as reserves of soldiers and nurses. Considered to be the "lifeblood of the nation" (Jp. *kokka katsuryoku no gensen*), the colonial authority first organized youth groups in 1930 to intensify *dōka*.[25] Youth group membership was drawn from upper-class graduates of primary schools before 1939, and lower-middle-class youths, regardless of whether they had completed primary school education, were included beginning in 1939. In April 1937, there were a total of 25,909 youth group members. By 1944, there were 421,000 male youth group members and 313,000 female youth group members.[26] The colonial authority mainly targeted primary school graduates to be members of the youth groups because the colonial state trusted them to be patriotic in contrast to middle school graduates, who were deemed "arrogant" and "lack[ing] practical ability."[27] Besides "lectures, reading, and character-building activities" and military exercises, youth groups likely attracted members through theatrical shows, sport games, singing and dancing parties, and festivals with "sociable interactions, leisure and learning" as the "core elements in youth training."[28] Their wartime contributions included "providing agricultural and construction labor" and Japanese-language lessons.[29] In the youth groups, young women received physical training and "learn[ed] skills and manners associated with feminine attributes of Japanese culture, including cooking, sewing, music, flower arrangement, archery, and dancing."[30] Sayaka Chatani argues that these youth groups helped incorporate young men, especially rural youth, into Japan's nation-empire building and identify themselves as patriotic "Japanese."[31] In other words, these young Taiwanese men seemed to be truly Japanized and made *dōka* a success.

CHAPTER 3

Most young women stayed on the home front, but a few joined the front line. Between 1942 and 1944, approximately 900 unmarried Taiwanese women between the ages of sixteen and twenty-five worked as assistant nurses or qualified nurses abroad, mostly in Guangdong, Hong Kong, and the Philippines.[32] Some women were recruited to serve as nurses, waitresses, or kitchen assistants on the front line only to discover their real task was to serve as "comfort women" (military sex slaves) once they had arrived in mainland China or Southeast Asia. Similar to their Korean and Japanese counterparts, Han Taiwanese and Taiwanese indigene "comfort women" sent to China and Southeast Asia were unmarried and married women of poor, lower-class background who were tricked by recruiters or forced into the role by police officers. Official counts stated that a total of 385 Taiwanese "comfort women" were sent to mainland China between November 1938 and December 1939.[33] Women's participation on the front line shows that wartime mobilization was gendered like that of the home front.

The targeted population and the training of the youth centers showed that, as Taiwanese male youths were mobilized for military service, Taiwanese women and girls had to fill the gaps in the labor force left by the male recruits. Each county and local government organized the labor force differently. For example, Taihoku (Taipei) County organized the labor force into three groups: the general public, schools, and youth. In contrast, Shinchiku (Hsinchu) County organized the labor force into groups of young women, married women, and workers by profession. Overall, the youth corps and the schools performed more than half of all labor on the home front.[34] With able-bodied men working in the military and in the factories, women and youth became major sources of labor on the home front.

The training and mobilization of Taiwanese youth were part of an effort that spanned the entire Japanese empire. In the metropole, the state legalized its control of human and material resources in 1938 with the National General Mobilization Law.[35] Students were mobilized after the Patriotic Labor Association Law in 1941 and fully integrated into wartime mobilization with the Student Labor Law of 1944 to deal with labor shortages.[36] The government encouraged women to organize patriotic labor corps to support the war from their school, workplace, and

MOBILIZING FOR THE WAR

97

neighborhood in the metropole.[37] In November 1941, unmarried women between the ages of sixteen and twenty-five were required to register for wartime labor. Starting in January 1944, the state organized Japanese women into Women's Labor Volunteer Corps to build aircraft and other essentials.[38] By August 1944, the government also required women to provide one year of industrial work. Women worked in various sectors, ranging from agriculture, forestry, fishing, and mining, to manufacturing, construction, transportation, and communication. When the war ended, approximately three million Japanese women had worked outside the domestic sphere.[39] Women in the colonies of Taiwan and Korea also had to serve the state. Korean women who served in women's volunteer corps were called "flowers of Japanese-Korean unity."[40] In both the metropole and the colony, the government mobilized single women and exempted married women from labor conscription. This policy suggests that Japanese officials valued women's reproductive contribution more than their industrial labor, which suggests that the family unit and women's role at home were seen as essential to winning the war.

With its emphasis on women's responsibilities in the home and its reluctance to mobilize married women, Japanese official policy differed from how other great powers mobilized women. On the extreme opposite end of the "good wife, wise mother" ideal, the Soviet Union passed a universal military duty law in September 1939 that accepted women into the military. The Soviet Union trained women to fire weapons as women comprised 8 percent of all combatants, and eight hundred thousand women served in the Red Army during the war. A more moderate and perhaps more practical mobilization of women was accomplished through women's auxiliary units in Great Britain and Germany, where the official or public stance on ideal womanhood (cult of domesticity) led to restrictions on whether women were allowed to fire weapons. Great Britain organized mixed-gender units to target enemy aircraft and buzz bombs with a limited number of people to protect the home, while male soldiers focused on offensive missions.[41] Germany, Japan's ally, initially followed the "good wife, wise mother" ideal closely because women were deemed necessary to preserve the Aryan race. However, some began performing clerical work for the military through the Female Auxiliary Units in 1941. The German state then drafted women into industry starting in

January 1943 and began military conscription of women in 1944. By the end of the war, 450,000 German women had joined women's auxiliaries, and women made up 85 percent of formerly male posts such as accountants, interpreters, laboratory workers, and administrative workers and 50 percent of the "clerical and administrative posts in high-level field headquarters."[42] The United States considered using women in combat after seeing Great Britain's success. However, top US officials' fear of a negative public reaction, along with the reality that women were intended to be employed only in "clerical and administrative jobs" in women's auxiliary units unless battles were to take place on mainland United States, ended up preventing the government from taking such measures.[43] Furthermore, American men, "mostly male soldiers[,] were strongly opposed to the Women's Army Corps and urgently advised their sisters and friends not to join" because military service symbolized manhood and there were rumors of sexual promiscuity and lesbianism in the Women's Army Corps.[44] The absence of military threat to the continental United States and Canada helps explain why the US government used propaganda campaigns to promote the iconic Rosie the Riveter and Canada publicized the Bren Gun Girl, both of whom were portrayed as contributing to the war through their industrial labor.[45] Female labor was needed on the industrial front in North America, not as combatants on the front line.

Interestingly, the mobilization of women in the Japanese nation-empire was more similar to that in the United States than Germany or Great Britain, based on their level of wartime combat permitted by the government. The presence of battles in Europe no doubt forced European leaders to mobilize women into combat even if they were initially reluctant; but American and Canadian leaders, who did not experience battles on their homeland, did not do so. The Soviets allowed women to become combatants, Great Britain allowed limited combat, Germany permitted less involvement than Great Britain but more than the United States, and the United States focused on women's industrial power, while Japan only mobilized unmarried women in the late years of the war. In contrast to the Rosie the Riveter propaganda campaign in the United States, which successfully mobilized 6.3 million mothers, Japan did not promote an image of wartime womanhood because of its insistence on the "good wife, wise mother" ideal.[46] As discussed in previous chapters, a "good wife, wise mother" was crucial to the home, which formed the foundation of the Japanese nation. Japanese officials might have feared the collapse of the empire-nation without a strong foundation that relied on "good wives, wise mothers." They likely recognized the importance of domestic labor and did not want married women with children to work outside of the home, which reduced their time spent on domestic labor. It was also possible that Japanese officials did not have the capacity to deal with "motherless home[s]" like in the United States, where the federal and state governments spent more than US$75 million building childcare centers, or "war nurseries," to support the Rosie the Riveter campaign.[47] Another explanation for the limited mobilization of women's industrial contribution could be that unmarried women, with men who remained on the home front, made up a sufficient labor force to produce supplies and weaponry for the war without compromising the "good wife, wise mother" ideal. Also, Japan's military volunteer system and military conscription of Korean and Taiwanese men, labor conscription within its expanding nation-empire, and extraction of resources from Southeast Asia likely provided enough support for Japan's imperial expansion.[48]

Thus, female and child labor filled the vacuum in the educational, service, and agricultural sectors on the home front in Taiwan. Women who had graduated from primary school were active in a wide range of fields; certain factory work required some education, and clerical jobs required a degree from primary school or girls' middle school.[49] These jobs required workers to speak Japanese with Japanese supervisors, co-workers, and clients. Han Taiwanese women had been active in various manufacturing jobs before 1937. Lower-class women had been working in light industries, and middle- and upper-class women had been working in the educational and medical sectors since before the war.[50] For example, women comprised 98.3 percent of the workforce in the woven-hat industry (154,781 women), 35 percent (15,293 women) of the workforce in the food-processing industry, and 52.5 percent (3,199 women) of all tea production workers in 1936.[51] An increasing number of women had begun to work outside the home before the war, but the job vacancies left by men who joined the military accelerated this process and expanded it into new fields.

CHAPTER 3

MOBILIZING PATRIOTIC THINKING
THROUGH *KOKUGO* LESSONS

School was the most important site where the state trained children of different backgrounds to be loyal and skillful patriots. The teaching of the Japanese language was the most important course in the *kokugo* education. It was fundamental in mobilizing young minds to accomplish gendered assimilation and perform patriotic acts during the war. When government officials were revising the fourth edition of language textbooks (1937–42) in 1935, Katō Harumasa, the director of the textbook editing team, explicitly stated that the accompanying illustrations in the language textbooks were deployed to reform Han Taiwanese customs and to assimilate Taiwanese into Japanese, with the ultimate goal of Taiwanese children embracing the Japanese image as their own.[52] The final edition (1943–44) pushed *kōminka* to its height as Japan engaged in full-scale war against the United States and the Allied forces in the Pacific. Alongside the accompanying illustrations, the increased presence of and role played by Taiwanese girls and women in the two wartime editions of the primary school language textbooks suggests that gender training was fundamental to the success of gendered mobilization during the war.

From wartime language textbooks, primary schoolchildren learned about the *kokugo* campaign and the *kokugo no ie* (Japanese-language household) campaign. Both sought to erase Han Taiwanese identity and culture while emphasizing various roles that women served in the *kōminka* process. In the 1937–42 edition, a second-grade lesson titled "Kokugo no ie," tells of Michio's visit to his friend Yūichi's place on a Sunday. The lesson reveals that Yūichi's grandfather has learned *kokugo* after attending a *kokugo* workshop. It also tells how Yūichi's grandmother, who is unable to go to the language workshop because of her weak legs, is learning some *kokugo* after Yūichi's grandfather started going to the workshop, presumably from her husband. In the lesson, Yūichi's grandfather tells Michio, "From now on, I will study *kokugo* with Yūichi. I want to be able to speak *kokugo* at home." Upon hearing that Yūichi's parents do speak *kokugo* as primary school graduates, Michio's father comments that Yūichi's family will likely become a *kokugo no ie*.[53] The accompanying illustration shows an elderly man dressed in a Western-style shirt and

FIG. 11 "Kokugo Household" (1937–42). Courtesy of the Institute of Taiwan History Archive, Academia Sinica.

pants, talking to two primary-school-age boys dressed in school uniforms in front of a brick house (fig. 11).[54] Their outward appearance would be considered modern and fits the image of subjects in the nation-empire. Although both boys have Japanese names, likely part of the name-changing campaign of *kōminka*, students could infer that Yūichi's family is not ethnically Japanese because ethnic Japanese residing in Taiwan were not targeted to learn Japanese, nor did any Japanese household become *kokugo no ie*, because ethnic Japanese in Taiwan were presumed to be proficient in Japanese and loyal to the nation-empire. After reading the lesson, second-grade Taiwanese children could tell their elderly grandparents to attend a *kokugo* workshop so that everyone in the family could speak Japanese, as Yūichi's grandfather has done. The *kokugo* campaign of *kōminka* targeted those without primary school educations, likely to be the elderly, who were from a time when education was less widespread in Taiwan. Thus, Yūichi's grandmother is significant to the *kokugo* campaign because her Japanese proficiency is key to achieving the ideal wartime household goal of *kokugo no ie*. The basic qualification of a *kokugo no ie* was that every family member had to be proficient in Japanese before a household could apply for this status. The incentives included a certificate with some privileges, including admission to Japanese elementary schools, priority admissions to middle schools, priority hiring in government jobs, and higher chances of obtaining business licenses.[55]

The replacement of the lesson "Kokugo no ie" in the 1937–42 edition by "Grandmother's Kokugo" in the 1943–44 edition of textbooks reveals the attention that colonial officials and educators gave to assimilating women in the absence of the men who were mobilized and away from home during the later years of the war. Similar to the narrator's name in the previous lesson, Hana, the narrator, has a Japanese name. She talks about the progress that her grandmother has made in learning *kokugo*. Her grandmother finds asking Hana to help her read a book troublesome in a household where everyone except her is *kokugo* proficient. However, Hana's grandmother started attending the *kokugo* workshop with a woman neighbor three months ago and has not missed any lessons. Hana's grandmother is happy to comply with Hana's mother's request to read the telegram that Hana's father has sent from Taihoku. Hana's mother then compliments Hana's grandmother.[56] The colored illustration shows three people sitting on tatami floor: an elderly woman in glasses and a Western-style button-up blouse holding a piece of paper, a primary school–age girl with short hair in a Western dress, and an adult woman in a collared shirt with a sweater (fig. 12).[57] Everyone is dressed in Western clothing, not traditional Han Taiwanese or Japanese clothing.

The concept of acquiring Japanese proficiency through the *kokugo* workshop and seeking an educated grandchild's help is similar to the message in the 1937–42 edition of the textbooks, but the all-female cast in the 1943–44 edition suggests that the *kōminka* movement sought to expand the reach of *dōka* into Taiwanese homes, continuing the vision colonial officials and educators had had since the early colonial period. Hana's grandmother might have been motivated to learn Japanese to not feel left out when her family speaks Japanese, but the focus of the lesson remains that of *dōka*. *Dōka* had always targeted the home through educated girls and women, and thus it was no surprise that the *kokugo* campaign included a domestic side where women were mobilized to help

MOBILIZING FOR THE WAR

Fig. 12 "Grandmother's Kokugo." Courtesy of SMC Publishing.

increase its success. Currently attending school, Hana teaches *kokugo* to her grandmother. The lesson shows that Hana's family remains in contact with Hana's father through letter writing, which requires literacy that was presumed to be Japanese. Although the lesson does not specify why Hana's father is away from home, the wartime context suggests that he has been mobilized. Thus, Japanese proficiency also links the home with those mobilized by the war, in addition to marking one's membership in the nation-empire. If school was the main site to learn how to become Japanese, then Taiwanese elderly like Yūichi's grandparents and Hana's grandmother were the only ones left in Taiwan who had not had Japanese schools to attend when they were children. They represent the old Taiwan, and their assimilation would symbolize the success of *dōka* in Taiwan. Younger generations like Hana could help Japanize the elderly into the nation-empire. *Dōka* had expanded to non-schoolchildren who would learn Japanese during the war.

From the final edition of the language textbooks, third-grade Taiwanese learned that Taiwanese households should become *kokugo no ie* with clear gender and age divisions. In contrast to the 1937–42 edition, where Yūichi's family was behaving like a *kokugo no ie*, the family in a lesson from the

1943–44 edition had already received the designation. Students read about Masao visiting Yū's home, where Yū's family is already a *kokugo no ie*, and Masao's family is about to receive the certification. Yū's younger siblings speak good Japanese and are playing in the sand. When Masao arrives, Yū is reading a book, Yū's father is reading the newspaper, and Yū's mother is working with a sewing machine. Then Masao and Yū read Yū's diary, which includes beautiful drawings of soldiers in Southeast Asia who are holding Japan's national flag (*hi no maru* flag) while shouting, "*Banzai!*" (Long live!) to the emperor. Yū's father joins in their activity after hearing "Banzai." Yū's father says to both boys that they are "children of Japan" and will also serve the emperor as soldiers even in death when they grow up.[58] The accompanying illustration shows two boys sitting on straw mats (*tatami*), reading while a man looks over their shoulders. The three of them wear Western-style collared shirts. A woman with her hair in a bun wearing an apron and dress or skirt is working on a sewing machine, and two children are playing in the back (fig. 13).[59] Again, these characters have Japanese names but are likely Taiwanese because of their *kokugo no*

FIG. 13 "Kokugo Household" (1943–44). Courtesy of SMC Publishing.

MOBILIZING FOR THE WAR

ie status. The illustrations in this lesson and "Grandmother's Kokugo" suggest that colonial officials characterized modern Taiwan as having incorporated both Japanese (flooring) and Western (clothing) practices.

Through these language lessons, Taiwanese students learned that an ideal modern household, *kokugo no ie*, presumes a set of gender roles where the father embodies patriotism by keeping up with current events and encouraging one's sacrifice for the nation-empire while the mother looks like a "good wife, wise mother," caring for and watching her family from the side. By choosing to place the setting of these lessons, "Grandmother's Kokugo" and "Kokugo no ie," inside the home space with family members, colonial officials continued to emphasize the home as the target of *dōka*. Colonial officials insisted on maintaining ethnic hierarchy by continuing to encourage Taiwanese to desire full assimilation through *kokugo no ie*, even after forty years of colonization. These language lessons show that a *kokugo no ie* symbolized the completion of *dōka*. Unfortunately for the Taiwanese, colonial officials did not issue many *kokugo no ie* certifications, even by the end of the war. For example, only 3,448 out of 252,719 households, or 1.3 percent, in the Taihoku Prefecture, where colonial power was likely the strongest as the location of the colonial capital city, received such certification between 1937 and 1943.[60]

Ironically, although *kokugo* education during *kōminka* seemed to uphold gender difference while erasing Taiwanese identity to create loyal Japanese, Taiwanese students learned that the only force that could erase gender difference was the ultimate sacrifice as they read about the deaths of two historical Taiwanese in the final edition of the language textbooks. These last editions included Zhan Dekun, a Han boy, and Sayo, an Atayal indigenous young teenage girl, to illustrate Taiwanese patriotism toward the nation-empire. Fourth-graders read "National Anthem Boy" (Jp. Kimi ga yo shōnen), a lesson based on a true story, which tells of the dying wish of a third-grade boy, Zhan Dekun, who suffers a fatal injury in the 1921 earthquake in Taiwan. Dekun wants to return to school to see his teacher one more time before he dies. He dies after singing "Kimi ga yo," the Japanese national anthem.[61] The lesson tells the reader that the boy is determined to not speak Taiwanese Hoklo or Hakka (Jp. Taiwango) because his teacher taught them that "Japanese people speak *kokugo*" even though he was not completely comfortable speaking *kokugo*.[62] Singing "Kimi ga yo" shows Dekun's assimilation through his use of the Japanese language and choice of song, which was an embodiment of one's nationality. His death tells students not only that patriotism crosses the ethnic boundary but that the ultimate sacrifice does not have an age requirement.

After the Pacific War began in 1941, fifth-grade Taiwanese read "Sayo's Bell," a lesson based on the true story of a seventeen-year-old girl whose death symbolizes another type of patriotic sacrifice. Her patriotism came from the fact that she fell off a bridge in a thunderstorm while carrying the luggage of her former teacher, who was drafted into the military. In 1941, Hasegawa Kiyoshi (1883–1970), the eighteenth governor-general of Taiwan (1940–44), celebrated Sayo by placing a bell with the label "The Bell of Patriotic Maiden Sayo" at the educational center where Sayo received her education.[63] Unable to join the military, Sayo supported the war effort by sending off her Japanese teacher, a soldier leaving for the front line. Colonial officials reinterpreted her death as an alternative sacrifice for the nation-empire. While Dekun was Han Taiwanese, Sayo was a member of the Atayal group of Taiwanese indigenes from Yilan in eastern Taiwan.[64] Taiwanese students learned that even if they were young and had not yet mastered the Japanese language like Dekun, who dies from a fatal injury as a result of a natural disaster, or could not become a soldier because they were girls, like Sayo, they could still die as patriots. Therefore, even though it might seem strange that the colonial government included two historical Taiwanese youths in the language textbooks for the first time toward the end of the war, the message of *dōka* and the ultimate sacrifice regardless of one's ethnicity, age, and gender were crucial to wartime mobilization.

With young girls acting as facilitators of *dōka* and elderly women as the last remainder of old Taiwan in the wartime language textbooks, students learned that learning *kokugo* and sacrificing one's life embodied patriotism. The four pillars of *kōminka*—the spread of the Japanese language, name changing, shrine worshiping, and military service—were prominently shown in the language textbooks.[65] Although there were a few exceptions when the protagonist in the language lesson was explicitly Taiwanese, such as Zhan Dekun in "Kimi ga yo" and Sayo in "Sayo's Bell," for the most part, the colonial government erased Taiwanese names and culture in the wartime language textbooks. The wartime language textbook lessons showed that *kokugo* proficiency was foundational to *dōka* and *kōminka*. Specifically for girls and women, their Japanese proficiency signaled their responsibilities inside the home and link to men who were mobilized outside the home.

MOBILIZING SCHOOLGIRLS INSIDE THE SCHOOL GROUNDS

While the *kokugo* course was important for training Taiwanese children's minds, bodily and physical training were equally important in producing loyal and skillful patriots in school using gendered patriotism to highlight the roles of girls and women on the home front. Children in Taiwan received military training, participated in marching and metal recycling, and were expected to live a thrifty and simple life that defined the "bodily practice of everyday life" that scholar Tomiyama Ichirō has argued was an important part of becoming Japanese.[66] The bodily discipline involved in such activities and training speaks to the virtues of obedience, good manners, cooperation, and teamwork championed by the colonial officials.

Military exercises became part of school training in primary schools during the wartime period. Many former schoolgirls recalled their lessons. Consider Ying Xinrui, who grew up in a farming household as a child bride in Taipei, and Xu Kuidi, who was the daughter of a tea merchant family in Xiluo, Yunlin, in southern Taiwan. Although they were from different backgrounds and went to different schools, Ying to Hokutō (Beitou) Primary School and Xu to Seira (Xiluo) Girls' Primary School, they received the same military lessons. For example, they were taught how to use a bamboo or wooden stick to attack the enemy.[67] These lessons continued into middle school. Born to a gold mine owner (father) and a former primary school teacher (mother), Lin Xianyan also remembered receiving military training as a student at Taichū (Taichung) Girls' No. 2 Middle School:

> [We] girls also learned swordsmanship [Jp. *kendō*]. We used a long knife [and learned] how to carry [and] use it. We also received training on how to use old-style guns from hundreds of years ago. . . . We also used bamboo sticks with sharp ends. We were taught

to use them to fight against the Americans if they came, to attack them while wearing white headbands around our heads. We trained with the bamboo stick every day. We were taught that the Americans despised us, and if they saw us girls, they would definitely want to violate us. Therefore, we were taught that we had to kill Americans with bamboo sticks.[68]

Lin's narrative of their bamboo spear training echoed how the Japanese government portrayed Japan and its enemies during the wartime period. Japanese officials portrayed Japan as "the purifying sun or the sword of righteousness" in contrast to the image of the United States/Great Britain as demons (Jp. *oni*) who were violent and destructive.[69] The bayonet was seen as the "Japanese common man's sword of righteousness," and Japanese government propaganda posters depicted the Americans and the British as demons that could be brought down by a bayonet.[70] Instead of a bayonet, Lin and her classmates used bamboo spears to practice thrusting at their target. Schools required military training, where boys practiced with loaded weapons and girls practiced with bamboo spears, halberds, and hand grenades in Japan.[71] By August 1945, the Japanese state demanded that women kill themselves if faced with American soldiers as a new ideal feminine virtue to mobilize the public to fight to the end.[72] While *dōka* and wartime mobilization were gendered, death seems to be the only universal sacrifice for the nation-empire.

In the process of demonizing Americans, Lin's teacher taught them to defend themselves to protect their own chastity. Thus the lesson had two purposes: to imbue schoolgirls with the idea of defending their chastity and to impart military skills on a practical level. The self-defense training that these primary and middle school girls received also suggested that the colonial government was preparing for an invasion of the home front, including the colony of Taiwan. Just as male youths were mobilized for military training on school grounds and in youth groups, so were female youths in middle schools. The justification for military training was gendered: male training to fight for one's country, and female training to defend one's virtue.

While military training focused more on fighting or defending oneself against the external enemy, physical education had been important since

MOBILIZING FOR THE WAR

109

the early colonial period as a way to create healthy national subjects, and it came to reinforce men's role on the front line and women's role on the home front during the wartime period. Starting in 1898, colonial educators sought to create physically and spiritually healthy Japanese subjects through physical education.[73] Physical education included marching, the basic training of group coordination, and dumbbell exercises.[74] The physical education course was complemented with outside-classroom activities such as walking tours, field trips, and hiking.[75] In the early colonial period, instructors accommodated girls, many of whom had bound feet, by doing simple games like team formation and singing.[76] In contrast, boys did more active exercises. For example, in 1901, boys at Taikakan (Dakekan) Primary School in Shin'nan Town in Shinchiku participated in running races and competitions whereas girls participated in marching and games.[77] Also in the early colonial period, teachers accommodated the Han Taiwanese custom of foot-binding and implemented gendered exercises in order to create healthy women who would then produce healthy children.[78] Schoolgirls' mobility, limited by their bound feet, shaped gender-specific exercises in the early colonial period. However, as discussed in chapter 1, the success of the anti-foot-binding campaign and government efforts in the 1900s meant that foot-binding ceased to be the reason for gender-specific exercises by the 1920s.

Although physical education was required of all students, gender differences continued into the wartime period. A 1937 manual on physical education for all primary-level schools included gender-specific lessons in section 3 of the manual *Games and Sports*. Out of twenty-seven activities in the first chapter, titled "Instructions for Competitive Games," there were seven boys-only exercises that involved mostly pulling and pushing bamboo sticks against one's opponent as an individual or group activity. The following chapter, titled "Instructions for Marching and Singing Games," included six activities that were all girls-only and involved dancing or marching with two or more people. All activities involved dance moves. Teachers taught music pieces such as "Mountain March" and "Waving the Japanese Flag" and songs such as "Four Seasons in the Countryside" and "Moon over the Ruined Castle" to schoolgirls. The last chapter in this section, titled "Instructions for Running, Jumping, Throwing, and Ball Playing Activities," included three gender-specific

CHAPTER 3

activities out of fifteen exercises. The gender-specific activities were the girls-only fifty-meter relay race, the boys-only one-hundred-meter relay race, and the boys-only shot put.[79]

Although most lessons in the 1937 manual on physical education applied to all children, these lessons revealed the specific gender roles that the colonial government imagined for its subjects starting at a young age. The inclusion of boys-only activities yet no girls-only ones in the chapter on competitive games, and the inclusion of all-girl activities in the chapter on marching and singing games illustrated a clear gender divide. Boys-only activities involved using one's strength and competing against an opponent, both as individual and team exercises. These exercises sought to increase a boy's physical strength to fight against the enemy, alone and collectively, with the skills necessary to fight on the front line. In contrast, girls-only exercises of marching, dancing, and singing emphasized collective, uniform coordination. Girls were supposed to receive more training in marching than boys, but the 1937 manual nevertheless included a lesson for both girls and boys on moving around while holding large and small lanterns because all children would be mobilized to march.[80] This is likely because more women than men would contribute to the war effort as soldiers' moral support and the empire's additional labor force on the home front. Schoolgirls such as Xu Kuidi and her classmates had to practice marching every afternoon in the fifth and sixth grades at Seira Girls' Primary School.[81] The training in physical education helped prepare them for their participation in war celebration marches in the early war period.

Like other schoolgirls and schoolboys, Xu Kuidi and her classmates showed off their training at victory parades sponsored by the colonial government as an opportunity for Taiwanese to exhibit their patriotism and loyalty. However, their participation was more likely a demonstration of their wartime training rather than an expression of genuine patriotism. Lantern victory parades (Jp. *chōchin gyōretsu*) began two months after the start of full-scale war between China and Japan. *Taiwan nichinichi shimpō* reported that the Japanese army had scored victories in China, and, thus, the colonial government planned an island-wide lantern parade on the evening of September 27, 1937. The parade's purpose was to "show gratitude to the imperial army, to pray for the continued victorious battles of the imperial army, and to rally the morale of the residents of Taiwan."[82] Wu Surong, born as the daughter of a woodcraft factory owner in Daxi in northern Taiwan, remembered that as fourth- or fifth-graders in Daikei (Daxi) Primary School, she and her classmates participated in lantern parades at Daxi Town whenever Japan won a battle.

Wu Surong explained that students had to wear uniforms and meet on the school grounds. Their teachers then led them to downtown Daxi for the victory parade. They held lanterns and sang military songs while marching around the downtown area for about an hour.[83] These types of parades were held across the island. For example, on May 20, 1938, a total of thirty thousand people, including Taiwanese and Japanese students and eighty other groups, participated in a lantern parade at Tainan Shrine to show their loyalty to the nation-empire.[84] A year later, on February 11, 1939, Takao (Kaohsiung) City held a lantern parade to celebrate the takeover of Hainan Island in China. More than ten thousand participants, comprising local soldiers, home defense groups, students, and women's groups, gathered at 6:30 p.m. and began marching at 7:00 p.m. They sang patriotic songs and marched to the Takao Bridge, the closest point to Hainan Island.[85] These parades coincided with military victories, serving to construct an image of the Japanese empire as strong and its territory as ever expanding. The unofficial rule of school- and group-based participation showed that institutions were the basic units of mobilization.

In addition to singing patriotic songs during marches and parades, schoolchildren also demonstrated their singing skills in school-organized concerts to support soldiers and military families. Students learned song lyrics that correlated to contents from the Japanese-language course that aimed to increase patriotism.[86] Japanese and Taiwanese children's elementary schools and female youth groups in Xiluo planned to hold a four-hour joint concert for soldiers and their families on February 20, 1938.[87] Primary schools and kindergartens in Takao City planned a similar joint event for the imperial army on March 8, 1938.[88] Shinchiku Girls' Middle School also organized a concert for families of deceased soldiers and active-duty soldiers on March 5, 1938.[89] Female youth groups and faculty at Giran (Yilan) Girls' Primary School sang for the families of soldiers (Jp. *kazoku i'ankai*) on March 6, 1938.[90] Generally speaking, musical performers can bring joy and comfort to their audience. Therefore,

CHAPTER 3

these wartime performances likely served to comfort soldiers and their families before and during the times when soldiers were sent to the front line and to comfort families who lost their loved ones on the battlefield. Symbolically, students singing patriotic songs at these events served to demonstrate the success of colonial education as students singing in Japanese represented their patriotic spirits. Their performances also likely reassured soldiers and their families that their sacrifice was worthwhile to preserve the lives of these children on the home front.

In addition to training their minds and bodies for the war, teachers showcased the success of the *kokugo* lessons through letter writing and making care packages. Nearly seven decades later, Ying Xinrui, a former Hokutō Primary School student in northern Taiwan, recited a letter she wrote during the wartime period: "Thanks to you soldiers, we are able to lead a happy life; we are able to go to school."[91] Wu Surong recalled that the letter she wrote in Japanese won first place in her class and was then sent to the battlefield.[92] As the best student in her class, Zhu Qiufeng wrote many letters, also a merit-based activity, on behalf of her classmates at Tansui (Tamsui) Girls' Primary School in northern Taiwan. Zhu cried upon reading replies from soldiers, who sent letters of gratitude.[93] These letters were often sent with care packages. Zhu's school, Tansui Girls' Primary School, Tansui Boys' Primary School, and Tansui Elementary School each sent letters in fifty bags of care packages in 1938.[94] Lin Xianyan, a student at a Japanese children's elementary school in Taipei, and her mostly Japanese classmates made care packages as instructed by their teachers. "The teacher taught us what to write on the bag, such as 'Hang in there!' (Jp. *ganbatte*) or 'Come home quickly after defeating the enemy,'" she recalled.[95] Care packages generally included letters, towels, soap, cologne, and snacks. Soldiers were reportedly joyful when receiving these care packages.[96] The experiences of these former schoolgirls revealed that teachers played an important role in students' performance of patriotic actions as they directed and selected student works to be sent to the front line. In a sense, these activities assessed students' Japanese-language proficiency while encouraging young Taiwanese children, as the colonized, to appreciate the sacrifice the colonizers made in order to maintain their lifestyle on the home front, where children and women stayed behind to provide moral and material support for those on the front line. Through letter writing, students recognized soldiers as protectors of their home. Written in Japanese, these letters and packages also symbolized the success of colonial education in creating Japanese-proficient colonial subjects.

As part of their training, teachers required students to perform acts of thrift combined with patriotic acts in the name of the empire. The rising sun lunch box (Jp. *hinomaru bentō*) was an important item that embodied both concepts. The idea behind the lunch box originated from a girls' school in Hiroshima Prefecture in 1937. The school administration wanted to encourage students to be thrifty by requiring them to bring rice and one salted plum on Mondays. Because the resulting image of the lunch box resembled the Japanese flag, it became immensely popular in the metropole. The idea of this lunch box was exported to Taiwan, and some teachers required primary school students to bring it to class or on field trips (Jp. *ensoku*).[97] Li Piqing of Hokutō Primary School associated this lunch with *kamikaze* missions: "During the wartime period, we had to bring a lunch box with white rice and red plum whenever a *kamikaze* mission succeeded. . . . We were not allowed to bring vegetables that day. Our teacher instructed us to bring white rice and a red plum only. It was the Japanese flag."[98] Although Li ate her lunch to celebrate a strategic success, Lü Zhunju at Minato (Gang) Primary School in Tainan in southern Taiwan recalled the purpose of the lunch differently. She said it was for praying for safety. "Once a week or month, we had to have a lunch box with nothing but a salty plum in it. It was required [by the school]," Lü explained. However, she also remembered that some students resisted this rule: "Some students wouldn't eat just that, so they hid some goodies underneath the rice."[99] Both Li's and Lü's accounts revealed that there was still enough rice for students to fulfill this assignment in the earlier period of the war. Rice rationing began in October 1939. This type of lunch disappeared after intensive air raids hit Taiwan in 1944 and 1945, when rice production decreased because of cold weather, drought, and air raids, so residents consumed yams.[100]

Students' outward appearances were also regulated to reflect thrift and simplicity. In November 1940, the colonial government implemented the Ordinance of the National Uniform of the Greater Japanese Empire (Jp. Dai Nippon Teikoku Kokuminfuku Rei) in Taiwan, which mandated that all schoolboys and men wear ¥50 uniforms of earth-yellow or auburn-amber color, instead of the ¥100 Western suit. Secondary school boys changed their uniform to the mandated colors and shaved their heads. Women and girls were told not to perm their hair and not to wear Western dresses or hats, high heels, or makeup. Women and girls were also asked to wear *monpe*, a simple farmwoman's work clothes.[101] Gao Sumei, a student in Yunlin during the war, remembered the activity to mark her excellence: "My teacher asked who would like to learn how to make *monpe*, and I was the only one in my entire class to volunteer to learn it."[102] Gao's account suggests that *monpe*-making symbolized voluntary patriotism. The teacher did not teach it to every student, instead teaching only those who wished to learn it. Teachers acted as government agents in instilling the virtues of thrift and simplicity through a type of dress code, with more enforcement power inside state institutions such as schools.

To show their patriotism and thrift, students were also mobilized to participate in the metal recycling program during the wartime period. In September 1942, the colonial government requested that residents in Taiwan donate metals for weapon production, including copper, iron, copper-mixed gold, aluminum, white gold, tin, lead, diamond, and gold. People were forced to donate items such as postal boxes, billboards, copper statues, metal doors, temple bells, metal fencing, and streetlights.[103] Tōseki County in Bokushi (Puzi) in Southern Taiwan ordered all of its primary schools and village organizations to donate scraps (Jp. *haibutsu*) that resulted in ¥624 and 24 *sen*.[104] Taiwanese women were especially sad to have to sell their jewelry, usually part of their dowries, to the government at a low price.[105] For example, the Takao Branch of the Women's Patriotic Association (Jp. Aifu Takao shibu) in southern Taiwan mobilized its members to sell wristwatches, locks, hairpins, and other gold-material accessories to raise money for the nation-empire on August 9, 1938. Schools in Takao also instructed their students to encourage their families to participate in this activity.[106] Li Piqing recalled a metal collection school assignment at her school, Hokutō Primary School. Her teacher gave them a vacation assignment: to collect glass bottles, metal nails, iron, and anything that could be made into bombs. "We would get points for objects we collected and submitted to her. Each item was assigned a point value. We did it for two consecutive years [approximately in 1942 and 1943].[107] The assignment began when I was in the fifth grade," Li recounted. She happily recalled that she always submitted plenty of objects thanks to her father's position as the owner of a major hot spring resort in the local area, which allowed her to gather many bottles and cans.[108] Her classmate Ying Xinrui also remembered this assignment: "At that time, we had to pick up a bottle and even one broken iron nail. . . . Those [scraps] were going to be made into weapons."[109] During the wartime period across the globe, it was common for children to collect scraps to allow adults time to perform other tasks. In addition to patriotism, if they understood the concept, children were motivated to perform this task because of actual rewards for individuals, such as free movie tickets given in the United States.[110] In the case of Li and Ying, the task would count toward their academic grade in school. This low-skill yet potentially time-consuming and dirty task had no age limit as it only required hand-eye coordination and the ability to identify and collect needed objects. Their labor was necessary when metal scraps and glass became important resources as material goods became even scarcer and the war intensified. However, it was unclear if these scraps were made into weapons or other military supplies.

Training students to have healthy bodies and thrifty habits in the name of patriotism was crucial to keeping the war machine in operation. Military training and physical education were gendered to reinforce the roles of strong soldiers and "good wives, and wise mothers." Children wrote letters to soldiers, ate and dressed simply, and salvaged scraps to provide resources for the front line. Firsthand accounts have illustrated the degree to which the war permeated the lives of schoolchildren. It was a total war. However, oral interviews reveal that mobilization was not always centralized as local governments, schools, and teachers implemented different activities to show their patriotism and support for the war.

MOBILIZING SCHOOLGIRL LABOR
OUTSIDE OF THE SCHOOL GROUNDS

In addition to training and activities inside the school grounds, the "bodily practice of everyday life" of schoolgirls was extended to outside of the school grounds. Schoolgirls worked as agricultural laborers, made food for the military, and participated in the making of *senninbari*, a piece of white cloth with good luck messages sewn on. Their training and roles were limited to the feminine sphere of sewing, cooking, and caring for others, but because these activities were performed with teamwork and cooperation, school and the war created a new space for schoolgirls to make new friends and to work in public. Many former schoolgirls remembered these collective activities with their classmates, suggesting that wartime mobilization created a "feminine" space of a community of care and friendship outside the usual classroom space.

After the onset of the Pacific War in December 1941, students became fully mobilized. In January 1942, the colonial government mandated that students from the middle school and up were to form student public service teams (Jp. *gakusei hōkō tai*) to mobilize students for various military training, agricultural production, and other manual labor tasks. Two years later, in November 1944, the colonial government issued the Enforcement Regulation to the Ordinance on Student Labor (Jp. Gakusei Kinrō Rei Shikō Kisoku), based on the Student Labor Law (August 1944) to intensify the mobilization effort by assigning students to work in military factories, military base construction, military service, agricultural production, to do combat training and shrine cleaning, and go on hospital visits.[111] Secondary school students, male and female, were mobilized for military construction during a period of high demand for labor.

Activities that students performed outside of school grounds were performed in groups. As part of the new regulations on student mobilization, schoolgirls performed many tasks in the agricultural sector as temporary workers. Taihoku County was the first place to try implementing this plan, which targeted young women in female youth groups; the county formed a women's special patriotic agriculture volunteer corps in 1941.[112] Shinchiku County also sought to mobilize its 800,000 residents by targeting women, children, and primary school and vocational school students to work on rice transplanting.[113] Mobilization included students at girls' middle schools, who were the cream of the crop—they came from upper-middle-class backgrounds and had good enough grades to receive secondary education. Their family backgrounds allowed them to focus on schoolwork with little to no knowledge of chores and labor. During the wartime period, however, schools mobilized their labor. Lin Xianyan remembered the agricultural tasks that her school required students at Taichū Girls' No. 2 Middle School to perform: "On the school grounds, we planted yams, vegetables, and even carried fertilizer. . . . I learned how to plant crops from that time period."[114] Because of the war, girls from wealthy family backgrounds learned manual labor skills at school that they would not have acquired otherwise.

Agricultural production was one key role that Taiwan played in the empire during the wartime period. Taiwan became an important grain supplier within the Japanese empire because of the intensifying industrialization and urbanization in the metropole, an increasingly large military because of military conscription, the redirection of resources to the military, and droughts in Korea and the Kansai area in Japan in 1939. The purpose of the wartime agricultural system was to provide food for the war effort and to move agricultural surplus to the industrial sector. To accomplish these two goals, agricultural production had to increase with capital investment and technology. However, even with the incorporation of technology into agricultural production, manual labor was still necessary. The colonial government also forced Taiwanese farmers to achieve a certain quota of production to sell to the state.[115] The colonial government mandated that only rice, sugarcane, sweet potatoes, vegetables, *Corchorus* (Jp. *kōma*), and a few other crops could be planted. These restrictions served to ensure sufficient production of important crops that supported two important elements of the war—food and fuel.[116] Because Taiwan's agricultural production was crucial to the empire, girls and women, including middle school girls like Lin Xianyan and her classmates, were mobilized to farm.

The need for laborers to increase agricultural production during the wartime period resulted in the training and labor mobilization of not only girls' middle school students but also of young children at primary schools. They performed various tasks that were crucial to agricultural production. As a child bride in a farming household in Taipei, Ying Xinrui had not done any chores as a child. She still vividly recalled the sickening experience of picking out Asiatic rice borers with her classmates in the fields as a student at Hokutō Primary School.[117] Her classmate, Tang Yanyan, who helped out with farmwork at home, recalled the different reactions her classmates had to rice borers: "We countryside kids weren't

CHAPTER 3

scared when we saw the worms. But those city kids were screaming when they saw them. They were more fortunate and didn't have to work on the farm."[118] Lin Tiantian, the daughter of a taxi and bus driver, and her classmates at Seira Girls' Primary School were assigned to catch tree-eating insects and Asiatic rice borers during vacation. Lin and her fellow schoolmate Xu Kuidi, daughter of a local tea merchant, remembered that they also had to make compost.[119] Ying Xinrui recalled gathering grass and plants, and working with her classmates to cover the pile at Hokutō Primary School.[120] As reported in *Taiwan nichinichi shimpō*, sixth-graders at Shinten Minami (Xindian nan) Primary School and local youth group members visited a model farm and watched how farmers made compost.[121] One's age determined one's task. A student at Akebono (Shu) Primary School in Taichū City from 1939 to 1945, Lan Qinhua remembered age-specific tasks at her school: "In the fifth grade, we had to go to a place that was five to seven kilometers away, and carried rocks to pave an airplane runway.... But younger students would harvest rice for the military.... The younger students would also grow castor oil plants. This was how all of us were required to do manual labor, and thus didn't study much. We didn't really have school lessons in the fifth and the sixth grades."[122] Instead of acquiring academic knowledge, these accounts revealed, students spent school hours on agricultural production. With reduced instruction in academics, the war had transformed students into amateur farmers regardless of prior experience or socioeconomic background.

Regardless of their age and family background, these accounts revealed that primary school students were required to participate in agricultural production, from planting to harvesting, during the wartime period. Most of these students did not come from farming families and did not help out at home. Nevertheless, the war required the labor of amateurs, including students. This was why school became the place to teach students some agricultural skills. While commerce and handiwork courses continued to be boys-only courses, agriculture became part of the girls' educational curriculum in the late 1920s. *Agricultural Education for Primary School*, a 1927 manual, claimed that it was important for girls to receive instruction in sericulture, chicken-raising, and gardening as future housewives.[123] This manual shows that agricultural lessons for schoolgirls focused on tasks other than crop production, a task specific to boys. A decade later during the wartime period, colonial officials emphasized the importance of girls' education in primary schools in a 1939 manual on educating primary schoolgirls on agriculture.[124] The manual stated a challenge in its introduction: "Although Taiwanese women do not like to do laboring tasks outdoors, we need to guide them to correct that attitude. It is important for a housewife to understand completely the importance of agriculture."[125] The manual presumed an inevitable link between female agricultural production and home economics in the larger context that agricultural development was linked to the imperial family, and thus agricultural education was central to children's education.[126] The manual instructed teachers to make sure students understood the need to thank the imperial family, the nation, and society as they worked on agricultural production with "a sense of gratitude and repayment."[127] Schoolgirls were to learn how to cultivate crops such as sweet potatoes, beans, Chinese broccoli, cucumbers, tomato, white radishes, and green onions, how to harvest rice and grow flowers such as chrysanthemum and carnation, and how to raise chickens and pigs.[128] Agricultural lessons at school thus became useful during wartime mobilization. Although not all young children, especially those from wealthy backgrounds, did manual labor at home, the war entered their schools, where students, young and old, of all socioeconomic backgrounds, had to become amateur agricultural laborers to help feed the soldiers on the front line.

Schoolgirls were also mobilized to participate in the creation of *senninbari,* "thousand-person stitches," another symbol of women's gendered role during the wartime period. *Senninbari* were white pieces of cloth with red stitches sewn on them, supposedly by one thousand women. It represented female handiwork and unity on the home front. Created during the Russo-Japanese War (1904–5), *senninbari* represented one thousand women's good wishes for the soldiers. The phrase "Continued Luck in the Fortunes of War" (Jp. *bu'unchōkyō*) and the image of a tiger were sewn on the cloth. The tiger image, representing a safe return, came from a Japanese proverb: a tiger will return home safely even when it travels far away.[129] In October 1941, *Taiwan nichinichi shimpō* reported that Taiwanese women had embraced this activity at a time when Japanese and Taiwanese people had come together for the sake of the country. The

FIG. 14 Sixth-grade sewing lesson at Meiji Primary School in Tainan. Courtesy of Chenggong Elementary School, West Central District, Tainan Municipal.

report emphasized that each stitch on the *senninbari* came to represent the unity of all women on the home front.[130] All female residents of the empire, young and old, could be asked to sew one stitch on the cloth, likely because they were expected to have received homemaking training in school.[131] Many Taiwanese schoolgirls and young working women recalled sewing stitches on *senninbari*. Wu Surong recalled making *senninbari* outside of the school grounds when she was a primary school student in Daxi.[132] Li Piqing recalled that some students from her school tied the *senninbari* to soldiers who were teachers from her school.[133] Lin Xianyan remembered that no one dared to refuse to sew because refusal meant being unpatriotic (Jp. *hi-kokumin*).[134] Schoolgirls, who started learning to sew in the third, fourth, or fifth grade, were excellent candidates for the *senninbari* project because it tied them to the war effort (fig. 14). Sewing became not only a feminine skill but also a patriotic one, linking an individual act of sewing a piece of clothing to a collective activity for the nation-empire. A symbol of Japanese feminine patriotism, the production of *senninbari* across all ethnic groups in Taiwan represented the unity of the colonizer and the colonized fighting to win the war. Because only girls and women could participate, *senninbari* also created a feminine communal space where female friends and strangers came together to make this going-away lucky charm for soldiers.

MOBILIZING FOR THE WAR

In addition to sewing, the colonial government put schoolgirls' cooking skills to practical use during the wartime period. Some girls like Ying Xinrui learned how to make fried rice at primary school while some like Zhou Lianyu learned to make curry and omelette rice later at girls' middle school in Tainan.[135] Foods made during class became lunch for teachers and students.[136] This skill became useful during the war. Lin Xianyan, a student from 1941 to 1944 at Taichū Girls' No. 2 Middle School, recalled:

> I was the class president then. The class president had to call on each classmate [to help out]. It was dark, with no electricity. But we had to walk toward the school in the dark and made rice and sushi from this big pot. . . . Rice was scarce then, but we had to make it. While [the rice] was still hot, we had to make rice balls (Jp. *onigiri*). It was where I learned how to make triangular rice balls. . . . It was all scarce stuff. But not one of us schoolgirls ate any. We students were obedient then. We wrapped the stuff. In the early morning, the rice balls were transported to the soldiers by truck. [The rice balls] were made by every schoolgirl in my school, and not just people in my class. [The task] required the [labor of the] entire school, or else we wouldn't make it in time. Goods were scarce but we didn't eat any of them. We did this when I was in my third or fourth year in girls' middle school during high wartime. It was toward the end of the war when there weren't many material goods available.[137]

Lin's narrative highlights several focuses of the colonial education of girls: the virtues of cooking, helping the nation, teamwork, and obedience. Working as a team, Lin and her schoolmates put their cooking training to use (fig. 15). Instead of sleeping, they worked through the night to feed soldiers who were defending the nation-empire. At a time when food was scarce, these schoolgirls obeyed the teachers' instruction to make rice balls without eating any. This task shows schoolgirls' loyalty and obedience to the empire. Lin's family was wealthy, so house servants performed every chore at home, but Lin had to learn to do many tasks in school. Her account also reinforces her narrative of being an excellent student who was chosen as the class leader by her teacher, as a class leader was always the top student in each class. She fulfilled her role as a good student who was responsible and honest. These characteristics also represented Lin's

FIG. 15 Sixth-grade cooking lesson at Meiji Primary School in Tainan. Courtesy of Chenggong Elementary School, West Central District, Tainan Municipal.

evaluation of the values that Japanese education taught her and other members of her generation, which will be discussed further in chapter 5.

Another role that schoolgirls played was to express gratitude to and provide comfort (Jp. *irō*) to the soldiers. Showing gratitude to soldiers was something every civilian was expected to do, from officials, married Japanese women, and elderly Taiwanese women to students of all levels. To do this, teachers took elementary and secondary school students to visit military hospitals. For example, three hundred male and female students at Taihoku No. 1 Normal School, where most students were Japanese, visited a military hospital in Taihoku and cleaned up patient rooms on February 16, 1938. Later on the same day, two hundred second-year schoolgirls from Taihoku Girls' No. 1 Middle School, another predominantly Japanese school, brought flowers and helped clean the hospital.[138] While these older students showed their appreciation with hospital cleanup, younger students made donations to the soldiers in person. In February 1938, primary school students, along with women's patriotic groups, donated money and goods during their visits to the military hospital in Taihoku.[139] Zhu Qiufeng remembered that from second to sixth grade, her teacher regularly took her class to visit soldiers stationed in Tamsui. During the visit, her class sang Japanese songs for these soldiers that they had learned at school.[140] Although both school-girls and schoolboys were taken to visit injured veterans, these visits likely also reaffirmed the feminine quality of schoolgirls, who were to become major players on the home front. As potential future wives and mothers of imperial soldiers, these visits highlighted their nurturing and supportive nature and unity during the war. Hence, while the "good wife, wise mother" training had moved from the home to the school setting from the Qing to Japanese rule, the practice and the performance of the "good wife, wise mother" had expanded from the individual home setting to the public setting during the war.

Gender and age remained the sole divisions during the wartime period. Education and the war separated the female from the male population. The male population had a more militant experience of the war: school-boys received intensive military training, and youths and able-bodied men worked in factories or served on the front line. In contrast, the female population stepped outside the home sphere and established a wider social network on school grounds and at work than had the generations before them. The emergence of a community of care and friendship was one unintended consequence of wartime mobilization. In cases such as the making of *senninbari* and hospital visits, wartime mobilization created a feminine space to show community care. This sense of community might have contributed to many former schoolgirls' fond memories of Japanese education and the wartime period. Also worthy of note, the government did not mobilize students with the intention of flattening class divisions in Taiwan, but its plan to mobilize everyone for the war effort did result in some kind of equality in the sense that one's ethnicity, socioeconomic status, and educational background did not exempt one from wartime labor and contribution. All were equal when faced with war.

DISRUPTED SCHOOL LIFE

Starting around 1943, when American and Chinese air raids began in Taiwan, the balance between school lessons and wartime labor became increasingly disrupted by the intensifying war. Former students remembered that the American air raids eventually stopped them from attending school. Although Taiwan was the first Japanese territory to come under aerial attack after the Second Sino-Japanese War began (1937–45), when Chinese aircraft bombed Taipei and Hsinchu in February 1938, the start of the Asia-Pacific War (1941–45) brought the most intense aerial attacks on Taiwan. Students who lived in Hsinchu were the first to experience this series of attacks when Americans and Chinese attacked Shinchiku Airport on November 25, 1943. After that, the colonial government began to have more drills across the island. During these drills, women mainly worked on tasks like nursing and ration distribution. However, during the air raids at the end of the war, women also had to fight fires caused by the bombing and take care of unexploded bombs because there was not enough manpower available.[141]

Air raids on Taiwan became more intense as time went on. The most devastating air battle in the Pacific War took place on October 12, 1944. This air battle continued for five days, and about 600 of the 4,320 aircraft used were damaged. Students residing in major cities in Taiwan experienced intense air raids between October 12 and October 18. Aircraft dropped more than 4,800 explosive bombs, 710 firebombs, and 11,000 propaganda pamphlets. The air raids resulted in 738 deaths, 366 seriously injured, 748 people with minor injuries, and 6,042 buildings damaged. Takao was the most seriously hit area in the October attack. The American aircraft targeted airports, factories, and the transportation infrastructure. In Taipei, the capital of the colony, Matsuyama Airport, Taihoku Tobacco Factory, Taihoku Railway Factory, bridges in Taipei, Taihoku Commercial School, and Wakamatsu Primary School were hit in the October 1944 attack. Beginning in January 1945, after the Americans took over Luzon and gained control of the Philippines, American aircraft flew directly to Taiwan. The air raids became regular, occurring at 8:00 p.m., 10:00 p.m., midnight, and 2:00 a.m. The bombing focused on airports, mostly in central and southern Taiwan. However, the bombings eventually spread out, and by the beginning of June 1945, the bombing had flattened most urban areas in Taiwan and turned them into a wasteland. By this time, most school functions had stopped, and students had evacuated with their families to more remote areas. American aircraft attacked Shinchiku Airport, Takao's Okayama Airport, Takao Harbor, Tainan Airport, Sun Moon Lake Electricity Plant, military buildings and residential areas in Tainan, sugar refineries, and Keelung Harbor. Besides explosive bombs, firebombs, and propaganda pamphlets, the American aircraft sometimes dropped tobacco and sushi.[142] The Americans probably hoped to gain the support of the starving Taiwanese people as food became scarcer in the final two years of the war. The colonial government, through the police and the Public Service Association of Imperial Subjects (Jp. Kōmin Hōkō Kai), ordered residents of Taiwan to turn in American propaganda pamphlets to the police station.[143] American surveys in the postwar years found that most Taiwanese followed that order. Police received 11,620 pamphlets.[144]

The intensity of air raids prompted the Japanese leadership to act. By March 1945, the Japanese cabinet in the metropole passed the Outline for Education in the Decisive Battle and ordered the closure of school for a year, from April 1945 to March 30, 1946, at all levels except the elementary level. In Taiwan, all the upperclassmen in secondary schools, and students in vocational schools and universities were called to serve at military bases and work on defense projects along the coast, while students from the advanced courses (Jp. *kōtōka*) at primary schools and lowerclassmen at secondary schools were called to work at military factories.[145]

Before school was closed, teachers and students at primary and secondary schools tried to continue their daily routine even as it became increasingly difficult due to military attacks. Students continued to attend school as the war intensified and the threat of air raids became ever greater. Xu Kuidi remembered the older students had to be responsible for the younger students at Seira Girls' Primary School. In the morning, everyone gathered at the specified meeting place, and older primary school students (fifth- and sixth-graders) had to lead younger students to school. As fifth- and sixth-graders in the 1943–44 academic year, Xu and her classmates also had to lead first-graders to the bomb shelter when the air raid siren sounded.[146] Xu's schoolmate Lin Tiantian recalled that their graduation trip and talent shows (Jp. *yūkeikai*) were canceled because of the war.[147] Lan Qinhua at Akebono Primary School in Taichung lamented that they did not even hold commencement when she finished primary school in March 1945.[148] The cancellation was probably because resources had become scarcer, and the colonial government was concerned about air raids. Going to school in the same city of Taichung, Lin Xianyan and her classmates at Taichū Girls' No. 2 Middle School attended their commencement in March 1944. However, the air raid siren sounded in the midst of the ceremony. Half of the students quickly emptied the auditorium to return to their families.[149] Farther south of Taichung, Zhou Yingying, an eighteen-year-old teacher in Yunlin in 1945, led her students to the nearby bomb shelter when an air raid happened during class time.[150] These personal experiences show that while normal school instructions had become impossible, children were expected to continue to attend school because school was a primary site of wartime training and mobilization.

In the north, Zhu Qiufeng's fellow classmates at Taihoku Girls' No. 3 Middle School were worried about her because she lived in Tamsui, an important port in northern Taiwan. Tamsui suffered severely from the air raid: "Bombs burned Tamsui all night. My Taipei classmates were worried about me, because they could see Tamsui burning. Some bombs were dropped in the bomb shelters. People died, and rice balls had bloodstains on them. We had an underground shelter in my house. [That place] had many bullet holes. We didn't dare to stay in the house."[151] A second-year student in girls' middle school, Zhu stopped going to school and returned to her family during the intense air raids in 1945.[152]

Although evacuation was a family-based act, the war brought the colonizers and the colonized populations together in new places. An eleven- or twelve-year-old student during the evacuation, Hong Zhimei evacuated with her family to a remote area in central Taiwan, where they came in contact with Japanese soldiers:

One could feel [the intensity of] the war more in the cities. So the evacuation began. My father's friend lived in Nantun [in central Taiwan], a more remote area. . . . His friend's house was big. He rented two rooms to us. [We lived there because] it was the wartime period, and we didn't dare to live in the city. . . . Some [Japanese] soldiers lived at the local vocational school of agriculture [Jp. *nōgyō gakkō*]. Whenever the air raid began, those soldiers would come to hide in our place. That house was big, with fruit trees and a yard. . . . There were about twenty soldiers. . . . There was a Japanese soldier who told me that I looked like his younger sister who was in Japan. . . . One time a bomb landed on the school. We saw a big piece of bombshell [metal] near our place. One soldier who didn't run fast enough had his hearing damaged by the bombing. We were scared. ... We chatted with Japanese soldiers but didn't eat together.[153]

Hong's account illustrates that air raids had destroyed homes in the cities and military buildings to the point that Japanese soldiers and Taiwanese civilians evacuated to the same place. Taiwanese schoolgirls and their families feared for their lives and lived under constant threat from air raids. Hong's account shows that the colonizers' war brought the colonizers and the colonized together. They shared the same space and the same experience during the air raids. In her narrative, Hong expressed no fear or any negative feelings toward the Japanese soldiers. Instead, her account suggests that soldiers were as vulnerable as civilians, if not more, whenever they had to evacuate to where Hong's family was.[154] Although many like Hong witnessed the vulnerability of Japanese soldiers in Taiwan, they did not lose respect for these soldiers. In fact, many characterized Japanese imperial soldiers as "orderly" in contrast to Chinese Nationalist soldiers. The vivid descriptions of their fear and memories of wartime air raids reveal that Hong's generation continues to live with those experiences today.

As Hong Zhimei's account suggests, although the air raids caused fear and the evacuation was chaotic, these were not completely miserable memories. Zeng Chamei, a recent primary school graduate during the air raids, evacuated with her mother, sister, and their relatives to an area near Shinten (Xindian) in northern Taiwan. She played in the graveyard with relatives, classmates, and neighbors in Shinten.[155] Playing in the graveyard was something that city dwellers like Zeng and her classmates did not have the chance to do at home. Zhu Qiufeng, a Tamsui native, evacuated to her grandparents' home and had fun there:

We were in the mountains, so we didn't have to worry about food. We ate rice, and raised chickens, and so we had chicken and eggs. Other people would eat yams and dry *daikon*. We also had bamboo shoots. ... I was happy. Sometimes we would catch shrimp from the stream. We used rope, and got some type of grass, and made a loop. We put some [worms] on it, then lured shrimp. We then pushed them into the net to catch them. It was fun. We also had a mandarin orange garden so we would pick some, too. We had plentiful food then. We had rice.[156]

Zhu was having fun while not going to school. Her enjoyment was likely partly intensified by her hesitation about attending girls' middle school in Taipei. Zhu did not want to attend school in Taipei because she would be away from home. She envied her older sister, who had failed the entrance exam to Taihoku Girls' No. 3 Middle School (Jp. Taihoku Daisan Kōtō Jogakkō) and instead attended the local private Christian school, Tansui Girls' Academy (Jp. Tansui Jogakuin). Watching how her older sister enjoyed a good home life with frequent visits from her sister's teachers, Zhu wanted the same lifestyle. She enjoyed her primary school life but was depressed because she had long commutes to her school in Taipei.[157] However, she could not do anything about it because Taihoku Girls' No. 3 Middle School was the best school for Taiwanese girls, and her parents were happy that she was admitted. Thus, Zhu probably welcomed the change brought by the evacuation. Having plenty of food to eat and catching shrimp in the mountains probably also made Zhu happy even though she was away from home in a new environment. Having to commute far to school and later witnessing the horror of the air raids in her hometown of Tamsui, Zhu was probably glad that her new life was harmonious and close to her family. All evacuees were city dwellers who had to adjust their lives to the new environment in remote areas. Thankfully, they were with their families.

The optimism and organized activities in the early war years disappeared as air raids intensified in the later years of the war. Although colonial officials continued to require students to attend school, the reality of the war forced the school authority to cancel events and many students to evacuate during school hours. Students remembered the war as a scary time, but they also learned to live with it as they adjusted and enjoyed various aspects of the war—hiding from the air raids, going into evacuation, dealing with rations, and sharing space with strangers. In contrast to adults, who had the responsibilities to care for their families, the young age of schoolgirls likely helped them find joy during the war.

School was an important site for mobilizing female subjects during the war effort in colonial Taiwan, and the government tried to keep the schools in operation for as long as possible. School and the war mobilized schoolgirls of all backgrounds to learn and to work together for the empire and for the war. The colonial government sought to create Japanese-proficient, patriotic, obedient, and cooperative schoolgirls through individual and group activities. Individual activities tended to cultivate their characters and establish a connection with soldiers, while collective activities showcased their patriotic spirits and teamwork. The reduced number of men on the home front required schoolgirls and women to enter the labor force. Although some war-support activities were expected of every person in the empire, many activities relied on the feminine training of cooking and sewing that the schoolgirls received in school. School was the space and the medium that created groups of schoolgirls with strong friendship bonds, because in addition to formal instruction time, they also spent time marching and catching Asiatic borers together during the wartime period. The time spent outside school grounds strengthened the bond between schoolchildren, creating a community of friendship that likely contributed to the organization of reunions in the postwar years starting in the 1960s and 1970s.[158] Organized during the postwar period, these reunions also probably colored the memories former schoolchildren had about Japanese colonial rule and wartime mobilization as positively sweet, with some scary stories.

Wartime mobilization redefined gendered assimilation in colonial Taiwan as it shifted the training and focus of "good wives, wise mothers" from the individual households only to the entire nation-empire, which meant that schoolgirls were trained to become the "good wife, wise mother" of the nation-empire. It was no longer sufficient for schoolgirls and women to keep their individual homes strong and healthy. They had to work together to keep the nation-empire strong and healthy, mentally and physically, by showing their support through patriotic activities and mobilized labor. In the process of receiving spiritual and physical training and participating in agricultural production and patriotic activities, schoolgirls became Japanese imperial subjects during the *kōminka* movement. Although there were a few similarities, what defined the loyalty of schoolgirls was different from that of schoolboys because they played different gender roles within and for the empire.

This chapter incorporated oral histories with contemporary news reports to evaluate the implementation and the success of wartime mobilization. As expected, news media focused on Japanese success and a united front on the Taiwanese home front. Former schoolgirls recalled experiences that confirmed the many wartime mobilization activities that contemporary newspapers reported. However, their personal experiences also raised questions as to the degree of centralized control that colonial officials had in implementing patriotic activities, which was most obvious in their comments about the meaning of the rising sun lunch box and about who was required or chosen to write letters to soldiers. Their memories also filled potential gaps in knowledge about the later years of the war, especially since the intense air raids destroyed materials or made the printing of newspapers difficult, and the intentional destruction of government documents at the end of the war left few sources from which to recover the history of that period.

Although personal recollections are useful in filling some historical gaps, oral histories often minimized the structural discrimination based on gendered assimilation and wartime mobilization. Former schoolgirls and schoolboys provided positive wartime memories about their individual academic accomplishments, as seen with Wu Surong and Zhu Qiufeng, who highlighted their letter-writing skills. Their strong desire to showcase their academic accomplishments in the midst of wartime hardships outweighed their criticism of structural discrimination; however, the educational system remained inherently discriminatory. Furthermore, the implementation of a military draft of Taiwanese men in the late stage of the war revealed that the colonial authority continued to treat the Taiwanese differently from the Japanese population because it remained skeptical of the loyalty of the Taiwanese. Despite institutionalized discrimination, Taiwanese students were proud of their academic excellence at a time when not every girl or boy received an education. As will be discussed further in the concluding chapter, this construction of their identity based on their historical experiences became the backdrop of their nostalgia for Japanese colonial rule. Many believed that Japanese education had produced fine students, such as themselves, in contrast to the misbehaving and disrespectful children who received a postwar Chinese Nationalist education.

4

❀

REMAKING THE HOME

Previous chapters have covered how colonial officials and educators linked women's domestic roles with the level of civilization to make the "good wife, wise mother" training a success and how the wartime training and mobilization of schoolgirls and unmarried women affirmed educated girls and women as the embodiment of the ideal woman in the nation-empire. This chapter examines women's marriage and work to show that the colonial authority failed to produce such an ideal. Let us begin with Lin Jiao'e, who exemplifies limited success as a Japanese imperial subject, yet contributed greatly to herself, her family, and Taiwan's economy. Lin Jiao'e was born as an only child in 1931 in Yilan in eastern Taiwan. With classical Chinese training and a primary school diploma, her father worked at irrigation, a sugar manufacturing company, and a farmer's group under Japanese rule. Lin learned embroidery from her grandmother and knitting from her female cousin at home, while she learned how to make handbags, waistbands, and exercise pants at school in fifth and sixth grades. She sewed her own sailor uniform when she entered girls' middle school, where she learned how to make dishcloths and children's shirts. After completing her education, she worked as a teacher. Unfortunately, her salary was insufficient to support her family by herself. Lin decided to make, knit, and embroider clothes to supplement the family income. She even took a six-month sewing class with a Japanese instructor in 1956 and then 1969 to perfect her skills. When she was twenty-eight, Lin eventually opened her own sewing class to further increase her income. She supported six members of her household on her own because her Chinese Indonesian husband was unreliable in this arranged marriage.[1]

Lin's life speaks to the impact of girls' education under Japanese rule during and after the colonial period. Education helped Lin become a teacher, albeit one with an insufficient income to support her family. Sewing, a part of the "good wife, wise mother" training at home and in school, became an important skill that Lin utilized to supplement family income. Along with doing laundry, making clothes was one of the most common ways that Han Taiwanese women supplemented family income after marriage during and after Japanese rule. Since the Qing period, women who were not skillful at sewing would hand-wash clothes for people to supplement family income.[2] Lin was exceptional in her high level of education and sewing skills, but she still did not completely fulfill the ideal of "good wife, wise mother" according to the colonial officials' vision for Taiwanese women because she was a working mom with two jobs who did not devote all of her time to the household. Lin's mother cared for her children while she worked.[3]

The "good wife, wise mother" is a powerful imaginative construct in which a woman who does not earn money is the anchor of the imagined nuclear family. Yet, contrary to this ideal, the political and economic developments in the postwar era required women to participate directly in the economy. The "good wife, wise mother" ideal was only compatible with the assimilation of Taiwan into the Japanese nation-empire, not the Cold War political economy that pulled Taiwan into the United States' capitalist camp.

This chapter joins existing studies on the impact of education on Taiwanese women from the late colonial period to the early postcolonial period, roughly the 1940s and the 1950s, but considers different angles from previous studies. Scholars have mainly focused on the impact of girls' education in the public sphere and women's activism. Through her discussion of primary school, secondary school, and teacher training for girls and women under Japanese rule, Zhang Subi concludes that its impact was limited because girls' education focused on basic, low-level knowledge instead of high-level knowledge.[4] Her conclusion presumes that an education must include high-level knowledge to have value and

REMAKING THE HOME

a profound effect on the student, but this was not the case for Taiwanese women. In agreement with Zhang, Yu Chien-ming points out that primary education was limited to those of upper-middle-class backgrounds or urbanites. Yu concludes that the limitation of and discrimination in the educational system led to Taiwanese women working in lower-middle-class positions. Further, Yu argues it caused the lack or ineffectiveness of an independent women's movement and limited occupations for a few women of upper-middle-class backgrounds.[5] By criticizing Japanese officials for limiting educational opportunities for Taiwanese girls, Zhang and Yu are concerned about the impact of education on women's status and rights. In contrast, Ko Ikujo has a more positive evaluation of Japanese education. Through her analysis of girls' middle school education, Ko argues that its impact was the creation of the "new woman" in Taiwanese society, one who had natural feet and a modern education.[6] Whether a critical or positive evaluation, these studies have focused on the effect of education on Taiwanese women as a group and society as a whole.

To enrich our understanding of the impact of education on the lives of Han Taiwanese women, this chapter discusses the homemaking training at home, the practice of gender segregation, and the use of the Japanese language at home and in school. This will show how socioeconomic status and home training complemented school training in shaping women's work and marriage and how it affected the Japanese colonial legacy in postwar Taiwan.[7] Although Japanese schools failed to produce the next generation of "good wives, wise mothers" for the nation-empire, this chapter finds that the *kokugo* education and home training produced a hybrid—Taiwanese women with Han Taiwanese and Japanese cultural influences who knew Taiwanese, Japanese, and Western sewing styles and used their Japanese proficiency to learn and to socialize during and after Japanese colonization. Home training had been important from the Qing to the Japanese period because it marked a woman's marriageability. The biggest change between the two periods was that the training site expanded from the home to include the school under Japanese rule. Nevertheless, the sewing and cooking lessons in primary schools and the more extensive training in homemaking skills in girls' secondary schools were insufficient in preparing women for a stressful married life.

I want to note here one of the main reasons I did not follow other

CHAPTER 4

scholars' research methods of assessing the impact of Japanese education through the educational options or educational levels available to Taiwanese girls and women: We should not compare the nascent modern educational system in the early twentieth century with the more mature system that developed after World War II, where economic transformations led to higher educational expectations and increased employment opportunities. We should not use our contemporary educational system and employment infrastructure to judge the educational and work opportunities available to the Taiwanese under Japanese rule. Taiwanese who completed their primary education in the first half of the twentieth century would have had many work options, similar to the case for high school graduates in the United States at the turn of the twenty-first century. Therefore, Taiwanese women and men with primary education under Japanese rule should be considered educated and skilled. It also goes without saying that access to more educational options and higher levels of education favors the upper classes, and thus a focus on greater educational opportunities neglects the impact of education on the lower classes. What I hope to trace are the changes that this colonial education brought to Taiwanese society and women's lives across various socioeconomic statuses.

By relying on oral histories and interviews to provide insights and details that have been left out of written documentation to understand the impact of girls' education, this chapter argues that Japanese education brought more profound changes to women of lower socioeconomic backgrounds than those of upper-class backgrounds in work opportunities and marriage networks. This was because as women were trained to become a hybrid of "good wives, wise mothers," Han Taiwanese patriarchal and Japanese colonial influences reinforced gender division and hierarchy. Through the gendered training of the "good wife, wise mother" ideal, the Japanese colonial state found ways to use the patriarchal household to help implement *dōka*. Han Taiwanese households shared a similar desire to the colonial state in reinforcing gender roles appropriate to Taiwanese society. Namely, patriarchal homes and colonial schools did not work against each other; they actually imparted different yet related skills to ensure stability and social reproduction. The colonial state also accommodated and allowed old Han Taiwanese customs to remain culturally strong through the legal system. The "good wife, wise mother" training shows that the upper- and upper-middle-class families had already incorporated girls' education as a status symbol to maintain their socioeconomic status and to reinforce Han Taiwanese customs with expanded social networks through school, including friends and marriage partners, while lower-and lower-middle-class families saw an expansion of work opportunities that increased economic gains and choices of marriage partners. If one considers economic gains and marriage choice as markers of improved status, then women of lower-class backgrounds seemed to have benefited more than those from the upper- and upper-middle-class backgrounds under Japanese rule.

Even when considering the uneven effects of education on Taiwanese women of different backgrounds, colonial education and home training, nevertheless, produced a hybrid "good wife, wise mother" with Japanese and Taiwanese characteristics. This hybrid "good wife, wise mother" displayed learning from both Taiwanese and Japanese knowledge of and skills in sewing and child-rearing. In particular, the *kokugo* education taught Han Taiwanese, Japanese, and Western sewing styles, and Western sewing styles would become commercially successful in postwar Taiwan, when many women became seamstresses to help jump-start Taiwan's postwar economic miracle. Thus the postwar working women with Japanese education stood in contrast to the Japanese ideal, even when we consider how wartime mobilization had brought "good wives, wise mothers" out of the household and into the public realm with parades, air raid drills, and other patriotic activities. The "good wife, wise mother" training that aimed to modernize the home with stay-at-home housewives ended up producing working women whose labor supported their families and helped develop Taiwan's economy during the wartime and postwar periods. Although their sewing work continued to be viewed as feminine and thus suggests a gendered division of employment, their income-earning status in the family and their participation in the country's economy reveal the public and commercial implications of their labor.

CHAPTER 4

THE "GOOD WIFE, WISE MOTHER"
TRAINING AT SCHOOL AND AT HOME

The continuous importance of the homemaking training in Han Taiwanese society from the Qing to the Japanese period suggests that Han Taiwanese patriarchal customs would complement the goal of producing "good wives, wise mothers" for the inherently gendered assimilation found in *dōka*. Under Qing rule, most women received training to fulfill their roles as wives and mothers at home with the understanding that a woman would secure her social status after giving birth to sons.[8] By the time they were twelve or thirteen years old, Han Taiwanese girls from the Qing period had learned sewing and embroidery while assisting with laundry and cooking at home.[9] Before the onset of Japanese colonization in the late nineteenth century, a few upper-class girls received some reading and writing lessons at Chinese academies, and a few Taiwanese indigene girls were enrolled in missionary schools, such as Tamsui Girls' Academy in Taipei in the north and Xinlou Girls' School in Tainan in southern Taiwan. Before Japanese arrival, girls learned basic literacy and feminine virtues at these learning institutions and received homemaking training at home.[10] While the homemaking training continued from the Qing to the Japanese period, the major changes that happened under Japanese rule were that the majority of women did not bind their feet, and more girls and women were able to acquire new knowledge in schools that allowed them to become part of the labor force, including in new industries under colonial capitalism.[11] Japanese colonial rule thus expanded educational opportunities for girls and women to receive homemaking training in addition to acquiring the practical knowledge and skills necessary to be part of the workforce.

To achieve *dōka*, the educational curriculum at the primary school level was gendered throughout the colonial period to train boys to be skilled workers and girls to be "good wives, wise mothers." By 1904, the colonial government had incorporated gendered training into primary education by requiring schoolgirls to take three hours of sewing lessons starting in the third grade, while boys were to take handiwork, agriculture, or commerce beginning in the fifth grade.[12] The government required schoolgirls to learn the virtues of diligence, thrift, organization, and meticulousness through sewing and home economics lessons. In sewing lessons, the government indicated that schoolgirls should learn the basics, which included sewing, mending, washing, and embroidering. Home economics included a basic knowledge of clothing, food, shelter, caretaking, livestock raising, furniture selection, and food preservation. Effective 1913, schoolgirls were mandated to receive more instruction hours in sewing and home economics lessons as they moved up in grade level: from three hours in third and fourth grades to seven hours in fifth and sixth grades. In contrast, schoolboys received only two hours of lessons in agriculture, commerce, or industry as third- and fourth-graders and only three hours in fifth and sixth grades. Both the agriculture and the commerce lessons emphasized the importance of cultivating diligence and honesty in schoolboys. The Educational Ordinance of Taiwan of 1919 and the New Educational Ordinance of Taiwan of 1922 continued this gendered training in primary school with the same goals and content as the previous regulations. In the 1919 ordinance, girls' training remained the same as in the previous regulations, while the instructional hours increased from three hours to five hours in fifth and sixth grades in 1919 for boys' vocational training in agriculture, commerce, or industry. In the 1922 new ordinance, girls' training began later in the fourth grade with fewer hours, at two hours per week, and increased to five hours in the fifth and sixth grades, which meant two fewer hours than previously, while boys were to receive four hours per week in the fifth and sixth grades, one fewer hour than previously.[13]

These regulations on primary education reveal the importance that the colonial state placed on beginning gender training at a young age for Han Taiwanese children from early in the colonial period to achieve *dōka* through the gendered *kokugo* education. They suggest that colonial educators valued women's role at home since girls began their homemaking training one or two years before boys began their vocational training. Even when colonial officials changed the number of instructional hours of these trainings, girls consistently received more instructional hours than boys in these types of courses. By starting girls' training for domestic duties at an earlier age and with more instructional hours than boys' vocational training, colonial officials seemed to consider having homes with trained housewives to be more important than an economy with skilled laborers, which reflects the idea that the home formed the foundation of the Japanese nation-empire. This gendered training has a colonial dimension to it as the curriculum adopted Japanese as the language of instruction. Japanese was the medium in which students learned all lessons, including this gendered training, and Japanese proficiency marked one's Japaneseness. Ultimately, the goal of the homemaking training for Taiwanese girls and the vocational training for Taiwanese schoolboys was the creation of Japanese-proficient "good wives, wise mothers" in the home setting and productive workers in the public setting. The primary school curriculum revealed that colonial officials had the same gender-specific goal for all Taiwanese, regardless of one's socioeconomic status. Even children from upper-class backgrounds, not accustomed to performing manual labor, had to receive vocational training designed to produce skilled laborers for the Japanese empire. By retaining the same gendered training from the early to the late colonial period, Japanese education officials revealed their consistent expectation of the gender roles that Han Taiwanese children would perform as Japanese subjects, roles that proved to be consistent with Han Taiwanese customs.

To produce this hybrid of "good wives, wise mothers," sewing textbooks and lessons indicate that Han and non–Han Taiwanese sewing styles were taught in school under Japanese rule, in contrast to learning only the Han Taiwanese style at home during the Qing period. A manual titled *Main Principles for Instructing Sewing and Home Economics in Primary School*, published in 1913, stated that schoolgirls would learn Han Taiwanese-style sewing until the second semester of fifth grade.[14] Starting in the third semester of fifth grade, schoolgirls began learning Japanese-style sewing, making items such as aprons for cooking, infant aprons, unlined kimonos, and underskirts. In the 1910s, the government incorporated Japanese-style sewing, different from the previous Han Taiwanese style in techniques and products. Colonial officials also introduced Western style in addition to the existing Taiwanese and Japanese styles in the 1920s.[15] The incorporation of different sewing styles revealed the modernizing process in colonial Taiwan. The colonial authority approved the continuation of Han Taiwanese style, which symbolized the old and the traditional, while including Western style alongside Japanese style to modernize Taiwan, as the West and Japan represented modernity within

REMAKING THE HOME

139

the nation-empire at the turn of the twentieth century. Primary education thus incorporated Japanese and Western knowledge as "modern" for Taiwanese children to learn, which was part of *dōka*. The Western-style lessons would prove useful to some girls in the postwar era, when their skills were required to make clothes for Taiwan's rising manufacturing sector.

Sewing was a marker of a woman's marriageability during the Qing and the Japanese periods, and sewing lessons provided in primary education sought to produce Japanese-proficient "good wives, wise mothers" whose literacy would help extend their training after formal schooling. For example, Gao Sumei recalled that sewing lessons began in the fifth grade in primary school, where she learned the basics, such as sewing buttons. Gao remembered beginning to make clothes in her sixth-grade lessons. She also recalled that when she later attended a girls' middle school, most students chose sewing over the English language as an elective course because of its practicality. Her father was a local official, which meant she belonged to the upper classes and likely did not need to do any menial chores and could afford to attend middle school. After completing her education, Gao purchased instructional sewing books so that she could continue to learn to make clothes, including for her children after marriage.[16] Since the social expectation of girls was that they become good housewives, it made sense that Gao and her classmates valued sewing skills over English proficiency when considering their futures. After formal schooling, Gao continued to self-train because of her Japanese proficiency, which allowed her to study sewing textbooks. While Gao's experience suggests that sewing was important to her household, Lin Jiao'e's life described at the beginning of this chapter also speaks to the importance of sewing as a way to supplement household income. Although Gao and Lin made clothes for different purposes because of their differing financial situations, both acquired the skills in Japanese schools during and after formal schooling. No doubt both women's middle school education provided a higher Japanese proficiency that allowed them to self-study or pursue further training more successfully than primary school graduates. Nonetheless, sewing lessons in a formal school setting constituted an important part of a girl's homemaking training because it met an old requirement of Han Taiwanese brides, dating back to the

Qing period, and furthered the production of "good wives, wise mothers" under Japanese rule.

Although the colonial state intended the household training for home uses only, the practical implication of sewing in primary and secondary schools suggests that sewing could be seen as vocational training that would bring income to the household, which led to the emergence of seamstresses in the postwar era. By requiring sewing as part of the "good wife, wise mother" training of *dōka*, an unintended positive consequence was that future seamstresses could use their language proficiency to continue their training after graduation. Enrolled in Hōrai Girls' Primary School in Taipei, Shi Suyun (b. 1923) recalled practicing how to hold a needle before formal sewing lessons began in the third grade. She and her classmates could make a lunch bag by fourth grade, then undershirts and underpants in the fifth grade, and finally progressed to aprons in the sixth grade.[17] After finishing primary education, girls and women would find that homemaking training was included in the curriculum of all twenty-three girls' middle schools, five teacher-training programs, and eight women's vocational secondary schools (Jp. *jikka kōjo*) in Taiwan. All of these girls' schools and programs included home economics, sewing, and handicraft courses. Two women's vocational schools in Taipei specifically focused on teaching women's virtues and knowledge and skills for daily life. The title of one academy in Tainan and one in Taipei contained the word *sewing* when they were established.[18] As a former student of Taihoku Girls' No. 3 Middle School, Shi recalled learning Taiwanese, Japanese, and Western sewing styles over three years. First, Taiwanese teachers taught Taiwanese-style sewing. Then, students learned how to make children's *yukata* and then kimonos using Japanese-style sewing. And finally, third-year students learned how to make school uniform shirts and skirts in Western-style sewing classes in addition to mending and fabric dyeing.[19] Shi's experience shows a continual training in different sewing styles during middle school education and sharpening her skill after primary education. Girls' middle schools mandated nine to eleven hours of instructional time on sewing and handicrafts out of thirty-one hours total instruction for Taiwanese girls before the promulgation of the New Educational Ordinance of Taiwan in 1922, which reduced instruction to four out of twenty-eight total instructional hours for all middle school girls to accommodate Japanese girls' academic education after the legal coeducation of Taiwanese and Japanese that same year. For students enrolled in women's vocational supplementary programs, sewing took up eight to ten hours of instructional time, double that in girls' middle schools. Although it was initially established as supplementary to primary school training, Enomoto Miyuki argues that home economics education, which included sewing lessons, should have been considered comparable to other vocational schools (Jp. *shokugyō gakkō*) of business, industry, and agriculture after practical learning legally became a separate training from primary schools in 1922. During wartime mobilization, colonial officials emphasized home economics courses at girls' middle schools as having similar importance to the Japanese language, ethics, geography, and history that constituted "national courses" (Jp. *kokumin ka*). Enomoto observes that official regulations on vocational training were passed simultaneously with the increase of home economics schools in the 1930s as girls' middle school was seen as providing insufficient homemaking training for girls. The popularity of home economics schools increased.[20] In sum, the sewing lessons in primary school formed the basis for further training and produced a group of seamstresses. Hence, the sewing part of the "good wife, wise mother" training could be considered vocational training in the same way that business, agricultural, and industry training were vocational training for boys and men. It also turned out that some women took up sewing as their main occupation to support their families. Perhaps the colonial government and educators thought that the sewing lessons would strengthen the "good wife, wise mother" training. However, this focus inadvertently produced public and commercial implications that contradict the original purpose of the "good wife, wise mother" education for the home.

The popularity of Western-style clothes that emerged in the late colonial period helped create an economic space for these "good wife, wise mother" hybrids as seamstresses who were familiar with Western-style sewing. Western-style clothes became popular among the younger generations of Taiwan starting in the 1930s and the 1940s because it was "the symbol of civilization and progress" with similar aesthetic standards for both Taiwanese and Japanese instead of having to conform to Japanese aesthetics and bodily movements to match the Japanese kimono that colonial officials campaigned for Taiwanese women to adopt.[21] In addition to potentially anticolonial reasons, most Taiwanese women did not wear kimonos because the material was expensive and the many layers were too warm for the climate in Taiwan. Kimonos also restricted mobility when walking, sitting, and working, and might reveal one's body because the lack of underpants at the time might expose women's private parts. And their ankles would be revealed while walking. Taiwanese women's reluctance to adopt kimonos led them to turn to Western clothes to avoid catching official attention if they continued to wear traditional Han Taiwanese clothing. By the 1960s, with the development of the textile industry that produced Western-style clothes, the majority of Taiwanese women chose to wear Western-style clothes. To meet the increasing demand for Western-style clothing in the early postwar period, various public group and private individual sewing lessons, including apprenticeships, were created to meet the demand to train women to make clothes.[22] The Japanese-educated "good wife, wise mother" hybrid would be in a good position to meet the demand for making clothes, receiving additional sewing training, and giving sewing lessons with the skills they had acquired in school and at home. Their skill and labor contribution thus expanded from the home to the public realm as Taiwan developed its textile industry in the early postwar era.

This increased demand for Western-style clothes since the late Japanese period coupled with the postwar state economic policy to engender a reliance on sewing as one main source of family income for women of lower-middle-class backgrounds, especially those who received the "good wife, wise mother" training, allowing them to work from home while taking care of their families in the early postwar period. As Chen Peiting argues, Japanese rule and Chinese Nationalist government policies turned the sewing occupation from a male-dominated industry during the Qing period to a female-dominated one from the 1930s to the 1960s with the increasing popularity of Western-style clothes and after the Japanese colonial education made sewing a popular marriage requirement. In the early postwar years, inflation had led women of lower-class backgrounds to use durable cotton materials to make new clothes and mend torn clothes for their families. Concurrently at the state level, Chinese Nationalist officials started to encourage the mechanization of the textile industry after prioritizing textiles along with electric power and fertilizer industries in 1949, and the United States also began providing raw cotton to help develop the textile industry after the Korean War (1950–53) began. Chen notes that this textile development would have been difficult without the sewing training that Japanese and Taiwanese women had received before 1945. The convergence of these economic and geopolitical developments helped shift sewing from a side job to supplement family income to an occupation as Taiwan shifted from an agricultural to an industrial economy during the Cold War period.[23]

The political change and economic problems created more professional opportunities for Japanese-educated women in the early postwar era, such as Shi Suyun, who had years of training in Western-style sewing. Shi actually focused on studying English instead of embroidery in her last two years of girls' middle school and majored in early childhood education (Jp. *hoiku jisshū-ka*) at Tokyo Women's Higher Normal School after graduating from a middle school in Taipei. She took additional Western-sewing lessons after completing teacher's training around 1941, likely because Western clothes became popular, and she wanted to make and wear them. She became a teacher at Jinxiu (Seishū) Girls' Academy in Taipei right after the 2-28 Incident in 1947, which is discussed further in the concluding chapter. Her marital family was greatly affected by the 2-28 Incident when the entire family, including children and women, were arrested and much of their property confiscated by the government. Her husband's income was insufficient to support the entire family, so she decided to work after hearing about a vacancy at Jinxiu Girls' Academy, where she taught home economics, cooking, early childhood education, and sewing. After the Chinese Nationalist government banned the use of Japanese and Taiwanese languages in school instruction, Shi wanted to quit her full-time teaching job because she did not speak the new mandatory language, Mandarin Chinese. But the school principal asked her to teach one or two nighttime classes while starting and operating Shi's own Western-sewing class during the day. The number of Shi's students increased, and she offered more classes, including home economics, hygiene, and cooking.[24] She represents one of many women who became involved in the sewing business and shows how the postwar development of seamstress as a women's profession helped propel Taiwan from an agricultural to an industrial economy. In other words, the emphasis and implementation of sewing lessons in the "good wife, wise mother" training in primary and secondary educational curricula under Japanese rule contributed to the development and success of industrializing Taiwan, an unintended consequence of Japanese colonialism.

While sewing had become a good occupation for women to support their families during the postwar period, women working to supplement their family income was nothing new; many women had done so since the Qing period. However, the educational system instituted by the colonial authority and the economic developments of the Japanese period expanded the fields in which women worked. While the main form of economic production in Qing Taiwan had been subsistence agriculture, the economy under the Japanese became export agriculture. Major infrastructural changes took place in agriculture, trade, transport, communications, banking, public health, and education, leading to their commercialization.[25] These new industries produced new positions for men and women in Taiwan. During the wartime period, the shortage of male labor in all sectors encouraged companies to hire women. In 1943, the workforce in all companies was 93 percent women, mostly primary school graduates. Those with middle school or higher degrees comprised 38 percent of this group.[26] Under Japanese rule, the major change in the correlation between women's educational level and their work was that more primary school graduates entered the workforce compared with girls' middle school graduates as more Han Taiwanese girls received an education starting in the midcolonial period.

Women's education level correlated to their socioeconomic backgrounds as more primary school graduates from lower- and lower-middle-class backgrounds entered the workforce than those from upper- and upper-middle-class backgrounds who had completed middle school. From 1908 to 1936, two-thirds of girls with a primary school degree did not continue their education. Between 1908 and 1923, approximately 80 percent of these graduates were unemployed or stayed at home to help out. From 1924 to 1936, unemployed/at-home graduates declined from 44 percent to 16 percent. Graduates pursued work in commerce, agriculture, industry, and domestic service.[27] The drastic change took place in the mid-1920s because both colonial officials and Taiwanese intellectuals encouraged women to work after the end of World War I. World War I mobilization motivated some individuals in Japan to value women's work outside the home, and Taiwanese intellectuals who studied in Japan absorbed their ideas. In the fall of 1920, *Taiwan nichinichi shimpō* published a series of articles on the benefits of side jobs for women: training women to be diligent and to assist with planning the family budget.[28] Advocating for more radical changes, *Taiwan seinen* and its successor, *Taiwan minbao*, published twenty-one articles between 1920 and 1932 that focused on women's economic independence in which writers emphasized that work, having more career options, would allow women to be economically independent from men and would ultimately elevate a woman's status. These writers criticized patriarchy for enslaving women to be economically dependent on men and treating girls and women like commodities to be sold and bought, arguing that it, along with capitalism, had forced lower-class women to become concubines and prostitutes.[29] In other words, *Taiwan minbao* writers believed that if women held jobs and earned money, they would not be commodified by men through the bride price, concubinage, or servitude. Ultimately, both groups encouraged women to work with different motivations—the colonial authority wanted women to strengthen the nation-empire through home as the core, and some Taiwanese intellectuals wanted to modernize Taiwan through women's economic independence.

Although sewing became an important skill commercially, other skills remained essential to girls' training at home alongside school education as Han Taiwanese home training sometimes interfered with the success of Japanese schooling. Women of lower-class backgrounds were more likely than their upper-class counterparts to perform household chores before marriage because their families needed their labor. For example, Tang Yanyan, the daughter of a railroad repairman and a seamstress in Beitou in northern Taiwan, performed chores at the expense of her education. Tang had to wake up at 5:00 a.m. every day to carry water, two buckets at a time, for nine trips between her home and the well. Sometimes she went to get water at midnight before bedtime. After carrying the water in the morning, she had to cook rice porridge for her parents before school began. After school, she did not stay to play because she had to do chores at home. She pounded rice, worked on the farm, dug up yams, fed the chickens, and cooked dinner. Tang said that because her parents were busy and there were not enough helping hands, she had to do chores. Therefore, she did not have time to do her homework and always received corporal punishment from her teacher the next day.[30] Tang's labor was necessary because her parents were working in lower- to middle-class jobs. Her experience suggests a clash between home training and school training. Tang's obligations at home provided more experiences with the household than her school training did, but her obligations also meant she was unable to complete her schoolwork and, thus, was less likely to fully immerse in the *kokugo* education to achieve *dōka*. Her experience differed from that of upper- and middle-class girls, who were able to focus on their studies or relax at home because their labor was unnecessary. Schooling was more likely a disruption to families of lower-class backgrounds than those of the upper classes.

While doing chores at home likely interfered with the schoolwork of those of lower- and lower-middle-class backgrounds, daughters of upper- and upper-middle-class families were not idle. Some acquired other knowledge and skills at home before marriage, which suggests a complementary relationship between Taiwanese home training and Japanese education in these families. For example, political activist and feminist Feng Shou'e recalled that her father used a Taiwanese Hoklo textbook printed in the missionary romanization system to instruct her and her siblings about the teachings of Mencius. She was born in 1930 to a farming household in rural Yilan, but her father later opened his own business. Her father also created some arithmetic questions for the children to solve as part of their homework.[31] Another example is Hong Zhimei, who was born to a business family in Lugang in central Taiwan. Her father taught her how to use an abacus and required her to observe him and her mother cook.[32] There is also Lü Zhunju from Tainan, whose businessman father taught her and her siblings how to swim. He also told them stories from *Romance of the Three Kingdoms* (Ch. Sanguo yanyi) and a folktale on why dogs attack roosters on sight. Lü recalled proudly that the folktale explained the attack by saying that dogs wanted roosters to return the combs that roosters had borrowed from dogs in the past.[33] Zhu Qiufeng, from Tamsui, learned classical Chinese from her grandfather at home before attending primary school. Her grandfather was a local official, and her family owned a school supplies shop in the Tamsui area in northern Taiwan. She also enjoyed listening to stories from *Romance of the Three Kingdoms* that her grandfather told her.[34] These fatherly figures were business owners, people of upper-middle-class backgrounds, which meant these men were almost certainly more educated than those in lower-class families. They imparted Confucian values and moral lessons using Chinese stories, arithmetic and abacus skills that would be useful in accounting, and Taiwanese Hoklo language literacy to their daughters or granddaughters at home. The moral, cultural, and practical training at home likely complemented the knowledge and skills they learned at school. Some moral lessons and practical skills that girls of upper-class backgrounds received at home likely reinforced the imperial ethics lessons of filial piety and arithmetic skills they also learned in Japanese schools.

Families of upper- and upper-middle-class backgrounds did not train their daughters to do chores because they envisioned them playing a different role upon marriage, one that signified their socioeconomic status. Upper-middle-class families such as Xu Xianxian's did not need their children to do chores because they hired servants. Although both parents were teachers with servants, Xu nonetheless had to observe her mother's cooking. Xu explained, "My mother said that you must know how to do something yourself before you can supervise others to do the same," like how teachers fulfill their duties.[35] Her story hints at one of the duties of an upper-middle-class housewife in addition to the presumed feminine skill of cooking for one's household—the ability to supervise house servants. Du Pan Fangge, a Hakka poet, saw from her mother that supervising servants was part of women's responsibilities. Du recounted that her mother, born in 1907, who had completed her education at Taihoku Girls' No. 3 Middle School, had to manage household matters and servants, carry out her mother-in-law's orders, and dress up beautifully for potential guests visiting their household.[36] Du's mother showed that household management, obedience to the mother-in-law, and hospitality were duties of married women under Japanese rule. These personal accounts suggest that upper- and upper-middle-class families deemed certain skills, especially the ability to supervise others, as crucial to a married woman's success even when she might not have any experience in them before marriage. Many parents seemed to believe that observation was sufficient to prepare their daughters for marital life, perhaps because they deemed chores to be something easy to learn, such as in Zhang Yue'e's case. Zhang was born in 1927 in Yilan to a father who was a business owner and Chinese medicine doctor. Her mother told her to go study instead of learning chores because her mother believed it would be easy to learn chores at a later time. Zhang obeyed and completed her education at Ranyō (Lanyang) Girls' Middle School.[37] Her experience reveals that the motivation behind these families sending their daughters to school was to bolster family status rather than to provide housewife training. Throughout the entire colonial period, over 80 percent of Taiwanese girls never attended school because families were unwilling to pay tuition for future housewives who only needed to learn sewing and household matters. For those who completed primary school, over 80 percent of educated girls did not receive more education.[38] The few lucky ones from upper- and middle-class backgrounds could choose further educational opportunities from the limited options of advanced course study (Jp. *kōtōka*) and girls' middle schools that the colonial government provided. After they finished middle school, most women likely stayed home to wait for marriage. Between 59 percent and 93 percent of girls' middle school graduates did not indicate their jobs between 1924 and 1936, presumably because they were unemployed.[39] Unlike lower- and lower-middle-class families with economic incentives, these families of upper- and upper-middle-class backgrounds were motivated to educate their daughters only to reinforce their social status.

According to Ko Ikujo, daughters of upper-middle-class families who were highly proficient in Japanese attended girls' middle school to become wives of government officials and businessmen who could socialize with Japanese guests. In traditional practices during the Qing period, upper-class women only left their marital homes to visit temples or their natal families. When visitors were present in their marital households, women hid in their rooms. Under Japanese rule, schools allowed upper-middle-class Taiwanese women to become visible in public, first as schoolgirls and then also as visitors to scenic and popular sites. Attending to their guests at home also became part of their household responsibilities. Middle school education in Taiwan produced women well versed in

REMAKING THE HOME

149

upper-middle-class hobbies and culture, with knowledge in areas such as science and home economics, cultural aesthetic practices such as flower arrangement and tea ceremony, and training in Western-style etiquette and social dance.[40] In sum, girls' middle school sought to prepare Taiwanese women to become the ideal "good wives, wise mothers" who could assist with their husbands' business and position by properly socializing with Japanese officials and their wives.

Upper-and upper-middle-class families thus found secondary education for their daughters a valuable investment. Only families of their backgrounds could send their daughters to receive a middle school education as tuition at girls' middle schools cost 3.6 to 29 times as much as primary school—from ¥2.5 to ¥2.9 per month compared with 10 to 70 *sen* per month at primary schools, where 100 *sen* equaled ¥1. For schoolgirls who lived in the dormitory, monthly lodging and food cost about ¥16 at Taihoku Girls' No. 3 Middle School in 1939, enough to purchase 141 kilograms of rice.[41] A primary school teacher's annual salary was ¥633 (or ¥52.75 per month) in 1922, while a carpenter in Taipei earned ¥1.4 daily (or ¥42 per month) in 1930.[42] A teacher could afford to send his daughter to girls' middle school, but a carpenter would have to think twice because of its cost. For example, guardians of students at Taihoku Girls' No. 3 Middle School, a predominantly Taiwanese school, were mostly working in business, government, manufacturing, and agriculture, with property worth ranging from ¥5,000 to ¥100,000 between 1925 and 1940. Between 1927 and 1940, 56 percent to 68 percent of these guardians were civil servants or businessmen.[43] Students of higher socioeconomic status were more likely to pursue further education because they could afford the cost and their parents were motivated by it as a status symbol.[44] Although daughters of upper-middle-class backgrounds were more likely to receive secondary education, their education seemed to serve their families by reinforcing their socioeconomic status through marriage arrangements rather than providing emotional or economic benefits for the women themselves.

However, the status symbol of education did not help reduce the stress of new daughters-in-law who were overwhelmed, especially for those who had never performed chores at home before marriage, which suggests that the Japanese "good wife, wise mother" training at school had failed these women. Lü Zhunju's traumatizing experience after marriage reveals the importance of homemaking training before marriage. She was born in Tainan, and her father was a well-to-do business owner. Her family hired cooks at home, so she had never cooked until after marriage. She noted that her mother told her it was sufficient to observe cooking before marriage without cooking herself. As expected, she was told to cook after marriage. Her marital family's business was making miso, and they hired thirty to forty workers. Every day, Lü had to cook one meal with rice porridge and two meals with rice for all the workers. Cooking made her cry because she had never done it before marriage.[45] Lü was not the only woman overwhelmed by her duties after marriage. Born in 1925, Liu Duan, an adopted daughter of a business owner in Yilan, completed girls' middle school and worked as a teacher and nurse before marriage. She faced challenges after marriage:

> I did not have to do any chores at home before but had to cook and raise pigs immediately after marriage. There were three big pigs. Every time I saw the pig opening its large mouth and making the loud noise, "Oink, oink," I was very scared! I did not know how to put the feed into the pig's large mouth. But there was nothing else I could do. I could not escape my responsibility. Because I've never done any heavy physical labor before, I was unable to lift heavy objects. Every time I carried the pig feed, I could only carry a half bucket one at a time. . . . I was always the last one to eat. . . . There were endless chores every day and I did not have enough to eat.[46]

Liu's account reveals that marriage required not only cooking skills but also physical strength and knowledge of family businesses. A daughter-in-law had to perform whatever tasks her mother-in-law ordered. Both Lü and Liu recalled those early times as full of feelings of helplessness and sorrow. Their accounts reveal that their transition from girlhood to wifehood was challenging and stressful. Their homemaking training at school did not seem to alleviate their stress, especially since virtually all of them had to live with and obey their mother-in-law, a living arrangement and hierarchy that remained dominant in postwar Taiwan.

Primary school was supposed to teach girls basic skills such as cooking and livestock-raising as part of the "good wife, wise mother" training, but accounts from Lü and Liu suggest that the homemaking training was likely unevenly implemented in Taiwan, as some girls received such training in school while others did not. And the lack of such training at home for some meant that they had little practical experience before marriage. Even for those who received such practical training in primary and/or secondary schools, basic cooking and sewing skills were likely insufficient to reduce the stress of newly married women, who also had to worry about having and raising children under the careful supervision of their mothers-in-law. A possible reason primary education lacked some practical housewife skills was that the "good wife, wise mother" was part of the *kokugo* education, which focused on teaching the Japanese language and basic knowledge of a modern society. As discussed in chapter 1, colonial officials seemed to emphasize the motherhood training over the wifehood training. A "wise mother" was expected to teach her children the Japanese language and basic knowledge before starting school. Although primary school education taught duties and values such as frugality expected of "good wives, wise mothers" in language and ethics lessons, it devoted little time to instructing practical skills needed in a marriage.

The "good wife, wise mother" training of the *kokugo* education sought to prepare Taiwanese women for marriage and child-rearing for the nation-empire, but oral histories and interviews suggest that the training fell short of preparing them for their new role upon marriage during and after Japanese rule. Although lower classes benefited from gaining a vocational skill that was useful in the postwar economy, the upper classes benefited mainly from reinforcing their socioeconomic status. After they completed their education or had worked outside their homes for a few years, most educated women got married and had to do chores in their marital household, and their socioeconomic backgrounds shaped their experience and training.[47] Women of lower-class backgrounds likely adjusted faster to their new life as wives and daughters-in-law because they were more likely to have done chores at home before marriage. Although many did not do chores at home before marriage, some women of upper classes received moral, cultural, and practical lessons at home that reflected their higher socioeconomic status. For daughters in the upper classes, education became a status symbol and likely complemented the home lessons some received. Regardless of their socioeconomic status, many women benefited from the sewing lessons in school. Their Japanese proficiency and basic sewing skills allowed some women to train further to make clothes for their family members or to supplement family income. Women of lower-class backgrounds might have received home training at the expense of their schooling, but they were more likely to have the economic incentive to use their sewing skills as professionals in the postwar economy, whereas women of upper-class backgrounds were more likely to receive complementary training from home and school to reinforce their status but faced more challenges as a new wife and daughter-in-law. The type of women's home training one received was strongly dependent on their socioeconomic status, and school training to fully prepare them for marriage was implemented unevenly and insufficiently. Women of lower-class backgrounds benefited economically, while women of upper-class backgrounds benefited socially.

ROMANCE AND MARRIAGE: WHEN GIRLS AND WOMEN MEET BOYS AND MEN

While many Taiwanese families had embraced the change in the home-making training site from the home to the school, they likely did not expect Japanese schools to contribute to the rise of romantic love and free-choice marriage, which challenged their authority. Even as Han Taiwanese customs and colonial educators likely limited the growth of romantic love and free-choice marriage by enforcing gender segregation, schools established during the Japanese period nonetheless provided a space for students of all genders to interact, something that had not been permitted during the Qing period. Schools also indirectly encouraged romantic relationships between women and men by equipping them with the literacy to communicate with each other and the skills required to work after completing their education, where they had more opportunity to interact with coworkers of the opposite gender. The increased opportunities to share the same space and the discussions of romantic love and free-choice marriage in *Taiwan minbao* in the 1920s as influenced by the feminist movement in Japan and the New Culture Movement in China likely helped popularize the concept of romantic love among educated Taiwanese intellectuals and youths. As William M. Reddy asserts, romantic love is seen as a "self-consciously chosen modern practice" in "vernacular literature, music, and the decorative arts," "songs or folklore," and fiction to show "modernity" and "personal freedom" in opposition to arranged marriage.[48] Even though arranged marriages remained dominant, some Taiwanese women and men began to practice romantic love through love-letter writing, where the Japanese language was likely the language of love, at least in writing, because children acquired Japanese proficiency in their *kokugo* education.

Influenced by the Han Taiwanese custom of gender segregation since colonization, Japanese colonial officials implemented gender segregation in primary school to make it easier to provide gender training and preparation for the single-gender middle school entrance exams, which were gender specific. To conform to the traditional Han Chinese idea that boys and girls over the age of seven should not share the same room, colonial officials implemented gender segregation when they established the Girls' Department at the National Language School, which later became the Third Attached School in 1897. Although some argued it was more cost-efficient to have coed classes, colonial officials set a policy on gender segregation starting in 1899, with various revisions afterward, to help increase the school enrollment rate of Han Taiwanese girls.[49] As more girls enrolled in schools over time, the administration changed the minimum grade level and the number of schoolgirls at which gender segregation was to be implemented in Taiwanese primary schools between third and fifth grade. The Primary School Organization Regulations of Taiwan (Jp. Kōgakkō Hensei Kitei) from 1899 stated that when more than twenty girls enrolled in a primary school, girls had to be segregated from the boys to form their own class. In September 1901, the new regulations changed the required number from twenty to thirty girl enrollees. Later in 1907, the requirement indicated a grade level for gender segregation—thirty or more girl fifth-graders would form their own class. This policy was later revised to forty or more girl third-graders and older in the Educational Ordinance of Taiwan in 1919.[50] The policy again changed to begin gender segregation starting in the fifth grade with more than fifty girls in 1921, and to sixty girl third-graders and older in 1943.[51] The change in the number of schoolgirls to form their own class correlated to the increase in female enrollees over time. The grade-level requirement for gender segregation likely had to do with gender training—sewing lessons began in third or

CHAPTER 4

fourth grade for girls, and vocational training lessons began in the fifth grade for boys. In coed schools, because there were fewer schoolgirls than in girls' schools, school administrators usually combined different grade levels or classes of girls to give sewing and home economics lessons.[52] Shi Suyun recalled that the school began soliciting students' postgraduation plans in the third grade and divided them into different classes in the fifth grade, where the class with students who planned to pursue secondary education had to stay to study from 4:00 p.m. to 7:00 p.m. or later.[53] Gender segregation allowed instructors to teach gender-specific lessons without having to take the extra step of segregating students each time a gendered lesson was given, and in fifth and sixth grades it also allowed teachers to focus on preparing students for middle school entrance exams. Middle schools were segregated by gender.

Beyond the practical reasons some schools and classes were segregated by gender, interviews with former schoolgirls illustrate how both school authorities and families actively discouraged interactions between the genders, reinforcing Han customs with government support. Several girls' middle school students recalled gender segregation in their commute to and from school. Lan Linlin, an interviewee from Hsinchu, commuted to school as a middle school student during the wartime period. She recalled that when she first became a commuter, there were few students, and thus girls attending Shinchiku Girls' Middle School and boys attending Shinchiku Middle School rode on the same bus. But in the midst of her first year at the middle school, both schools banned coed buses, resulting in gender segregation on buses. After departing from the bus at Shinchiku Station, girls would line up on the left side and boys on the right before walking to their respective schools. Lan explained that gender segregation was also practiced in the cafés, where boys sat in the front and girls in the back.[54] Gender segregation was not limited to Hsinchu; Zhang Yue'e also recalled gender segregation on the train when she began commuting to school in her second year at Ranyō Girls' Middle School in Yilan. Her teacher warned her class, "You have grown up. You are students of Ranyō. You must behave and not walk with boys."[55] Not only did officials and the school authority extend gender segregation outside school grounds, families also reinforced this concept by punishing their daughters if they seemed to have transgressed gender boundaries, including by using corporal punishment to achieve their goal. Lin Tiantian from Yunlin in southern Taiwan recalled that she did not "dare to talk to boys" because otherwise she would be punished. She recalled that boys often called out her name and two other girls' names in public. "We didn't even know who those boys were, let alone talking to them. They would call out our names [in public]. . . . And then our parents would misunderstand. . . . [They] hit us because [some boys] called our names." Both Lin and her friend received beatings at home after their families heard about their "improper behavior" with boys.[56] This was likely because having one's name called constituted acquaintanceship, and schoolgirls and young women were not permitted to interact with boys and young men unless they were engaged. The idea was that girls and women needed to remain proper, and interactions with boys and men from outside their family would imply sexual promiscuity. Both Zhang's and Lin's accounts suggest that gender segregation was implemented because schoolgirls' sexual purity helped define the reputation of families and schools.

Gender segregation at school and in public places established by school authorities and families likely had some effects in preserving the Han Taiwanese idea of female chastity to maintain patriarchy, but young people nevertheless used their Japanese proficiency to make connections during their commute to school or work. For example, Lin Tiantian met her husband when she was a middle school student commuting to school. Her husband saw her on the train. For five years, he wrote love letters to her.[57] Lan Linlin also met her first husband when she was commuting to work. He was a local policeman, and she was a teacher. He greeted her every morning and eventually wrote her a love letter.[58] Both accounts showed that letter writing was an important medium in facilitating romantic relationships because both the sender and the recipient were literate, which was made possible by the *kokugo* education. Although earlier accounts revealed that the school authority and parents reinforced gender segregation in public areas through policy and punishment, school attendance and consequently increased work opportunities inevitably created social space for girls and boys and then women and men to interact.

Besides regulations from school and family authorities, former schoolgirls illustrate the persistence of the Han Taiwanese custom of gender segregation in limiting the growth of romantic love and free-choice marriage as some girls and women practiced self-imposed gender segregation at different ages due to social expectations. For example, Lai Huazhu remembered that girls and boys played separately in primary school in Miaoli in central Taiwan. Although she was in a coed classroom, she characterized potential interaction as "shameful, embarrassing. . . . Teachers didn't tell us [not to interact with the opposite gender]. Parents didn't tell us either. It was we ourselves who felt embarrassed. Boys didn't come to play with us. Boys didn't try to mess with girls, at least not boys in my class."[59] Xia Yujia, from an all-girl class in Taichung in central Taiwan in the 1930s, provided a similar account: "We didn't really play together. 'Men and women must keep their distance from each other.'[60] No one taught us; it was the natural way. Sometimes both [girls' and boys'] classes had to do joint activities together. Boys didn't really want to hold girls' hands. [Therefore they] barely held onto each other's fingertips."[61]

Age seems to be key in understanding when gender segregation was implemented, as Lai and Xia discussed interactions in primary school while Zhang Yue'e and Lin Tiantian recalled their experiences as middle school students. Teachers and parents did not seem to actively forbid primary school students from having physical contact with each other but were more likely to intervene once students became older, such as in middle school. Although Xia claimed it was "natural" and not taught, social expectations produced strong feelings of shame and embarrassment that limited interactions. This self-segregation and self-policing continued into adulthood, as Xu Xianxian called gender segregation an "automatic" part of proper and good behavior of any professional woman: "We girls back in the day behaved. If my mother hadn't said anything about marriage, I wouldn't have thought about it. We girls didn't go see movies with boys. No, we didn't do that. Back then, we would go home after work. When it was time to work, we worked. . . . We didn't go out with people causally. . . . We men and women were not casual, unlike people today. . . . In the workplace, we also didn't talk to men casually.[62] Xu's characterization of a girl's good and proper behavior in regards to boys provides a glimpse of how unmarried girls and women behaved in a society that did not favor romantic love. Gender segregation was the norm and marked a girl's chastity and virtue, and that was contradictory to romantic love, which might lead to multiple consecutive partners without marriage in sight.

Although gender segregation limited the growth of romantic love and free-choice marriage, Japanese schools nevertheless increased the number of working women from lower- and lower-middle-class backgrounds while enabling girls' middle school graduates from upper- and upper-middle-class backgrounds to use their Japanese literacy to create more free romantic relationships and marriages. Families of middle- and lower-class backgrounds sent their daughters to school in the hope that their degree would lead to employment to help supplement family income. Thus, workingwomen were more likely from lower- and lower-middle-class backgrounds because of the economic incentives. Their work then created opportunities for them to meet their future husbands at work or through social networks outside their family's intervention. This meant these families might be unwilling to let their daughters marry too early or marry with a low bride price because of the financial losses the family would suffer once their married daughter shifted to giving their income to their marital home.

Even under Japanese rule, parents continued to hold on to their power to accept marriage proposals. Consider Zeng Jinjin, whose large lower-class family was supported by her father selling chicken at the market and her mother working as a full-time housewife with fourteen children. Zeng met her husband in the early postwar years when she worked as a waitress and her husband was a cook at the same restaurant. They dated for a couple of years before she married him at the age of eighteen. Her mother was against their marriage because she wanted Zeng to continue to work to bring money home and only agreed to the marriage after receiving a sizable bride price from the groom, who was also of a lower-class background.[63] In contrast, Lai Huazhu got married without obstacles because her parents were already deceased. She was working as a cook for Japanese teachers when she met her husband, a tailor who made suit jackets and pants across the street. They met without introduction by a third party. She got married at the age of twenty-two, during the Japanese period.[64] Clearly, family backgrounds helped decide their fate after completing primary school. After completing primary education, Zeng worked to supplement family income and Lai worked to support herself.

CHAPTER 4

Their work allowed them to meet their partners and go on dates without parental intervention. Nevertheless, these two accounts illustrate the power the older generations had in deciding the marriage of the younger generation. Zeng ultimately married her chosen partner, although not without some challenges, while Lai did not have any obstacles because she was an orphan. Coming from lower-class backgrounds, both found their love and marriage partners through work that required some skills or Japanese proficiency, which they acquired from schooling.

While school and work provided the space and social networks for romantic love and free-choice marriage to begin and propagate, the campaign for marriage based on romantic love contributed to the spread of the concept of such relationships starting in the 1920s, which challenged the Han Taiwanese custom of arranged marriage. Taiwanese intellectuals advocated romantic love as the condition for marriage in their campaign for women's rights.[65] They reported on the Chinese women's movement in fifty-eight articles published in *Taiwan minbao*, no doubt inspired by the campaign for women's liberation in the New Culture Movement on mainland China, which called for free-choice marriage and family reform, economic independence, equal educational opportunities, a ban on prostitution, and women's political participation. Writers of *Taiwan minbao* also republished works by Hu Shi, Chen Duxiu, and Lu Xun, major thinkers of the New Culture Movement. Hu Shi's play *Life Event: Marriage* was influential among Taiwanese intellectuals and was performed in Taiwan.[66] Taiwanese intellectuals were also influenced by leftist and feminist movements in Japan. They published articles on the equal education movement, the rights of workingwomen, women's political participation, and the antiprostitution movement.[67] Inspired by ideas from both mainland China and Japan, *Taiwan minbao* discussed and spread the idea of love-based, free-choice marriage as more Taiwanese women and men became educated.

The new form of schooling made these romantic encounters possible, but Han Taiwanese customs as embodied by parents proved strong in dictating marriages even when young Taiwanese formed such relationships through school and work. For example, Lin Yuzhu, who was born around 1905 and had completed girls' middle school education, had maintained contact with her law-school boyfriend through letter writing and occasional meetings. Unfortunately, Lin's family arranged for her to marry someone else because of the historical feud between her family and her boyfriend's family.[68] Another tragic account comes from Zhang Yue'e's family. Her older sister died before her wedding day and at the age of fifteen because of apparent heartbreak over her father's disapproval of her boyfriend and a subsequent arranged marriage.[69] *Taiwan nichinichi shimpō* also reported a tragedy on October 4, 1930, when a twenty-one-year-old factory worker who was three months pregnant died by suicide after her father discovered her relationship with a fellow worker in June 1930.[70] Gao Zhuyuan, from Tainan with a primary school diploma, emphasizes children's obedience to their parents as key to upholding the practice of arranged marriages for people of her generation, who were born in the 1920s and the 1930s: "Yeah, some people had romantic love, but parents didn't recognize it. So [marriage] was always [arranged] through matchmaking. Back in the day, parents decided for you, and people obeyed their parents. One didn't know if the match was good or bad. We didn't think about it. We thought marriage was marriage. We didn't think about divorce either."[71] Historian Doris Chang attributes this obedience to filial piety.[72] Although these girls received an education and some even completed postprimary education, they were bound by social expectations and obeyed their families' decisions, which were sanctioned by the colonial state. Disobedience led to tragedies because women could not survive independently from their family in a patriarchal society that was supported by the government.

Although new forms of schooling helped increase the number of romantic-love relationships, interviews I conducted suggest that it could also terminate such relationships just as it had created them. Romantic love made infidelity less acceptable to many women, and it sometimes resulted in divorce, which had become more plausible for women to pursue thanks to the increased educational and work opportunities for women under Japanese rule. As noted by William M. Reddy, romantic love differs from lust and needs to be proven by showing fidelity.[73] For women who married for love, heartbreak continued decades after the betrayal ended, as seen in Lin Tiantian's experience. She married for love, but her husband cheated on her repeatedly after marriage. She expressed her anger and pain with tears during the interview when she was in her eighties.[74] Another example is Lan Linlin, whose police officer husband courted her but then cheated on her with a married Japanese woman. Although her parents-in-law asked her to return home for the sake of their three children, Lan eventually divorced him after her then husband refused to leave the woman.[75] Similarly, Lin wanted to divorce her husband after she found out about his infidelity, but her neighbors and family convinced her to stay in the marriage for the sake of her young children.[76] Although the reasons these two women made different choices were unclear, it was possible that Lan was able to get a divorce because she continued to work after marriage, whereas Lin had quit her job.[77] New educational opportunities, such as midwife training, allowed divorced women to support themselves and their children, such as in the case of Zeng Qinglian's mother. Zeng's mother moved back to her natal family to receive financial and childcare support after her divorce. Zeng's grandmother paid for the midwife training for her mother, who then supported the entire family as a midwife and even promoted the establishment of childcare centers in Yilan.[78] Although society did not approve of divorce, Zeng's mother was lucky to have the support of her rich family, like other upper-class women who could divorce their husbands for taking a concubine or being physically abusive.[79]

Besides financial support, parents continued to exert great control over their children's lives. Parental power was supported by the colonial government when it upheld old customs such as requiring the parents' approval, in addition to that of the couple, in obtaining a divorce.[80] Men had greater actual power and could initiate divorce on these grounds—"infertility, not serving in-laws, talkative, theft, jealousy, and illness"—while women had little power, but parents could file for their daughter's divorce under Qing rule.[81] However, women's power to file for divorce in court increased under Japanese rule. A woman could apply for a divorce on the grounds of her husband having "committed a 'dishonest crime,' refused to reside with her, or married another woman as wife (not as concubine) and lived with this woman."[82] Under Japanese rule, women filed more lawsuits for divorce than men because women remained weaker than men in obtaining a divorce agreement without state intervention via the court.[83] The divorce rates were 14.4 percent to 22.3 percent in 1906 and 7.7 percent to 9.4 percent in 1925.[84] Extramarital relationships and actions threatened marriage, although only women who were able to access new educational and work opportunities or rely on family support would obtain divorce because they could become financially independent.

Although there were examples of love-based, free-choice marriages and women-initiated divorces in Taiwan under Japanese rule, Taiwanese families continued to practice arranged marriage with support from the colonial state, which reinforced parental authority and gender hierarchy from Han Taiwanese customs. Marriage and family relations were considered civil matters, and colonial officials treated old Han Taiwanese customs as part of civil matters until 1923, when most of the Japanese civil substantive laws were finally applied to Taiwanese civil matters, but family-related issues remained under the old custom laws. This meant that arranged marriage, child brides, and bride price were allowed, even when the colonial court disapproved of the embedded monetary transactions. Colonial court also allowed concubinage in 1906 but gave concubines the power to end the relationship in 1922.[85] Many upper-class women had fathers with multiple wives, such as Shi Suyun's father, who had three wives. Her mother was the principal wife, and she constantly argued with him about this practice. Shi explained that her father had to do social drinking in places with sex workers and would marry women he met there.[86] By continuing to designate family-related matters to follow old Taiwanese custom law throughout the colonial period, the colonial government upheld the power of the patriarchal family, especially of men.

Gender segregation and parental decision likely had greater power over the marriage of women of upper-class backgrounds than their lower-class counterparts as extended family connections and school networks often produced marriage candidates. Examples included classmates introducing their cousins as potential partners and sometimes men asking their parents to arrange their marriage.[87] For example, Shi Suyun's father arranged her marriage with the Yan family of Keelung in northern Taiwan, which matched the prestige of her family, the Shi family of Lugang in southern Taiwan. Her marriage was decided after she graduated from primary school when her future father-in-law found out she had graduated as the valedictorian and passed the entrance exam into the prestigious Taihoku Girls' No. 3 Middle School. Shi claimed that the only qualification in choosing a marriage match was if that person was studious.

CHAPTER 4

"No one had boyfriends back then. We never heard of anyone having a boyfriend while we were studying at girls' middle school. If someone got a boyfriend, she would be called a bad girl (Ch. *buliang shaonü*)," she commented.[88] She only saw a photograph of her future husband before their engagement, and they got married a year after becoming engaged.[89] It is interesting that Shi did not know of anyone with a boyfriend, even though there are oral histories and interviews that included accounts of romantic love and/or free-choice marriage. Her unawareness suggests that romantic love was very limited or hidden among those from upper-class families. Perhaps unsurprisingly, upper-class families extended their marriage networks through Japanese education. For example, Wang Feimei, whose family worked for the famous Lin Family in Banqiao in Taipei, got married through family connections. Her future husband was a classmate of her brother; her brother and her husband played rugby together and listened to classical music. Wang's brother knew her future husband to be an honest man. Her brother also took her frail body into consideration and thought her husband would be a good match for her because of his medical training. Following the old Han Chinese custom of not showing her face in front of strangers, she peeked at him from her backyard whenever he visited her house.[90] Other examples include Zheng Rongrong's and Li Piqing's fathers, who arranged for their daughters to marry one of their employees, from a construction company and at a hot spring hotel respectively.[91] Zheng recalled, "My father made the decision for me. I didn't dare to protest."[92] Family members had many considerations when they searched for potential partners for their children, including health, diligence, and marital happiness. Although there were stories of resistance that ended tragically, Taiwanese women and men tended to follow decisions made by their family members instead of resisting them.

Even as those of upper- and middle-class backgrounds had less choice than those of lower-middle and lower classes in choosing their own partners because of their insistence on following old marriage practices, their higher levels of education implied higher literacy that could be key to finding their own partners. As mentioned earlier, Lin Tiantian and Lan Linlin received love letters from their future husbands. Another account comes from the poet Du Pan Fangge. Du's mother often wrote to her younger brother (Du's uncle), who was studying in Taichū Middle School, urging him to study diligently. An upperclassman at her brother's school once accidentally saw the letter and fell in love with her. This person became Du's father. Du quoted her father: "I was curious about letters from a girls' middle school student. I picked it up and felt that this girl seems determined and talented; her writing is methodical. I thought then, this girl would be a good wife. I can delegate child-rearing to her without worries."[93] However, Du's father's family did not deem Du's mother a compatible match due to her socioeconomic status, unbound feet, and lack of beauty. Moreover, Du's mother's family had already chosen another marriage partner, and the engagement ceremony was approaching. Du's father then threatened suicide if he could not marry her. Du's father was the oldest son, which meant that he was valued in the family as the one to continue the patrilineal line. The two ended up getting married at the age of eighteen.[94] The story of Du's parents reveals the impact of education in Taiwan. First, letter writing became common for Taiwanese to communicate with their family when they were away from home. Second, one's writing could plant the seed for romance to blossom. Without the *kokugo* education, Du's parents would not have met because there would not have been a school for Du's uncle and father to meet in, the letter that Du's father encountered would not have been written, and Du's mother would not have had the literacy to produce the letter.

These educated women continued to use their Japanese proficiency to communicate, to socialize, and to learn in the postwar period. According to Ueno Hiroko, girls' middle school graduates continued to embrace the Japanese practices they had learned in school in the postwar years because their middle school education symbolized their upper-middle-class social status. Her research shows that Taiwanese girls' middle school graduates embraced sewing, especially Western style, and made clothes for their family members as a symbol of their middle school education in the postwar years. Ueno has found that Han Taiwanese women continued to write and read in Japanese in the postwar years, such as perusing Japanese magazines on knitting. She observes that girls' middle school graduates continued to obtain new knowledge through Japanese magazines, books, and newspapers. She argues that unlike Taiwanese men, who had to learn Chinese to work in the public realm, Taiwanese girls' middle school graduates retained their Japanese proficiency and further developed the skills and knowledge they had begun learning under Japanese rule through these Japanese publications. These women also wrote letters in Japanese to their friends after Japanese rule ended.[95] Overall, educated women's proficiency in Japanese helped increase their homemaking skills, and they maintained their Japanese proficiency into the postwar years.

The use of Japanese proficiency in creating and maintaining familial and social relationships during and after Japanese rule could be seen as a success of the *kokugo* education. Japanese speaking and writing proficiency helped create and maintain romantic relationships. Many, like Lan Linlin, used Japanese as a common language for communication. After her divorce, Lan remarried, but because Lan was Taiwanese Hakka and her second husband was Taiwanese Hoklo, they could not communicate in their own native language.[96] Taiwan was already a multiethnic society when Japanese became its lingua franca under Japanese rule and into the early postwar era. Most of my interviews were conducted in Taiwanese Hoklo, mixing a few Japanese words throughout. Interviews and existing studies have documented that children and grandchildren of the last Japanese-educated generation of Han Taiwanese grew up knowing some basic Japanese vocabulary, shown by how this generation of Taiwanese mixed Japanese vocabulary into their daily conversations. Some of their children and grandchildren even learned some Japanese nursery rhymes such as "Peach Boy" (Jp. Momotarō), which was part of first-graders' curriculum until 1941.[97] A few Japanese-educated Han Taiwanese, such as Lin Xianyan from Taipei, only spoke Japanese before 1945 because her parents spoke Japanese and she attended a kindergarten and elementary school (Jp. shōgakkō) for Japanese children. Lin had to learn Mandarin Chinese and Taiwanese Hoklo after Japanese rule ended.[98] No doubt the adaptation of Japanese music and the retention of Japanese lyrics and place-names in popular Taiwanese Hoklo songs performed by Japanese-educated singers contributed to the ubiquitous influence of Japanese language and culture in postwar Taiwan.[99] Even though the Sinification campaign under the Chinese Nationalist government banned the use of Japanese language and the sale of Japanese songs in the early postwar era, demand from the Japanese-educated and the postwar generations of Taiwanese popularized the Japanese *enka* music genre and other aspects of Japanese culture.[100] Japanese proficiency, although mostly low-level, can be considered the biggest legacy of the *kokugo* education in Han Taiwanese society and households.

Published oral history accounts and interviews I have conducted suggest that arranged marriages might have taken place more often for the more educated women of upper- and upper-middle-class backgrounds than for the less educated ones of lower- and lower-middle-class backgrounds. Women of lower- and lower-middle-class backgrounds were more likely to work after graduation and thus meet their future partners. In contrast, women of upper-middle-class backgrounds tended to stay at home because there was no economic incentive to work like their counterparts from lower-class backgrounds. Another reason was that their parents did not want them to show their faces in public, since not being seen in public was a marker of feminine virtue.[101] Their family members sought to preserve the virtue of their daughters. Marriages were arranged with someone of equivalent status. Besides arranged marriages, minor marriages were still common in many parts of Taiwan until the early postwar era, where child brides were adopted into the family at a young age to give the household an additional helping hand, to train the girl to be an obedient daughter-in-law, and to save wedding expenses.[102] Japanese education did not remove many oppressive practices, but I want to point out the changes, however small, that the *kokugo* education brought to Taiwanese marriage practices. Although women of upper- and upper-middle-class backgrounds received more educational opportunities than those of lower- and lower-middle-class backgrounds, one can consider those of lower- and lower-middle-class backgrounds as having benefited more from the educational system in the sense that it allowed them to enter the workforce and to experience love-based, free-choice marriage. It also allowed these women to gain work experience even if they did not keep all of their income because it was given to their families. If increased economic opportunities and the ability to choose one's marriage partner were the two measures of the impact of girls' education in Taiwan, then the impact was greater for women of lower- and lower-middle-class backgrounds than for those of the upper and upper-middle classes. From this angle, this pattern of the working-class women having more freedom in some sense seems to conform with the public mobility of nineteenth-century English working-class women, who became increasingly visible in the public spaces such as factories for work and dance classes and gardens for leisure. English middle-class women would reject the level of public visibility of the working-class women because such visibility would cast doubt on their respectability.[103] However, Taiwanese women of all backgrounds under Japanese rule differed from these nineteenth-century Englishwomen in that they did not seem to solely equate public visibility with their respectability because of increasing educational and work opportunities and the later wartime mobilization that encouraged all women to participate, even though the school enrollment numbers reveal that many remained outside the educational system at the end of colonial rule.

The complementary relationship between Taiwanese homes and Japanese schools produced a hybrid group of "good wives, wise mothers" with Han Taiwanese and Japanese characteristics whose experiences varied depending on their socioeconomic status. Women's life stories revealed that training at home varied depending on one's socioeconomic status, as those of lower-class backgrounds acquired homemaking skills, and those of upper-class backgrounds learned life lessons through stories and acquired classical Chinese literacy and abacus skill. Although it is difficult to conclude that Han Taiwanese women benefited more from the sewing lessons in Japanese schools than from the lessons at home during the Qing period, women certainly made use of the sewing skills they had acquired from Japanese schools as some turned to their skills to supplement family income or fully support the entire household while others made clothes for their family members. Cooking lessons seemed to have less impact than sewing lessons during the Japanese period because most Taiwanese schoolgirls either learned to cook from their mothers before marriage or from their mothers-in-law after marriage. In other words, the effect of Japanese primary education in Han Taiwanese households was limited if sewing and cooking skills were the only measures of the success of the "good wife, wise mother" training. However, if we view the school and the home as complementary sites in training girls and women to be ready for a married life with children, then a hybrid "good wife, wise mother" with Han Taiwanese and Japanese knowledge and skills was created at the end of Japanese rule.

Influenced by the Confucian idea that women and men from different families shall not have physical contact (Ch. *nan nü shou shou bu qin*), the old Han Chinese idea of gender segregation and the seclusion of girls to safeguard girls' virtue continued to affect Han Taiwanese schoolgirls and schoolboys under Japanese rule. Colonial and school officials implemented gender segregation for the practical reason of institutionalizing gender education that also implemented the Han Taiwanese idea of maintaining girls' virtue. Han Taiwanese families imposed corporal punishment to enforce the cultural idea that their daughters must not interact with boys in any manner, regardless of who initiated the interaction. At a young age, Han Taiwanese schoolgirls themselves absorbed social expectations of gender segregation and policed themselves. Thus, official policies, family rules, and individual actions helped enforce this old Han Chinese concept of gender segregation in many increasingly mixed-gender sites under Japanese rule.

Japanese education had an uneven impact on women, whose socio-economic backgrounds helped shape when and what knowledge and skills they received before marriage. Women of lower-class backgrounds were more likely to have experience with household chores than those of upper-class backgrounds, which likely made their life in the marital household more emotionally manageable than those of upper-class backgrounds. Their backgrounds also shaped what educational level women obtained, the likelihood of holding a job after completing their education, and the type of marriage they attained. Women with only a primary education degree were more likely to work after graduation and be in a love-based, free-choice marriage than their counterparts who received a girls' middle school education, who then stayed at home and had an arranged marriage. There were a few success stories of romantic-love marriages among women of upper-middle-class backgrounds because their Japanese proficiency allowed them to write and read love letters. Japanese literacy not only affected romantic relationships under Japanese rule, but Japanese-educated Taiwanese of all genders incorporated Japanese language and some aspects of Japanese culture into their lives in the postwar era. In particular, girls' middle school graduates were more likely than primary school graduates to use their Japanese proficiency in their marriage life in the postwar era to acquire new knowledge from Japan. Educated women made economic and cultural differences in their households during and after Japanese rule. Although Sayaka Chatani hesitates to discuss colonial legacy in her study on male youth groups because she believes that term is too simplistic, given that Japanese-educated Taiwanese had to infuse ideas and experiences acquired from Japanese rule to survive under the postwar Chinese Nationalist rule, this chapter shows that Japanese education changed Han Taiwanese women, their homes, and society at large.[104] Their historical experiences and cultural legacy likely contributed to the formation of a unique identity of being "Taiwanese" with Japanese, Chinese, and American influences during the postwar era. The concluding chapter will discuss how these Japanese-educated women and men assessed the two authoritarian regimes they lived under—the Japanese and the Chinese Nationalist governments—as they incorporated their personal experiences to construct colonial nostalgia in the early 2010s.

5

✵

COLONIAL NOSTALGIA

Although *dōka* was inherently discriminatory and reinforced ethnic and gender divisions, in the 2010s, many educated Taiwanese remembered Japanese colonial rule along gender lines fondly. The unintended utilities of the *kokugo* education and "good wife, wise mother" training, which provided the sewing skills and Japanese proficiency for Taiwanese women to work in the postwar era, contradicted the "good wife, wise mother" ideology of the Japanese nation-state. Women might not have noticed this contradiction because their main concerns were economic well-being and moral behaviors, not the political implications of *dōka* and the *kokugo* education. Along with men, women focused on the positive characterization of their Japanese education and teachers to affirm their identity as skillful members of society with proper manners as a result of this *kokugo* education. While some were very critical of Japanese colonial rule, Zhou Lianyu, the only daughter of a Monopoly Bureau (Jp. Hanbaikyoku) employee, was not alone when she fondly remembered her Japanese teachers and reflected on Japanese colonialism: "Teachers didn't hit students. Everyone was a good teacher. Everyone took care of me. Even though we were Taiwanese children, teachers took care of us. That's why, even today, every Taiwanese feels nostalgic about Japan. Even now, it's nostalgic for me. . . . We weren't bullied, we were taken care of, and we were helped. We received an education from them. That's why we're thankful." The absence of corporal punishment and bullying in her experiences, the caring the colonizer Japanese teachers showed to the colonized Taiwanese students, and the gratitude that Zhou felt toward her teachers created a strong nostalgia for Japanese rule.[1] Zhou earned a middle school diploma and taught in Xiamen, China, in the last two to three years of the war, where she worked with other Japanese teachers.[2] Zhou's use of Japanese teachers as symbols of Japanese colonialism was not unusual among her generation.

This chapter examines how former Taiwanese students' experiences, especially those of schoolgirls, shaped their own nostalgia for Japanese colonialism as memories of Japanese imperialism remain contentious in the region. Historical memory of Japanese aggression in Korea and China continues to spark anti-Japanese sentiments today. These sentiments become especially visible when the Chinese and Korean governments protest against Japan over revisionist history in Japanese textbooks and when top Japanese officials visit the Yasukuni Shrine, which houses top World War II war criminals. In contrast, these events do not lead to anti-Japan protests in Taiwan, likely because of Taiwanese people's positive view of Japan today. A 2021 survey of Taiwanese favorability toward other countries found that Japan topped the ranking: 60 percent of Taiwanese named Japan as their favorite country, 46 percent believed Japan should be Taiwan's closest ally in the future, and 77 percent felt close to Japan.[3] In contrast to strong anti-Japanese and nationalist sentiments on the Korean peninsula during and after the Korean colonial experience, many older Taiwanese were less critical of Japanese colonialism because of their experiences under the postwar Chinese Nationalist government.[4] According to Leo Ching, some in Taiwan even embrace Japanese colonialism to "[construct] a uniquely Taiwanese subjectivity."[5] Colonial nostalgia toward Japan became a tool to criticize the postwar government and society in Taiwan, express their concerns about social ills, and showcase their good character by comparing the Chinese Nationalist rule with Japanese colonization.

Scholars have found, unsurprisingly, that former colonizers around the world often express nostalgia for the colonial past, remembering their successful modernizing and civilizing efforts with collaboration from the colonized population.[6] Literary scholar Dennis Walder looks at postcolonial nostalgia as an "uncertain zone between memory and history" where historical actors turned to nostalgia to "represent or explore their own memories" when they felt that their connections with the past "ha[d] been severed by migration or displacement."[7] However, there are two

COLONIAL NOSTALGIA

forms of postcolonial nostalgia, according to historian Patricia Lorcin: imperial and colonial. Imperial nostalgia is defined as the "embellishment of lived experiences . . . associated with loss of empire," whereas colonial nostalgia is "the misinterpretation or incomprehension of the colonized territory and its people or the fabrication of a nonexistent dimension of colonial life . . . [associated] with the loss of socio-cultural standing."[8] Japanese neoconservatives practice both forms of nostalgia whenever they highlight the Taiwanese colonial experience to glorify Japan's imperial past. Their nostalgia reveals what Walder observes as a moment when people feel the "need to redefine the self" with "increased globalisation, ethnic tension, and national self-questioning."[9] Emphasizing the fond memories about Japanese teachers expressed by the Japanese-educated Taiwanese elderly, Japanese (neo)conservatives seek to maintain Japan's regional power and status to counter China's regional (and global) rise while rejecting Japan's wartime atrocities and depicting Japanese colonialism positively. According to Tetsushi Marukawa's study, Kobayashi Yoshinori's (in)famous manga *Taiwan ron* (2000) is one prime example of a neoconservative using the memories of Japanese-educated Taiwanese to argue that Japanese colonialism created and laid the foundation for Taiwan's modernization and economic success with values opposite those of Communist China. Kobayashi depicted his grandfather's generation and Japanese-educated Taiwanese as "'victims' of postwar culture," which sought to "silence" their wartime contribution and sacrifice.[10] He also links the anti-China rhetoric from Taiwanese independence activists in Japan to the anti-China feelings among many Japanese.[11]

Most studies have focused on nostalgia about former colonizers, but colonized people sometimes invoke their colonial experiences to express their anxiety over social changes and economic uncertainties as well. In his study of Zanzibar City, anthropologist William Cunningham Bissell found that even Zanzibar residents born after British colonial rule talked nostalgically about British rule to criticize their present urban life. During his fieldwork in Zanzibar in the mid-1990s, Bissell heard residents talking about British rule as a period when laws and rules were enforced, government planning and management were effective, and their city was "clean and orderly."[12] Zanzibar residents blamed the current state of affairs on "a failure of moral will" where people were no longer faithful, the government was incompetent or had become indifferent to people's livelihood, and people had become selfish and greedy.[13] My research shows that formerly colonized Taiwanese also feel nostalgic about the colonial past. As Bissell notes, nostalgia is "shaped by cultural concerns and struggles. . . . [I]t can only be understood in particular historical and spatial contexts."[14] Particularly, postcolonial nostalgia has been used by both the colonized and the colonizer to increase nationalist sentiment in former colonies.[15] Japanese-educated Taiwanese certainly experienced some cultural shock when Japanese rule shifted to Chinese Nationalist rule after World War II, which contributed to their nostalgia for Japanese rule. While Japanese (neo)conservatives have used Taiwanese elderly to increase Japanese patriotism, the Japanese-educated Taiwanese have also asserted their identity against the Chinese Nationalist regime by citing their experiences under Japanese rule.

Based on interviews conducted between 2010 and 2013 with former Taiwanese schoolgirls and a few schoolboys born between 1915 and 1936, this chapter shows that these students express "social critique and protest" as nostalgia "conjoin[s] space and time, placing them in a state of creative tension and mobilizing them for reciprocal comment and contrast" in ways similar to the accounts of Zanzibar residents.[16] These Japanese-educated Taiwanese often cite good manners under Japanese rule as the standard of measurement for a good society, which stood in contrast to the corrupt postwar Chinese Nationalist rule. One common argument states that the 2-28 Incident of 1947 was the single most important factor in turning many Taiwanese, particularly victims of the Incident, against the Chinese Nationalist government, helping to create this nostalgia for the "good old [Japanese] days." On February 28, 1947, Chinese Nationalist troops fired on Taiwanese protesters who demanded the government punish some government workers and police officers for beating a woman who had been selling tobacco illegally. The firing on protesters sparked widespread angry resistance from the Taiwanese.[17] As a result, the Nationalist government, then based in Nanjing, sent more troops to Taiwan. In the subsequent weeks, Chinese troops rounded up and executed at least eighteen thousand Taiwanese, including many high school students and educated elites who were community leaders.[18] Although the 2-28 Incident shaped Taiwanese identity formation and turned some against the Chinese Nationalist government, not everyone was affected by or aware of the urban- and Taipei-centric 2-28 Incident.

Wan-yao Chou, Cai Jintang, and Leo Ching have decentered the 2-28 Incident as the main cause of anti-Nationalist sentiments and offered different explanations for colonial nostalgia in Taiwan. Analyzing the wartime experience of the final generation of the Japanese-educated, those born between 1920 and 1930, Wan-yao Chou and Cai Jintang found that wartime hardship reduced political and economic differences between the Taiwanese and the Japanese.[19] Chou argues that this nostalgia was shaped by the wartime patriotism that was felt by that generation of Taiwanese.[20] Cai stretches his analysis further back in time and argues that the final generation of Japanese-educated Taiwanese is nostalgic for Japanese rule because most of them were too young or not elite enough to know about the history of movements for autonomy and against the Japanese in the 1920s.[21] Ching uses the "personable and Taiwanized term *dōsan*," to refer to this generation who "spent their formative years of schooling during the period of imperialization (kōminka) and war mobilization" and "were traumatized by the ensuing recolonization by the Kuomintang (KMT)."[22] He shows that the *dōsan* generation writes nostalgically about Japanese rule after being mobilized by neoconservatives in Japan to voice their sentiment and existence because they felt "abandoned by Japanese colonialism after Japan's defeat, [and] oppressed by the KMT because of their Japanese heritage."[23] Whether they based their analysis on historical experience or contemporary geopolitics, these scholars have identified the colonial nostalgia of the last generation of Japanese-educated Taiwanese.

Joining the discussion initiated by Chou, Cai, and Ching, this chapter argues that gendered assimilation led to gendered nostalgia for Japanese rule to emphasize the importance of gender. Following Lorcin's argument that colonial nostalgia is "a collective sentiment that remains grounded in personal or familial experience" and "the belief in benevolent modernity, and the relative bonhomie of the colonial lifestyle," this chapter focuses on students' interaction with their teachers to examine the colonizer-colonized relationship on school grounds as a modern institution that served the interests of the colonial regime.[24] Specifically, a gender lens allows an examination of how *dōka* helped create gendered memory.

CHAPTER 5

Although both women and men criticized the Chinese Nationalist regime with similar talking points, they focused on different experiences in constructing their colonial nostalgia, which revealed their gendered education under the Japanese. This chapter finds that Taiwanese women anchored their colonial nostalgia in personal and individual interactions compared with men, who tended to focus on institutions when criticizing the postwar Chinese Nationalist government.

CONSTRUCTING COLONIAL NOSTALGIA: DOWNPLAYING JAPANESE DISCRIMINATION

Colonial nostalgia for Japanese rule was shared by Taiwanese of diverse socioeconomic, regional, and educational backgrounds, ranging from wealthy landlords to poor manual laborers, whose birthplaces ranged from Taipei in the north to Kaohsiung in the south, and educational levels from primary school to college. Although the exploitation of the Taiwanese was evident in Japanese political, social, and economic policies, which privileged the ethnic Japanese at the expense of the colonized, the narratives of many Taiwanese downplayed the inherent discrimination in colonialism and highlighted the improvement of Taiwan under Japanese rule. No doubt their nostalgia was shaped by the insecurity and chaos they experienced in the immediate postwar era, when inflation and the transfer of Taiwanese resources to aid the Nationalists in the Chinese Civil War destabilized the Taiwanese economy, with the situation coming to a head in the 2-8 Incident in 1947. The Chinese Nationalist suppression of the 2-28 Incident, the subsequent forty years of martial law, and oppression under an authoritarian government consolidated the view of the Chinese Nationalist government in the eyes of Japanese-educated Taiwanese as a corrupt, dishonest, disorderly, and oppressive regime. These Taiwanese reminisced about Japanese rule to express their dissatisfaction with the new government, because the Japanese rule was the only other regime with which they were familiar. They sometimes expressed hesitancy in voicing their political views and criticisms of the Chinese Nationalist government during the interview. Those who did not offer any criticism of the postwar regime provided narratives that told of individual successes that overcame or erased the chaos caused by the regime change in 1945.

Comparisons between the two regimes emerged soon after the Japanese surrender on August 15, 1945. When Taiwan came under Chinese Nationalist rule on October 25, 1945, there was an initial enthusiasm that quickly waned as Taiwanese preferred the law and order that existed under Japanese rule to the ineffective Chinese Nationalist regime. Han Taiwanese people were initially joyous as they returned to the embrace of their ancestral land.[25] The Chinese Nationalist government taught the Taiwanese some songs to celebrate "the return of Taiwan to its ancestral land."[26] George Kerr, a US Department of State vice consul who was stationed in Taiwan from 1946 to 1947, observed that parades composed of office workers and schoolchildren who had been "standing many hours in the sun" welcomed Chinese troops as liberators when the troops landed in Taiwan.[27] However, with the arrival of "the shambling, poorly disciplined, and very dirty Chinese troops" who had fought eight years of war against the Japanese, the Taiwanese people's enthusiasm dwindled.[28]

The Taiwanese noted the stark contrast between the disorderly Chinese troops in ragged uniforms and the more disciplined and better-equipped Japanese troops. Many Taiwanese were upset by the behaviors of newly arrived officials and soldiers, ranging from rampant corruption, bribery, nepotism, and seizure of Japanese properties to theft, cheating, robbery, sexual harassment, spitting, and line-cutting at bus stops, in addition to high unemployment rates and a rapid decline in food production.[29] By February 1947, the Taiwanese had become frustrated with the new Chinese Nationalist government. In an article published in the periodical *Damingbao* on January 20, 1947, the Taiwan Political Reconstruction Association appealed to the central government in Nanjing, requesting the provincial government to rebuild war-torn Taiwan by "reform[ing] their own inefficient system and noxious attitude" with existing infrastructure and human resources.[30] In other words, this association believed that it was the Chinese Nationalist government that impeded Taiwan's postwar rebuilding, not the lack of resources in Taiwan or the Taiwanese people. Taiwanese intellectuals also assumed that they would "attain political dignity and equality" because of US sponsorship of the Chinese Nationalist government in contrast to institutionalized discrimination under Japanese rule.[31]

However, similar to the Japanese colonial regime, the Chinese Na-

CHAPTER 5

176

tionalist government established political and economic hierarchy along ethnic lines based on the assumption that the Taiwanese had been completely assimilated under the *kokugo* education and could not be trusted. The Nationalist government installed Chinese Mainlanders (Ch. Waishengren) into senior political and economic positions formerly held by Japanese despite the presence of highly educated and qualified Taiwanese candidates.[32] The population of Taiwan was six million Taiwanese (Han and indigenes) and one million Chinese Mainlanders in 1946.[33] Yet, in the civil service exam of 1950, Mainlanders comprised 83 percent of the accepted candidates.[34] In 1956, over 35 percent of people working in the combined public and education sectors were Mainlanders.[35] Two decades later, in 1974, although Mainlanders comprised 15.5 percent of the population in Taiwan, their representation in the public sector was 46.1 percent.[36] The government also gave preferential treatment to Mainlanders by setting lower passing scores and a higher quota in civil service exams for Mainlanders compared with Taiwanese.[37] Between 1954 and 1960, Mainlanders comprised 39 percent of students at National Taiwan University, the top university in Taiwan. They made up over 45 percent of the student population in the 1960s, and 41 percent in the 1970s.[38] Institutionalized discrimination reflected how Chinese Nationalist officials viewed colonized Taiwan. Lieutenant General Keh King-en, who was the nominal mission chief who arrived in Taiwan with the American forces on October 5, 1945, called Taiwan "a degraded territory" that was "beyond the pale of true Chinese civilization" and the residents "a degraded people."[39] Chinese Nationalist officials trusted the loyalty of Mainlanders who had worked with them since before 1949 and "felt obligated to take care of them" by employing them in the public sector, which led to what sociologist Hong-zen Wang calls "refugee shelters" for these Mainlanders.[40] Taiwanese thus remained mostly outside of the powerful political and economic circles under both the Japanese and the Chinese Nationalist regimes.

Although the Chinese Nationalist government instituted discriminatory policies against the Taiwanese, the economy improved over time alongside school enrollments during the postwar period, which some might expect to produce a positive view of the regime compared to the Japanese regime. Trade as a percentage of GNP increased from 27.45

percent in 1960 to 95.6 percent in 1988.[41] Between 1968 and 1979, the per-capita income in Taiwan increased from US$719 to US$1,370. Wealth disparity also decreased. In 1952, the top 20 percent of people earned fifteen times the amount of the bottom 20 percent of people, although the gap narrowed to five times in 1964. The average annual increase in GNP in Taiwan between 1952 and 1973 exceeded 8.74 percent. The unemployment rate was less than 1 percent before 1974, and only increased to 3.2 percent after 1974. Taiwan led other Asian countries in getting itself out of a recession in the mid-1970s.[42] The postwar economic growth could be correlated to education, as more students eventually received education under Chinese Nationalist rule than during the Japanese period. Over 71 percent of school-age Taiwanese children attended primary school under Japanese rule in 1944, compared to 99.57 percent under Chinese Nationalist rule in 1978.[43] Over 94 percent of junior high school–age students attended junior high school in 1978, and 29 percent of students who took college entrance exams received placement in 1977.[44] These statistics reveal that most girls received an education and that the gender gap in school enrollment had narrowed under Chinese Nationalist rule compared with Japanese rule. However, the increased educational rates and the economic growth that this Japanese-educated generation and their children experienced during Taiwan's economic miracle did not end criticism against the Chinese Nationalist regime or reduce praise for Japanese colonial education in the construction of colonial nostalgia among many Japanese-educated Taiwanese.

Despite having experienced established ethnic discrimination under both regimes, Japanese-educated Taiwanese claimed no discrimination had existed in their construction of colonial nostalgia by remembering their lives under Japanese rule. As a former local government staff and then a nursing assistant under Japanese rule, Wu Surong recalled, "I have a very good impression of the Japanese people. The Japanese teachers treated students well. . . . They didn't discriminate against us."[45] Here, Wu equated Japanese people with her Japanese teachers. Similarly, Lin Xianyan, a seventeen-year-old graduate of Taichū Girls' No. 2 Middle School when the war ended in 1945, insisted that no discrimination existed under Japanese rule. When asked if her teachers treated students differently based on one's ethnicity, Lin proudly cited the equal number

CHAPTER 5

of Japanese and Taiwanese enrollees at her middle school as proof. Interestingly, she did not find it unfair that her school enrolled equal numbers of Japanese and Taiwanese students when Japanese only comprised 5 percent of the total population in Taiwan. She also insisted that discrimination did not exist among students by claiming that one's academic performance, and not ethnicity, determined how her peers treated her. She believed that good grades led to respect. Lin focused on merit, not ethnicity.[46] Born in Kaohsiung, Lin Cairong emphasized how one's skills and handwork could receive promotion and be successful even if one only completed primary school education under Japanese rule.[47] This focus on merit might be a result of an image that the colonial state created to pacify any anger from the colonized population over inequality. For example, as part of the military service program of the *kōminka* movement, Takashi Fujitani has found that Japanese officers were supposed to welcome Korean military volunteers and promote them based on merit.[48] In this way, merit meant everyone could compete equally, an idea that was important during the wartime period when the colonial state mobilized everyone, including the colonized, to make sacrifices for the empire. Both Lin Xianyan and Lin Cairong chose to focus on merit to prove that one's ability was the basis of how one was treated, not ethnicity. To focus on ethnicity would reveal preferential practices embedded in the educational system and workplace. This idea of merit continued into the postwar era, and other Taiwanese have also highlighted merit as one marker of superior Japanese rule over corrupt Chinese Nationalist rule.

Interestingly enough, the constitution of the Republic of China (ROC) under Nationalist rule had actually legalized merit, through the civil service exams, as a criterion for hiring civil servants, even though these Taiwanese claimed that Chinese Nationalist rule was guided by nepotism, which stood in contrast to merit as an indicator of one's success under Japanese rule. The Nationalist government claimed to have used schools to build the nation-state in Taiwan by "remov[ing] the evil left" by the Japanese regime.[49] However, education alone did not determine one's success in becoming a civil servant. Through the Examination Yuan, the government agency that administers the civil service exams, the Nationalist government used Mandarin Chinese proficiency, and not intelligence or academic performance, to determine successful candidates. Although the 1947 ROC constitution proclaimed that the civil service exams were "open and competitive," Shui On Chu's research finds that the Examination Yuan's unlimited power to create any special examination and the provincial quota system, which determined the acceptance rate "based on the population of pre-1949 mainland Chinese provinces," opened the door to the "favoritism and corruption" that the Nationalist government claimed to fight against.[50] The Chinese Nationalist government used the civil service exams to favor high-ranking military veteran Mainlanders and advanced-degree holders in official posts to preserve and reproduce Mainlander networks in Taiwan. The government accepted five times more candidates from special exams than regular exams between 1950 and 1992, with more Mainlander civil servants than Taiwanese ones in the early twenty-first century even after the provincial quota was abolished in 1992.[51] Considering the number of Chinese Mainlander bureaucrats compared to their percentage of the population and the advantages that Chinese Mainlanders had in the Mandarin Chinese language–based special exams, it would seem that Taiwanese had some basis for criticizing the corruption and nepotism of the Chinese Nationalist government.

The Taiwanese Hoklo–, Taiwanese Hakka–, and Japanese-speaking generation of Taiwanese who did not know Mandarin Chinese before 1945 was likely unhappy with the requirement to use Mandarin Chinese on civil exams, which constituted the path to government jobs, and as the language of instruction at schools, which sought to reinforce the Sinicization programs that the Chinese Nationalist government forced on the postwar Taiwanese society. The government forced Taiwanese intellectuals to be "passive objects of re-Sinicization" that needed to be "saved," "reeducated," and "reconfigured" culturally by the self-proclaimed "superior" Nationalists, who viewed and treated the Taiwanese as "slaves of the Japanese."[52] The Nationalist government promulgated educational guidelines to instill Chinese nationalism and to train the Taiwanese to speak Mandarin Chinese. Using Mandarin Chinese as the language of instruction, the school curriculum focused on teaching Chinese history, literature, traditions, and geography. Students were punished for speaking their native languages of Taiwanese Hoklo, Taiwanese Hakka, and any of the Taiwanese indigene languages. The purpose of the educational curriculum was to create loyal Chinese nationalists who would appreciate

"Sun Yat-sen's *Three Principles of the People*—nationalism, democracy, and livelihood"—which the Chinese Nationalists claimed to have been fulfilled in Taiwan, making Taiwan "a revival base for the KMT government's future reunification of China."[53] Ironically, many Japanese-educated Taiwanese called this Sinicization campaign "the new *kōminka* movement" because of its resemblance to forced cultural assimilation.[54] Under the party-state education of the Chinese Nationalist government, post-1945 generations of Taiwanese children learned that Japan was an aggressive and ambitious nation and that Japanese rule in Taiwan had been an illegal encroachment on Chinese sovereignty. They also learned that the Japanese colonizers exploited Taiwanese people and resources and that Taiwanese people suffered from the lack of freedom of speech and rights to private property. The official narrative taught students that the Taiwanese resisted Japanese colonial rule because of their loyalty to their home country, China.[55] For the Japanese-educated generation who had had positive and personal connections to Japanese education and people, the postwar school curriculum contradicted their own experiences and became another critique against the Chinese Nationalist government.

Some Japanese-educated Taiwanese voiced their disapproval of the Chinese Nationalist government's characterization of Japanese rule, which "marginalized and discredited" Taiwan's "historical memories and cultural traditions," to praise Japanese colonial accomplishments.[56] For example, Zhang Taishan was a seventeen-year-old attending a commercial vocational school in Tainan in 1945. He was an elementary school teacher for forty years in the postwar period. He criticized the Nationalist government's attempt to change Taiwanese people's favorable view of Japan. Zhang asserted that it was wrong for the Nationalist government to ignore Japanese modernization efforts as he praised the Japanese for building modern infrastructure, such as dams, and for the establishment of public education to elevate Taiwan's standard of living and culture.[57] Also disapproving of the Chinese Nationalist depiction of Japanese colonizers as evil, Zeng Xiuying, who received six years of primary education and worked several years in the factory under Japanese rule, reflected, "I thought they were fine, no bully. I have a good impression of the Japanese people. . . . Nowadays, the Taiwanese are educated by the Chinese Mainlanders to criticize the Japanese severely."[58] Taiwanese such as Zhang and Zeng constructed their nostalgia by countering the Chinese Nationalist narrative of pure Japanese exploitation with a focus on Japanese colonial accomplishments. Taiwanese nostalgia for Japanese modernization was not baseless. Scholars have found that the standards of living and economic development in Taiwan under Japanese rule rose in comparison to before the Japanese arrival, which helped contribute to Taiwanese people's positive evaluation of Japanese colonialism.[59] Leo Ching observes that among many Taiwanese of the wartime generation, "the contradistinction between Japanese rule and Chinese rule is usually posited between modernity and primitivity."[60]

Perhaps unsurprisingly, education is where colonial nostalgia of Taiwanese students and imperial nostalgia of Japanese teachers came together to praise Japanese modernization, as former students insisted that no discrimination existed under Japanese rule, and former teachers concurred with their claim of impartiality as one of their guiding principles in educating Taiwanese children. For example, Watanabe Yaeko was a former Taiwanese primary schoolteacher in Taihoku from 1926 to the end of World War II who evoked impartiality as the main principle of teaching in Taiwan. She proudly recalled that her students thought she was fair, treating students of different nationalities, socioeconomic backgrounds, and levels of literacy the same way.[61] Tōyama Waketsuyoshi, a former Japanese elementary teacher in Taiwan, tied this principle to the Shizangan spirit: "[The] main goal of education in Taiwan was impartiality (Jp. *isshi dōjin*) and the Shizangan spirit. . . . We followed the goal of Izawa Shuji [(1851–1917), the first chief of the educational bureau in Taiwan] that stated 'Let's educate the Taiwanese until they become Japanese subjects [Jp. *kokumin*].'"[62] Shizangan spirit was cited as the foundation of education in Taiwan by many former Japanese educators in *Bridge to Taiwan*, a collection of remembered experiences of Japanese living in colonial Taiwan that was published in Japan in 1981. Shizangan was a place in Shilin, Taipei, where Taiwanese resistance fighters had killed six Japanese educators in January 1896.[63] The colonial government honored these educators as martyrs for the education of Taiwanese children. The colonial government used their deaths to symbolize the greatest sacrifice an educator could make in Taiwan. Teacher-training programs then indoctrinated students with this idea.[64] Having taught at

CHAPTER 5

182

Taiwanese primary schools, Ueda Sumio defined the Shizangan spirit as "[the] heart to sacrifice for education [in Taiwan]. It's the same spirit as that of those who would die for the nation. The basis of it is to love one's country, one's family, and the students you teach."[65] Teaching in Taiwan from 1910 to 1923, Kitō Eiji said the Shizangan spirit made him realize that an educator had to be prepared to "throw one's life away at any time."[66] He claimed that these two goals guided his teaching: "to improve Taiwan's culture and to cultivate moral national subjects."[67] Another teacher, Miyazaki Saiji, believed that by focusing on training national subjects using the Shizangan spirit and the Imperial Rescript on Education as the guiding principles, he and other teachers helped make education in Taiwan a success.[68] By linking impartiality with the *kokugo* education, these educators assumed that education provided an equal opportunity for all non-ethnic-Japanese subjects to become Japanese. They insisted that their willingness to sacrifice their life to teaching Taiwanese children helped create loyal and moral Japanese subjects. Their invocation of sacrifice, regardless of gender, convinces them that colonial education was for the sake of the colonized population, not the colonizers. They saw the Japanization of Taiwanese children as a marker of educational success and disregarded the effect of *dōka* in erasing local cultures. Although they were part of a segregated school system where Japanese children enjoyed better-quality instructions and facilities than Taiwanese children, these teachers claimed impartiality, which revealed that they embraced and implemented *dōka* completely per the official policy.

Despite improvement in the postwar economy and educational opportunities, many Japanese-educated Taiwanese constructed colonial nostalgia in favor of Japanese rule while criticizing the Chinese Nationalist regime by insisting there had been equality under Japanese rule, a view that both students and teachers shared by claiming teachers were impartial. Former students praised Japanese modernization and educational opportunities to condemn attempts by the Chinese Nationalist government to shape the historical memory of Japanese colonialism in the minds of the younger generations. Recounting their experiences in the early 1980s, former teachers emphasized their sacrifice by teaching Taiwanese children in Taiwan instead of remaining in the comfort of their homeland. The publication of their accounts coincided with a slowed economic growth in Japan after decades of rapid growth in the late 1970s, and the Japanese neoconservatives' second wave of attacks on history textbooks as "biased and/or communist-inspired" when describing Japanese wartime atrocities in the Nanjing Massacre and the Battle of Okinawa.[69] The Nixon Shock of 1970–72 that led to the United States reestablishing formal diplomatic relations with China in 1979, the oil shock of 1973, and the United States' defeat in the Vietnam War in 1975 all contributed to diplomatic and economic uncertainties.[70] It is difficult to know if any former teachers became neoconservatives, but their positive depiction of their actions in a colony would find support in Japan. Their book could also contribute to the revisionist history movement that began in Japan in the mid-1990s, although the movement targeted military sex slavery and the Nanjing Massacre.[71] Eika Tai observes that "some teachers believed that assimilation would end discrimination against the Taiwanese. But because the aim of assimilation was to foster voluntary submission to the emperor . . . even teachers' devotion and good intentions were destined to serve the goal of Japanese imperialism."[72] Hence, regardless of their intentions, former teachers acted as colonial agents who helped propagate *dōka* that reinforced colonial and gender hierarchy and discrimination. The publication of former teachers' accounts of their teaching in Taiwan in 1981 was timely as Japan was undergoing some economic, diplomatic, and social changes that would likely make their positive depictions of colonialism more acceptable in Japanese society. Although both groups created positive images of Japanese colonialism in their nostalgia, former students sought to criticize the postwar government while former teachers likely sought to validate their complicity in the colonial project.

REMEMBERING QUALIFIED AND CARING (JAPANESE) TEACHERS

Women were more likely than men to anchor their colonial nostalgia in their interactions with their teachers that depicted their teachers as qualified and caring educators. Their memories of personal interactions with their Japanese teachers were perhaps the strongest factor in creating and strengthening this colonial nostalgia for Japanese rule. Japanese teachers might be the only Japanese people these Taiwanese interacted with regularly under Japanese rule. Japanese teachers were public servants who justified *dōka* by claiming the "superiority of Japanese culture" and citing the trust that their students placed in them.[73] Despite these teachers' discriminatory attitude that supported and was supported by the segregated educational system, former Taiwanese students remembered that their Japanese teachers were devoted to, cared for, and protected students. The students' fondness can be understood if we follow Lorcin and other research that shows how colonial nostalgia allows female colonizers to emphasize familial and compassionate memories. Colonizers were not the only ones with this perspective. I argue that Taiwanese women who were colonized also "anchored" their nostalgia in the "familial" and "compassionate" elements of their past experiences to create this nostalgia.[74] They depicted their teachers as more qualified and virtuous than teachers in the postwar period. This depiction reveals their concerns about the state of education in Taiwan in their old age in the early twenty-first century. In these former students' criticism of the Chinese Nationalist education, Japanese teachers became synonymous with Japanese education, Japanese rule, and all Japanese people in the colonial nostalgia that these Japanese-educated Taiwanese constructed.

As part of their colonial nostalgia, former students characterized their teachers as protective and caring to illustrate their close connection with their teachers. Wu Surong recalled that her fifth- to sixth-grade homeroom teacher, a Japanese man, almost started a physical fight with a Taiwanese teacher next door, after Wu's teacher disciplined the next-door students for being naughty with Wu's class. Before that, her Japanese teacher used to trade calligraphy lessons for music lessons with the Taiwanese teacher. Wu's teacher's response to bullying created such bitterness between the two teachers that the lesson exchange stopped for an entire year.[75] A primary school graduate, Zeng Yuanyuan, compared teachers of both periods: "It wasn't like today's society where if a student kisses up or if the student's family has money, then the teacher would take more care of that student. No, it wasn't like that back then. Back then, teachers would take care of you if you worked hard in your studies and followed [their instructions]."[76] Zeng praised her teachers for truly caring for students while criticizing teachers in the postwar era for being superficial. Lin Jiao'e, whose experience was summarized at the beginning of chapter 4, remembered a Japanese woman teacher she had from first through third grade who really loved and cared for them. She then had two Taiwanese and a Japanese teacher from fourth through sixth grade who worked hard to tutor students after school and provided free sample exams. Her teachers also remained in contact with parents and persuaded parents to let their children continue schooling.[77] Former students provided these accounts to illustrate the caring, diligence, and fairness of Japanese teachers who held the interests of their students at heart, even though, in reality, some teachers might have only tried to increase their students' success rates to bolster their career portfolio. Likely, most teachers were simply focused on implementing *dōka* through the *kokugo* education, which was what their training sought to accomplish. By anchoring their memories in the "familial" and "compassionate" parts of their educational experiences, these women, some with grandchildren and even great-grandchildren still in school, likely did not think teachers of the postwar educational system were doing enough to help students succeed and pass entrance exams into the early twenty-first century, in contrast to their teachers before 1945.

Regardless of their personal motivations, these teachers earned praise from their students for helping the few fortunate Taiwanese students climb the educational ladder to earn the educational degrees required for their desired professions or to maintain social status while these educators promoted *dōka*. The colonial government could not stop teachers from preparing students for middle school entrance exams. According to Wu Wenxing's study, some teachers replaced instruction time for arts, music, exercises, or calligraphy with Japanese language and arithmetic to prepare students for the entrance exams. But colonial officials disapproved of this practice because it ran contrary to the *kokugo* education, which emphasized a well-rounded education in producing imperial subjects. In 1937, colonial officials banned teachers from using Japanese elementary school (Jp. *shōgakkō*) textbooks in Taiwanese primary school (Jp. *kōgakkō*).[78] Undoubtedly, the administration wanted Taiwanese students to learn from the primary school textbooks that were designed for them, as discussed in chapter 1, instead of studying textbooks intended for Japanese children. Wu also finds that the colonial government banned Taiwanese students from using teacher's manuals to study for entrance

CHAPTER 5

186

exams. However, as Wu points out, the middle school entrance exam was based on the curriculum in Japanese elementary schools, not Taiwanese primary schools. Without extra tutoring or additional reference materials, Taiwanese students had little chance of passing the exam.[79] By breaking official rules and adjusting the curriculum as needed, teachers seemed to act on behalf of students' interests, and their actions help explain why many former Taiwanese students recalled their teachers as kind and diligent in helping them prepare for the entrance exams. Wu's interviews show that some students recalled that some teachers tutored students during winter or summer vacations and used their own money to reward and help poorer students. Parents could volunteer to pay for tutoring fees, but many gave gifts instead. Wu asserts that Japanese teachers provided free tutoring because teachers would feel highly rewarded if their students passed the entrance exam in such a highly competitive environment.[80] These accounts portrayed Japanese teachers as selfless, caring, and compassionate educators who disregarded official policy to help students succeed instead of enriching themselves. From the student perspective, they appreciated their teachers' efforts. This feeling likely strengthened their colonial nostalgia despite their teachers' official mission or ulterior motives of career advancement.

The strength of this colonial nostalgia, created and/or multiplied by their fondness for their teachers, can be illustrated by students' attitude toward corporal punishment. Not only did these punishments not diminish their fondness, former students actually cited corporal punishment in explaining good student behavior under Japanese rule, in contrast to the ban on corporal punishment in schools in twenty-first-century Taiwan. Working as a twenty-one-year-old chef-in-training after graduating from primary school under Japanese rule, Huang Jinde believed he received a good education because "Japanese education was stricter" and employed corporal punishment. His approval of corporal punishment became the basis of his criticism of misbehaving students in democratized Taiwan: "The time [now] is not as good [as the Japanese period]. . . . Nowadays, kids don't follow rules."[81] Zeng Xiuying, who worked at a sock factory after graduating from primary school in Taipei, agreed with Huang. She equated corporal punishment with strict teaching.[82] Although it was unclear if Huang or Zeng received such punishment, not only did they not resent such punishment, but they considered it part of effective teaching. This link between behavior and corporal punishment was similar between women and men. They cited the absence of corporal punishment in Taiwanese schools as why education in early twenty-first-century society failed to train the younger generations to be rule-abiding citizens. Note that this criticism was possible only in the early twenty-first century because corporal punishment was used throughout postwar Taiwan.

If students could praise corporal punishment as effective pedagogy, it was not surprising that former schoolgirls characterized the free manual labor that they performed for their teachers as highlighting that they were special and worthy of their teachers' attention instead of as labor exploitation. To these students, being allowed to spend time with their teachers by performing labor for them indicated that they had acquired their teachers' favor. As the daughter of a taxi and bus driver, Lin Tiantian recalled that her male Japanese teacher called on students to clean his residence on the weekends. Her teacher was married but had come to Taiwan alone. With a smile, Lin recalled proudly:

> Every weekend [our teacher] would call on three to four students to mop the floor at his place. Those students who were called on by the teacher were happy. Those who weren't called would chant, "Teacher's pet, teacher's pet!" I was always called on by the teacher. Those four students who were chosen were happy to have been chosen. We would get the bucket and water, and then clean his room. . . . The four of us always got called on by the teacher. . . . All of us really liked to be called on by the teacher. . . . The teacher didn't treat us to anything afterwards. There was no need. . . . It was once a week.[83]

Students like Lin did not feel that their teachers were taking advantage of them; instead, they felt honored to have been chosen because it was an experience not shared by most of their classmates. Lin's account suggests that students who performed chores for their teacher considered it to be a recognition of them as good students and not workers for hire. Performing these manual labor tasks made students feel closer to their teachers. The familial sentiment that students felt through performing these tasks strengthened their nostalgia. Interestingly, no former schoolboys provided such accounts; only schoolgirls did. It was likely that cleaning was considered domestic, which was linked to women's household responsibilities, not those of men. Hence, only schoolgirls had provided such free domestic service, not schoolboys. Their memories and nostalgia were thus gendered because of their expected gender roles, with their gender being connected to their labor.

While schoolgirls remembered unpaid labor to show how they were special in the eyes of their Japanese teachers, which likely contributed to their colonial nostalgia, some teachers recalled paid work as part of the established child labor system. For example, Mikami Takatoshi, a sixth-grade teacher at Kannonyama (Guanyinshan) Primary School, recalled paying ¥3 to students who were on duty at the teacher's dormitory to clean his place, heat up his bath water, and help with cooking.[84] Lü Lietong also remembered a similar system—he worked part-time as a fifth-grader running errands, cleaning the hot bath area, and carrying and heating up bath water for teachers.[85] The arrangement suggests that teachers considered the practice to be normal, especially when there were students already stationed in the teachers' dormitory. Provided that both paid and unpaid work existed, students who performed free labor likely recalled it to mark themselves as exceptional and worthy of recognition, as shown in Lin's narrative. That child domestic labor was available meant that the predominantly male teachers from Japan could use the students' labor to supplement whatever domestic help they hired or were provided. As Wu Wenxing notes, these teachers usually took their jobs without a family in Taiwan to serve the country in the first half of the colonial period, and shifted to monetary incentives in the second half of the colonial period.[86] Although the gender of students was not mentioned, it was likely that schoolgirls were targeted if one presumed that teachers followed the expected gender roles at the time. Taking into consideration the goal of *dōka* and its *kokugo* education, perhaps teachers considered these tasks to be part of schoolgirls' training as diligent homemakers.

Furthermore, interviews I have conducted suggest that what seems to be inappropriate behavior today was not understood that way in 1930s and 1940s Taiwan, as students wove such experiences into their colonial nostalgia to highlight their excellent skills. Based on my interviews, although eating lunch with or singing for one's teacher was likely an innocent activity that created a familial space for students and teachers, it is difficult to consider physical touch as appropriate.[87] Born to a business family in Lugang in central Taiwan, Hong Zhimei recalled that her music teacher would call on her to sing for teachers during lunch breaks. Another teacher would call on her to massage his back during lunchtime. Hong described these times spent with her teachers as fun and recalled that her classmates were jealous and resentful of her.[88] One wonders how often Hong was called on because she sang for and massaged different teachers during lunchtime, which implied reduced time to eat. Nevertheless, these callings likely made her feel closer to her teachers. Although former students such as Hong did not feel that their teachers were taking advantage of them, contemporary reports from the colonial era showed that Taiwanese parents were anxious about sexual harassment by schoolteachers, especially older students in girls' middle schools. Newspapers reported on teachers taking advantage of schoolgirls in various ways, including the sexual harassment and labor exploitation that were discussed in chapter 2.

Given that colonial nostalgia and news reports were clearly gendered, there are several ways to reconcile colonial nostalgia in the early 2010s and contemporary reports from the 1920s, almost a century apart. One explanation is that those who felt they were victims might not have wanted to share their experiences. In contrast, those who shared their experience sought to depict themselves as excellent students serving their teachers. It was possible that some families were anxious about exposing their daughters to outside dangers, which was why elite families kept girls and women inside the house during the Qing period and why many Taiwanese families were hesitant about sending their daughters to school in the early and midcolonial period. Another explanation, as discussed in chapter 2, is that Taiwanese elites of the 1920s viewed predatory teachers who targeted schoolgirls as a symbol of the vulnerability of the colonized. Despite Taiwanese families' concerns, the colonial government only focused on teaching Japanese elementary school students how to protect themselves from sexual harassment, not Taiwanese students.[89] The different responses, or the absence of responses, to protecting girls suggest that the colonial government valued Japanese female chastity, not Taiwanese, or that colonial leaders presumed Japanese teachers would not violate Taiwanese female chastity because of ethnic differences or hierarchy. Ethnic hierarchy holding Japanese superior to the Taiwanese had been the basis of a segregated educational system since the early colonial period. And gender deepened ethnic hierarchy.

Considering that their positive interactions with teachers were central to the creation of this gendered nostalgia, it is no surprise that some Japanese-educated Taiwanese linked the quality of teachers to their nostalgia for Japanese rule and their criticism of the Chinese Nationalist government. The teaching profession was highly respected in Taiwan before, during, and after Japanese rule because of highly qualified candidates in the profession.[90] The classical Chinese training during the Qing period and the highly competitive normal school examination system under the Japanese and the Chinese Nationalist governments produced a small, high-quality group of teachers. Under Japanese rule, however, very few Taiwanese could enter the teaching profession.

The Japanese colonial administration set up teacher-training programs soon after colonization began. Officials recruited male teachers from Japan in the early period because they could only entrust the *dōka* mission through the *kokugo* education to Japanese, not non-Japanese. Those recruited before September 1896 were Japanese men with prior teaching experience who had gone through the two- to six-month programs. Starting in September 1896, the colonial government targeted Japanese middle school graduates and set up a more formal training program. These programs required recruits to take courses to learn the Taiwanese Hoklo or Hakka language. After completing this free two-year training, graduates were required to fulfill a minimum three years of teaching service. The colonial government attracted Japanese by giving recruits more benefits than teachers in Japan. For instance, the starting monthly salary for Japanese teachers in Taiwan ranged from ¥40 to ¥50, compared to ¥25 in Japan. With higher prices and standard of living in the metropole, many Japanese men began looking for opportunities outside their homeland and found teaching in Taiwan became an attractive option.[91] In his research, Yasumura Kensuke found that the teaching program attracted Okinawans because of its good career and economic returns.[92]

By 1899, the colonial government formally set up teacher's normal schools in Taipei with Japanese and Taiwanese male recruits. Most recruits for teacher-training programs came directly from Japan with middle school education, although starting in the second half of the 1920s, Japanese who had grown up in Taiwan began to enroll in these programs. The admission procedure set a higher quota for Japanese than Taiwanese. The average admission rate for Japanese applicants was 23 percent, reaching its highest rate, 60 percent, in 1939. The average admission rate for Taiwanese applicants was 5 percent. In addition to uneven acceptance rates, Wu Wenxing has found that Japanese preference for middle school over normal school and Taiwanese preference for normal school over middle school meant that as a whole, Taiwanese students were more academically prepared than Japanese students. Wu also shows that these school preferences revealed applicants' class backgrounds, as Taiwanese candidates came from upper- and upper-middle-class backgrounds, while Japanese candidates came from lower-middle and middle-class backgrounds.[93] The normal school admission quota and the socioeconomic background of Taiwanese students produced the reality that the teaching profession was competitive and gendered as men dominated the profession under Japanese rule. Normal schools were established for men, not women. Men, Japanese and Taiwanese, dominated the teaching profession because men were expected to have careers, unlike women, who were expected to become full-time homemakers.

After the Nationalists lost control of mainland China and fled to Taiwan, the Nationalist policy on teacher recruits caused them to hire a group of professionals who were subpar in the eyes of Japanese-educated Taiwanese, who criticized the less-qualified teachers as the reason for the lower quality of education and behavior of the younger generations in the postwar era. The Chinese Nationalist government indeed lowered qualifications by recruiting candidates without teacher's training to meet teacher shortages in its early administration in Taiwan. In November 1945, the Department of Education of the Chinese Nationalist government announced the qualifications for a primary or secondary school teacher: a degree from a normal school; a teacher-training program certificate from a high school in mainland China; or a senior high school degree in the Japanese colonial system. Other qualifications included: a degree from a high school in mainland China with one year of teaching experience; a degree from a middle school, girls' middle school or vocational school from the Japanese colonial system with two years of teaching experience;

or three years of teaching experience at primary schools or traditional Chinese academies under Japanese rule.[94] While it is difficult to calculate the number of Mainlander teachers who met the degree qualifications, as a whole, Mainlanders who moved to Taiwan were more highly educated than the Taiwanese. Over 34 percent of Mainlanders born before 1949 received higher education, compared to 7 percent of Taiwanese. The ethnic disparity persisted in postwar Taiwan as nearly 35 percent of Mainlander men and 3.5 percent of Mainlander women had a college degree, compared to 5.3 percent of Taiwanese men and 0.8 percent of Taiwanese women among those born in 1940.[95] The reason for this disparity was that Japanese officials discouraged most Taiwanese from receiving post-primary-level education because of discriminatory admission practices that ensured Japanese dominance at these institutions.[96] Although qualifications were lowered in the initial postwar period, teaching remained competitive, with only the top 10 percent of junior high school graduates passing the entrance exam to enter normal junior colleges in Taiwan.[97]

Despite how these statistics showed the competitiveness of the profession, many Japanese-educated Taiwanese, in their critique of the Nationalist government, criticized Chinese Mainlander teachers for their lack of proper educational training, which strengthened their colonial nostalgia. For example, Zhang Jintu, a teacher during and after Japanese rule, questioned the quality of these Mainlander teachers as a whole. He recalled being at a teacher's workshop at Tamsui Elementary School where the Mainlander instructors, an army captain and an air force lieutenant, did not know how to teach *bopomofo*, a phonetic alphabet of Mandarin Chinese. He said over half its teachers were war veterans who could not speak Mandarin Chinese well and taught math terribly.[98] Zhou Yingying, a substitute teacher at a Taiwanese primary school during the wartime period who taught for decades after 1945, shared a similar assessment to Zhang. She said that in the postwar society, jobs in fields such as banking and the postal services provided more benefits than teaching, resulting in many Taiwanese men feeling reluctant to enter the profession. She complained, "[The teaching profession] was cheap and bad. That is why Taiwan's education has failed [students]. It was all the [Mainlander] war veterans who came to teach. Their [Mandarin Chinese] pronunciation wasn't standard. They [also] didn't know how to teach math. . . . They didn't have proper schooling [or training], yet they became teachers."[99] She saw that well-qualified candidates would work elsewhere, while unqualified candidates would apply and get the teaching position. Having been trained as a teacher under Japanese rule, Zhou was disappointed with the quality of teachers in the postwar years. Zhou's criticism of the lack of proper schooling of teachers in the postwar years is especially interesting considering the fact that Zhou herself was not a normal school graduate but a girls' home economics school graduate with some training in a normal school. Yet she shared the same criticism as many Taiwanese teachers, women and men, who cited nonstandard Mandarin Chinese enunciation and ineffective math pedagogy as evidence of unqualified Chinese Mainlander teachers. Additionally, women had access to fewer formal teacher-training opportunities than men did under Japanese rule, yet both genders seemed to share similar views of Mainlander teachers. Given that most Mainlanders who arrived in Taiwan with the Chinese Nationalist government were men and many were soldiers, they were likely not criticizing the gender of the teachers but the deprofessionalization of teaching caused by hiring former soldiers.

Moreover, the Taiwanese perception of the discriminatory pay scale based on ethnicity under the Chinese Nationalist government, without mentioning such a system based on ethnicity and gender under Japanese rule, suggests that the profession remained male dominated as Taiwanese used teaching qualifications to criticize the Nationalist regime. According to Wu Sheng, a former teacher, Taiwanese and Chinese Mainlanders were on different pay scales. Born to a farming household in Shulin, Taipei, in 1919, Wu completed one year of advanced-course study and passed the exam to enter Taihoku No. 2 Middle School. From 1941 until 1948, he taught at Dojō (Tucheng) Primary School, later switching to Shulin Elementary School, where he remained until retirement. Under Nationalist rule, Wu did not receive a pay raise during his fifteen years of teaching because his school considered his salary sufficient. He claimed the Nationalist government considered Taiwanese teachers to be half Japanese and refused to raise their salary. According to Wu, although the government claimed that Mainlanders were more highly educated than the Taiwanese and continued to raise their salary, one of his coworkers, a Mainlander, told Wu that he did not even graduate from middle school.

Supposedly, according to Wu, a Mainlander teacher was able to become a teacher by finding three witnesses to testify that he had finished a normal school education. This Mainlander was able to become a principal until retirement. In contrast, Wu, who graduated from a top middle school in Taiwan, could not even become the dean of students at his school. He remained frustrated, saying, "You can see how the KMT insulted us!"[100] Wu's experience suggests that the teacher-selection method the Chinese Nationalist government established was not the issue but that the verification of qualifications was a major issue because some Mainlanders falsified their qualifications by finding witnesses, an accommodation the Nationalist government likely made because the wars (Second Sino-Japanese War and the Chinese Civil War) and the mass migrations (inside mainland China and to Taiwan) had led to the loss of many documents. Taiwanese also deemed their middle school education under Japanese rule to be superior to those in mainland China. Although Wu believed that he was discriminated against because of his Taiwanese ethnicity, his narrative focused on qualifications. Considering that many Taiwanese believed in merit-based promotion, Wu and others suggest that Taiwanese were more talented and well trained than Chinese Mainlander teachers and thus were qualified for and deserving of pay and promotions that reflected their educational accomplishments. Merit was thus linked to ethnicity. In contrast to ethnicity, gender differences were not raised during interviews as no female teachers complained about their pay, probably because they were less likely than men to be the sole income earners and thus, under less financial pressure, less likely to mark the difference.

Former Taiwanese students fondly recalled their teachers while simultaneously emphasizing their merit and training in their narratives, which revealed colonial nostalgia as gendered. In their eyes, Japanese teachers were selfless in providing free tutoring and sample exams to help students pass middle school entrance exams, thus showing their compassion for students. Students even praised corporal punishment for producing law-abiding citizens and saw themselves as exceptional when asked to perform unpaid manual labor and spend one-on-one time with their teachers in a familial-feeling classroom. The likelihood that it was schoolgirls performing these manual tasks meant that women were more likely than men to focus on the personal and familial relationships with their teachers in constructing colonial nostalgia. In contrast, men were more likely than women to focus on the teachers' qualifications in criticizing the Chinese Nationalist government when constructing colonial nostalgia because men were more likely to become professionals in patriarchal Taiwan. Taiwanese expressed anger over the lower qualifications required of Mainlander teachers, although no significant difference existed between the educational level of teachers under Japanese rule and under Chinese Nationalist rule. Their criticisms were imbued with personal and political messages of the postwar regime that contributed to the colonial nostalgia for the Japanese regime. Seeing themselves as trained in a merit-based system, Taiwanese were clearly frustrated by having to compete and work with less-qualified Mainlanders in the postwar era, especially when they believed that ethnicity determined one's pay and promotion. While criticisms and accusations were often directed at their Mainlander colleagues, ultimately, Taiwanese critique was directed at the Chinese Nationalist government—a corrupt authoritarian regime that shattered Taiwanese expectations of being treated as equals after Japanese rule ended, when Taiwanese continued to be treated as second-class citizens. By focusing on their interactions with Japanese teachers and the teachers' qualification in their narratives, Taiwanese transformed their nostalgia for their Japanese teachers into nostalgia for Japanese rule and contemporary Japan. To them, merit motivated teachers and students under Japanese rule, whereas ethnicity produced nepotism under Chinese Nationalist rule.

GOOD MANNERS: CULTIVATING PERSONAL QUALITIES AND SKILLS IN SCHOOL

Praising their own behavior and practical skills was part of their colonial nostalgia to show the success of gendered assimilation, which was best illustrated during the wartime period when Taiwanese women recalled it as a time when good behavior was cultivated and practical skills acquired in contrast to men, who remembered the war less fondly because they were mobilized to serve in the military. Women acknowledged that their life during the wartime period was difficult, especially when the government began food rationing in 1939 and when air raids intensified in 1945, as noted in chapter 3. Nevertheless, women cited their law-abiding behavior and the sewing and cooking skills they had learned under Japanese rule to set themselves apart from the younger generations who were educated under the postwar educational system. In their critique of the younger generations, these women bolster their sense of identity and place in society by praising their Japanese education and blaming the contemporary educational curriculum for failing to produce well-mannered youths. Their focus on youths stood in contrast to men, who did not comment on the younger generations, as men were more likely than women to criticize the Chinese Nationalist government directly.

Acquiring practical life skills was one major point that many woman interviewees emphasized to demonstrate the success of Japanese education in constructing their colonial nostalgia. This contrasts with what they perceived to be the failed Chinese Nationalist education that did not prepare graduates for the professional world. Some women, such as Lü Zhungju, cited their sewing and cooking training as evidence that their education was more practical and, thus, better than the one in democratized Taiwan. Born in Tainan, Lü said that primary school graduates of her generation had acquired the necessary skills from their schooling to hold a job. After graduation, she worked at the broadcasting station for several years until the Japanese left Taiwan. She believes that elementary school graduates in democratized Taiwan since the 1990s would not have sufficient training from school to succeed in the workplace.[101] Whether it was sewing, cooking, or other work skills, former students attributed their homemaking and work training to their education. As discussed in chapter 4, these women had reasons to hold this view as their sewing training proved its vocational usefulness during the postwar years. They are disappointed that primary and secondary school graduates in democratized Taiwan would not be able to perform tasks that the Japanese-educated generation was capable of doing. It is worthwhile to note that their narratives did not consider how social and family expectations affected the educational curriculum in both periods. Under Japanese rule, both the family and the colonial state wanted and expected most Taiwanese to work at a young age. Where the difference lies is that Taiwanese families expected their children to contribute to household income with or without education, whereas the colonial state expected all Taiwanese to complete only primary education to make *dōka* a success by training Japanese-speaking, skilled, and loyal subjects for the nation-empire. Under Chinese Nationalist control and then after democratization, expectations changed over time as Taiwan's economy shifted from an agricultural society to an industrial and service economy. In the early twenty-first century, when the interviews were conducted, most families expected their children to complete college-level education, and the state supported this view by converting many technical and vocational schools into colleges.[102] Nonetheless, many former schoolgirls valued practical skills in their daily life because of their gendered training in the *kokugo* education instead of abstract knowledge from higher levels of education that may be useful for working professionals in industrialized and service economies.

Perhaps more important than practical skills, many Taiwanese women focus on the cultivation of their character to highlight the success of the *kokugo* education in their colonial nostalgia. Lin Jiao'e, a seamstress with a middle school diploma who taught sewing in postwar Taiwan, summed up her education this way: "I think Japanese education trained us to have manners, to respect the elderly and our teachers, to value ethics, to be patriotic and do teamwork."[103] Although she did not explicitly cite the source, her comment was likely shaped by the Imperial Rescript on Education, which students were required to memorize and which most Taiwanese probably remembered as the foundation of their self-described good character. Attending a school with mostly Japanese children, Lin Xianyan recalled that her elementary school teacher required her class to recite the Rescript while standing outdoors in the cold. Thinking back, she appreciated the lessons listed in the Rescript: harmonious relationship with siblings and friends, filial piety, and the meaning of being a good person. She linked the memorization of this Rescript to the cultivation of a "Japanese spirit" (Tw. Hoklo, *jı̍t-pún cheng-sîn*, Jp. *nihonseishin*) among people who received Japanese education before 1945.[104]

The Japanese government had issued the Rescript in 1890 as the guiding principle of education within the nation-empire. The Taiwanese I interviewed linked the Rescript to "Japanese spirit" and claimed that this spirit embodied virtues such as honesty, loyalty, purity, filial piety, diligence, lawfulness, fairness, accountability, and hygiene. However, Leo Ching has clarified that the Taiwanese definition of "Japanese spirit"

CHAPTER 5

during the postwar era differs from the original Japanese definition from the wartime period. The Japanese term refers to "a sense of dedication and commitment to the Japanese nation and the emperor," whereas the Taiwanese "*ribunjinshin* defines a more quotidian and practical understanding of social etiquette and communal conduct . . . and more about everyday lives and their organization."[105] He points out that the Taiwanese Hoklo term speaks to "moral and ethical virtues" and "a wide spectrum of conducts and behaviors that are associated with a greater whole: punctuality, justice, diligence, willingness to abide by the law, responsibility, sincerity, humaneness, and other virtues" that are independent from Japan or the nation-state.[106] Living under a different political regime with historical and cultural differences in the postwar era, Japanese-educated Taiwanese had internalized and localized the term to be applicable first under Chinese Nationalist rule and then in a democratized society.

The localization of this "Japanese spirit" terminology was applied in some Taiwanese women's criticism of Mainlanders in postwar and democratized Taiwan, as they were more likely than men to focus on the behaviors and characters of the younger generations because the gendered assimilation embedded in the *kokugo* education had trained them to be mothers to educate the younger generations at home. For example, Lan Qinhua, who completed six years of primary education in 1945 and junior high and teacher-training school in the postwar years, discussed the "Japanese spirit" to criticize Mainlanders as cheaters, swindlers, tricksters, and thieves. She defined this spirit as obedience, honesty, decisiveness, loyalty to Japan, and uprightness. Lan compared the teaching and the actions of Japanese and Chinese (Mainlanders) residing in Taiwan. She said Japanese people practiced what they preached: teaching students how to be upright, serious, diligent people. In contrast, she claimed that the Chinese Nationalist education taught Taiwanese students to be upright, but Mainlanders in Taiwan were the opposite—liars and swindlers.[107]

Also criticizing the postwar education under Chinese Nationalist rule, Wu Surong believed that Japanese education taught "Japanese spirit." She proclaimed, "We Taiwanese over the age of seventy still have this 'Japanese spirit.' How do you define it? It's being honest as a person, [and] being thrifty."[108] She asserted that her Japanese education had trained her generation to adopt the virtues of honesty and thrift, two qualities that Wu believes are lacking in youths in democratized Taiwan. The invocation of the term *Japanese spirit* simultaneously distinguished her generation of Taiwanese from the younger ones and marked Japanese colonial education as superior to that of the Nationalists. Leo Ching argues that this generation of Taiwanese linked this "Japanese spirit" "with a modern moral and ethical form of conduct for the greater 'good' . . . a philosophy of the public . . . [to] lament its passing in contemporary Japan, where they see rampant social ills that they attribute to an increasingly self-centered populace that had abandoned the notion of the common good."[109] He concludes that this generation of Taiwanese "shares a similar conservatism with Japanese neoconservatives" in viewing the younger generation as in need of rejuvenation.[110] It is interesting that Japanese neoconservatives like Kobayashi Yoshinori lament the loss of this "Japanese spirit" in contemporary Japan but argue that it could still be seen in postwar Taiwan.[111] In constructing their colonial nostalgia, both Kobayashi and Japanese-educated Taiwanese seem to treat "Japanese spirit" as a timeless concept, unchanged from the Japanese period to the early twenty-first century, even though they have different definitions.

While the Imperial Rescript on Education served as the foundation of the *kokugo* education, former schoolgirls discussed the *shūshin* (imperial ethics) course as central to cultivating good persons and depicted the *kokugo* education as effective in producing well-mannered and moral citizens, in contrast to the immoral and criminal acts of the ill-mannered younger generations educated by the Chinese Nationalist curriculum. Zhou Lianyu, whose memory begins this chapter, praised the *shūshin* course in her evaluation of Japanese education. She believes that the absence of the *shūshin* course was the key reason many people had become messed up (Jp. *mecha-mecha*), committing robbery and murder in democratized Taiwan. She concludes, "Chinese [Nationalist] education failed. . . . I think that when one compares the educational systems, Japanese education was the correct way of teaching, and the real way of education. . . . I strongly disapprove of the Chinese education in Taiwan right now."[112] Gao Sumei shares Zhou's view. Born as the daughter of a local official in Yunlin, Gao was a second-year student at Torao (Huwei) Girls' Middle School when Japan lost the war. She completed high school in the postwar years. She criticized the lack of manners of children in democratized Taiwan by invoking the *shūshin* course: "I'm saying that we should have the *shūshin* course so that children won't become bad. . . . [Children nowadays] have no manners. They are not courteous toward others. Nowadays they would kill their parents, beat them. Don't you agree?! It's no longer about lack of manners. It's more like the order of heaven and earth has been flipped. Some don't allow their parents to eat, and some swindle their parents' wealth. There was no such behavior in the old days."[113]

Lan's comment goes beyond public manners and etiquette and reveals her anxiety over the younger generation mistreating and murdering their parents, meaning her generation as they aged. She is concerned that the previous family hierarchy and expectations of obeying and caring for their elders are no longer observed by the younger generations, who grew up in a greed-guided capitalist and individualism-guided democratic society with less emphasis on absolute obedience to figures of authority in the household and/or government. Another interviewee, Zhou Yingying, a former teacher, explained that the *shūshin* course taught students about a daily-life routine and manners. She also said that her teacher instilled the spirit of perseverance in her fourth-grade class when her teacher forced them to walk several kilometers from school to the ocean and back in commemoration of Navy Day, even after they became exhausted in the heat. Zhou believed that the *shūshin* course trained the Taiwanese to be law-abiding people during the Japanese period, and thus society was more orderly then.[114]

These women viewed *shūshin* as a crucial part of creating an orderly and respectful society with law-abiding citizens inside and outside of the household. Their critique of the educational system in democratized Taiwan is obvious, and they compared it to the familiar Japanese system as the standard. Their disapproval of the younger generations' lack of proper behavior at home and in public made them nostalgic for Japanese rule because they attributed social ills in democratized Taiwanese society to education. Their narrative also marks their virtues and behaviors as superior to those of the younger generations. Their concerns over the manners and behaviors of the younger generations revealed their roles as mothers who were tasked with teaching their children, according to the "good wife, wise mother" training. These concerns were not necessarily personal, as none spoke of their children or grandchildren as misbehaving or criminal. However, their commentaries, based on observations and increased reports of crimes, show that they had transformed the duties of a "good wife, wise mother" from individual households to the societal scale. Identifying the roots of social ills can be seen as an expression of thinking for the collective good, a mentality that this wartime generation was trained and mobilized to cultivate during the wartime period.

While the Japanese-language course was the core of the *kokugo* education, the *shūshin* course was the most memorable course for many Taiwanese because it taught them "ethics," which ultimately meant learning how to be obedient, loyal subjects of Japan in a gendered course that bound men and women to specific roles at home and in society. The colonial government published a set of ethics textbooks for Taiwanese primary schools in 1914, 1928, 1930, 1942, and 1943. The major themes in all the *shūshin* textbooks were obedience, national spirit, diligence, and honesty, according to Chou Wan-yao's research. Other themes included: "non-superstition, selfless," "self-control, introspection, leniency, thrift," "responsibility, hygiene, manner, filial piety, gratitude, respect teachers, friendship, empathy, fraternity, mutual assistance," "charity, law-abiding, loyalty and patriotism, and god worshipping," all aimed to govern individual behaviors in the family, society, and the nation-empire.[115] To act according to themes that were essential to maintaining a harmonious household and a stable society in the *shūshin* course, students received moral lessons that were gendered. The Taiwan Primary School Regulation of 1907 stated that all courses, including *shūshin*, had to be particular to boys' and girls' character.[116] For example, in a lesson titled "Men's Duties and Women's Duties" from volume 6 of the *Primary School Ethics Textbook*, students learned that a man's supposed natural physical strength made him suitable to be the sole income earner as the head of the household who served society and the nation, while a woman's gentleness was suitable for managing household matters and child-rearing to maintain family harmony. By fulfilling their roles, the lesson concludes, men and women would increase the prosperity of the home and the nation.[117]

One major premise of *shūshin* was to train girls to be chaste and virtuous.[118] For instance, a Japanese woman named Nogi Shizuko was portrayed as the model woman in a lesson titled "Women's Virtue" in the *shūshin* textbook for Taiwanese children. Students learned that Nogi possessed the virtues of filial piety, kindness, thrift, and simplicity. She assisted her military-officer husband and was devoted to caring for her sick mother-in-law after marriage. Regardless of how many promotions her husband received, Nogi continued to live a simple and thrifty life, exemplified by actions such as making clothes from cotton instead of a more expensive material. She was kind to people, including servants. She watched military drills in support of students.[119] She was a dutiful wife and daughter-in-law even in her husband's absence. She continued to be thrifty even after her husband's promotions had increased family income. Nogi also did not act arrogantly toward others because of her socioeconomic status. She was a patriot who supported military activities. The fact that Nogi was Japanese suggests that the colonial government wanted Taiwanese schoolgirls to strive to become ideal Japanese women with the same virtues and skills as Nogi, who embodies the wifehood of the "good wife, wise mother" ideal.

While the "Japanese spirit" seemed universal and the *shūshin* course was gendered in cultivating good etiquette and behavior, Lin Xianyan's discussion of the virtue of *junjō* was gendered in demonstrating the success of schoolgirls' education and wartime mobilization, even though her definition of *junjō* as not stealing was not its exact definition during the war. The word *junjō* had two meanings during the wartime period: purity and self-sacrificing devotion.[120] According to John Dower, the Japanese evoked the concept of purity to distinguish themselves as racially different and superior as a nation in the twentieth century because they believed that this purity could only be appreciated and achieved by Japan and its people. The Japanese argued that they were "historically purer than other peoples genetically and morally" to support their belief in the "divine origins of the Yamato race."[121] Japanese military aggression in the 1930s and 1940s reflected the desire to purify the Japanese nation, Asia, and the world to achieve "a higher state of perfection and purity" to "restore a past racial and spiritual purity largely lost in recent times."[122] During the wartime period, this purity was exemplified by sacrificing one's life for the purpose of spiritual cleansing. The *kamikaze* mission was one example of purity through self-sacrifice.[123]

Interestingly enough, only one interviewee I spoke to mentioned the term *junjō*. Lin Xianyan, the only interviewee who attended a Japanese elementary school, explained that although wartime rations resulted in insufficient rice for ordinary people, no student from her middle school stole any of the rice balls they were preparing for the troops: "Everyone was *junjō*, so no one took [rice balls] home.... What we were happy about was that after cooking the rice on the metal pot/wok, we got to eat the remaining rice that was burned at the bottom. It became our breakfast. We were happy to eat it."[124] Students from her school were also assigned to make camouflage nets for military tanks. She recalled having to finish the nets at home, but no one stole any materials because "everyone was *junjō*, and didn't steal. Nowadays in the Chinese [Nationalist] period, people would steal parts to make things, but not back then."[125] Echoing one definition of self-sacrifice from the wartime period, Lin highlighted the sleepless nights that she and her classmates experienced for the war effort. By directly comparing her wartime law-abiding behavior to common stealing under Nationalist rule, she also offered a critique of the disorderly Nationalist regime in contrast to an orderly wartime society.

Lin Xianyan specified that this *junjō* was uniquely a schoolgirl virtue that was best illustrated by wartime mobilization, invoking age and gender as important factors in creating this virtue. In explaining a report on why schoolgirls from Taihoku Girls' No. 1 Middle School were sent to gather some precious metals that were dispersed in the hills, Lin said that the colonial authority "didn't dare to call on adults to gather those diamonds. Adults weren't as purehearted.... Girls back then had really pure hearts."[126] Lin recalled it as something that middle schoolers— schoolgirls—possessed. Lin also explained that the Japanese teachers presumed a certain virtue that educated Japanese women held. As discussed in chapter 3, Lin's teachers taught students how to use bamboo spears for self-defense should the Americans land and attempt to violate them.[127] Historian Vera Mackie has observed that the "preservation of women's chastity, purity, and fidelity was part of a gendered division of wartime labour" in Japan.[128] Rather than citing *junjō* to invoke the current definition of the naivete or innocence in Japanese, Lin used the term to describe purehearted and law-abiding actions. Lin's definition of *junjō* functions similarly to the "Japanese spirit" concept and the *shūshin* course in praising good etiquette and behavior under Japanese rule to construct colonial nostalgia among many Taiwanese. However, she has partially retained the original meaning of *junjō* from the wartime period. Her definition of *junjō* differs from the "Japanese spirit" definition in that she did not localize the *junjō* concept as many Taiwanese did to the "Japanese spirit" concept during the postwar era.

In constructing their nostalgia for Japanese rule, former schoolgirls emphasized practical skills acquired and good character developed from their colonial education. Some remembered concepts of "Japanese spirit" and *junjō*, which embodied virtues of obedience, honesty, uprightness, diligence, and perseverance. Many also recalled the Imperial Rescript on Education that they were required to memorize and the required course of *shūshin* as the essential ingredient to an orderly society. Although the Rescript and the course originally emphasized loyalty to Japan and its emperor, Taiwanese women largely ignored discussing the embedded patriotism and instead focused on universal virtues that were independent of the nation-empire to highlight their personal and Japanese educational successes while critiquing the Chinese Nationalist government's failure in educating its people in the postwar period with remnants into the contemporary period. In the end, the concepts and the course they cited matter less than their self-identification as law-abiding, respectful citizens who were educated under a different regime, in contrast to the chaos they see in the younger generations who were educated with the Chinese Nationalist curriculum.

Former Taiwanese students constructed their nostalgia for Japanese rule by insisting on the absence of discrimination from Japanese colonizers and characterizing Japanese teachers as compassionate people who imparted lifelong lessons to Taiwanese children. Reflecting on their educational experiences under Japanese rule in the 1930s and the 1940s and under Chinese Nationalist rule in the post-1945 era, most of my interviewees spoke fondly of their Japanese teachers and the orderly society they remembered while criticizing the postwar educational system. By incorporating their teachers into constructing their nostalgia, as Leo Ching has also observed, their "personal experiences [had] become testimonies to larger historical events, and historical events inform the trials and tribulations of individual lives: a dialecticism that underscores the connectivity and organicity between Taiwan and Japan."[129] Educated under a discriminatory system based on creating "good wives, wise mothers," most Taiwanese women interviewees had children and grandchildren and likely felt compelled to judge the impact of the postwar educational system as mothers, grandmothers, and members of the society. Their gendered training thus created gendered colonial nostalgia based on the personal, the familial, the compassionate.

Japanese teachers avoided discussing their complicity in the inherent discriminatory system decades after colonization ended. Shimadu Kenpō, a former principal at Tainan Elementary School,[130] proclaimed that the publication of *Bridge to Taiwan* in 1981 served to document the educational legacy of fifty years of Japanese rule. As the chairperson of the Hōrai Society, he claimed that the book is a record of former teachers' passion for their sacred profession.[131] Through this publication, he hoped, future generations would understand the legacy of fifty years of Japanese education in Taiwan.[132] Although former teachers such as Shimadu emphasized their selfless devotion to teaching Taiwanese children, the colonial teacher-training system reveals inherent discrimination against the native population. School admissions favored ethnic Japanese applicants; Japanese teachers earned higher salaries than Taiwanese teachers; and the goal of assimilating Taiwanese children presumed Japanese superiority and Taiwanese inferiority. It is ironic that Japanese teachers claimed that they sought to help Taiwanese children, even though their profession and their belief in Japan's superiority over Taiwan reinforced the unequal colonizer–colonized power relationship and hierarchy.

No doubt postwar reunions helped create and maintain colonial nostalgia. Former students began reunions starting in the 1960s and 1970s because they had more time after their children reached adulthood, and a few even had grandchildren by then.[133] They invited Japanese teachers to Taiwan. These reunions helped reinforce the bonds between the former colonized and colonizer.[134] They also provided an occasion for nostalgic expression during and after the gatherings. As Leo Ching has declared, the nostalgia of these Taiwanese "forces us to confront a violence that continues from the colonial past into the (post)colonial present."[135] He expresses sympathy for this generation of Taiwanese for wanting "recognition from the former colonizers of their marginalized existence since the end of formal colonialism."[136] Perhaps reminiscing about their young days under an orderly Japanese regime while pointing out the failures of the postwar Chinese Nationalist government helps this generation of Taiwanese carve out a space for themselves in a society that was ignorant of the complexity of having been born in and lived under Japanese colonialism. Their colonial nostalgia became a strategy for coping with changes, including unwelcome ones, in a society that has become increasingly different from that of their childhood.

The last generation of Japanese-educated Han Taiwanese dealt with two minority-rule governments during their lifetime, the Japanese and then the Chinese Nationalist regimes. They were aware that their ethnicity marked them as different from their teachers under Japanese rule, yet women and men saw impartiality and merit as the defining features of their educational and professional experiences when they recalled their educational experiences. In the postwar era, many Japanese-educated Taiwanese had initially believed in their shared ethnicity with Chinese Mainlanders, which implied an impartiality in which merit would dictate one's position in society. Unfortunately for these Taiwanese, ethnicity also became a marker of one's status and position under Chinese Nationalist control, characterized by rampant corruption and nepotism. Andrew Morris remarks that some Japanese-educated Taiwanese used "every instance of KMT misrule" to argue that the Nationalists were incompetent rulers of Taiwan while "appropriat[ing]" the long-gone "Japanese spirit."[137] Interestingly, while the first Japanese-educated Taiwanese turned to China's New Culture Movement to find inspiration to fight against Japanese discrimination in the 1920s, the last Japanese-educated Taiwanese turned to Japanese education to criticize the Chinese Nationalist oppression during the martial law period (1949–87) in their old age in the 2010s. By looking for outside inspiration to criticize the foreign rulers of Taiwan, Taiwanese people revealed their sense of being different from the ruling elites based on their ethnicity. The realization that they were different from Chinese Mainlanders helped construct their colonial nostalgia and likely contributed to the formation of a new Taiwanese identity.

As the Japanese-educated Taiwanese became retirees in their old age at the turn of the twenty-first century, Taiwan had become a vibrant democracy that permitted opposing and diverse viewpoints, including for Japan and against Chinese Nationalist rule. As Leo Ching maintains, Taiwanese colonial nostalgia was only possible because of "the historical trauma of another (post)colonial colonial rule" such that "the Japanese colonial period appears righteous, just, and orderly," even though Taiwanese clearly experienced the institutional "discrimination and injustice" under colonization. Taiwanese saw "the rampant corruption of the 'liberation' and the authoritarian regime of the KMT . . . with suspicion and disdain."[138] In other words, both the Japanese and Chinese Nationalists were colonial regimes. Throughout most of their (adult) life, members of the final generation of Japanese-educated Taiwanese were unable to publicly vent their frustrations about the Chinese Nationalist government during the martial law era if they did not wish to disappear or be imprisoned. However, after experiencing the democratization that began in the late 1980s and early 1990s, many Taiwanese became increasingly vocal in their criticisms of Chinese Nationalist rule, although some remain reserved about speaking negatively about the Nationalist regime even into the twenty-first century. On the whole, these Japanese-educated Taiwanese were able to voice their more honest assessment of the Japanese education and colonial rule and Chinese Nationalist rule with less fear in a young democracy in the early twenty-first century.

Japanese-educated Taiwanese grew up knowing that they were different from their Japanese rulers, and then they encountered Chinese Mainlanders as adults, as they lived in a society where being "Taiwanese" has transformed from an ethnic identity to a national identity. Scholars have noticed the drastic political, cultural, and social transformations in twentieth-century Taiwan in their studies of identity politics, which have traced the emergence of a Taiwanese identity since the martial law period, and some studies have even pushed the time back to the Japanese period, such as Evan Dawley's argument that an ethnic Taiwanese identity was formed between the late nineteenth and mid-twentieth century.[139] In the early postwar years, the Chinese Nationalist government grouped the Taiwanese Hoklo and Hakka people together as "Provincials" (Ch. Benshengren, literally "people of this province," meaning Taiwan), and recent migrants from mainland China who followed the Nationalist gov-

CHAPTER 5

208

ernment as "Mainlanders," and the differences and tension between the two groups increased after the 2-28 Incident.[140] The systematic privilege given to Mainlanders over Provincials in the early postwar era likely heightened the perception of differences between the two groups. As T. Y. Wang and I-Chou Liu argue, the shared culture and ethnicity, resistance to authoritarianism, and democratization contributed to the emergence of a Taiwanese national identity during the martial law and the democratization periods.[141] Many Japanese-educated Han Taiwanese had either worked with or resisted against the Chinese Nationalist government, inside and outside of Taiwan, in democratizing Taiwan and forming a separate and recognizable identity after 1945.

With democratization and the emergence of the Chinese economy in the region in the 1990s, the "new Taiwanese" identity emerged. This term, coined by Lee Teng-hui (1923–2020), refers to anyone living in Taiwan who is willing to fight for and serve Taiwan regardless of their heritage and place of origin.[142] Concerned with the regional and global rise of China, Lee's proposed "new Taiwanese" identity seeks to unite all residents of Taiwan against potential Chinese military invasion, in addition to the new "economic invasion" that would affect Taiwan's economy negatively. Lee was the first Taiwan-born and the only Japanese-educated Han Taiwanese to become president(1988–2000) of the Republic of China on Taiwan, which means he was the first such high-ranking official in Taiwan's history to represent the majority population.[143] After his victory in Taiwan's first democratic, direct presidential election in 1996, his government implemented new language and history programs. His government started the "mother-tongue policy" to teach Taiwanese Hoklo, Hakka, and indigene languages in elementary and junior high schools.[144] Under the directive of his administration, a Taiwan-centric curriculum replaced the Chinese Nationalists' Sino-Han-centric curriculum in the social science and history curriculum, *Knowing Taiwan* (Ch. Renshi Taiwan), which included the Japanese period and the Taiwanese indigenes and thus makes the argument for a pluralist society that creates a Taiwanese identity.[145] Japanese-educated Taiwanese likely found comfort in seeing that their history and experience would not be forgotten but remembered by the younger generations, who can construct an ethnic and/or national identity that Japanese-educated Taiwanese likely struggled with their entire life.

COLONIAL NOSTALGIA

209

However, film scholar Corrado Neri observes that an "attempt to redefine national identity is a compromise between the search for the roots and the need for independence" and "a centrifugal force aiming to move the Taiwanese identity away from China, and consequently, to draw it closer to Japan" during the reemergence of China as a superpower.[146] Even with the passing of the last Japanese-educated Taiwanese, Japanese studies specialist Jens Sejrup has concluded, Taiwan "continues to be defined by its Japanese—not Chinese—past" in the early twenty-first century.[147] Their legacy lives on in the younger generations of Taiwanese, who are taught their native language and learn pluralist Taiwan-centric history in schools, something that they did not have living under Japanese and Chinese Nationalist control. Having embraced cultural pluralism and moving toward gender equality, the early twenty-first-century Taiwan continues to move away from ethnic hierarchy and gender division, and become a society different from the one the final generation of Japanese-educated Taiwanese experienced in the twentieth century.

GLOSSARY

dōka (Jp.)   assimilation

kōgakkō (Jp.)   Taiwanese (children's) primary school (common school)

kokugo (Jp.)   (Japanese) national language

kokugo no ie (Jp.)   national language household

kōminka (Jp.)   imperial subjectification (imperialization)

kōtō jogakkō (Jp.)   girls' middle school (girls' higher school)

kōtōka (Jp.)   advanced course (higher than primary education but lower than secondary education)

ryōsai kenbo (Jp.)   "good wife, wise mother"

shōgakkō (Jp.)   Japanese (children's) primary school

shūshin (Jp.)   (imperial) ethics course

Taiwan nichinichi shimpō (Jp.)   Taiwan daily news

Taiwan minbao (Ch.)   Taiwan people's news

NOTES

INTRODUCTION

1. The interviewee states that her mother gave birth to six children, but her description suggests that it was seven children with four girls. She might have misspoken because her two older brothers died when she was very young (Li Que'niang, interview by Zhang Meifeng, in *Yilan nüsheng—Ama de gushi: Hangye pian*, ed. Li Suyue [Yilan: Yilan Xian Xian Shi Guan, 2015], 136–40, 148).

2. Fang Yu Hu, "Taiwanese Girls' Education, 1897–1945: Policy and Practice in a Gendered Colonial System," *Eras: Monash University School of Historical Studies Online Journal* 13, no. 1 (December 2011): 4.

3. Yu Chien-ming, *Ri ju shiqi Taiwan de nüzi jiaoyu* (Taibei: Guoli Taiwan Shifan Daxue Lishi Yanjiu Suo, 1988), 249–50.

4. Wang Jinque, *Ri zhi shiqi Taiwan gongmin jiaoyu yu gongmin texing* (Taibei: Taiwan Guji Chuban Youxian Gongsi, 2005), 6.

5. Alan Christy, "The Making of Imperial Subjects in Okinawa," in *Formations of Colonial Modernity in East Asia*, ed. Tani Barlow (Durham, NC: Duke University Press, 1997), 147; Wang Jinque, *Ri zhi shiqi Taiwan gongmin jiaoyu yu gongmin texing*, 36.

6. Kathleen Uno, "Womanhood, War, and Empire: Transmutations of 'Good Wife, Wise Mother' before 1931," in *Gendering Modern Japanese History*, ed. Barbara Molony and Kathleen Uno, Harvard East Asian Monographs 251 (Cambridge, MA: Harvard University Asia Center, 2005), 499. The quotation and paraphrase are from Hu, "Taiwanese Girls' Education, 1897–1945," 4.

7. Homi K. Bhabha, *The Location of Culture*, 2nd ed. (London: Routledge, 1994), 122, https://doi-org.proxy.lib.utc.edu/10.4324/9780203820551.

8. Bhabha, *The Location of Culture*, 126.

9. Bhabha, *The Location of Culture*, 129.

10. Evan Dawley, *Becoming Taiwanese: Ethnogenesis in a Colonial City 1880s–1950s* (Cambridge, MA: Harvard University Asia Center, 2019), 332.

11. Komagome Takeshi, *Shokuminchi teikoku nihon no bunka tōgō* (Tokyo: Iwanami Shoten, 1996), 73–74.

12. Komagome, *Shokuminchi teikoku nihon no bunka tōgō*, 358.

13. Komagome, *Shokuminchi teikoku nihon no bunka tōgō*, 68, 71, 186, 188.

14. Eika Tai, "*Kokugo* and Colonial Education in Taiwan," *positions* 7, no. 2 (1 May 1999): 504.

15. Dawley, *Becoming Taiwanese*, 44.

16. Sayaka Chatani, *Nation-Empire: Ideology and Rural Youth Mobilization in Japan and Its Colonies* (Ithaca, NY: Cornell University Press, 2018), 4.

17. Jun Uchida, *Brokers of Empire: Japanese Settler Colonialism in Korea, 1876–1945* (Cambridge, MA: Harvard University Asia Center, 2011), 146.

18. Uchida, *Brokers of Empire*, 119–20.

19. Uchida, *Brokers of Empire*, 119.

20. Dawley, *Becoming Taiwanese*, 15.

21. Chen Peifeng, *"Dōka" no dōshō imu: Nihon tōchi ka Taiwan no kokugo kyōikushi saikō* (Tokyo: Sangensha, 2001), 23.

22. Patricia Lorcin, *Historicizing Colonial Nostalgia: European Women's Narratives of Algeria and Kenya 1900–Present* (New York: Palgrave Macmillan, 2012), 13, ProQuest Ebook Central.

23. Lorcin, *Historicizing Colonial Nostalgia*, 13.

24. Dawley, *Becoming Taiwanese*, 43–44.

25. Byron K. Marshall, *Learning to Be Modern: Japanese Political Discourse on Education* (London: Routledge, 1994), 31–32, 88, https://doi-org.proxy.lib.utc .edu/10.4324/9780429499272.

26. Sheldon M. Garon, *Molding Japanese Minds: The State in Everyday Life* (Princeton, NJ: Princeton University Press, 1997), 5.

27. Annette Skovsted Hansen, "Practicing 'Kokugo': Teachers in Hokkaido and Okinawa Classrooms, 1895–1904," *Journal of Japanese Studies* 40, no. 2 (2014): 329–31.

28. Hansen, "Practicing 'Kokugo,'" 335.

29. Marshall, *Learning to Be Modern*, 30.

30. The full original text of the Imperial Rescript on Education in Japanese, a Chinese translation, and an English translation are available in "Kyōiku chokugo," in *Taiwan e no kakehashi*, ed. Yamamoto Ryōichi (Osaka: Hōrai Kai Kansai Shibu, 1981), 241–43. Byron Marshall has also provided an English translation (Marshall, *Learning to Be Modern*, 58–59).

31. Marshall, *Learning to Be Modern*, 35–37, 41, 72.

32. Marshall, *Learning to Be Modern*, 72, 74–77, 93, 116–17.

33. Spencer Segalla, *The Moroccan Soul: French Education, Colonial Ethnology, and Muslim Resistance, 1912–1956* (Lincoln: University of Nebraska Press, 2009), 64–66, ProQuest Ebook Central; Andrew Paterson, "'The Gospel of Work Does Not Save Souls': Conceptions of Industrial and Agricultural Education for Africans in the Cape Colony, 1890–1930," *History of Education Quarterly* 45, no. 3 (2005): 383, http://www.jstor.org/stable/20461986.

34. Patricia Tsurumi, *Japanese Colonial Education in Taiwan*, Harvard East Asian Series (Cambridge, MA: Harvard University Press, 1977), 15, 45, 88, 110.

35. Tsurumi, *Japanese Colonial Education in Taiwan*, 34; Yu, *Ri ju shiqi Taiwan de nüzi jiaoyu*, 286.

36. Tsurumi, *Japanese Colonial Education in Taiwan*, 45, 53, 73. The per-capita educational expenditure for Japanese elementary schools ranged from ¥47.3 to ¥63.5 between 1930 and 1940, compared to between ¥24 and ¥29.6 for Taiwanese primary schools during the same decade (Tsurumi, *Japanese Colonial Education in Taiwan*, 239–40; tables 3 and 4 list workers in each sector by their ethnic breakdown [54–58]).

37. Dawley, *Becoming Taiwanese*, 84–85.

38. Stefan Tanaka, *Japan's Orient: Rendering Pasts into History* (Berkeley: University of California Press, 1995), 4, 12–13.

39. Indigene primary schools had much lower standards than Han Taiwanese primary schools and had very few schools across Taiwan (Tsurumi, *Japanese Colonial Education in Taiwan*, 232–33). Indigene children's education centers were established in 1908 and reached more indigenous children than primary schools as colonial officials eventually established such centers in every administrative district with indigenes (Kitamura Kae, "Fantong jiaoyu suo jiuxuezhe zengjia de juti qingkuang: Yi Taiwan zongdu fu de ducu jiuxue ji qi xianshi jichu wei zhongxin," trans. Guo Tingyu, in *Taiwan shi luncong Jiaoyupian–Diguo de xuexiao Diyu de xuexiao*, ed. Xu Peixian [Taibei: Taida Chuban Zhongxin, 2020], 140; Tsurumi, *Japanese Colonial Education in Taiwan*, 233). For a brief description of Japanese schools, see Tsurumi, *Japanese Colonial Education in Taiwan*, 32–34, 110–14. For a brief description of education for Taiwanese indigenes, see Tsurumi, *Japanese Colonial Education in Taiwan*, 231–35.

40. Tsurumi, *Japanese Colonial Education in Taiwan*, 11, 231, 234. Within Taiwanese indigenes, the Sino-Manchu officials created two categories that Japanese officials adopted that revealed their "concept of historical stages of cultural development": one group was the plains indigenes (Jp. *heihozoku*, or the pre-1930s derogatory term *jukuban*, which means "cooked savages") who lived among the Han Taiwanese, engaged in agriculture, and had become slightly sinicized under the Sino-Manchu Qing empire as the lesser uncivilized when compared to the mountain indigenes (Jp. *kōzanzoku*, or the pre-1930s derogatory term of *seiban*, which means "raw savages"). Considered to be the most uncivilized, mountain indigenes lived in the mountains, had an animal-like appearance, supposedly, and engaged in hunting (Leo T. S. Ching, *Becoming Japanese: Colonial Taiwan and the Politics of Identity Formation* [Berkeley: University of California Press, 2001], 153; Emma Teng, *Taiwan's Imagined Geography: Chinese Colonial Travel Writing and Pictures, 1683–1895* [Cambridge, MA: Harvard University Asia Center, 2004], 130–32).

41. See Brett L. Walker's *The Conquest of Ainu Lands: Ecology and Culture in Japanese Expansion, 1590–1800* (Berkeley: University of California Press, 2001), 133–36, 204–5, 213, 216–17, 220, 228–32, for more on the Ainu in Ezo/Hokkaido. For an explanation of how Taiwanese indigenes were classified and viewed under the Sino-Manchu Qing empire, see Teng, *Taiwan's Imagined Geography*, 122–48.

42. Uchida, *Brokers of Empire*, 116.

43. Dawley, *Becoming Taiwanese*, 44.

NOTES TO PAGES 9–10

44. Paterson, "'The Gospel of Work Does Not Save Souls,'" 390, 392.

45. Max Weber, *The Protestant Ethic and the Spirit of Capitalism*, trans. Talcott Parsons (1930; repr., London: Routledge, 2005), 104, 125.

46. Kathleen S. Uno, "Women and Changes in the Household Division of Labor," in *Recreating Japanese Women, 1600–1945*, ed. Gail Lee Bernstein (Berkeley: University of California Press, 1991), 28.

47. Komagome, *Shokuminchi teikoku nihon no bunka tōgō*, 4.

48. Bob W. White, "Talk about School: Education and the Colonial Project in French and British Africa (1860–1960)," *Comparative Education* 32, no. 1 (1996): 14, http://www.jstor.org/stable/3099598.

49. White, "Talk about School," 15.

50. Evanson N. Wamagatta, "Changes of Government Policies towards Mission Education in Colonial Kenya and Their Effects on the Missions: The Case of the Gospel Missionary Society," *Journal of Religion in Africa* 38, no. 1 (2008): 10, http://www.jstor.org/stable/27594443.

51. Chatani, *Nation-Empire*, 6.

52. Chatani, *Nation-Empire*, 7.

53. Christin J. Mamiya, "Nineteenth-Century French Women, the Home, and the Colonial Vision: Les Sauvages de la Mer Pacifique *Wallpaper*," *Frontiers: A Journal of Women Studies* 28, no. 1/2 (2007): 113, http://www.jstor.org/stable/40071949.

54. Linda Kerber, "The Republican Mother: Women and the Enlightenment—An American Perspective," *American Quarterly* 28, no. 2 (1976): 202–3, https://doi.org/10.2307/2712349.

55. Kay Boardman, "The Ideology of Domesticity: The Regulation of the Household Economy in Victorian Women's Magazines," *Victorian Periodicals Review* 33, no. 2 (2000): 155–56, http://www.jstor.org/stable/20083724.

56. Sharon H. Nolte and Sally Ann Hastings, "The Meiji State's Policy toward Women, 1890–1910," in *Recreating the Japanese Women, 1600–1945*, ed. Gail Lee Bernstein (Berkeley: University of California Press, 1991), 152.

57. Hyaeweol Choi, "Wise Mother, Good Wife": A Transcultural Discursive Construct in Modern Korea," *Journal of Korean Studies* (1979-) 14, no. 1 (Fall 2009): 5; Joan Judge, "The Ideology of 'Good Wives and Wise Mothers': Meiji Japan and Feminine Modernity in Late-Qing China," in *Sagacious Monks and Bloodthirsty Warriors: Chinese Views of Japan in the Ming-Qing Period*, ed. Joshua A. Fogel (Norwalk, CT: East Bridge, 2002), 226.

58. Jin Jungwon, *Higashi ajia no ryōsai kenbo ron: Tsukurareta dentō* (Tokyo: Keisō Shobō, 2006), 20–22

59. Uno, "Womanhood, War, and Empire," 502.

60. Uno, "Womanhood, War, and Empire," 503. The quotation and paraphrase are from Hu, "Taiwanese Girls' Education, 1897-1945," 4.

61. Uno, "Womanhood, War, and Empire," 499. The quotation and paraphrase are from Hu, "Taiwanese Girls' Education, 1897–1945," 4.

62. Michel Foucault, *The History of Sexuality, Volume 1: An Introduction*, trans. Robert Hurley (1976; New York: Vintage, 1990), 12.

63. Foucault, *The History of Sexuality, Volume 1*, 11.

64. Foucault, *The History of Sexuality, Volume 1*, 12.

65. Edward W. Said, *Orientalism* (1978; New York: Vintage, 1994), 3, 5.

66. Dawley, *Becoming Taiwanese*, 13, 18.

67. Uchida, *Brokers of Empire*, 4–5, 21–22.

68. Chatani, *Nation-Empire*, 274.

69. Chatani, *Nation-Empire*, 270.

70. Wamagatta, "Changes of Government Policies towards Mission Education in Colonial Kenya and Their Effects on the Missions," 10.

71. Some studies on gender and colonial education: Gail Minault, *Secluded Scholars: Women's Education and Muslim Social Reform in Colonial India* (Delhi: Oxford University Press, 1998); Barbara Southard, *The Women's Movement and Colonial Politics in Bengal: The Quest for Political Rights, Education, and Social Reform Legislation, 1921–1936* (New Delhi: Manohar, 1995); Jean Taylor, "Education, Colonialism, and Feminism: An Indonesian Case Study," in *Education and the Colonial Experience*, ed. Philip G. Altbach and Gail P. Kelly (New York: Advent, 1991), 137–51.

1. INSTITUTIONALIZING GIRLS' EDUCATION

1. As the largest newspaper outlet in Taiwan, it received funding from the colonial government (Wu Micha, Huang Zhiwei, and Lin Xinyi, "Taiwan ri ri xin bao" [Jp. *Taiwan nichinichi shimpō*], in *Taiwan shi xiao shidian* [Taibei: Yuanliu Chuban Shiye Gufen Youxian Gongsi, 2000], 105). "Katō Tadatarō," *Taiwan zongdu fu zhiyuan lu xitong*, Institute of Taiwan History, Academia Sinica.

2. In the early colonial period, Japanese colonial officials actually categorized Han Taiwanese into two groups—Fujian and Guangdong people, with the assumption that Taiwanese Hoklo speakers traced their ancestry to Fujian and Taiwanese Hakka speakers traced their ancestry to Guangdong in China. This categorization thus is more revealing of one's native language and culture in Taiwan than of one's place of origin or ancestry. The mentioning of "Fujian" in the article thus refers to the Taiwanese Hoklo population, not Hakka women.

3. "Jiaoyu tanpian (Katō Mengjia gong xuexiao zhang tan)," *Kanbun Taiwan nichinichi shimpō*, January 23, 1910, 5.

4. Judge, "The Ideology of 'Good Wives and Wise Mothers,'" 223.

5. Uno, "Womanhood, War, and Empire," 498.

NOTES TO PAGES 13–24

6. Jin, *Higashi ajia no ryōsai kenbo ron*, 65–66.

7. Koyama Shizuko, *Ryōsai kenbo to iu kihan* (Tokyo: Keisō Shobō, 1991), 19.

8. Uno, "Women and Changes in the Household Division of Labor," 28, 30, 32.

9. Jin, *Higashi ajia no ryōsai kenbo ron*, 25.

10. Koyama, *Ryōsai kenbo to iu kihan*, 39–41, 43, 46, 85.

11. Koyama, *Ryōsai kenbo to iu kihan*, 41–42, 93.

12. Koyama, *Ryōsai kenbo to iu kihan*, 41–48.

13. Koyama, *Ryōsai kenbo to iu kihan*, 50.

14. Koyama, *Ryōsai kenbo to iu kihan*, 50–51, 76.

15. Koyama, *Ryōsai kenbo to iu kihan*, 100, 136–37, 146, 168.

16. Taiwan Kyōiku kai, ed., *Taiwan kyōiku enkaku shi* (Taihoku: Taiwan Kyōiku Kai, 1939), 14–15.

17. *Taiwan kyōiku enkaku shi*, 13.

18. Yu, *Ri ju shiqi Taiwan de nüzi jiaoyu*, 61, 262–64.

19. All Taiwanese primary schools and Japanese elementary schools were renamed "national schools" (Jp. *kokugo gakkō*) in 1941, with the promulgation of the National School Ordinance (Jp. Kokumin Gakkō Rei). Therefore, the distinction between Japanese and Taiwanese schools was no longer noted on government documents. However, in 1938, there were 146 Japanese elementary schools (main campuses) and 796 Taiwanese primary schools (main campuses) for a total of 942 schools. This means that 84.5 percent of primary educational institutions were for Taiwanese children. If the same ratio was applied to the number of schools in 1944, then there were 929 schools for Taiwanese children (*Taiwan sōtokufu dai yon jū ni tōkei sho Shōwa jusan nen* [Taihoku: *Taiwan sōtokufu*, 1940], 67, 73). "Biao 468 li nian quansheng xuexiao ji yuan sheng shu," in "Taiwan sheng wushi'nian lai tongji jiaoyu gaikuang," originally published in *Taiwan wushi'yi'nian lai tongji tiyao (1894–1945)*, ed. Taiwan sheng xingzheng zhangguan gongshu tongji shi (Taibei: Guting Shuwu, 1969), http://twstudy.iis.sinica.edu.tw/twstatistic50/Edu.htm.

20. For a complete list of school names and year of establishment of each school, see Yu, *Ri ju shiqi Taiwan de nüzi jiaoyu*, 302. Enomoto Miyuki listed each school by prefecture: six in Taihoku Prefecture, six in Taichū Prefecture, and ten in Tainan Prefecture. Most of them had *kasei jogakkō* in their school names. Some had *shokugyō gakkō, joshi kōtō gakuin, saihō gakuen, gigei jogakkō, and kasei senshū gakkō* in their names (Enomoto Miyuki, "Nihon tōchi jiki Taiwan no kasei kyōiku" [master's thesis, Hiroshima Daigaku, 2000], 62–63, https://ir.lib.hiroshima-u.ac.jp/20306/files/24235).

21. *Taiwan kyōiku enkaku shi*, 232–33, 278–80, 282–86. Reading and essay writing lessons were incorporated into the language lesson. Calligraphy was not mentioned in the language lesson, but it was probably part of the writing exercises (*Taiwan kyōiku enkaku shi*, 282, 284–85).

22. It was not always clear who the writer of an article in a periodical is, but most

contributors were colonial officials and educators. Although it was difficult to identify every writer, various viewpoints on "good wife, wise mother" existed in Taiwan. The author's name and language of the article, and the writer's job title, if known, are identified in the discussions followed to map out the viewpoints of Japanese and Taiwanese who engaged in this discourse on "good wife, wise mother."

23. A sample article in which the term "good wife, wise mother" was applied to Japanese secondary schoolgirls is Fukyū sei, "Rongi jogakusei (shita)," *Taiwan nichinichi shimpō*, September 8, 1905.

24. Yu, *Ri ju shiqi Taiwan de nüzi jiaoyu*, 43, 45.

25. Tanahashi Gentarō, "Shufu to kagaku," *Taiwan kyōiku*, no. 187 (January 1918): 63.

26. Uno does not indicate what year (Uno, "Womanhood, War, and Empire," 503).

27. The organization, the Educational Association of Taiwan (Taiwan Kyōikukai), published this periodical every two to three months from July 1901 to 1902, and then every month until 1943. In December 1912, the journal was renamed *Taiwan kyōiku* (Education of Taiwan). The Educational Association of Taiwan focused on "teaching the Japanese language to the natives" and the "advancement of the Formosan education" by publicizing its views, studying education, surveying issues of education, sponsoring public meetings or lectures on education and "Teachers' Training extension meetings," and "publishing educational periodicals and some other books and pamphlets related to education" ("A Review of Educational Work in Formosa, 1916," reprinted in *Nihon shokuminchi kyōiku seisaku shiryō shūsei, Taiwan hen dai 1-kan*, ed. Abe Hiroshi [Tokyo: Ryūkei Shosha, 2007], 99–100). Educators dominated its membership, and the membership increased with the number of schools, from 215 members in December 1901 to nearly 13,000 members in November 1940, including educators from Japanese schools in mainland China ("Kai'in meibo," *Taiwan kyōikukai zasshi*, no. 3 [December 1901]: 87–91; "Taiwan kyōikukai kai'in meibo," *Taiwan kyōiku*, November 1940, 71–72). "Tsūshin," *Taiwan kyōikukai zasshi*, no. 2 (July 1901): 78.

28. Zhou Dengxin, "Hontō joshi kyōiku no fushin naru genin," *Taiwan kyōiku*, no. 158 (June 1915): 45.

29. Zhou, "Hontō joshi kyōiku no fushin naru genin," 45.

30. Language and essay writing, reading, and calligraphy lessons were essentially the teaching of the Japanese language. The required weekly hours of instruction for the language and essay writing course were: five hours for first- and second-graders; six hours for third- and fourth-graders; and nine hours for fifth- and sixth-graders. The required hours of instruction of reading were twelve hours for all grade levels. The required hours of instruction for calligraphy were four hours for first- to fourth-graders; and two hours for fifth- and sixth-graders (*Taiwan kyōiku enkaku shi*, 233).

31. *Taiwan kyōiku enkaku shi*, 229, 231.

32. *Shotōka kokugo VIII*, lesson 2.

33. Tai, "*Kokugo* and Colonial Education in Taiwan," 507.

34. The publication years of the first edition of textbooks were incorrectly converted as 1900 to 1902; the correct years are 1901 to 1903 (Chou Wan-yao and Xu Peixian, "Taiwan gong xuexiao zhidu, jiaoke he jiaokeshu zongshuo," *Taiwan fengwu* 53, no. 4 [November 2003]: 139).

35. No furigana was included for her name, and thus I adopt the Japanese reading "gyoku," meaning precious stone or pearl.

36. *Taiwan kyōka-yō-sho kokumin yomihon VI*, lesson 16.

37. *Taiwan kyōka-yō-sho kokumin yomihon VI*, lesson 16.

38. *Taiwan kyōka-yō-sho kokumin yomihon VII*, lesson 12.

39. The Chinese character is accompanied by the furigana as "kao," but the actual reading of the character should be "kō," meaning aroma. *Kōgakkō yō kokumin yomihon IV*, lesson 9.

40. *Kōgakkō yō kokugo yomihon dai ichi shu IV*, lesson 20.

41. *Kōgakkō yō kokumin yomihon IV*, lessons 18–19; *Kōgakkō yō kokugo yomihon dai ichi shu IV*, lessons 6–7.

42. *Kōgakkō yō kokugo yomihon dai ichi shu IV*, lesson 7.

43. *Taiwan kyōka-yō-sho kokumin yomihon VII*, lesson 17.

44. Ming-cheng Miriam Lo, *Doctors within Borders: Profession, Ethnicity, and Modernity in Colonial Taiwan* (Berkeley: University of California Press, 2002), 5, ProQuest Ebook Central.

45. Michael Shiyung Liu, *Prescribing Colonization: The Role of Medical Practices and Policies in Japan-Ruled Taiwan, 1895–1945* (Ann Arbor, MI: Association for Asian Studies, 2009), 3, 5, 15.

46. *Taiwan kyōka-yō-sho kokumin yomihon III*, lesson 5.

47. In the section "Islanders' Evil Practices," Katō Harumasa listed uncleanliness as the first harmful practice (Jp. *akushūkan*), followed by opium smoking and foot-binding (Katō Harumasa, "Kōgakkō shūshin ka kyōju oite no zakkan," *Taiwan kyikukai zasshi*, no. 104 [November 1910]: 38).

48. For more detail on how the Japanese implemented hygiene campaigns in the colonies, see Ruth Rogaski, *Hygienic Modernity: Meanings of Health and Disease in Treaty-Port China* (Berkeley: University of California Press, 2004).

49. Akiyoshi Otoji, "Fujin no katsudō wa nani wo haikei to senupanaranu ka—ōkaji ga okuruzo himodo no yōjin wo negaimasu," *Fujin to katei* 1, no. 1 (December 1919): 21.

50. Tanaka Yujirō, "Shin kyōiku wo uketa hontō fujin," *Fujin to katei* 1, no. 2 (January 1920): 8.

51. Yu, *Ri ju shiqi Taiwan de nüzi jiaoyu*, 286.

52. I could not find Cai's current job title but found that he earned a primary school teaching certificate in 1915, which meant he completed the teacher-training program and was likely teaching at the time of writing ("Jiaoyuan mianxu zhuang shouyu [Dai Wenzhang (Li Yongchang, Cai Shitian, Yang Azong, Pan Yuanzhen, Su Dìng, Zhang

Qiming, Yang Chong'an, Fan Yapi, Song Linyou cang)]," in "Taishō 4-nen Taiwan sōtoku kōbunsho hensan towa hozon dai 64-kan kyōiku," *Taiwan zongdu fu dang'an: Zongdu fu gongwen leizuan*, archived at the Guoshi Guan Taiwan Wenxian Guan [Taiwan Historica], no. 00002404005, accessed May 1, 2023, https://onlinearchives.th.gov.tw/index.php?act=Display/image/1364389_gLvWaE#0JV5).

53. Cai Shitian, "Jiating jiaoyu," *Kanbun Taiwan kyōiku*, no. 186 (December 1917): 1.

54. Partha Chatterjee, *The Nation and Its Fragments: Colonial and Postcolonial Histories* (Princeton, NJ: Princeton University Press, 1993), 6, 8, 120, 126, 128.

55. Takagi Heirarō, "Hontō joji no kyōiku ni oite," *Taiwan kyōikukai zasshi*, no. 70 (January 1908): 18, 21. Takagi taught at various primary schools in Taichung and Hsinchu. His article lists his location as Hsinchu, which implies he was working at the said school listed on *Taiwan jinbutsu shi*, and specifically a document titled "Shizangan shi," 313.

56. Takagi Heirarō, "Hontō joji no kyōiku ni oite shōzen," *Taiwan kyōikukai zasshi* no. 71 (February 1908): 35.

57. Joan Judge, *The Precious Raft of History: The Past, the West, and the Woman Question in China* (Stanford, CA: Stanford University Press, 2022), 23, 115, 189.

58. I could not find information on Seosan's background (Seosan Gyodō, "Nüxue biyao shuo," *Taiwan kyōikukai zasshi kanbun*, no. 79 [October 1908]: 11–13).

59. The information on Dai Liang's workplace comes from the 1919 list of members of the Educational Association of Taiwan ("Kai'in meibo," *Taiwan kyōiku*, December 1919, 10).

60. Dai Liang, "Nüzi jiaoyu lun xu qian," *Kanbun Taiwan kyōiku*, no. 199 (January 1919): 4–5.

61. Yang Jiyin earned a primary school teaching certificate in 1915 and was assigned to teach at a primary school ("Jiaoyuan mianxu zhuang shou yu [Yang Jiyin] [1915-05-01], in "Taishō 4-nen Taiwan sōtoku kōbunsho hensan towa hozon dai 67-kan kyōiku," *Taiwan zongdu fu dang'an: Zongdu fu gongwen leizuan*, archived at the Guoshi Guan Taiwan Wenxian Guan, no. 00002407010, accessed May 1, 2023, https://onlinearchives.th.gov.tw/index.php?act=Display/image/1364390Dj=K84P#Osf9). Yang Jiyin, "Nüzi jiaoyu lun," *Kanbun Taiwan kyōiku*, no. 204 (May 1919): 3.

62. The article indicates that he lived in Beimen, Tainan, but I could not find further information on Ke Yuancheng's background (Ke Yuancheng, "Quan nüzi jiuxue shuo," *Kanbun Taiwan kyōiku*, no. 144 [April 1914]: 7).

63. *Kōgakkō yō kokumin yomihon I*, 28–29.

64. Taiwanese girls in braids and traditional clothing: lessons 4, 6, and 8 from *Taiwan kyōka-yō-sho kokumin yomihon II*; lessons 2, 6, and 11 from *Kōgakkō yō kokumin yomihon III*. Japanese girls in kimonos and Japanese-style tatami room: lesson 10 from *Taiwan kyōka-yō-sho kokumin yomihon II*.

65. *Taiwan kōgakkō yō kokumin yomihon. Kōgakkō yō kokugo yomihon dai ichi shu*. For further discussion of changes in girls' outward appearance in school language textbooks,

see Chou Wan-yao, "Xieshi yu guifan zhijian—gong xuexiao guoyu duben chahua zhong de Taiwan ren xingxiang," *Taida lishi xuebao* 34 (December 2004): 93–115.

66. Honda Okichi, "Kokugo fukyū nani miniku ue yori mitaru hontō-jin joshi kyōiku," *Taiwan kyōiku*, no. 177 (March 1917): 54.

67. *Fujin to katei* was a monthly magazine published from December 1919 to December 1920 in both Japanese and classical Chinese languages. The journal claimed that its goal was to improve the colonial and family life of both Japanese and Taiwanese residing in Taiwan via the mothers who would benefit from reading this magazine (*Fujin to katei* 1, no. 1 [December 1919] to *Fujin to katei* 2, no. 12 [December 1920]). Yoshikawa Seima, "'Fujin to katei' hakkan ni tsuite" [On the publication of *Women and Family*], *Fujin to katei* 1, no. 1 (December 1919), 3; *Fujin to Katei* 1, no. 1 (December 1919): 86. Yoshikawa Seima, chief editor of *Taiwan kodomo seikai* (Children's world of Taiwan) and *Fujin to katei*, emphasized the necessity of the publication because he presumed that the periodical would help all women, whom he believed to lack intellect, self-awareness, and the ability to reflect on their actions (Yoshikawa, "'Fujin to katei' hakkan ni tsuite," 2). Although it seemed that the periodical sought to include women's voices by searching for "upright" women writers between the ages of eighteen and thirty-five with an educational level of girls' middle school or higher to work for the magazine, it was unclear if it was successful in its effort (*Fujin to katei* 1, no. 1 [December 1919]: 81). Most of its readers and donors were Japanese women. A list of donors can be found in *Fujin to katei* 1, no. 2 (January 1920): 15–16. School enrollment rates suggest that some women, mostly Japanese and few Taiwanese, would be able to read and purchase the journal. It is safe to assume that the majority of the magazine's readers were Japanese. Nevertheless, the appearance of a Chinese section starting in April 1920 suggests that the journal attempted to appeal to Chinese intellectuals, especially those who were trained in classical Chinese but not literate in Japanese (*Fujin to katei* 2, no. 4 [April 1920]).

68. Hiromatsu Yoshiomi, "Hontō fujin to katei seikatsu no kaizen wa ikani subeki?," *Fujin to katei* 1, no. 2 (January 1920): 62.

69. Tanaka, "Shin kyōiku wo uketa hontō fujin no katagata ni," 4–5.

70. I could not find information on Mishima's background. Mishima Namaroku, "Jia ting ri chang wei sheng," *Fujin to katei* 2, no. 8 (September 1920): 71–73; Mishima Namaroku, "Jiating richang weisheng er," *Fujin to katei*. 2, no. 9 (October 1920): 64–65.

71. Liu, *Prescribing Colonization*, 41–42, 45, 56–58.

72. Tanaka Yujirō, "Bendao furen you xin shou jiaoyu zhi ren," *Fujin to katei* 2, no. 4 (April 1920): 74–76.

73. Wu Wenxing, "Ri ju shiqi Taiwan de fangzu duanfa yundong," originally published in *Zhongyang yanjiu yuan minzu xue yanjiu suo zhuankan yizhong zhi shiliu*, reprinted in *Zhongguo funü shi lunwen ji di er ji*, ed. Li Youning and Zhang Yufa (Taibei: Taiwan Shangwu Yinshu Guan, 1988), 466, 471, 486–87, 493–94, 499–500.

74. Bhabha, *The Location of Culture*, 96, 105.

75. Bhabha, *The Location of Culture*, 118–19.

76. Zheng Fengqin, "Ri ju shiqi xin nüxing de zai xian fenxi: Yi meiti jishi yu xiaoshuo chuangzuo wei zhongxin" (master's thesis, Guoli Qinghua Daxue, 2008), 23–24, https://hdl.handle.net/11296/48nau3.

77. *Taiwan kyōka-yō-sho kokumin yomihon IV*, lessons 12 and 13.

78. *Taiwan kyōka-yō-sho kokumin yomihon VI*, lesson 14.

79. For example, see Leo Ching, "Savage Construction and Civility Making: The Musha Incident and Aboriginal Representations in Colonial Taiwan," *Positions: East Asia Cultures Critique* 8, no. 3 (January 12, 2000); and human exhibits in Kristen Ziomek, *Lost Histories: Recovering the Lives of Japan's Colonial Peoples* (Cambridge, MA: Harvard University Asia Center, 2019).

80. Dai Liang, "Nüzi jiaoyu lun xu qian," *Kanbun Taiwan kyōiku*, no. 201 (February 1919): 3–4.

81. Zhang graduated from Taihoku National Language School and taught at a primary school and later at Shōka (Changhua) Girls' Middle School. He later worked for two newspapers. He quit his job and focused on writing in 1927 ("Zhang Shuzi," *Guojia wenhua jiyi ku*, Ministry of Culture of Taiwan, accessed June 13, 2023, https://memory.culture.tw/Home/Detail?Id=606608&IndexCode=Culture_People).

82. Zhang Shuzi, "Jiating jianghua (xu qian)," *Kanbun Taiwan kyōiku*, no. 270 (December 1924): 2.

83. "Arita Otomatsu (8th ed. [July 1928])," *Historical Information for Japanese Studies Jinjikoshinroku (who's who) Database*, Nagoya University Graduate School of Law, accessed March 8, 2024, https://jahis.law.nagoya-u.ac.jp/who/docs/who8-964.

84. Arita Otomatsu, "Jiyū ren'ai? Ryōsai kenbo ka," *Taiwan nichinichi shimpō*, November 25, 1925, 6.

85. "Kindai fujin to teisō no yōgo keizai teki seikatsu ishiki no henten," *Taiwan nichinichi shimpō*, January 19, 1931, 6.

86. "Kindai fujin to teisō no yōgo," 6.

87. Chapter 2 discusses the "new woman" and the "modern girl" in more detail.

88. Kōra's original name was Kōra Tomi, and her pen name was Kōra Tomiko. "Kōra Tomi [1896–1993]," Webcat Plus, National Institute of Informatics, accessed May 1, 2023, http://webcatplus.nii.ac.jp/webcatplus/details/creator/35554.html.

89. Kōra Tomiko, "Gakkō kyōiku dai ichi shugi wo shijo wo sokoneru ganmei na ryōsai kenbo shugi wo suteyo Kōra Tomiko on'nashi dan, *Taiwan nichinichi shimpō*, September 5, 1933, 6.

90. Kōra, "Gakkō kyōiku dai ichi shugi wo shijo wo sokoneru."

91. Theodore F. Cook Jr., "'Making "Soldiers': The Imperial Army and the Japanese Man in Meiji Society and State," and Donald Roden, "Thoughts on the Early Meiji Gentleman," both in *Gendering Modern Japanese History*, ed. Barbara Molony and Kath-

leen Uno. Harvard East Asian Monographs 251 (Cambridge, MA: Harvard University Asia Center, 2005), 259–94, 61–98. "Fukuzawa Yukichi," in *Portraits of Modern Japanese Historical Figures*.

92. Published monthly from May 1934 to June 1939, *Taiwan fujinkai* was founded and edited by Kakinuma Fumiaki, who had a background in journalism and was concerned with issues pertaining to women, children, and Buddhism. Kakinuma sought financial support from the political, financial, and industrial sectors, which resulted in the restructuring of the publication company, Taiwan Women, Inc., which ended up having forty-nine shareholders, including twenty-five Japanese women and two Taiwanese men. The company created ten branches all over Taiwan, one in Dalian, and one in Tokyo, with four Japanese women and eight Taiwanese men, out of twenty people, who had served as the branch manager. Readers of *Taiwan fujinkai* consisted of Japanese women living in Taiwan and upper-middle-class Taiwanese women. The magazine did well, and by December 1935, a total of 5,300 copies of the magazine were published monthly in Taiwan, Japan, Korea, and Manchuria, compared to 8,687 copies of the much older periodical *Taiwan kyōiku*. But its circulation decreased drastically in the subsequent years, and publication stopped altogether in 1939 (Zheng Hanyun, "Zhimin di Taiwan de funü zazhi *Taiwan furen jie* zhi yanjiu [1934–1939]" [master's thesis, Guoli Taiwan Shifan Daxue, 2017], 1, 3, 6–10, 16–24, https://hdl.handle.net/11296/w49yn7).

93. Suzuki Yuzusaburō, "Honshi nitaisuru kibō narabi ni chūmo," *Taiwan fujinkai*, May 1934, 40.

94. Kobayashi Jun'ichi was assigned to work as the police medical officer in Taihoku government ("Kobayashi Jun'ichi Taihoku chō keisatsu i nin-su," *Guojia wenhua jiyi ku*, Ministry of Culture of Taiwan, accessed May 1, 2023, https://memory.culture.tw/Home /Detail?Id=00001435066&IndexCode=th).

95. Kobayashi Jun'ichi, "Honda shi cho *Haha no Ai* wo yomite," *Taiwan fujinkai*, August 1937, 43.

96. Tsurumi, *Colonial Education in Taiwan*, 80, 85, 99.

97. *Taiwan kyōiku enkaku shi*, 361.

98. Chou Wan-yao, and Xu Peixian, "Taiwan gong xuexiao zhidu, jiaoke he jiaokeshu zongshuo," 127.

99. Chou Wan-yao, *Hai xing xi de niandai—Riben zhimin tongzhi moqi Taiwan shi lunji* (Taibei: Xunchen Wenhua Gongsi, 2003), 226.

100. Cheng Tun-jen argues that Taiwan follows the metropole-colony economic model of the metropole as the industrialized base and the colony as the agricultural base. Although camphor oil and tea were Taiwan's leading exports in the first decade of Japanese colonization, rice and sugar replaced them as the main exports to the metropole. Chemical fertilizer, metal, textile, and industrial chemical industries developed, but Taiwan remained a largely agricultural society under Japan (Cheng Tun-jen, "Transforming Taiwan's Economic Structure in the 20th Century," *China Quarterly*, no. 165 [2001]: 21–22, http://www.jstor.org/stable/3451104).

101. The article did not provide the birth year of Zhang Hongchou. However, it reported that Zhang was a sixteen-year-old in 1908. Her husband died in 1927. This meant that she was born in 1892 and was a thirty-five-year-old in 1927.

102. "Taiwan bunka wo irodoru hontōjin josei (ni) shin jidai ka 'unta' ryōsai kenbo no tenkei Taihoku dai san kōjo no dai senpai Sote wa jūroku sai no on'na kundō wakaki mibōjin Chō-shi Akachū on'na shi," *Taiwan nichinichi shimpō*, May 31, 1930.

103. Kakinuma's quote as cited in Zheng Hanyun, "Zhimin di Taiwan de funü zazhi *Taiwan furen jie* zhi yanjiu (1934–1939)," 7.

104. I could not find information on Miyazaki Naosuke's background (Miyazaki Naosuke, "Naichijin fujin no kotoba nokohi ni tsuit," *Taiwan fujinkai*, July 1937, 7).

105. Miyazaki Naosuke, "Naichijin fujin no kotoba nokohi ni tsuite," 9–13.

2. EMBRACING EDUCATED GIRLS AND WOMEN

1. Lin Zhimei, "Yang Qianhe," in *Ri ju yilai Taiwan nü zuojia xiaoshuo xuandu (shang)*, ed. Qiu Guifen (Taibei: Nü Shu Wenhua Shi Ye Youxian Gongsi, 2001), 65; Qiu Zuyin, "Taiwan shou wei nü jizhe Yang Qianhe gaobie zhuan qi rensheng," *Zhongguo shibao*, October 28, 2011, https://web.archive.org/web/20111031162657/http://news.chinatimes .com/reading/110513/112011102800538.html.

2. Yang Qianhe, "Hua kai shijie" (Riwen yuanzuo: Hana saku kisetsu), in *Ri ju yilai Taiwan nü zuojia xiaoshuo xuandu (shang)*, ed. Qiu Guifen (Taibei: Nü Shu Wenhua Shiye Youxian Gongsi, 2001), 73.

3. "Wu Zhuoliu," *Taiwan wenxue guan xianshang ziliao pingtai*, accessed June 14, 2023, https://db.nmtl.gov.tw/site4/s6/writerinfo?id=458.

4. Jinling University is the Ginling Women's College, a famous women's mission college in China (see Jin Feng, *The Making of a Family Saga: Ginling College* [Albany: State University of New York Press, 2009]).

5. Wu Zhuoliu, *Orphan of Asia*, trans. Ioannis Mentzas (New York: Columbia University Press, 2006), 124.

6. Wu Zhuoliu, *Orphan of Asia*, 130, 138–40.

7. Lin Zhimei, "Yang Qianhe," 65; Yang Qianhe, "Hua kai shijie."

8. Wu Zhuoliu, *Orphan of Asia*, 27–30, 53, 59–60, 114–24.

9. Oral histories of women born in the early colonial period were scant because there were fewer educated girls than in the middle and later periods. It was in the middle colonial period, starting in the 1920s, that the first generation of Japanese-educated Taiwanese emerged to finance a periodical dedicated to Taiwanese issues and to write fiction to express their views.

10. Yu, *Ri ju shiqi Taiwan de nüzi jiaoyu*, 286.

11. I did not find sources or studies that explain why the number increased in 1916.

12. Yu, *Ri ju shiqi Taiwan de nüzi jiaoyu*, 286; Tsurumi, *Colonial Education in Taiwan*, 113.

13. *Taiwan kyōiku enkaku shi*, 248.

14. Many accounts in these two volumes mention this reason to explain why they or their mothers received little or no education: Jiang Wenyu, ed., *Xiaoshi zhong de Taiwan ama* (Taibei: Yushan, 1995); and Jiang Wenyu, ed., *Amu de gushi* (Taibei: Meta Media International, 1998).

15. "Nüzi jiaoyu de quexian," *Taiwan minbao*, no. 202 (April 1928): 6.

16. Yu, *Ri ju shiqi Taiwan de nüzi jiaoyu*, 93–94, 97, 288, 290.

17. There were fewer schools in the countryside than in the cities, and thus an urban-rural gap existed. For example, 32.73 percent of Taiwanese girls living in the cities, 19.05 percent of girls living in towns, and 10.41 percent of girls in rural areas enrolled in school in 1928 (Yu, *Ri ju shiqi Taiwan de nüzi jiaoyu*, 287).

18. Ko Ikujo, *Kindai Taiwan josei shi: Nihon no shokumin tōchi to "Shinjosei" no tanjō* (Tokyo: Keisō Shobō, 2001), 140.

19. Ko, *Kindai Taiwan Josei shi*, 140–43.

20. Chen Peifeng *"Dōka" no dōshō imu*, 19.

21. Chen Peifeng *"Dōka" no dōshō imu*, 24–26, 29–31.

22. For example, upper- and middle-class Taiwanese demanded that the colonial government in Taiwan open middle schools for Taiwanese students. The colonial government agreed to their demands and set up Taichū Middle School (Jp. Taichū Chūgakkō) for boys in 1915 to appease these Taiwanese and to slow down the number of Taiwanese studying in Japan, where they were more likely to be exposed to ideas that threatened the colonial authority (Tsurumi, *Japanese Colonial Education in Taiwan*, 69, 79–80, 177–96).

23. Tsurumi, *Japanese Colonial Education in Taiwan*, 192.

24. Tsurumi, *Japanese Colonial Education in Taiwan*, 192, 198–99. For the ideology and activities of these conservative and liberal activists, see Tsurumi, *Japanese Colonial Education in Taiwan*, 180–211.

25. Wu Micha, Huang Zhiwei, and Lin Xinyi, "Taiwan seinen," in *Taiwan shi xiao shidian*, 126; Wu Micha, Huang Zhiwei, and Lin Xinyi, "Taiwan minbao," in *Taiwan shi xiao shidian*, 139; Wu Micha, Huang Zhiwei, and Lin Xinyi, "Taiwan xin minbao," in *Taiwan shi xiao shidian*, 142.

26. Ko, *Kindai Taiwan Josei shi*, 138. Ko Ikujo describes two types of ideology on female education among Taiwanese intellectuals before and after the 1920s. One type was the ideology of "governing the family makes a prosperous nation" (Jp. *seika kōkoku ron*). The "women's liberation ideology" (Jp. *kaihō ron*) was another ideology promoted mainly by Taiwanese men with Japanese education who studied in Japan in the 1920s (Ko, *Kindai Taiwan Josei shi*, 137–51).

27. Doris T. Chang, *Women's Movements in Twentieth-Century Taiwan* (Urbana: University of Illinois Press, 2009), 23.

28. In the inaugural issue of *Taiwan seinen* in 1920, a contributing writer emphasized the importance of writing Taiwanese literature in the vernacular form to reform society,

NOTES TO PAGES 64–68

an idea supported by other contributors in later issues of the journal. Zhang Wojun, who studied in Beijing and became an editor of *Taiwan minbao* in 1924, also called on Taiwanese intellectuals to write in vernacular Taiwanese Hoklo (Xu Junya, ed., *Ri zhi shiqi Taiwan xiaoshuo xuandu* [Taibei: Wanjuanlo Tushu Gufen Youxian Gongsi, 2003], 2–5).

29. While I won't analyze articles using the liberal–conservative lens because both factions agreed on the necessity of educating girls and women, I will make note of which faction likely influenced certain ideas to identify Japanese colonial official and Chinese progressive influences on *Taiwan minbao*.

30. Liang Qichao (1897), "On Women's Education," in *The Birth of Chinese Feminism: Essential Texts in Transnational Theory*, ed. Rebecca Karl, Dorothy Ko, and Lydia Liu (New York: Columbia University Press, 2013), 194.

31. Jin, *Higashi ajia no ryōsai kenbo ron*, 3, 6, 239–40.

32. Yang Cui, *Ri ju shiqi Taiwan funü jiefang yundong: Yi Taiwan minbao wei fenxi changyu, 1920–1932* (Taibei Shi: Shibao Wenhua Chuban Qiye Youxian Gongsi, 1993), 460.

33. In addition to education for girls and women, *Taiwan minbao* advocated these three main issues in the 1920s: a ban on prostitution; romantic love as the prerequisite for marriage; and women's economic independence (Hu, "The 'Modern Woman' in Colonial Taiwan: The Intellectuals' Construction in *Taiwan minbao*, 1924–1927" [master's thesis, University of Chicago, 2006], 41–42, 49).

34. Yang Cui, *Ri ju shiqi Taiwan funü jiefang yundong*, 456; for a list of topics Taiwanese women writers covered in the journal, see 521–25; and for information on the hometown of, educational background of, and topics written by Taiwanese men, see 449–54.

35. Yang Cui, *Ri ju shiqi Taiwan funü jiefang yundong*, 460.

36. Chen Ying, "Nüzi jiaoyu zhi biyao," *Taiwan seinen* 1, no. 2 (August 1920): 19–20.

37. "Xiwang nüzi jiaoyu de puji dangshe nüzi shifan," *Taiwan minbao* 2, no. 20 (October 1924): 1.

38. Ko, *Kindai Taiwan josei shi*, 127, 151, 159.

39. Ko Ikujo, "Shokuminchi Taiwan no 'modangāru' genshō to fasshon no seiji-ka," in *Modangāru to shokuminchi teki kindai—Higashiajia ni okeru teikoku shihon jendā*, ed. Itō Ruri, Sakamoto Hiroko, and Tani Barlow (Tokyo: Iwanami Shobō, 2010), 261, 263–65.

40. Laurel Rasplica Rodd, "Yasano Akiko and the Taisho Debate over the 'New Woman,'" in *Recreating the Japanese Women, 1600–1945*, ed. Gail Lee Bernstein (Berkeley: University of California Press, 1991), 175–76, 190, 193–94.

41. Miriam Silverberg, "The Modern Girl as Militant," in *Recreating the Japanese Women, 1600–1945*, ed. Gail Lee Bernstein (Berkeley: University of California Press, 1991), 239.

42. Silverberg, "The Modern Girl as Militant," 240, 242, 246, 250.

43. Silverberg, "The Modern Girl as Militant," 259.

44. Silverberg, "The Modern Girl as Militant," 258–59.

45. Alys Eve Weinbaum et al., "The Modern Girl as Heuristic Device," in *The Modern*

Girl around the World: Consumption, Modernity, and Globalization, ed. Weinbaum et al. (Durham, NC: Duke University Press, 2008), 1–2, ProQuest Ebook Central.

46. Jiyoung Suh, "The 'New Woman' and the Topography of Modernity in Colonial Korea," *Korean Studies* 37 (2013): 13, 18–20, http://www.jstor.org/stable/24575275.

47. Suh, "The 'New Woman' and the Topography of Modernity in Colonial Korea," 22.

48. Suh, "The 'New Woman' and the Topography of Modernity in Colonial Korea," 25.

49. Yang Cui, *Ri ju shiqi Taiwan funü jiefang yundong*, 458.

50. Ko, *Kindai Taiwan josei shi*, 190.

51. Lin Shuangsui, "Watashi no Taiwan fujo kan," *Taiwan seinen* 1, no. 4 (October 1920): 43–44.

52. "Xiwang nüzi jiaoyu de puji," *Taiwan minbao* 2, no. 20 (October 1924): 1.

53. Yu, *Ri ju shiqi Taiwan de nüzi jiaoyu*, 225, 231.

54. Yang Cui, *Ri ju shiqi Taiwan funü jiefang yundong*, 24.

55. Chang, *Women's Movements in Twentieth-Century Taiwan*, 17, 20.

56. By focusing on women "students and professional trainees in missionary schools and as educators, professionals, and activists" in East Asian societies, Garrett L. Washington argues that Christianity played an important role in redefining women's role as women "took advantage of distinct new opportunities and connections provided by Christianity. . . . Their efforts also provided momentum for new movements aimed at truly improving women's lives" (Garrett L. Washington, "Editor's Introduction," in *Christianity and the Modern Woman in East Asia*, ed. Washington [Leiden, the Netherlands: Brill, 2018], 5–6). For influence of a Christian school on Chinese women, see Feng, *The Making of a Family Saga: Ginling College*. To read about Korean women, see Hyaeweol Choi, *Gender and Mission Encounters in Korea: New Women, Old Ways*, Seoul-California Series in Korean Studies, vol. 1 (Berkeley: University of California Press, 2009).

57. For policies and restrictions on private schools in Taiwan, refer to Tsurumi, *Japanese Colonial Education in Taiwan*, 34–38. The Presbyterian Church from Canada established Tamsui Girls' Academy in 1884 and Tamsui Middle School for boys in 1914. The Presbyterian Church from England established the Tainan Presbyterian Girls' Academy in 1887 and a middle school for boys in 1885. Some Catholic priests established Seishū (Jinshou) Girls' Academy (Blessed Imelda's School) in 1916. Information comes from table 5.1 in Komagome Takeshi, "Dai ni ji Taiwan kyōikurei ka ni okeru shiritsu gakkō—'Shiritsu chūgakkō kōtō jogakkō setsuritsu ninka hyōjun' seitei ikisatsu," in *Chōsen Taiwan ni okeru shokuminchi shihai no seido kikō seisaku ni kansuru sōgō-teki kenkyū Heisei 13-nendo–15-nendo Kagaku kenkyūhi hojokin kenkyū seika hōkoku-sho* (May 2004): 125.

58. Jian Ru, "Furen can zheng yundong," *Taiwan minbao* 1, no. 1 (April 1923): 11.

59. Jian Ru, "Furen can zheng yundong," 11.

60. "Geng qi liang de qi geng qi xian de mu," *Taiwan minbao* 4, no. 99 (April 1926): 12.

61. "Za lu nüxiao chouwen," *Taiwan minbao* 1, no. 10 (November 1923): 5–6.

62. "Jiaoshi nongxi nü xuesheng zhi chouwen," *Taiwan minbao* 2, no. 14 (August 1924): 9.

63. "Shiotome kōgakkō no kaibun: On'na seito o tane ni shite, kai shashin o totta to ka," *Taiwan minbao*, no. 315 (May 1930): 12.

64. "Kelian de nü xuesheng! Bei ta jiaoshi roulin zhencao? Dangdi zhumin fanyan zeze," *Taiwan minbao* 11, no. 301 (February 1930): 7.

65. "Gao nü ne? Xia nü ne?," *Taiwan minbao* 2, no. 15 (August 1924): 13.

66. Ou Zongzhi, *Zou chu lishi de beiqing: Taiwan xiaoshuo pinglun ji wenxue pinglun ji* 62 (Banqiao: Taibei Xian Zhengfu Wenhua Ju Chuban, 2002), 25–28, 245.

67. Yang Cui, "Hai de nü'er 'Wu ji mu'—Geming nü doushi Ye Tao," in *Ama de gushi*, ed. Jiang Wenyu (Taibei: Yushan She Chuban, 1995), 36–43, 45, 49.

68. Yang Cui, "*Ai de jiejing* dao du," in *Ri ju yilai Taiwan nüzuo jia xiaoshuo xuandu (shang)*, ed. Qiu Guifen (Taibei: Nü Shu Wenhua Shiye Youxian Gongsi, 2001), 63.

69. Ye Tao, "Ai de jiejing," in *Ri ju yilai Taiwan nü zuojia xiaoshuo xuandu (shang)*, ed. Qiu Guifen (Taibei: Nü Shu Wenhua Shiye Youxian Gongsi, 2001), 54–59.

70. Long Yingzong, "Zhi you mugua shu de xiaozhen," trans. Zhang Liangze, in *Ri zhi shiqi Taiwan xiaoshuo xuandu*, ed. Xu Junya (Taibei: Wanjuanlo Tushu Gufen Youxian Gongsi, 2003), 260–62, 271–73.

71. Xu Junya, *Ri zhi shiqi Taiwan xiaoshuo xuandu*, 251–52.

72. Xu Junya, *Taiwan wenxue luncong: Cong xiandai dao dangdai* (Taibei: Shida Shuyuan Youxian Gongsi, 1997), 52–54.

73. Yang Qianhe, "Hua kai shijie," 70–73, 80–81, 84.

74. Yang Qianhe, "Hua kai shijie," 78–80, 92–93.

75. Xu Junya, *Taiwan wenxue luncong*, 74.

76. Xu Junya, *Taiwan wenxue luncong*, 73.

77. Xu Junya, *Taiwan wenxue luncong*, 71–72.

78. Xu Junya, *Taiwan wenxue luncong*, 71–72.

79. "Wu Zhuoliu," *Taiwan da baike quanshu* (Wenhua bu), accessed August 6, 2018, http://nrch.culture.tw/twpedia.aspx?id=2219.

80. Wu Zhuoliu, *Orphan of Asia*, 22, 32, 39–42, 51.

81. Wu Zhuoliu, *Orphan of Asia*, 28, 52–53, 99.

82. Wu Zhuoliu, *Orphan of Asia*, 124–30.

83. Wu Zhuoliu, *Orphan of Asia*, 128.

3. MOBILIZING FOR THE WAR

1. Xu Xianxian, interview by Fang Yu Hu, Taipei, Taiwan, July 9, 2012. When I cite interviews, Taipei includes both Taipei City and New Taipei City because the border of Taipei City expanded overtime and people often moved between the two cities. I don't refer them as the "greater Taipei area" because Keelung is included in it.

2. The concept of the "total war" meant that the line between soldiers and civilians blurred as all participated in the war to some degree (Belinda Davis, "Experience, Identity, and Memory: The Legacy of World War I," *Journal of Modern History* 75, no. 1 [2003]: 117, https://doi.org/10.1086/377750).

3. Joshua S. Goldstein, *War and Gender: How Gender Shapes the War System and Vice Versa* (Cambridge: Cambridge University Press, 2001), 6.

4. Goldstein, *War and Gender*, 249–50.

5. Sabine Frühstück, *Playing War: Children and the Paradoxes of Modern Militarism in Japan* (Oakland: University of California Press, 2017), 6, 35, 53.

6. Louise Young, *Japan's Total Empire: Manchuria and the Culture of Wartime Imperialism* (Berkeley: University of California Press, 1998), 4, 8, 11–13.

7. The National Eugenics Law (1940) and the "Outline for Establishing Population Growth Policy" (effective in 1942) revealed women's reproductive importance in the metropole (Yoshiko Miyake, "Doubling Expectations: Motherhood and Women's Factory Work under State Management in Japan in the 1930s and 1940s," in *Recreating Japanese Women, 1600–1945,* ed. Gail Lee Bernstein [Berkeley: University of California Press, 1991], 267, 277–78).

8. William B. Hauser, "Women and War: The Japanese Film Image," in *Recreating Japanese Women, 1600–1945,* ed. Gail Lee Bernstein (Berkeley: University of California Press, 1991), 297, 300. Thomas Havens showed that the government acted only to "urge" women to work in 1943, without mobilizing them until the formation of women's volunteer labor corps to produce airplanes and other crucial supplies in 1944 (Thomas R. H. Havens, "Women and War in Japan," *American Historical Review* 80, no. 4 [1975]: 921–22).

9. Yang Yahui, "Zhan shi tizhi xia de Taiwan funü (1937–1945): Riben zhimin zhengfu de jiaohua yu dongyuan" (master's thesis, Guoli Qinghua Daxue, 1993), 89, 93, https://hdl.handle.net/11296/xajk35.

10. One typical way to periodize Taiwan's history under Japanese rule is pacification and early establishment (1895–1919), civilian rule (1919–36), and wartime imperial subjectification (1936–45). The governors-general of the first and the last periods were from military backgrounds, either generals or admirals. Admiral Kobayashi Seizō's appointment (1936–40) marked the beginning of the third period. Admiral Hasegawa Kiyoshi (1940–44) and General Andō Rikichi (1944–45) served as the last two governors-general (Huang Zhaotang, *Taiwan zongdu fu*, trans. Huang Yingzhe [Taibei: Ziyou shidai, 1989], 70, 113, 165).

11. Wu Micha, Huang Zhiwei, and Lin Xinyi, "Kobayashi Seizō," in *Taiwan shi xiao shidian*, 151.

12. Wan-yao Chou, "The Kominka Movement in Taiwan and Korea: Comparisons and Interpretations," in *The Japanese Wartime Empire, 1931–1945,* ed. Peter Duus, Ramon H. Myers, and Mark R. Peattie (Princeton, NJ: Princeton University Press, 1996), 41; Hui-yu Caroline Ts'ai, "Total War, Labor Drafts, and Colonial Administration: Wartime

Mobilization in Taiwan (1936–1945)," in *Asian Labor in the Wartime Japanese Empire*, ed. Paul H. Kratoska (New York: M. E. Sharpe, 2005), 105.

13. Seiji Shirane, *Imperial Gateway: Colonial Taiwan and Japan's Expansion in South China and Southeast Asia, 1895–1945* (Ithaca, NY: Cornell University Press, 2022), 130, http://www.jstor.org/stable/10.7591/j.ctv310vk5n.

14. Ching, *Becoming "Japanese,"* 94, 97.

15. Cai Jintang, *Zhanzheng tizhi xia de Taiwan* (Taibei: Richuang She Wenhua, 2006), 16–17.

16. Cai, *Zhanzheng tizhi xia de Taiwan*, 17–18.

17. Ching, *Becoming "Japanese,"* 104.

18. Takashi Fujitani, *Race for Empire: Koreans as Japanese and Japanese as Americans during World War II* (Berkeley: University of California Press, 2011), 12, 27.

19. Fujitani, *Race for Empire*, 17, 25, 27.

20. Scholars often discuss military civilian employees alongside military porters. Chou Wan-yao explained that the nature of the civilian employees was top secret, and thus their records are not accessible (Chou Wan-yao, *Hai xing xi de niandai*, 68, 156).

21. Cai, *Zhanzheng tizhi xia de Taiwan*, 103–6; Ts'ai, "Total War, Labor Drafts, and Colonial Administration," 111–12.

22. Examples of civilian employees: military doctors, pharmacists, medical assistants, nurses, nursing assistants, veterinarians, and personnel who worked to prevent poultry diseases (Cai, *Zhanzheng tizhi xia de Taiwan*, 109).

23. Taiwanese males aged seventeen and older were recruited through the volunteer system, with more than 5,000 army and 16,000 navy recruits. According to a 1973 Japanese official record, a total of 80,433 Taiwanese served on the front line with military status, and 126,750 served as noncombatant personnel (Cai, *Zhanzheng tizhi xia de Taiwan*, 110, 113, 115, 121).

24. Ching, *Becoming "Japanese,"* 104.

25. Miyazaki Seiko, *Shokuminki Taiwan ni okeru seinendan to chiiki no henyō* (Tokyo: Ochanomizu Shobō, 2008), 131–32.

26. Miyazaki, *Shokuminki Taiwan ni okeru seinendan to chiiki no henyō*, 217–18, 345, 360.

27. Chatani, *Nation-Empire*, 142.

28. Chatani, *Nation-Empire*, 145.

29. Chatani, *Nation-Empire*, 152.

30. Chatani, *Nation-Empire*, 158.

31. Chatani, *Nation-Empire*, 15.

32. Ts'ai, "Total War, Labor Drafts, and Colonial Administration," 113.

33. Shu Tokuran (Zhu Delan), *Taiwan sōtokufu to ianfu* (Tokyo: Akashi shoten, 2005), 196–97, 207–11, 214, 216, 218. The colonial government established "comfort stations" in Keelung, Taipei, Chiayi, Tainan, Kaohsiung, and Pingtung, where Japanese, Korean, and Taiwanese women served as military sex slaves (Zhu Delan, *Taiwan wei'anfu* [Taibei: Wunan tushu, 2009], 214–25).

34. Ts'ai, "Total War, Labor Drafts, and Colonial Administration," 109.

35. W. Donald Smith, "Beyond 'The Bridge on the River Kwai': Labor Mobilization in the Greater East Asia Co-Prosperity Sphere," *International Labor and Working-Class History*, no. 58 (2000): 220, http://www.jstor.org/stable/27672681.

36. Janice C. H. Kim, "The Pacific War and Working Women in Late Colonial Korea," *Signs* 33, no. 1 (2007): 89, doi:10.1086/518392.

37. Miyake, "Doubling Expectations," 288.

38. Havens, "Women and War in Japan," 919, 922.

39. Miyake, "Doubling Expectations," 283, 288–89, 292.

40. Kim, "The Pacific War and Working Women in Late Colonial Korea," 96.

41. D'Ann Campbell, "Women in Combat: The World War II Experience in the United States, Great Britain, Germany, and the Soviet Union," *Journal of Military History* 57, no. 2 (1993): 312, 316, 318–20, https://doi.org/10.2307/2944060.

42. Campbell, "Women in Combat," 313–15.

43. Campbell, "Women in Combat," 302, 305–6.

44. Campbell, "Women in Combat," 320–21.

45. Pamela Wakewich and Helen Smith, "The Politics of 'Selective' Memory: Re-Visioning Canadian Women's Wartime Work in the Public Record," *Oral History* 34, no. 2 (2006): 58, http://www.jstor.org/stable/40179897.

46. Jessica Enoch, "There's No Place Like the Childcare Center: A Feminist Analysis of <Home> in the World War II Era," *Rhetoric Review* 31, no. 4 (2012): 422, http://www.jstor.org/stable/41697863.

47. Enoch, "There's No Place Like the Childcare Center," 423.

48. The Japanese state mobilized more than fifteen million nonethnic Japanese during the war (Smith, "Beyond 'The Bridge on the River Kwai,'" 220).

49. Yu Chien-ming, "Ri ju shiqi Taiwan de zhiye funü" (PhD diss., Guoli Taiwan Shifan Daxue, 1995), 32–33; Zheng Xiumei, "Ri zhi shiqi Taiwan funü laodong qun xiang" (master's thesis, Guoli Chenggong Daxue, 2007), 84–85, https://hdl.handle.net/11296/cqt397.

50. Women were working in rice paper, hat, tea, canned pineapple, textile, and tobacco industries before 1927 (Zheng Xiumei, "Ri zhi shiqi Taiwan funü laodong qun xiang," 41, 50–51, 65, 78, 82–83). Educated women worked in jobs ranging from teachers, midwives, physicians, nurses, and pharmacists, to bus conductors, telephone operators, stenographers, accountants, typists, store clerks, and insurance sales agents (Yu, "Ri ju shiqi Taiwan de zhiye funü," 30).

51. Zheng Xiumei, "Ri zhi shiqi Taiwan funü laodong qun xiang," 51, 65, 78.

52. Chou, "Xieshi yu guifan zhijian," 108–9; Chou, *Hai xing xi de niandai*, 220.

53. *Kōgakkō yō kokugo yomihon dai ichi shu IV* (1937–42), lesson 17.

54. *Kōgakkō yō kokugo yomihon dai ichi shu IV* (1937–42), 90.

55. Chou, "The Kominka Movement in Taiwan and Korea," 51–52; Chou, *Hai xing xi de niandai*, 94.

56. *Kokugo IV*, lesson 19.

57. *Kokugo IV*, 85.

58. *Shotōka kokugo I*, lesson 19.

59. *Shotōka kokugo I*, 115.

60. Chou, *Hai xing xi de niandai*, 93–94.

61. *Shotōka kokugo III*, lesson 6.

62. *Shotōka kokugo III*, 32.

63. *Shotōka kokugo V*, lesson 17. Chou, *Hai xing xi de niandai*, 17.

64. Chou, *Hai xing xi de niandai*, 13–14.

65. Chou, "The Kominka Movement in Taiwan and Korea," 45, 48–50, 55, 61–63.

66. Leo Ching cites Tomiyama Ichirō, who coined the term *discipline* (Jp: *kiritsu*) to describe the "materialization" of the ideology of Okinawans "becoming Japanese" (Ching, *Becoming "Japanese,"* 90).

67. Xu Kuidi, interview by Fang Yu Hu, Yunlin, Taiwan, September 20, 2012; Ying Xinrui, interview by Fang Yu Hu, Taipei, Taiwan, April 9, 2013.

68. Lin Xianyan, interview by Fang Yu Hu, Taipei, Taiwan, June 28, 2012.

69. John W. Dower, *War without Mercy: Race & Power in the Pacific War* (New York: Pantheon, 1986), 250.

70. Dower, *War without Mercy*, 43–44, 245–46.

71. Eric J. Johnson, "Under Ideological Fire: Illustrated Wartime Propaganda for Children," in *Under Fire: Childhood in the Shadow of War*, ed. Elizabeth Goodenough and Andrea Immel (Detroit, MI: Wayne State University Press, 2008), 74.

72. Haruko Taya Cook, "Women's Deaths as Weapons of War in Japan's 'Final Battle,'" in *Gendering Modern Japanese History*, ed. Barbara Molony and Kathleen Uno, Harvard East Asian Monographs 251 (Cambridge, MA: Harvard University Asia Center, 2005), 328, 345–46.

73. Yu Chien-ming, "Ri zhi shiqi Taiwan xuexiao nüzi tiyu de fazhan," *Zhongyang yanjiu yuan jindai shi yanjiu suo jikan* 33 (2000): 13–14.

74. Xu Peixian, *Zhimin di Taiwan de jindai xuexiao* (Taibei: Yuanliu Chuban She, 2005), 207.

75. Yu, "Ri zhi shiqi Taiwan xuexiao nüzi tiyu de fazhan," 27.

76. Yu Chien-ming has found that students at Girls' Attached School in 1898 did the following simple exercises: team formation, singing, and games for thirty minutes because many girls had bound feet and could not stand for an extended period of time (Yu, *Ri ju shiqi Taiwan de nüzi jiaoyu*, 115).

77. Xu Peixian, *Zhimin di Taiwan de jindai xuexiao*, 301.

78. The colonial government was undoubtedly influenced by ideas from the metropole. Naruse Jinzō, founder of Japan Women's College, explained that physical education created bigger and stronger Japanese women, who would then be able to produce "fit" offspring for the empire (Sumiko Otsubo, "Engendering Eugenics: Fem-

inists and Marriage Restriction Legislation in the 1920s," in *Gendering Modern Japanese History*, ed. Barbara Molony and Kathleen Uno, Harvard East Asian Monographs 251 [Cambridge, MA: Harvard University Asisa Center, 2005], 242–43).

79. Boys-only activities were single-leg wrestling, individual single-bamboo stick-pushing game, individual single-bamboo stick-pulling game, individual double-bamboo stick-pulling game, individual double-bamboo stick-pushing game, group bamboo stick-pushing/pulling game, and knocking down bamboo stick competition. Girls-only activities included titles such as breaking (Jp: *burekking*), mountain march (Jp: *mautein maachi*), skating (Jp: *sukei teingu*), and waving the Japanese flag. "Four Seasons in the Countryside" (Jp: *Inaka no Shiki*) and "Moon over the Ruined Castle" (Jp: *Kōjō no Tsuki*) were the two songs for girls only in the manual (Hayakawa Kidaisu, *Shō kōgakkō taiiku no tokushu teki shidō to jissai* [Taichū: Tanabe Shoten, 1937], 89–90, 94–98, 101–36).

80. Hayakawa Kidaisu, *Shō kōgakkō taiiku no tokushu teki shidō to jissai*, 81–82.

81. Xu Kuidi, interview by Fang Yu Hu.

82. "Kōgun kenshō wo shukuga zentō de chōchin gyōretsu asu isseini kyokō," *Taiwan nichinichi shimpō*, September 26, 1937, 7.

83. Wu Surong, interview by Fang Yu Hu, Taoyuan, Taiwan, November 29, 2012.

84. "Kanki no hi no umi shimin san man sanka shite chōchin gyōretsu-zu wa saiu tsuite hatagyōretsu," *Taiwan nichinichi shimpō*, May 21, 1938, 9.

85. "Endō wa hi no umi Takao no chōchin gyōretsu," *Taiwan nichinichi shimpō*, February 12, 1939, 5.

86. Mei-ling Lai Kou, "Development of Music Education in Taiwan (1895–1995)," *Journal of Historical Research in Music Education* 22, no. 2 (2001): 185, http://www.jstor.org/stable/41300442.

87. "Seira de imon no yoru," *Taiwan nichinichi shimpō*, February 18, 1938, 5.

88. "Rengō gakugeikai," *Taiwan nichinichi shimpō*, March 7, 1938, 5.

89. "Shinchiku kōjo no imon ongaku kai," *Taiwan nichinichi shimpō*, March 3, 1938, 2.

90. "Kazoku iankai joshi kō de kaisai," *Taiwan nichinichi shimpō*, March 7, 1938, 5.

91. Ying Xinrui, interview by Fang Yu Hu, Taipei, Taiwan, November 9, 2011.

92. Wu Surong, interview by Fang Yu Hu.

93. Zhu Qiufeng, interview by Fang Yu Hu, Taipei, Taiwan, October 27, 2012.

94. "Imon bukuro hyaku gojū gakkō ni kitaku tansui-gai Tada Eikichi-shi bikyo," *Taiwan nichinichi shimpō*, May 26, 1938, 9.

95. Lin Xianyan, interview by Fang Yu Hu, June 28, 2012.

96. "Imon bukuro wo tsuida hi: Heitai-san wa kon'nanimo yorokobu," *Taiwan nichinichi shimpō*, July 23, 1940, 2.

97. Cai, *Zhanzheng tizhi xia de Taiwan*, 144–45.

98. Li Piqing, interview by Fang Yu Hu, Taipei, Taiwan, May 20, 2012.

99. Lü Zhunju, interview by Fang Yu Hu, Tainan, Taiwan, July 12, 2012.

100. Li Liyong, "Riben diguo zhimindi de zhan shi liangshi tongzhi tizhi: Taiwan yu Chaoxian de bijiao yanjiu (1937–1945)," *Taiwan shi yanjiu* 16, no. 2 (2009): 77–78.

101. Cai, *Zhanzheng tizhi xia de Taiwan*, 143–44.

102. Gao Sumei, interview by Fang Yu Hu, Yunlin, Taiwan, September 10, 2012.

103. Cai, *Zhanzheng tizhi xia de Taiwan*, 152–53.

104. "Haihin wo keibai," *Taiwan nichinichi shimpō*, August 2, 1938, 5.

105. Cai, *Zhanzheng tizhi xia de Taiwan*, 153–54.

106. "Chiji fujin shihan sossen udedokei ya kusari, kanzashi wo baikyaku Aifu Takao ndo in katsuyaku," *Taiwan nichinichi shimpō*, August 10, 1938, 5.

107. The school year began on April 1 of each year and ended on March 31 the following year with three terms: Term 1 was April 1 to August 20; Term 2 was August 21 to December 31; and Term 3 was January 1 to March 31 (*Taiwan kyōiku enkaku shi*, 301–2). Li and her classmates belonged to the class of 1944. They began first grade in April 1937. Fifth grade was from April 1942 to March 1943, and sixth grade was from April 1943 to March 1944.

108. Li Piqing, interview by Fang Yu Hu.

109. Ying Xinrui, interview by Fang Yu Hu, November 9, 2011.

110. American children were mobilized to perform many tasks, including collecting scraps (see "Kids Salvage," chapter 3 of Lisa L. Ossian, *The Forgotten Generation: American Children and World War II* (Columbia: University of Missouri Press, 2011), 41–42, ProQuest Ebook Central.

111. Li Yuanhui, *Ri ju shiqi Taiwan shifan jiaoyu zhidu* (Taibei: Nan Tian Shuju, 1997), 282–83.

112. "Hontō no fu joshi gun wo nōkō ni dōin no keikaku Taihoku shū de kakkitekina kokoromi," *Taiwan nichinichi shimpō*, April 15, 1941, 3; "Hontōjin fu joshi mo suiden de hataraku nōgyō hōkoku teishin tai kessei," *Taiwan nichinichi shimpō*, May 13, 1941, 2.

113. "Fu joshi mo jidō mo suiden ni shutsudō zōsan e kyo shū kairō ndo chiji-san mo waraji haki de taue," *Taiwan nichinichi shimpō*, March 14, 1943, 4.

114. Lin Xianyan's memory of these crops corresponded to colonial policy of crop planting during the wartime period. See the next paragraph for more detail (Lin Xianyan, interview by Fang Yu Hu, June 28, 2012).

115. Lin Jiwen, *Riben ju Tai moqi zhanzheng dongyuan tixi zhi yanjiu* (Taibei: Daoxiang Chuban She, 1996), 110–11, 117–18, 120–21.

116. Zhang Jingyi, *Zhan shi tizhi xia Taiwan teyong zuowu zengchan zhengce zhi yanjiu (1934–1944)* (Gaoxiong: Gaoxiong Fu Wen, 2007), 173.

117. Ying Xinrui, interview by Fang Yu Hu, November 9, 2011.

118. Tang Yanyan, interview by Fang Yu Hu, Taipei, Taiwan, January 18, 2013.

119. Lin Tiantian, interview by Fang Yu Hu, Yunlin, Taiwan, September 20, 2012; Xu Kuidi, interview by Fang Yu Hu.

120. Ying Xinrui, interview by Fang Yu Hu, Taipei, Taiwan, April 9, 2013.

121. "Shinten kokuminkō seito taihi seizō ni shihan," *Taiwan nichinichi shimpō*, December 7, 1941, 3.

122. Lan Qinhua, interview by Fang Yu Hu, Taichung, Taiwan, June 19, 2012.

123. Inoue Tokuya, *Kōgakkō nōgyō kyōiku* (Taihoku: Taiwan Kodomo Seikai Sha, 1927), 6.

NOTES TO PAGES 115–119

124. Taihoku daini shihan gakkō fuzoku kōgakkō keimei kai, ed., *Kōgakkō joshi nōgyō kyōju saimoku dai go roku gakunen yō* (Taihoku: Taihoku Daini Shihan Gakkō Fuzoku Kōgakkō Keimei Kai, 1939), 1.

125. Taihoku daini shihan gakkō fuzoku kōgakkō keimei kai, ed., "Kōgakkō joshi nōgyō kyōju saimoku dai go gakunen yō," in *Kōgakkō joshi nōgyō kyōju saimoku dai go roku gakunen yō* (Taihoku: Taihoku Daini Shihan Gakkō Fuzoku Kōgakkō Keimei Kai, 1939), 1.

126. "Kōgakkō joshi nōgyō kyōju saimoku dai go gakunen yō," 1; *Kōgakkō joshi nōgyō kyōju saimoku dai go roku gakunen yō*, 3.

127. Taihoku daini shihan gakkō fuzoku kōgakkō keimei kai, ed., *Kōgakkō joshi nōgyō kyōju saimoku dai go roku gakunen yō* (Taihoku: Taihoku Daini Shihan Gakkō Fuzoku Kōgakkō Keimei Kai, 1939), 1.

128. "Kōgakkō joshi nōgyō kyōju saimoku dai go gakunen yō," 6–9.

129. Cai, *Zhanzheng tizhi xia de Taiwan*, 159–60.

130. "Senninbari ni jūgo otome no magokoro," *Taiwan nichinichi shimpō*, October 3, 1941, 4.

131. Lin Xianyan said that men wouldn't know how to sew. She said any female member of the empire who knew how to sew could stitch one knot on the *senninbari* (Lin Xianyan, interview by Fang Yu Hu, April 12, 2013).

132. Wu Surong, interview by Fang Yu Hu.

133. Li Piqing, interview by Fang Yu Hu.

134. Lin Xianyan, interview by Fang Yu Hu, Taipei, Taiwan, June 28, 2012.

135. Ying Xinrui, interview by Fang Yu Hu, Taipei, Taiwan, August 20, 2010; Zhou Lianyu, interview by Fang Yu Hu, Taipei, Taiwan, May 14, 2013.

136. Ying Xinrui, interview by Fang Yu Hu, August 20, 2010.

137. Lin Xianyan, interview by Fang Yu Hu, June 28, 2012.

138. "Ichi shi danjo seito to dai ichi kōjosei ga rikugun byōin no seisō ni hōshi," *Taiwan nichinichi shimpō*, February 17, 1938, 7.

139. "Rikugun byōin e no omonaru imon-sha," *Taiwan nichinichi shimpō*, February 22, 1938, 7.

140. Zhu Qiufeng, interview by Fang Yu Hu, October 27, 2012.

141. Zhuang Tianci, *Er ci dazhan xia de Taibei da kongxi* (Taipei: Taibei Shi Zhengfu Wenhua Ju Taibei Er Er Ba Ji'nian Guan, 2007), 15, 161–63.

142. Zhuang, *Er ci dazhan xia de Taibei da kongxi*, 33–35, 37–38, 40, 43–45.

143. Established in Taiwan on April 19, 1941, the association was headed by the governor-general. It incorporated all civilian and business groups, such as youth groups and women's patriotic association. The association aimed to provide labor and supplies for the war by sponsoring military and industrial training in agriculture, industry, commerce, and mining for young men and women (Cai, *Zhanzheng tizhi xia de Taiwan*, 91, 94–95).

144. Zhuang, *Er ci dazhan xia de Taibei da kongxi*, 35.

145. Li Yuanhui, *Ri ju shiqi Taiwan shifan jiaoyu zhidu*, 283.

146. Xu Kuidi, interview by Fang Yu Hu.

147. Lin Tiantian, interview by Fang Yu Hu.

148. Lan Qinhua, interview by Fang Yu Hu.

149. Lin Xianyan, interview by Fang Yu Hu, April 12, 2013.

150. Zhou Yingying, interview by Fang Yu Hu, Yunlin, Taiwan, September 21, 2012.

151. Zhu Qiufeng, interview by Fang Yu Hu, October 27, 2012.

152. Zhu Qiufeng, interview by Fang Yu Hu, October 27, 2012.

153. Hong Zhimei, interview by Fang Yu Hu, Taipei, Taiwan, May 29, 2012.

154. Hong Zhimei, interview by Fang Yu Hu.

155. Zeng Chamei, interview by Fang Yu Hu, Taipei, Taiwan, November 9, 2012.

156. Zhu Qiufeng, interview by Fang Yu Hu, October 27, 2012.

157. Zhu Qiufeng, interview by Fang Yu Hu, Taipei, Taiwan, November 24, 2012.

158. For example, Tanaka Kurō visited Taiwan to attend a reunion with his former students on August 10, 1967; it had been twenty-one years since he last saw them (Tanaka Kurō, "Inori tsuzuke te nijūichi nen," in *Taiwan e no kakehashi*, ed. Yamamoto Ryōichi [Osaka: Hōrai kai kansai shibu, 1981], 52). Miyazaki Saiji had a reunion with his former students in Taiwan in 1976 (Miyazaki Saiji, "Taiwan kyōiku o kaerimi te," in *Taiwan e no kakehashi*, ed. Yamamoto Ryōichi [Osaka: Hōrai kai kansai shibu, 1981], 209). For more individual accounts, see Yamamoto Ryōichi, ed., *Taiwan e no kakehashi* (Osaka: Hōrai Kai Kansai Shibu, 1981).

4. REMAKING THE HOME

1. Interview with Lin Jiao'e, in *Yilan nüsheng—Ama de gushi: Jiaoyu pian*, ed. Lai Shujuan and Zhang Meifeng (Yilan: Yilan Xian Shi Guan, 2014), 298–99, 302–3, 312, 316–17, 321, 324, 329.

2. Zeng Jinjin, an interviewee, and Li Wu Xianmei, quoted in published oral histories, did laundry to support their families (Li Yulan, "1920 niandai amu: Li Wu Xianmei—Yi zhi cao yi dian lu," in *Amu de gushi*, ed. Jiang Wenyu [Taibei: Wenzun Wenhua Qiye Gufen Youxian Gongsi, 1998], 138–39; Zeng Jinjin, interview by Fang Yu Hu, Los Angeles, CA, March 26, 2012; Zheng Xiumei, "Ri zhi shiqi Taiwan funü laodong qun xiang," 12–13).

3. Interview with Lin Jiao'e, in *Yilan nüsheng—Ama de gushi*, 321.

4. Zhang Subi, "Ri ju shiqi Taiwan nüzi jiaoyu yanjiu," in *Zhongguo funü shi lunwen ji di er ji*, ed. Li Youning and Zhang Yufa (Taibei: Taiwan Shang Wu Yin Shu Guan, 1988), 259, 373.

5. Yu, *Ri ju shiqi Taiwan de nüzi jiaoyu*, 106, 220, 232, 243.

6. Ko, *Kindai Taiwan josei shi*, 127–82.

7. This chapter uses the terms *class* and *socioeconomic status* interchangeably because it attempts to draw attention to how an educated woman's background shaped her life course. Unfortunately, historians of colonial Taiwan have not engaged with the concept of class, so women cannot be defined or classified accordingly in this chapter. Historians

of Japanese-colonized Taiwan have used the terminologies *upper class*, *middle class*, and *lower class* without defining or theorizing the concept of class. By using the terms *class* and *socioeconomic status*, this chapter points out the difference between those from more privileged backgrounds and those from less privileged households to discuss the uneven effect of Japanese education.

8. Zheng Xiumei, "Ri zhi shiqi Taiwan funü laodong qun xiang," 14.

9. Zhang Subi, "Ri ju shiqi Taiwan nüzi jiaoyu yanjiu," 322.

10. Yu, *Ri ju shiqi Taiwan de nüzi jiaoyu*, 28–33.

11. Zheng Xiumei, "Taiwan funü laodong qun xiang," 15.

12. *Taiwan kyōiku enkaku shi*, 271–72. Some primary schools provided six years of education, and some provided four years of education as acknowledged by the Primary School Ordinance of Taiwan in 1898 and subsequent revisions to the ordinance and regulations with specific rules in topics such as land area, class organization, and course curriculum. The instructional hours per course differed for the four-year school and the six-year school as first specified in the 1907 revision to Primary School By-laws. The 1907 revision even specified instructional hours for an eight-year primary school. In response to local governments supporting the removal of the four-year education and the retention of the eight-year education, the colonial government revised the by-laws to remove eight-year institutions to make the last two years purely vocational training while retaining the four-year schools. This chapter cites the instructional hours at six-year schools for comparison purposes because primary education was standardized to be six years with the promulgation of the Educational Ordinance of Taiwan in 1919 (*Taiwan kyōiku enkaku shi*, 249, 279, 282–86, 290, 292, 325).

13. *Taiwan kyōiku enkaku shi*, 291, 298–99, 314–16, 324, 337–38, 346–48, 356, 361, 379–81.

14. Schools in Taiwan were in operation for three semesters in the same academic year as in Japan, the metropole: from April to July, September to December, and January to March. Postwar Taiwan under Chinese Nationalist rule changed the academic calendar of schools to two semesters: September to January and February to June.

15. Takizawa Kanae, "Shokumin chi Taiwan ni okeru gigei kyōiku—Taihoku dai san kōtō jogakkō o chūshin ni" (master's thesis, Danjiang Daxue, 2005), 66, 69, https://hdl .handle.net/11296/n9hwct.

16. Gao Sumei, interview by Fang Yu Hu, September 10, 2012; Gao Sumei, interview by Fang Yu Hu, September 19, 2012.

17. Wu Meihui (recorded), *Yibeizi zhenxian yi jiazi jiaoxue: Shi Suyun nüzhi fangwen jilu*, interview by Xu Xueji, Wu Meihui, Lian Xiansheng, and Guo Yueru (Taibei shi: Zhongyang Yanjiu Yuan Taiwan Shi Yanjiu Suo, 2014), 68, 87.

18. Based on secondary sources, these are the eight women's vocational secondary schools established in Taiwan by 1943: Taihoku Women's Professional Private School in Taipei in 1920 (renamed to be Patriotic Higher Handicrafts Women's Academy in 1935), Tainan Home Economics Sewing Training School in Tainan in 1929 (renamed

Tainan Home Economics Women's Academy in 1932), Taihoku Women's Higher Private Academy in Taipei in 1931, Yoshimi Sewing Private Academy in Taipei in 1935, Kiryū Handicrafts Women's Private School in Keelung in 1935, and Women's Commerce School, Women's Agriculture School, and Practical Learning Training School (Jp. *jitsugyō hoshū gakkō*). A practical learning training school was established in 1922 and in 1935 as part of primary schools before 1935 (Yu, *Ri ju shiqi Taiwan de nüzi jiaoyu*, 271, 277–83, 302; Komagome, "Dai ni ji Taiwan kyōikurei ka ni okeru shiritsu gakkō," 125). Enomoto Miyuki states that there were thirty-two women's vocational continuation schools (Jp: *jitsugyō hoshū gakkō*) established by the city, town, or government-general with some private schools by 1943 (Enomoto, "Nihon tōchi jiki taiwan no kasei kyōiku," 5, 15, 58–59).

19. Separate from the sewing course, embroidery was required for all students in their first two years at Taihoku Girls' No. 3 Middle School, and majors would complete the training in the last two years (Wu Meihui, *Yibeizi zhenxian yijiazi jiaoxue*, 123–25).

20. Enomoto, "Nihon tōchi jiki taiwan no kasei kyōiku," 15–17, 19.

21. Ko, "Shokuminchi Taiwan no 'modangāru' genshō to fasshon no seiji-ka," 269–70, 276–77, 279–81.

22. Chen Peiting, "Taiwan shan dao yangfu: Taiwan funü yangcai fazhan lishi (1895–1917)" (master's thesis, Fengjia Daxue, 2009), 42–44, 50, 70–80, https://hdl.handle.net/11296/gnf9w6.

23. Chen Peiting, "Taiwan shan dao yangfu," 5, 44–48, 68–70, 100–105, 113.

24. Shi Suyun became engaged right after graduating from Tokyo Women's Higher Normal School and got married a year later in 1942. Therefore, she graduated in 1941 or beforehand (Wu Meihui, *Yibeizi zhenxian yi jiazi jiaoxue*, 120, 145, 168, 177, 215–21, 228–31, 233–34, 237).

25. Chang Han-Yu and Ramon H. Myers, "Japanese Colonial Development Policy in Taiwan, 1895–1906: A Case of Bureaucratic Entrepreneurship," *Journal of Asian Studies* 22, no. 4 (August 1963): 433, 436, 440, 442.

26. Yu, *Ri ju shiqi Taiwan de nüzi jiaoyu*, 219.

27. Yu, *Ri ju shiqi Taiwan de nüzi jiaoyu*, 213–14.

28. Yu, *Ri ju shiqi Taiwan de nüzi jiaoyu*, 218.

29. Yang Cui, *Ri ju shiqi Taiwan funü jiefang yundong*, 205–8, 210.

30. Tang Yanyan, interview by Fang Yu Hu.

31. "Fennu de baige: Feng Shou'e," in *Fennu de baige: Zouguo Taiwan bainian lishi de nüxing*, ed. Zhou Fenlin (Taibei shi: Wenzun Wenhua Qiye Gufen Youxian Gongsi, 1998), 46–48, 50, 56–58.

32. Hong Zhimei, interview by Fang Yu Hu.

33. Lü Zhunju, interview by Fang Yu Hu.

34. Zhu Qiufeng, interview by Fang Yu Hu, October 27, 2012.

35. Xu Xianxian, interview by Fang Yu Hu.

36. Zeng Qiumei, interviews with Du Pan Fangge, Taibei, Taiwan, August 18, 1994, October 20, 1994, and June 14, 1995, "Fumu qin, Nü'er pian—Kejia nü shiren: Du Pan Fangge," in *Xiaoshi zhong de Taiwan ama*, interview by Zeng Qiumei, ed. Jiang Wenyu (Taibei: Yushan She, 1995), 2, 5, 8, 12.

37. Interview with Zhang Yue'e, in *Yilan nüsheng—Ama de gushi: Jiaoyu pian*, ed. Lai Shujuan and Zhang Meifeng (Yilan: Yilan Xian Shi Guan, 2014), 140, 144.

38. Yu, *Ri ju shiqi Taiwan de nüzi jiaoyu*, 94–95, 103, 323.

39. Yu, *Ri ju shiqi Taiwan de nüzi jiaoyu*, 328.

40. Ko, *Kindai Taiwan josei shi*, 114–15, 122–23, 168.

41. For simplicity, I divided the maximum tuition at girls' middle school (¥2.9) by the minimum tuition cost at primary school (10 *sen* after 1923) to get the biggest difference between the two costs. I divided the minimum tuition at girls' middle school (¥2.5) by the maximum tuition cost at primary school (70 *sen*) to get the smallest difference between the two costs. The 1922 regulation stipulated tuition at girls' middle school to be ¥24 per year, but gave individual schools the flexibility to make adjustments. Tuition ranged from ¥30 to ¥35 per year. Dividing ¥30 and ¥35 annually by twelve months yields ¥2.5 to ¥2.91 per month. Adding the cost of uniforms, books, supplies, field trip, and other fees, the total cost of sending a daughter to middle school ranged from ¥93.60 to ¥180.30 per year. Primary school tuition changed over time. The lowest cost between 1905 and 1921 was 2.7 *sen*, and the highest was 36.7 *sen* per month. In 1922, the lowest cost was 7 *sen*, which increased to 10 *sen* after 1923, and the highest was 70 *sen* per month (Yu, *Ri ju shiqi Taiwan de nüzi jiaoyu*, 149–51, 297).

42. Ko, *Kindai Taiwan josei shi*, 156–57.

43. Yu, *Ri ju shiqi Taiwan de nüzi jiaoyu*, 151, 311, 313.

44. Ko, *Kindai Taiwan josei shi*, 123.

45. Lü Zhunju, interview by Fang Yu Hu.

46. Interview with Liu Duan, in Zhang Meifeng, *Yilan nüsheng—Ama de gushi: Tong-yangxi yangnü pian* (Yilan: Yilan Xian Shi guan, 2015), 102–3, 126–27.

47. Every one of my interviewees got married, women and men, except for Lin Meihui, who remained single. Her family members forbade me from asking for more detail (Lin Meihui, interview by Fang Yu Hu, Yunlin, Taiwan, July 11, 2012).

48. William M. Reddy, *The Making of Romantic Love: Longing and Sexuality in Europe, South Asia, and Japan, 900–1200 CE* (Chicago: University of Chicago Press, 2012), 5, 16, 18, 20, ProQuest Ebook Central.

49. Yu, *Ri ju shiqi Taiwan de nüzi jiaoyu*, 60–61, 98.

50. *Taiwan kyōiku enkaku shi*, 247–48, 251, 329.

51. Yu, *Ri ju shiqi Taiwan de nüzi jiaoyu*, 64, 68.

52. Yu, *Ri ju shiqi Taiwan de nüzi jiaoyu*, 123.

53. Wu Meihui, *Yibeizi zhenxian yijiazi jiaoxue*, 91.

54. Lan Linlin, interview by Fang Yu Hu, Hsinchu, Taiwan, September 22, 2012.

55. Interview with Zhang Yue'e, in *Yilan nüsheng—Ama de gushi: Jiaoyu pian*, 146.

56. Lin Tiantian, interview by Fang Yu Hu.

57. Lin Tiantian, interview by Fang Yu Hu.

58. Lan Linlin, interview by Fang Yu Hu.

59. Lai Huazhu, interview by Fang Yu Hu, Taipei, Taiwan, August 18, 2012.

60. Yujia said this phrase in Mandarin Chinese, "Men and women must keep their distance from each other" [Ch. *nan nü shou shou bu qin*]. This is a classical Chinese proverb that literally means men and women should not give or accept things from each other directly with their hands. It offers moral guidance for men and women to make sure they do not become involved with each other unless they are married (Xia Yujia, interview by Fang Yu Hu, Taichung, Taiwan, June 19, 2012).

61. Xia Yujia, interview by Fang Yu Hu.

62. Xu Xianxian, interview by Fang Yu Hu.

63. Zeng Jinjin gave birth to her first child before she was nineteen years old. She likely got married when she was eighteen years of age (Zeng Jinjin, interview by Fang Yu Hu).

64. Lai Huazhu, interview by Fang Yu Hu.

65. Doris T. Chang, *Women's Movements in Twentieth-Century Taiwan*, 24.

66. Yang Cui, *Ri ju shiqi Taiwan funü jiefang yundong*, 151, 153.

67. Yang Cui, *Ri ju shiqi Taiwan funü jiefang yundong*, 143.

68. Wang Lingyi, the writer of the account, is Lin Yuzhu's child, who did not indicate Lin's birth year. Assuming the time of writing is the publication year of 1998 and Lin's tenth-year death commemoration, she passed away in 1988 at the age of eighty-four years. She was likely born in 1904 or 1905, depending on her birthday (Wang Lingyi, "1900 niandai amu: Lin Yuzhu—Chamo jian zai cai zi ming," in *Amu de gushi*, ed. Jiang Wenyu [Taibei: Meta Media International, 1998], 114, 119–20).

69. Interview with Zhang Yue'e, in *Yilan nüsheng—Ama de gushi: Jiaoyu pian*, 169.

70. The report was cited in Zheng Xiumei, "Taiwan funü laodong qun xiang," 110.

71. Gao Zhuyuan, interview by Fang Yu Hu, Tainan, Taiwan, July 13, 2012.

72. Doris T. Chang, *Women's Movements in Twentieth-Century Taiwan*, 24.

73. Reddy, *The Making of Romantic Love*, 18.

74. Lin Tiantian, interview by Fang Yu Hu.

75. Lan Linlin, interview by Fang Yu Hu.

76. Lin Tiantian, interview by Fang Yu Hu.

77. Lin Tiantian, interview by Fang Yu Hu; Lan Linlin, interview by Fang Yu Hu.

78. Interview with Zeng Qinglian, in *Yilan nüsheng—Ama de gushi: Hangye pian*, 10–12.

79. Chin-ju Lin, "Modern Daughters-in-Law in Colonial Taiwanese Families," *Journal of Family History* 30, no. 2 (April 2005): 204.

80. Tay-sheng Wang, *Legal Reform in Taiwan under Japanese Colonial Rule, 1895–1945: The Reception of Western Law* (Seattle: University of Washington Press, 1999), 166, ProQuest Ebook Central.

NOTES TO PAGES 155–161

81. Zhuo Yiwen, *Qingdai Taiwan funü de shenghuo* (Taibei: Zili Wanbao She Wenhua Chuban Bu, 2004), 56–57.

82. Tay-sheng Wang, *Legal Reform in Taiwan under Japanese Colonial Rule*, 166.

83. Tay-sheng Wang, *Legal Reform in Taiwan under Japanese Colonial Rule*, 167.

84. Chin-ju Lin, "Modern Daughters-in-Law in Colonial Taiwanese Families," 204.

85. Tay-sheng Wang, *Legal Reform in Taiwan under Japanese Colonial Rule*, 140–41, 145, 164–66.

86. Wu Meihui, *Yibeizi zhenxian yijiazi jiaoxue*, 38.

87. Note 55 in Chin-ju Lin's study discusses the typical definition of romantic courtship that involved the man's free choice with parents' arrangement in colonial Taiwan. Cousins and classmates of male youths would introduce them to potential partners, and these young men would then ask their parents to arrange the marriage on their behalf after they had chosen their partners (Lin, "Modern Daughters-in-Law in Colonial Taiwanese Families," 209).

88. Wu Meihui, *Yibeizi zhenxian yijiazi jiaoxue*, 176–77.

89. Wu Meihui, *Yibeizi zhenxian yijiazi jiaoxue*, 177.

90. This narrative on her marriage was told by Wang Feimei's daughter because Wang was too shy during the interview to recount how she met her husband. Wang nodded or added more details during her daughter's narrative (Wang Feimei, interview by Fang Yu Hu, Taipei, Taiwan, April 20, 2013).

91. Zheng's father owned a construction company that built bridges and dikes. Li's father owned two hot spring hotels (Li Piqing, interview by Fang Yu Hu; Zheng Rongrong, interview by Fang Yu Hu, Yunlin, Taiwan, September 21, 2012).

92. Zheng Rongrong, interview by Fang Yu Hu.

93. Zeng Qiumei, interview with Du Pan Fangge, 9.

94. Zeng Qiumei, interview with Du Pan Fangge, 10.

95. Ueno Hiroko, "Shokuminchi Taiwan niokeru kōtō jōgakkōsei no 'nihon'—seigatsu bunka no henyō ni kansuru shiron," in *Sengo Taiwan ni okeru nihon: Shokuminchi keiken no renzoku henbō riyō*, ed. Igarashi Masako and Mio Yūko (Tokyo: Fūkyō Sha, 2006), 136–37, 144, 146.

96. Lan Linlin, interview by Fang Yu Hu.

97. One interviewee, Wang Zhirui, from Taichung, taught "Peach Boy" to her grandson (Wang Zhirui, interview by Fang Yu Hu, Taipei, Taiwan, January 14, 2013). Lin Xianyan also taught "Peach Boy" to her children (Lin Xianyan, interview by Fang Yu Hu, April 12, 2013). Other scholars also heard from interviewees whose parents spoke Japanese or listened to Japanese songs while growing up in the postwar era (Huang Ling'e, "Yan'ge zai Taiwan de fazhan yu bianqian—touguo yan'ge aihao zhe de diaocha" [master's thesis, Donghai Daxue, 2019], 84, 87–88, https://hdl.handle.net/11296/wmpkz3). The song "Momotaro-san" was removed from the school curriculum in 1941 because the lyrics were deemed to glorify wartime aggression (Sun Manlin, "Qingting

yu jilu—Taiwan zai rishi shiqi xia de Riben tongyao" [master's thesis, Guoli Taiwan Shifan Daxue, 2017], 55, https://hdl.handle.net/11296/8wacg5).

98. Lin Xianyan, interview by Fang Yu Hu, April 12, 2013.

99. Japanese educated Taiwanese enjoyed singing Japanese songs in the postwar era (Tsuruta Jun, "1950–60 niandai Riben qu Taiyu ge yanjiu" [master's thesis, Guoli Chenggong Daxue, 2008], 4–6, 25, 40, 50–51, https://hdl.handle.net/11296/9fyh28).

100. Huang Ling'e, "Yan'ge zai Taiwan de fazhan yu bianqian," 30–32, 36–38, 45–46, 109, 116–17.

101. Yu, *Ri ju shiqi Taiwan de nüzi jiaoyu*, 216.

102. Girls were taken to and grew up in their future marital household. Once they were of age, around late teens, they would be ordered to consummate the marriage with their husbands, with whom they grew up like siblings. Although some Taiwanese fought successfully against this order, many ultimately consummated their marriage. See Zhang Meifeng, *Yilan nüsheng—Ama de gushi: Tongyangsi yangnü pian* (Yilan: Yilan xian shi guan, 2015), 38, 61, 87, 208–9; and Chen Huiwen, *Dadaocheng chabolang ditu: Dadaocheng funü de huodong kongjian jin bainian lai de bianqian* (Taibei: Boyang, 1999), 50–53.

103. Teresa Gerrard and Alexis Weedon, "Working-Class Women's Education in Huddersfield: A Case Study of the Female Educational Institute Library, 1856–1857," *Information & Culture* 49, no. 2 (2014): 242, http://www.jstor.org/stable/43737487.

104. Chatani, *Nation-Empire*, 250–51.

5. COLONIAL NOSTALGIA

1. Zhou Lianyu, interview by Fang Yu Hu, April 30, 2013.

2. Japan had set up Taiwanese schools in Xiamen/Amoy for children of Taiwanese, who were Japanese subjects conducting business in Xiamen as of 1910 (*Taiwan kyōiku enkaku shi*, 512).

3. The survey was published in both Japanese and Chinese, and I refer to the Chinese survey because the survey was presumably conducted in Mandarin Chinese ("2021 niandu Taiwan minzhong dui Riben guangan yanjiu," conducted by Nihon Taiwan kōryū gakukai, 5, 7, 11, accessed March 12, 2022, https://www.koryu.or.jp/Portals/0/culture/%E4%B8%96%E8%AB%96/2021/2021_seron_shosai_CH.pdf).

4. The democratization process that began in the late 1980s in South Korea provided the opportunity for Koreans to express their anger toward Japan (David Hundt and Roland Bleiker, "Colonial Memories in Korea and Japan," in "Reconciliation between China and Japan," special issue, *Asian Perspective* 31 (2007): 68–69. In contrast, democratization in 1990s Taiwanese society led to the creation of Taiwan studies, where many scholars reevaluated Japanese rule in a more comprehensive narrative with negative and positive impact on Taiwan. This means that although both societies shared similar political developments in the postwar period and began to assess the impact of Japa-

NOTES TO PAGES 165–171

nese colonization in the same time period, most Koreans continued to express strong anti-Japanese sentiment while many Taiwanese openly praised Japan.

5. Leo T. S. Ching, "Give Me Japan and Nothing Else!": Postcoloniality, Identity, and the Traces of Colonialism," *South Atlantic Quarterly* 99, no. 4 (2000): 764, https://www.muse.jhu.edu/article/30676.

6. Patricia M. E. Lorcin lists "coffee-table books" by Nigel Pavitt, Mirella Ricciardi, Marie Cardinal, and Serge Durieux that focus on mutual cooperation and harmony between the colonizer and the colonized populations in Africa. In the case of the Japanese empire, Barak Kushner notes that some Japanese groups sought to create "a more positive national memory of Japanese colonialism" by portraying "Japan as the harbinger of the future, as the country best suited to bring civilization, along with urbanization and increased trade, to a backward continent," something they believed Japan achieved before and during World War II (Barak Kushner, "Nationality and Nostalgia: The Manipulation of Memory in Japan, Taiwan, and China since 1990," *International History Review* 29, no. 4 [December 2007]: 803, http://www.jstor.org/stable/40110927; Patricia M. E. Lorcin, "Imperial Nostalgia, Colonial Nostalgia: Differences of Theory, Similarities of Practice?," in "Nostalgia in Modern France: Bright New Ideas about a Melancholy Subject," special issue, *Historical Reflections/Réflexions Historiques* 39, no. 3 [Winter 2013]: 103–5, http://www.jstor.org/stable/42703774).

7. Dennis Walder, *Postcolonial Nostalgias: Writing, Representation and Memory* (London: Taylor & Francis, 2010), 2, 3, ProQuest Ebook Central.

8. Lorcin, *Historicizing Colonial Nostalgia*, 2, 9.

9. Walder, *Postcolonial Nostalgias*, 4.

10. Tetsushi Marukawa, "Situating Yoshinori Kobayashi's Taiwan ron ('The Taiwan Question') in East Asia," *Postcolonial Studies: Culture, Politics, Economy*, 6, no. 2 (2003): 240, doi:10.1080/13688790308102.

11. Marukawa, "Situating Yoshinori Kobayashi's Taiwan ron ('The Taiwan Question') in East Asia," 240–41.

12. William Cunningham Bissell, "Engaging Colonial Nostalgia," *Cultural Anthropology* 20, no. 2 (May 2005): 215, 222, 237, http://www.jstor.org/stable/3651534215.

13. Bissell, "Engaging Colonial Nostalgia," 222.

14. Bissell, "Engaging Colonial Nostalgia," 216.

15. Walder, *Postcolonial Nostalgias*, 11, 16.

16. Bissell, "Engaging Colonial Nostalgia," 239.

17. The catalyst of the 2-28 Incident occurred on February 27, 1947. Several workers from the Monopoly Bureau (Ch. Zhuan Mai Ju) and a few police officers confiscated a woman tobacco vendor's tobacco and cash because only the government was allowed to sell tobacco. The woman begged for forgiveness but received a beating, and bystanders became angry. During the conflict, one civilian was killed by gunshot. The following day, on February 28, some Taiwanese protesters gathered in front of the Monopoly Bureau.

For more detail, see Chen Cuilian, "Er er ba Shijian," in *Taiwan da baike quanshu*, last modified September 24, 2009, https://nrch.culture.tw/twpedia.aspx?id=3838; and Wu Micha, Huang, and Lin, "Er er ba shijian," in *Taiwan shi xiao shidian*, 162–63.

18. Lindi Gail Arrigo, "Fifty Years after '2-2-8': The Lingering Legacy of State Terror in the Consolidation of Bourgeois Democracy in Taiwan": *Humboldt Journal of Social Relations* 23, no. 1/2 (1997): 47, http://www.jstor.org/stable/23263489. The period of martial law overlapped with the period of White Terror in Taiwan, and scholars and people in Taiwan have used the two terms interchangeably. Martial law was declared three times in Taiwan: during the 2-28 Incident, December 1947, and May 1949, ending on July 15, 1987. Thus, the martial law period is commonly treated as having started in 1947 and lasted until 1987. However, in July 1947, Chiang Kai-shek enacted the Temporary Provisions during the period of the "Communist Rebellion" to give himself and the president great executive power to punish Chinese communists. It was effective in Taiwan until April 30, 1991. Thus, the period of Chinese Nationalist political oppression in Taiwan, or sometimes termed *martial law*, is often considered to be from 1947 until 1991. During this period, the government limited freedom of expression and media. The Chinese Nationalist government arrested, imprisoned, and executed dissidents, mainly political leftists and Taiwan-independence activists from both leftist and rightist camps, by accusing them of rebelling against the government or committing espionage. The Chinese Nationalist government abolished the provisions on April 30, 1991. Other relevant provisions were banned or passed to formally end the White Terror period in 1992. For more detail, see Liu Hengwen, "Jieyan," in *Taiwan da baike quanshu*, last modified September 24, 2009, https://nrch.culture.tw/twpedia.aspx?id=3861; Su Ruiqiang, "Baise kongbu," in *Taiwan da baike quanshu*, last modified March 21, 2012, https://nrch.culture .tw/twpedia.aspx?id=3864; and Xue Huayuan, "Donyuan kanluan shiqi linshi tiaokuan," in *Taiwan da baike quanshu*, last modified September 24, 2009, https://nrch.culture.tw /twpedia.aspx?id=3860.

19. Chou, *Hai xing xi de niandai*, (2).

20. Chou, *Hai xing xi de niandai*, (9)–(11).

21. Cai Jintang, "Nihon jidai tōji jidai to Kokumintō tōchi jidai ni koette ikita Taiwanjin no nihonkan," in *Sengo Taiwan ni okeru nihon: Shokuminchi keiken no renzoku henbō riyō*, ed. Igarashi Masako and Mio Yūko (Tokyo: Fūkyousha, 2006), 22.

22. Leo T. S. Ching, *Anti-Japan: The Politics of Sentiment in Postcolonial East Asia* (Durham, NC: Duke University Press, 2019), 82–83, 86, https://doi.org/10.2307 /j.ctv113166n.

23. Ching, *Anti-Japan*, 83, 88, 95.

24. Lorcin, "Imperial Nostalgia, Colonial Nostalgia," 103–4.

25. Li Xiaofeng, "Zhan hou chuqi Taiwan shehui de wenhua chongtu," in *Taiwan shi lunwen jingxuan xia*, ed. Zhang Yanxian, Li Xiaofeng, and Dai Baocun (Taibei: Yushan She Chuban, 1996), 273.

NOTES TO PAGES 173–176

26. Xia Yujia recalled and sang some songs in Taiwanese Hoklo during the interview (Xia Yujia, interview by Fang Yu Hu).

27. Lisa Miller, "Register of the George H. Kerr papers," Online Archive of California, last updated 2003, https://oac.cdlib.org/findaid/ark:/13030/kt558013kc/entire_text/; George Kerr, "The Surrender on Formosa, 1945," chapter 3 of *Formosa Betrayed* (Upland, CA: Taiwan Publishing, 2005), http://www.romanization.com/books/formosabetrayed/chap03.html.

28. Kerr, "The Surrender on Formosa, 1945."

29. Chatani, *Nation-Empire*, 261; Li Xiaofeng, "Zhan hou chuqi Taiwan shehui de wenhua chongtu," 289–97. One of my interviewees, Xia Yujia, expressed obvious disdain for Chinese soldiers when she talked about her impression of those who arrived in Taiwan after World War II. She admired how clean and orderly Japanese soldiers looked (Xia Yujia, interview by Fang Yu Hu).

30. Kerr quoted the article from the periodical *Damingbao* (*Ta Ming Pao*) in his book. George Kerr, "On the Eve of Disaster," chapter 11 of *Formosa Betrayed* (Upland, CA: Taiwan Publishing, 2005, http://www.romanization.com/books/formosabetrayed/chap11.html.

31. Kerr, "The Surrender on Formosa, 1945."

32. Hong-zen Wang, "Class Structures and Social Mobility in Taiwan in the Initial Post-War Period," *China Journal*, no. 48 (2002): 57, 59–61, 68, https://doi.org/10.2307/3182441.

33. Luo Mingqing, "Jiaoyu chengjiu de shengji yu xingbie chayi," *Jingji lunwen congkan* 29, no. 2 (2001): 146–47, http://homepage.ntu.edu.tw/~luohm/attainment.pdf.

34. Luo Mingqing, "Gao pukao fen sheng qu ding e luqu yu tezhong kaoshi de sheng ji shaixuan xiaoguo," *Jingji lunwen congkan* 31, no. 1 (2003): 90, http://homepage.ntu.edu.tw/~luohm/selection.pdf.

35. Luo, "Jiaoyu chengjiu de shengji yu xingbie chayi," 147.

36. Luo, "Gao pukao fen sheng qu ding e luqu yu tezhong kaoshi de sheng ji shaixuan xiaoguo," 88, 90.

37. For example, the minimum passing score for the civil service exam was 60 points in 1978. The government accepted Chinese Mainlanders who scored 10 points below this minimum. A total of 606 Taiwanese passed the exam with a score of 60 points or higher. After score adjustment, only 172 Mainlanders scored 50 points or higher. The government allocated a total of 570 spots to Chinese Mainlanders but made adjustments. As a result, the government placed 606 Taiwanese and 172 Mainlanders in 1978 (Luo, "Gao pukao fen sheng qu ding e luqu yu tezhong kaoshi de sheng ji shaixuan xiaoguo," 92).

38. Luo Mingqing, "Shui shi Tai da xuesheng?—Xingbie, shengji yu chengxiang chayi," *Jingji lunwen congkan* 30, 1 (March 2002): 122, http://homepage.ntu.edu.tw/~luohm/papers/NTU.htm.

39. Kerr, "The Surrender on Formosa, 1945."

40. Hong-zen Wang, "Class Structures and Social Mobility in Taiwan in the Initial Post-War Period," 75.

41. Christopher Howe, "Taiwan in the 20th Century: Model or Victim? Development Problems in a Small Asian Economy," *China Quarterly* (March 2001): 52, http://www.jstor.org/stable/3451105.

42. Christopher J. Lucas, "The Politics of National Development and Education in Taiwan," *Comparative Politics* 14, no. 2 (January 1982): 211, 217, 220, http://www.jstor.org/stable/421587.

43. Tsurumi, *Japanese Colonial Education in Taiwan*, 113.

44. Lucas, "The Politics of National Development and Education in Taiwan," 212–13, 224.

45. Wu Surong, interview by Fang Yu Hu.

46. Lin Xianyan, interview by Fang Yu Hu, June 28, 2012.

47. Zhang Taishan, interview by Fang Yu Hu, Kaohisung, Taiwan, July 15, 2012.

48. Fujitani, *Race for Empire*, 268, 295.

49. Shiu On Chu, "The Fifth Great Chinese Invention: Examination and State Power in Twentieth Century China and Taiwan" (PhD diss., Brown University, 2018), 10.

50. Chu, "The Fifth Great Chinese Invention," 99–100, 154, 179.

51. Chu, "The Fifth Great Chinese Invention," 182–83, 194–95.

52. Ching, *Anti-Japan*, 93.

53. Ya-Chen Su, "Ideological Representations of Taiwan's History: An Analysis of Elementary Social Studies Textbooks, 1978–1995," *Curriculum Inquiry* 37, no. 3 (September 2007): 209–10, http://www.jstor.org/stable/30053219.

54. Chatani, *Nation-Empire*, 262.

55. Ya-Chen Su analyzed two series of social studies textbooks, 1978–89, and 1989–95, and provided an account of the portrayal of Japanese colonial rule in the first series, 1978–89. Although she only provided analysis of textbooks used after 1978, the negative portrayal of Japanese colonialism was unlikely less so in the pre-1978 period, when the Nationalist government worked to de-Japanize and re-Sinicize the Taiwanese population through education (Su, "Ideological Representations of Taiwan's History," 215–16, 222–23, 225).

56. Kushner, "Nationality and Nostalgia," 808.

57. Zhang Taishan used these terms: *standard of living* (Tw. Hoklo *chúi-chún*; Ch. *shuizhun*) and *level of civilization* (Tw. Hoklo *būn-hòa thêng-tō*; Ch. *wenhua chengdu*) (Zhang Taishan, interview by Fang Yu Hu).

58. Zeng Xiuying, interview by Fang Yu Hu, Taipei, Taiwan, April 9, 2013.

59. Dennis McNamara portrays Taiwan's domestic economy before Japanese arrival as having had little growth, although foreign trade grew in the nineteenth century. Christopher Howe's study focuses on foreign trade and shows that Taiwan was integral to East Asian trade in the late sixteenth century and to international trade under Dutch

and Qing control from the seventeenth to the mid-nineteenth century with impact on domestic economy (Howe, "Taiwan in the 20th Century," 38–40; Dennis L. McNamara, "Comparative Colonial Response: Korea and Taiwan," *Korean Studies* 10 [1986]: 57, http://www.jstor.org/stable/23718831).

60. Ching, *Anti-Japan*, 92.

61. Tai, "Kokugo and Colonial Education in Taiwan," 510; Watanabe Yaeko, "Isshi dōjin," in *Taiwan e no kakehashi*, ed. Yamamoto Ryōichi (Osaka: Hōrai Kai Kansai Shibu, 1981), 212–13.

62. Tōyama Waketsuyoshi, "Hōtai ni omō hō'on kansha," in *Taiwan e no kakehashi*, ed. Yamamoto Ryōichi (Osaka: Hōrai Kai Kansai Shibu, 1981), 64–65. Izawa Shuji set up the first *kokugo* programs for Taiwanese in July 1895 and the first teacher-training program by recruiting "thirteen education bureau officials and thirty-six teacher train-ees" with teaching degrees from Japan to teach in Taiwan in 1896 (Tsurumi, *Japanese Colonial Education in Taiwan*, 13–16). For a brief description of the early teacher-training programs, see Yoshino Hidetomo, *Taiwan kyōiku shi* (1927; repr., Taibei: Nantian Shuju Youxian Gongsi, 1997), 10–13. For a more comprehensive discussion of different train-ing programs, years of training, and years of compulsory service after completing the program throughout the colonial period, see Wu Wenxing, *Ri ju shiqi Taiwan shifan jiaoyu zhi yanjiu, Guoli Taiwan shifan daxue lishi yanjiu suo zhuankan*, ser. 8 (Taibei: Guoli Taiwan Shifan Daxue Lishi Yanjiu Suo, 1983).

63. This manuscript adopts Eika Tai's romanization for "Shizangan" (Tai, "Kokugo and Colonial Education in Taiwan," 510).

64. Tai, "Kokugo and Colonial Education in Taiwan," 511. An official account of the killing can be found in *Taiwan kyōiku enkaku shi*, 22–31.

65. Ueda Sumio, "Sōshiju Taiwan no tsuioku," in *Taiwan e no kakehashi*, ed. Yamamoto Ryōichi (Osaka: Hōrai Kai Kansai Shibu, 1981), 211.

66. Kitō Eiji, "Watashi no ashiato," in *Taiwan e no kakehashi*, ed. Yamamoto Ryōichi (Osaka: Hōrai Kai Kansai Shibu, 1981), 155.

67. Kitō Eiji, "Watashi no ashiato," 155.

68. Miyazaki Saiji, "Taiwan kyōiku o kaerimi te," in *Taiwan e no kakehashi*, ed. Yamamoto Ryōichi (Osaka: Hōrai Kai Kansai Shibu, 1981), 209.

69. Mark Selden and Yoshiko Nozaki, "Japanese Textbook Controversies, National-ism, and Historical Memory: Intra- and Inter-national Conflicts," *Asia-Pacific Journal—Japan Focus* 7, issue 24, no. 5 (June 2009): 6–8, https://apjjf.org/-Yoshiko-Nozaki—Mark-Selden/3173/article.pdf.

70. Selden and Nozaki, "Japanese Textbook Controversies, Nationalism, and His-torical Memory," 6.

71. Selden and Nozaki, "Japanese Textbook Controversies, Nationalism, and His-torical Memory," 12.

72. Tai, "Kokugo and Colonial Education in Taiwan," 527.

73. Tai, "Kokugo and Colonial Education in Taiwan," 526–27

74. Lorcin, *Historicizing Colonial Nostalgia*, 11.

75. Wu Surong, interview by Fang Yu Hu.

76. Zeng Yuanyuan, interview by Fang Yu Hu, Taipei, Taiwan, August 25, 2010.

77. Interview with Lin Jiao'e, *Yilan wenxian congkan 9—Yilan qilao tan Ri zhi xia de junshi yu jiaoyu*, ed. Lin Huiyu (Yilan: Fucheng Yinshua Xingye Gufen Youxian Gongsi, 1996), 186. A brief interview with Lin Jiao'e is included in this volume that includes interviews with both men and women. Another volume, containing only interviews with women, treats Lin's life in more detail, as cited in chapter 4.

78. Wu, *Ri ju shiqi Taiwan shifan jiaoyu zhi yanjiu*, 194.

79. Wu, *Ri ju shiqi Taiwan shifan jiaoyu zhi yanjiu*, 194–95.

80. Wu, *Ri ju shiqi Taiwan shifan jiaoyu zhi yanjiu*, 194.

81. Huang Jinde, interview by Fang Yu Hu, Taipei, September 23, 2012.

82. Zeng Xiuying, interview by Fang Yu Hu.

83. Lin Tiantian, interview by Fang Yu Hu.

84. Mikami Takatoshi, "Waga kokoro no 'Karenkō," in *Taiwan e no kakehashi*, ed. Yamamoto Ryōichi (Osaka: Hōrai Kai Kansai Shibu, 1981), 41.

85. Ro Retsu-tsu (Lü Lietong), "Watashi wa kekkon shiki hikaeshitsu no shinzoku—ippan dochira ni hairu beki ka," in *Taiwan e no kakehashi*, ed. Yamamoto Ryōichi (Osaka: Hōrai Kai Kansai Shibu, 1981), 109.

86. Wu Wenxing, *Ri ju shiqi Taiwan shifan jiaoyu zhi yanjiu*, 92. For the statistics of graduates from teacher-training school by ethnic and gender breakdown between 1896 and 1943, see table 4–2 in Wu Wenxing, *Ri ju shiqi Taiwan shifan jiaoyu zhi yanjiu*, 156-1-156-2. For statistics on married Japanese women living in Taiwan between 1905 and 1935, see George W. Barclay, *Colonial Development and Population in Taiwan* (Princeton, NJ: Princeton University Press, 1954), 213, ProQuest Ebook Central.

87. Born to a business family in Taichung City in central Taiwan, Xia Yujia remembered eating lunch with her teachers, all Japanese men (Xia Yujia, interview by Fang Yu Hu).

88. Hong Zhimei, interview by Fang Yu Hu.

89. Zheng Fengqin, "Ri ju shiqi xin nüxing de zaixian fenxi," 36–37.

90. As part of the social elite in Qing-period Taiwan, some Confucian scholars were teachers. Under Japanese rule, teacher- and medical-training programs offered the most prestigious education, and thus teachers and physicians became social elites active in shaping political, social, and economic developments in Taiwan (Bih-Jen Fwu and Hsiou-Huai Wang, "The Social Status of Teachers in Taiwan," *Comparative Education* 38, no. 2 [May 2002]: 212, http://www.jstor.org/stable/3099785; Wu Wenxing, *Ri ju shiqi Taiwan shehui lingdao jieji zhi yanjiu* [Taibei: Wu'nan Shuju, 1992], 5, 102; Wu Wenxing, *Ri ju shiqi Taiwan shifan jiaoyu zhi yanjiu*, 100).

91. Wu Wenxing, *Ri ju shiqi Taiwan shifan jiaoyu zhi yanjiu*, 15–17, 19, 79–83.

92. Yasumura Kensuke, *Nihon tōchi ka no Taiwan to Okinawa shusshin kyōin* (Yabusachi: Yamaneko Shuppan, 2012), 67. Hiroko Matsuda has found that Taiwan provided great educational, career, and financial opportunities for Okinawans because Japanese officials devoted many resources to develop Taiwan and few to Okinawa after annexation (see Hiroko Matsuda, *Liminality of the Japanese Empire: Border Crossings from Okinawa to Colonial Taiwan* [Honolulu: University of Hawai'i Press, 2019], http://www.jstor.org/stable/j.ctvvn7ng).

93. Wu, *Ri ju shiqi Taiwan shifan jiaoyu zhi yanjiu*, 18, 87, 89, 100, 102–8.

94. Shen Cuilian, *Taiwan xiaoxue shizi peiyu shi* (Taibei: Wu'nan Tushu Chuban Gufen Youxian Gongsi, 2004), 56.

95. Luo, "Jiaoyu chengjiu de shengji yu xinbie chayi," 126.

96. Tsurumi, *Japanese Colonial Education in Taiwan,* 45–47, 116–24.

97. Fwu and Wang, "The Social Status of Teachers in Taiwan," 214.

98. Zhang Jintu, interview by Zhang Wenlong, in *Taiwan ren jiaoshi de shidai jingyan*, ed. Zhang Yanxian (Taibei: Taibei Xian Li Wenhua Zhongxin, 1996), 31.

99. Zhou Yingying, interview by Fang Yu Hu.

100. Wu Sheng, interview by Zhang Wenlong, in *Taiwan ren jiaoshi de shidai jinyan*, ed. Zhang Yanxian (Taibei: Taibei Xian Li Wenhua Zhongxin, 1996), 35, 37, 41.

101. Even though Japan lost in 1945, Lü Zhunju likely worked until 1947–48. She began schooling when she was eight years old (*sui*), which would be around 1937–38, and would have graduated in 1943 or 1944. She said she worked at the Broadcasting Company for four years (Lü Zhunju, interview by Fang Yu Hu).

102. Lin and Lin, "Does Higher Education Expansion Reduce Credentialism and Gender Discrimination in Education?," 283.

103. Interview with Lin Jiao'e, *Yilan wenxian congkan 9*, 186.

104. During the interview, Lin Xianyan said that General MacArthur removed the teaching of the Rescript from the Japanese school curriculum because the Americans believed the Rescript was the force behind the cultivation of the Japanese spirit (Lin Xianyan, interview by Fang Yu Hu, June 28, 2012).

105. Ching, *Anti-Japan*, 91. I adopt the romanization system used in the *Maryknoll Dictionary* for all Taiwanese Hoklo terms in this book. I do not know what system Leo Ching uses, but the romanization of *ribunjinshin* sounds like the Taiwanese Hoklo pronunciation written in Japanese romanization, and not the Mandarin Chinese pronunciation.

106. Ching, *Anti-Japan*, 91.

107. Lan Qinhua, interview by Fang Yu Hu.

108. Wu Surong, interview by Fang Yu Hu.

109. Ching, *Anti-Japan*, 92.

110. Ching, *Anti-Japan*, 92.

111. Ching, *Anti-Japan*, 91–92.

112. Zhou Lianyu, interview by Fang Yu Hu, May 14, 2013.

113. Gao Sumei, interview by Fang Yu Hu, September 10, 2012.

114. Zhou Yingying, interview by Fang Yu Hu.

115. Chou, *Hai xing xi de niandai*, 306, 317, 321–22.

116. *Taiwan kyōiku enkaku shi*, 295.

117. The lesson was cited in Wang Jinque, *Ri zhi shiqi Taiwan gongmin jiaoyu yu gongmin texing*, 173.

118. *Taiwan kyōiku enkaku shi*, 295.

119. Lesson as cited in Wang Jinque, *Ri zhi shiqi Taiwan gongmin jiaoyu yu gongmin texing*, 172.

120. *Junjō* is written in Japanese here, but Lin Xianyan actually pronounced this word in Taiwanese Hoklo (*sūn-chêng*). I use the Japanese romanization because the word was originally Japanese. It does not exist in Taiwanese Hoklo.

121. Dower, *War without Mercy*, 215–16.

122. Dower, *War without Mercy*, 215.

123. Dower, *War without Mercy*, 232–33.

124. Lin Xianyan, interview by Fang Yu Hu, April 12, 2013.

125. Lin Xianyan, interview by Fang Yu Hu, April 12, 2013.

126. Lin Xianyan used the term *pure* (Jp: *jun*; Tw. Hoklo *sūn*; Ch. *chun*). The term literally means purity, but the context in which Lin used the term means "pure heart" (Lin Xianyan, interview by Fang Yu Hu, April 12, 2013).

127. Lin Xianyan, interview by Fang Yu Hu, April 12, 2013.

128. Vera Mackie, *Feminism in Modern Japan: Citizenship, Embodiment and Sexuality* (Cambridge: Cambridge University Press, 2003), 110.

129. Ching, *Anti-Japan*, 88.

130. A member of Japan's Diet wrote that Shimadu Kenpō was the principal of Taitō (Taitung) Elementary School and a national school (Jp. kokumin gakkō) in Tainan in his introduction to the volume *Bridge to Taiwan* (Ozawa Tarō, "Tsuide ni kaete," in *Taiwan e no kakehashi*, ed. Yamamoto Ryōichi [Osaka: Hōrai Kai Kansai Shibu, 1981]).

131. Hōrai Society is a national group in Japan made up of educators who taught in prewar/wartime Taiwan (Yamamoto Ryōichi, *Taiwan e no kakehashi*, 388). "Hōrai" likely refers to Taiwan, as Japanese colonial officials developed the hōrai rice in Taiwan to meet Japanese demands (Howe, "Taiwan in the 20th Century," 46).

132. Shimadu Kenpō, "Hakkan ni atte," in *Taiwan e no kakehashi*, ed. Yamamoto Ryōichi (Osaka: Hōrai Kai Kansai Shibu, 1981).

133. Wu Surong explained that when she and her classmates were in their thirties, they were too busy with working and child-rearing. They found more time in their forties and fifties, after their children had grown up, to organize reunions (Wu Surong, interview by Fang Yu Hu).

134. For example, Tanaka Kurō visited Taiwan to attend a reunion with his former students on August 10, 1967, twenty-one years since he last saw them (Tanaka, "Inori

NOTES TO PAGES 201–206

tsuzuke te nijūichi nen," 52). Miyazaki Saiji had a reunion with his former students in Taiwan in 1976 (Miyazaki, "Taiwan kyōiku o kaerimi te," 209). For more individual accounts, see *Taiwan e no kakehashi*.

135. Ching, *Anti-Japan*, 86.

136. Ching, *Anti-Japan*, 18.

137. Andrew D. Morris, "Introduction: Living as Left Behind in Postcolonial Taiwan," in *Japanese Taiwan: Colonial Rule and Its Contested Legacy*, ed. Morris (London: Bloomsbury Academic, 2016), 22.

138. Ching, *Anti-Japan*, 92.

139. Dawley, *Becoming Taiwanese*. Evan Dawley provides an overview of some recent studies on identity and history in "The Question of Identity in Recent Scholarship on the History of Taiwan," *China Quarterly*, no. 198 (June 2009): 442–52, http://www.jstor.org/stable/27756461. On the evolution of ethnic identities in Taiwan over time, see Melissa J. Brown, "Changing Authentic Identities: Evidence from Taiwan and China," *Journal of the Royal Anthropological Institute* 16, no. 3 (2010): 459–79, http://www.jstor.org/stable/40926117.

140. "Provincials" is my translation, which is more literal. Interestingly, the Japanese also labeled Han Taiwanese "Islanders" (Jp: Hontōjin); the more literal translation is "those of this island." As a common translation, Dominic Yang translates it as "Taiwanese" but uses "Benshengren" throughout his book (Dominic Meng-Hsuan Yang, *The Great Exodus from China: Trauma, Memory, and Identity in Modern Taiwan* [Cambridge: Cambridge University Press, 2020], 15, doi:10.1017/9781108784306). T. Y. Wang and I-Chou Liu, "Contending Identities in Taiwan: Implications for Cross-Strait Relations," *Asian Survey* 44, no. 4 (2004): 571, https://doi.org/10.1525/as.2004.44.4.568.

141. Wang and Liu, "Contending Identities in Taiwan," 571.

142. Lee Teng-hui, "Understanding Taiwan: Bridging the Perception Gap," *Foreign Affairs* 78, no. 6 (1999): 9, https://doi.org/10.2307/20049528.

143. Daniel C. Lynch, "Taiwan's Self-Conscious Nation-Building Project," *Asian Survey* 44, no. 4 (2004): 515, https://doi.org/10.1525/as.2004.44.4.513.

144. Rou-Lan Chen, "Beyond National Identity in Taiwan: A Multidimensional and Evolutionary Conceptualization," *Asian Survey* 52, no. 5 (2012): 853, https://doi.org/10.1525/as.2012.52.5.845.

145. Lynch incorrectly states that the history curriculum change was in high school (Rou-Lan Chen, "Beyond National Identity in Taiwan," 853; Lynch, "Taiwan's Self-Conscious Nation-Building Project," 515).

146. Corrado Neri, "Haunted Island: Reflections on the Japanese Colonial Era in Taiwanese Cinema," in *Japanese Taiwan: Colonial Rule and Its Contested Legacy*, ed. Andrew D. Morris (London: Bloomsbury Academic, 2016), 182.

147. Jens Sejrup, "Reliving the Past: The Narrative Themes of Repetition and Continuity in Japan-Taiwan News Coverage," in *Japanese Taiwan: Colonial Rule and Its Contested Legacy*, ed. Andrew D. Morris (London: Bloomsbury Academic, 2016), 200.

BIBLIOGRAPHY

In addition to the sections titled "Primary Sources" and "Secondary Sources," "Oral Histories and Interviews" highlights the extensive interviews and oral histories conducted, compiled, and published by researchers based in Taiwan. Besides acknowledging the work of these researchers, I hope to encourage Taiwan specialists, especially junior researchers, to consider incorporating interviews and oral histories into their studies. I use "Primary Sources" and not "Archival Sources" because many sources are located or available outside of archives in different forms, such as fictions, digitalized surveys and certificates, and a bound compilation of historical documents by a Japanese researcher.

ORAL HISTORIES AND INTERVIEWS

Hu, Fang Yu. Personal interviews conducted in Taiwan. August 2010, October 2011–April 2013.

——. Personal interview conducted in the United States. March 2012.

Jiang Wenyu 江文瑜, ed. *Amu de gushi* 阿母的故事 [Mothers' stories]. Taibei: Wenzun Wenhua Qiye Gufen Youxian Gongsi [Meta Media International], 1998.

——. *Xiaoshi zhong de Taiwan ama* 消失中的臺灣阿媽 [The disappearing grandmothers of Taiwan]. Taibei: Yushan She, 1995.

Lai Shujuan 賴淑娟 and Zhang Meifeng 張美鳳, eds. *Yilan nü sheng—Ama de gushi: Jiaoyu pian* 宜蘭女聲 阿媽的故事 教育篇 [Voices of women of Yilan—Stories of grandmothers: Education]. Yilan: Yilan Xian Xian Shi Guan, 2014.

Li Suyue 李素月, ed. *Yilan nü sheng—Ama de gushi: Hangye pian* 宜蘭女聲 阿媽的故事 行業篇 [Voices of women of Yilan—Stories of grandmothers: Career professionals]. Yilan: Yilan Xian Xian Shi Guan, 2015.

——. *Yilan nü sheng—Ama de gushi: Tongyangxi yangnü pian* 宜蘭女聲 阿媽的故事 童養媳 養女篇 [Voices of women of Yilan—Stories of grandmothers: Child brides and adopted daughters]. Yilan: Yilan Xian Xian Shi Guan, 2015.

Lin Huiyu 林惠玉, ed. *Yilan wenxian congkan 9—Yilan qilao tan Ri zhi xia de junshi yu jiaoyu* 宜蘭文獻叢刊 9—宜蘭耆老談 日治下的軍事與教育 [Collection of Yilan primary documents: Discussion of military matters and education under Japanese rule by Yilan seniors]. Yilan: Fu Cheng Yinshua Xingye Gufen Youxian Gongsi, 1996.

Wu Meihui 吳美慧. Recorded. *Yibeizi zhenxian yi jiazi jiaoxue: Shi Suyun nüshi fangwen jilu*輩子針線 一甲子教學：施素筠女士訪問紀錄 [Whole life of sewing, sixty years of teaching: Interview with Ms. Shi Suyun]. Interview by Xu Xueji 許雪姬, Wu Meihui 吳美慧, Lian Xiansheng 連憲升, and Guo Yueru郭月如. Taibei: Zhongyang Yanjiu Yuan Taiwan Shi Yanjiu Suo, 2014.

Zhang Yanxian 張炎憲, ed. *Taiwanren jiaoshi de shidai jingyan* 臺灣人教師的時代經驗 [Experiences of Taiwanese teachers]. Taibei: Taibei Xian Li Wenhua Zhongxin, 1996.

Zhou Fenling 周芬伶, ed. *Fennu de baige: Zouguo Taiwan bainian lishi de nüxing* 憤怒的白鴿—走過台灣百年歷史的女性 [The wrath pigeon: Women who walked through one hundred years in Taiwan]. Taibei: Wenzun Wenhua Qiye Gufen Youxian Gongsi [Meta Media International], 1998.

PRIMARY SOURCES

"2021 niandu Taiwan minzhong dui Riben guangan yanjiu" 年度台灣民眾對日本觀感研究. Conducted by Nihon Taiwan kōryū gakukai 日本台湾交流学会 [Japan–Taiwan Exchange Association]. Accessed March 12, 2022. https://www.koryu .or.jp/Portals/0/culture/%E4%B8%96%E8%AB%96/2021/2021_seron_shosai_CH.pdf.

"Biao 468 li'nian quan sheng xuexiao ji yuan sheng shu" 表468歷年全省學校及員生數 [List 468: The total numbers of schools and students]. In "Taiwan sheng wushi'nian lai tongji jiaoyu gaikuang" 台灣省五十年來統計教育概況 [Statistical overview of education in Taiwan province in the past fifty years]. Originally published in *Taiwan sheng wushi'yi'nian lai tongji tiyao* (1894–1945) 台灣省五十一年來統計提要 (1894–1945) [Statistical overview of the Taiwan province in the past fifty-one years], edited by Taiwan sheng xingzheng zhangguan gongshu tongji shi 臺灣省行政長官公署統計室. Taibei: Guting Shuwu, 1946. Accessed June 13, 2023. http://twstudy.iis.sinica.edu.tw/twstatistic50/Edu.htm.

Fujin to katei 婦人と家庭 (Women and family), 1919–20. Archived at the National Taiwan Library, New Taipei City, Taiwan.

Hayakawa Kidaisu 早川喜代須. *Shō kōgakkō taiiku no tokushu teki shidō to jissai*小公學校體育の特殊的指導と實際 [Particular instructions and practices for physical education at primary and common schools]. Taichū: Tanabe Shoten, 1937. Archived at the National Taiwan Library, New Taipei City, Taiwan.

Inoue Tokuya 井上德彌. *Kōgakkō nōgyō kyōiku* 公學校農業教育 [Agriculture education for primary school]. Taihoku: Taiwan Kodomo Seikai Sha, 1927. Archived at the National Taiwan Library, New Taipei City, Taiwan.

"Jiaoyuan mianxu zhuang shou yu (Dai Wenzhang, [Li Yongchang, Cai Shitian, Yang Azong, Pan Yuanzhen, Su Dìng, Zhang Qiming, Yang Chong'an, Fan Yapi, Song Linyou cang])" (1915–04–01) 教員免許狀授與（戴文章、〔李永昌、蔡士添、楊阿宗、潘元貞、蘇定、張啟明、楊崇安、范亞丕、松林猶藏〕）(1915–04–01). In "Taishō 4-nen Taiwan sōtoku kōbunsho hensan towa hozon dai

64-kan kyōiku" 大正四年臺灣總督府公文類纂永久保存第六十四卷教育. *Taiwan zongdu fu dan'an: Zongdu fu gongwen leizuan* 臺灣總督府檔案/總督府公文類纂. Archived at the Guoshi Guan Taiwan Wenxian Guan (Taiwan Historica), No. 00002404005. Accessed May 1, 2023. https://onlinearchives.th.gov.tw/index.php?act=Display/image/1364389_gLvWaE#0JV5.

"Jiaoyuan mianxu zhuang shou yu (Yang Jiyin) (1915–05–01) 教員免許狀授與（楊基印）」(1915–05–01)." In "Taishō 4-nen Taiwan sōtoku kōbunsho hensan towa hozon dai 67-kan kyōiku" 大正四年臺灣總督府公文類纂永久保存第六十七卷教育. *Taiwan zongdu fu dan'an: Zongdu fu gongwen leizuan* 臺灣總督府檔案/總督府公文類纂. Archived at the Guoshi Guan Taiwan Wenxian Guan (Taiwan Historica), No. 00002407010. https://onlinearchives.th.gov.tw/index.php?act=Display/image/1364390Dj=K84P#Osf9.

Kanbun Taiwan kyōiku 漢文臺灣教育 [Chinese Edition, Educational journal of Taiwan], no. 186-270, 1914-1924. Archived at the National Taiwan Library, New Taipei City, Taiwan.

Kanbun Taiwan nichinichi shimpō 漢文臺灣日日新報 [Taiwan Daily News classical Chinese edition], 1915–19. Digital Archive Access on Transmission Beyond More Classic Books. https://tbmcxb.tbmc.com.tw/item-8.

"Katō Tadatarō." *Taiwan zongdu fu zhiyuan lu xitong.* Institute of Taiwan History, Academia Sinica. https://who.ith.sinica.edu.tw/search2result.html?h=ViY8yoHTz6rgCdlnotub8q2tCb5ngT6P2oxl%2FVoA8%2BJx8W3soe1afMAbYKGxfDYYoWpHfmxIHciLM1vSLO28DQ%3D%3D.

Kōgakkō yō kokugo yomihon dai ichi shu 公學校用國民讀本 第一種 [Primary school use national reader first kind]. Vols. 1–12. Tokyo: Taiwan Sōtokufu, 1923–26. Archived at the National Taiwan Library, New Taipei City, Taiwan.

Kokugo コクゴ [National language]. Vols. 1–4. Taihoku: Taiwan Sōtokufu, 1942. Archived at the National Taiwan Library, New Taipei City, Taiwan.

Liang, Qichao (1897). "On Women's Education." In *The Birth of Chinese Feminism: Essential Texts in Transnational Theory*, edited by Rebecca Karl, Dorothy Ko, and Lydia Liu, 189–203. New York: Columbia University Press, 2013.

Long Yingzong 龍瑛宗. "Zhi you mugua shu de xiaozhen" 植有木瓜樹的小鎮 [The town with papaya trees]. Translated by Zhang Liangze 張良澤. In *Ri zhi shiqi Taiwan xiaoshuo xuandu* 日治時期台灣小說選讀 [Selected short fictions of Taiwan under Japanese rule], edited by Xu Junya 許俊雅, 251–313. Taibei: Wanjuanlo Tushu Gufen Youxian Gongsi, 2003.

Office of the Governor-General of Formosa. "A Review of Educational Work in Formosa, 1916." Originally published by the Department of Educational Affairs of the Office of the Governor-General of Formosa, 1916. Collected in *Nihon shokuminchi kyōiku seisaku shiryō shūsei Taiwan hen dai 1-kan* 日本植民地教育政策資料集成 台湾編第1卷 [Collection of Japanese colonial educational policy: Section on Taiwan, vol. 1], edited by Abe Hiroshi 阿部洋. Tokyo: Ryūkei Shosha, 2007.

Shotōka kokugo 初等科國語 [Elementary-level national language]. Vols. 1–6. Taihoku: Taiwan Sōtokufu, 1943–44. Archived at the National Taiwan Library, New Taipei City, Taiwan.

Taihoku daini shihan gakkō fuzoku kōgakkō keimei kai 台北第二師範学校付属公学校啓明会 [Enlightenment Society at Taihoku No. 2 Normal School Attached Primary School], ed. *Kōgakkō joshi nōgyō kyōju saimoku dai go roku gakunen yō* 公學校女子農業教授細目第五六學年用 [Details for instruction on agriculture for primary school girl—For fifth- and sixth-graders' use]. Taihoku: Taihoku Daini Shihan Gakkō Fuzoku Kōgakkō Keimei Kai, 1939. Archived at the National Taiwan Library, New Taipei City, Taiwan.

Taiwan Fujinkai 台灣婦人界 [Taiwan women's world], 1934–37. Archived at the National Taiwan Library, New Taipei City, Taiwan.

Taiwan jinbutsu shi 臺灣人物誌 [Persons of Taiwan]. Digital database. Academia Sinica.

Taiwan kōgakkō yō kokumin yomihon 臺灣公學校用國民讀本 [Primary school use national reader]. Vols. 1–12. Taihoku: Taiwan Sōtokufu, 1913–14. Archived at the National Taiwan Library, New Taipei City, Taiwan.

Taiwan kyōiku 臺灣教育 [Educational journal of Taiwan], no. 117–no. 497, 1912–43. Archived at the National Taiwan Library, New Taipei City, Taiwan.

Taiwan kyōiku kai 台湾教育会, ed. *Taiwan kyōiku enkaku shi* 台湾教育沿革誌 [Historical account of education in Taiwan]. Taihoku: Taiwan Kyōiku Kai, 1939. Archived at the National Taiwan Library, New Taipei City, Taiwan.

Taiwan kyōikukai zasshi kanbun 臺灣教育會雜誌漢文 [Journal of the Educational Association of Taiwan Chinese edition], no. 79 (October 1908). Archived at the National Taiwan Library, New Taipei City, Taiwan.

Taiwan kyōikukai zasshi 臺灣教育會雜誌 [Journal of the Educational Association of Taiwan], no. 1–no. 116, 1901–11. Archived at the National Taiwan Library, New Taipei City, Taiwan.

Taiwan kyōka-yō-sho kokumin yomihon 臺灣教科用書國民讀本 [National reader for instructional use in Taiwan]. Vols. 1–12. Taihoku: Taiwan Sōtokufu, 1901–3. Archived at the National Taiwan Library, New Taipei City, Taiwan.

Taiwan minbao 台灣民報 [Taiwan people's news], 1924–28. Reprint, Taibei: Dongfang Wenhua Shuju, 1974.

Taiwan nichinichi shimpō 臺灣日日新報 [Taiwan daily news], 1898–1944. Digital Archive Access on Transmission Beyond More Classic Books. https://tbmcxb.tbmc.com.tw/item-8.

Taiwan seinen 台灣青年 [Taiwan youth]. 1920. Reprint, Taibei: Dongfang Wenhua Shuju, 1974.

Taiwan sōtokufu dai yon jū ni tōkei sho Shōwa jusan nen 台湾総督府第四十二統計書昭和十三年 [Taiwan Government-General statistics no. 42, Showa 13th year].

Taihoku: Taiwan Sōtokufu, 1940. Archived at the National Taiwan Library, New Taipei City, Taiwan.

Wu, Zhuoliu. *Orphan of Asia*. Translated by Ioannis Mentzas. New York: Columbia University Press, 2006.

Yamamoto Ryōichi 山本良一. *Taiwan e no kakehashi* 台湾への架け橋 [Bridge to Taiwan]. Osaka: Hōrai Kai Kansai Shibu, 1981.

Yang Qianhe 楊千鶴. "Hua kai shijie" (Riwen yuanzuo: Hana saku kisetsu) 花開時節 (日文原作：花咲く季節) [When flowers blossom (original Japanese title: When flowers blossom)]. In *Ri ju yilai Taiwan nü zuojia xiaoshuo xuandu* (shang) 日據以來台灣女作家小說選讀(上) [Selected short fictions by women writers in Taiwan since Japanese occupation, vol. 1], edited by Qiu Guifen 邱貴芬, 66–93. Taibei: Nü Shu Wenhua Shiye Youxian Gongsi, 2001.

Ye Tao 葉陶. "Ai de jie jing" 愛的結晶 [Beloved child]. In *Ri ju yilai Taiwan nu zuojia xiaoshuo xuandu (shang)* 日據以來台灣女作家小說選讀(上) [Selected short fictions by women writers in Taiwan since Japanese occupation, vol. 1], edited by Qiu Guifen 邱貴芬, 54–59. Taibei: Nü Shu Wenhua Shiye Youxian Gongsi, 2001.

Yoshino Hidetomo 吉野秀公. *Taiwan kyōiku shi* 台湾教育史 [History of education in Taiwan]. 1927. Reprint, Taibei: Nantian Shuju Youxian Gongsi, 1997.

SECONDARY SOURCES

"Arita Otomatsu 有田音松 (8th ed. [July 1928])." *Historical Information for Japanese Studies Jinjikoshinroku (who's who) Database.* Nagoya University Graduate School of Law. Accessed March 8, 2024, https://jahis.law.nagoya-u.ac.jp/who/docs/who8-964.

Arrigo, Linda Gail. "Fifty Years after '2-2-8': The Lingering Legacy of State Terror in the Consolidation of Bourgeois Democracy in Taiwan." *Humboldt Journal of Social Relations* 23, no. 1/2 (1997): 47–69. http://www.jstor.org/stable/23263489.

Barclay, George W. *Colonial Development and Population in Taiwan.* Princeton, NJ: Princeton University Press, 1954. ProQuest Ebook Central.

Bhabha, Homi K. *The Location of Culture.* 2nd ed. London: Routledge, 2004. https://doi-org.proxy.lib.utc.edu/10.4324/9780203820551.

Bissell, William Cunningham. "Engaging Colonial Nostalgia." *Cultural Anthropology* 20, no. 2 (May 2005): 215–48. http://www.jstor.org/stable/3651534.

Boardman, Kay. "The Ideology of Domesticity: The Regulation of the Household Economy in Victorian Women's Magazines." *Victorian Periodicals Review* 33, no. 2 (2000): 150–64. http://www.jstor.org/stable/20083724.

Brown, Melissa J. "Changing Authentic Identities: Evidence from Taiwan and China." *Journal of the Royal Anthropological Institute* 16, no. 3 (2010): 459–79. http://www.jstor.org/stable/40926117.

Cai Jintang 蔡錦堂. "Nihon jidai tōji jidai to Kokumintō tōchi jidai ni koette ikita

Taiwanjin no nihonkan" 日本時代統治時代と国民党統治時代に跨つて生きた台湾人の日本観 [Views of Japan from Taiwanese who lived under Japanese rule and Chinese Nationalist rule]. In *Sengo Taiwan ni okeru nihon: Shokuminchi keiken no renzoku henbō riyō* 戦後台湾における〈日本〉:植民地経験の連続·変貌·利用 [The "Japan" in postwar Taiwan: The formation, transformation, and use of colonial experience], edited by Igarashi Masako 五十嵐真子 and Mio Yūko 三尾裕子, 19–60. Tokyo: Fūkyousha, 2006.

———. *Zhan zheng tizhi xia de Taiwan* 戰爭體制下的台灣 [Taiwan under the wartime organization]. Taibei: Richuang She Wenhua, 2006.

Campbell, D'Ann. "Women in Combat: The World War II Experience in the United States, Great Britain, Germany, and the Soviet Union." *Journal of Military History* 57, no. 2 (1993): 301–23. https://doi.org/10.2307/2944060.

Chang, Doris T. *Women's Movements in Twentieth-Century Taiwan*. Urbana: University of Illinois Press, 2009.

Chang, Han-Yu, and Ramon H. Myers. "Japanese Colonial Development Policy in Taiwan, 1895–1906: A Case of Bureaucratic Entrepreneurship." *Journal of Asian Studies* 22, no. 4 (August 1963): 433–49. http://www.jstor.org/stable/2049857.

Chatani, Sayaka. *Nation-Empire: Ideology and Rural Youth Mobilization in Japan and Its Colonies*. Ithaca, NY: Cornell University Press, 2018.

Chatterjee, Partha. *The Nation and Its Fragments: Colonial and Postcolonial Histories*. Princeton, NJ: Princeton University Press, 1993.

Chen Cuilian 陳翠蓮. "Er er ba shijian" 二二八事件 [2-28 Incident]. In *Taiwan dabaike quanshu* 台灣大百科全書 [Encyclopedia of Taiwan]. Last modified September 24, 2009. https://nrch.culture.tw/twpedia.aspx?id=3838.

Chen Huiwen 陳惠雯. *Dadaocheng chabolang ditu: Dadaocheng funü de huodong kongjian jin bainian lai de bianqian* 大稻埕查某人地圖:大稻埕婦女的活動空間近百年來的變遷 [Map of women of Dadaocheng: Transformation of Dadaocheng women's space in the past 100 years]. Taibei: Boyang, 1999.

Chen Peifeng 陳培豐. *"Dōka" no dōshō imu: Nihon tōchi ka Taiwan no kokugo kyōikushi saikō* 同化の同床異夢:日本統治下台湾の国語教育史再考 [Diverging goals of assimilation: Reconsideration of the history of language education in Taiwan under Japanese rule]. Tokyo: Sangensha, 2001.

Chen Peiting 陳佩婷. "Taiwan shan dao yangfu: Taiwan funü yangcai de fazhan lishi (1895–1970)" 台灣衫到洋服—台灣婦女洋裁的發展歷史 [From Taiwanese traditional clothes to Western clothes: History of Taiwanese women's Western sewing (1895–1970)]. Master's thesis, Fengjia Daxue, 2009. https://hdl.handle.net/11296/gnf9w6.

Chen, Rou-Lan. "Beyond National Identity in Taiwan: A Multidimensional and Evolutionary Conceptualization." *Asian Survey* 52, no. 5 (2012): 845–71. https://doi.org/10.1525/as.2012.52.5.845.

Cheng, Tun-jen. "Transforming Taiwan's Economic Structure in the 20th Century." *China Quarterly*, no. 165 (2001): 19–36. http://www.jstor.org/stable/3451104.

Ching, Leo T. S. *Anti-Japan: The Politics of Sentiment in Postcolonial East Asia*. Durham, NC: Duke University Press, 2019. https://doi.org/10.2307/j.ctv113166n.

———. *Becoming "Japanese": Colonial Taiwan and the Politics of Identity Formation*. Berkeley: University of California Press, 2001.

———. "'Give Me Japan and Nothing Else!': Postcoloniality, Identity, and the Traces of Colonialism." *South Atlantic Quarterly* 99, no. 4 (2000): 763–88. https://www.muse.jhu.edu/article/30676.

———. "Savage Construction and Civility Making: The Musha Incident and Aboriginal Representations in Colonial Taiwan." *positions* 8, no. 3 (2000): 795–818. https://muse-jhu-edu.oca.ucsc.edu/journals/positions/v008/8.3ching.html.

Choi, Hyaeweol. *Gender and Mission Encounters in Korea: New Women, Old Ways*. Seoul-California Series in Korean Studies, vol. 1. Berkeley: University of California Press, 2009. ProQuest Ebook Central.

———. "Wise Mother, Good Wife": A Transcultural Discursive Construct in Modern Korea." *Journal of Korean Studies* 14, no. 1 (2009): 1–33. http://www.jstor.org/stable/43998361.

Chou, Wan-yao 周婉窈. *Hai xing xi de niandai—Riben zhimin tongzhi moqi Taiwan shi lunji* 海行兮的年代—日本殖民統治末期臺灣史論集 [The era of "When I go to the sea" ("Umi yukaba"): Collection of essays of Taiwanese history from the late Japanese colonial rule]. Taibei: Xunchen Wenhua Gongsi, 2003.

———. "The Kominka Movement in Taiwan and Korea: Comparisons and Interpretations." In *The Japanese Wartime Empire, 1931–1945*, edited by Peter Duus, Ramon H. Myers, and Mark R. Peattie, 40–70. Princeton, NJ: Princeton University Press, 1996.

———. "Xieshi yu guifan zhijian—gong xuexiao guoyu duben chahua zhong de Taiwanren xingxiang" 寫實與規範之間—公學校國語讀本插畫中的臺灣人形象 [Between reality and ideal: Images of Taiwanese in the illustrations from Kokugo readers in primary schools]. *Taida lishi xuebao* 34 qi (December 2004): 87–147.

Chou, Wan-yao周婉窈, and Xu Peixian 許佩賢. "Taiwan gong xuexiao zhidu, jiaoke he jiaokeshu zongshuo" 臺灣公學校制度、教科和教科書總說 [An overview of system, curriculum, and textbooks in Taiwanese primary schools]. *Taiwan fengwu* 臺灣風物 [The Taiwan folkways] 53, no. 4 (November 2003): 119–45.

Christy, Alan. "The Making of Imperial Subjects in Okinawa." In *Formations of Colonial Modernity in East Asia*, edited by Tani Barlow, 141–69. Durham, NC: Duke University Press, 1997.

Chu, Shiu On. "The Fifth Great Chinese Invention: Examination and State Power in Twentieth Century China and Taiwan." PhD diss., Brown University, 2018.

Cook, Haruko Taya. "Women's Deaths as Weapons of War in Japan's 'Final Battle.'" In *Gendering Modern Japanese History*, edited by Barbara Molony and Kathleen Uno,

326–56. Harvard East Asian Monographs 251. Cambridge, MA: Harvard University Asia Center, 2005.

Cook, Theodore F., Jr. "Making 'Soldiers': The Imperial Army and the Japanese Man in Meiji Society and State." In *Gendering Modern Japanese History*, edited by Barbara Molony and Kathleen Uno, 259–94. Harvard East Asian Monographs 251. Cambridge, MA: Harvard University Asia Center, 2005.

Davis, Belinda. "Experience, Identity, and Memory: The Legacy of World War I." *Journal of Modern History* 75, no. 1 (2003): 111–31. https://doi.org/10.1086/377750.

Dawley, Evan N. *Becoming Taiwanese: Ethnogenesis in a Colonial City, 1880s–1950s.* Cambridge, MA: Harvard University Asia Center, 2019.

———. "The Question of Identity in Recent Scholarship on the History of Taiwan." *China Quarterly*, no. 198 (June 2009): 442–52. http://www.jstor.org/stable/27756461.

Dower, John W. *War without Mercy: Race & Power in the Pacific War.* New York: Pantheon, 1986.

Enoch, Jessica. "There's No Place Like the Childcare Center: A Feminist Analysis of <Home> in the World War II Era." *Rhetoric Review* 31, no. 4 (2012): 422–42. http://www.jstor.org/stable/41697863.

Enomoto, Miyuki 榎本美由紀. "Nihon tōchi jiki Taiwan no kasei kyōiku" 日本統治時期台湾の家政教育 [Home economics education in Taiwan under Japanese rule]. Master's thesis, Hiroshima Daigaku, 2000. https://ir.lib.hiroshima-u.ac.jp/20306/files/24235.

Feng, Jin. *The Making of a Family Saga: Ginling College.* Albany: State University of New York Press, 2009.

Foucault, Michel. *The History of Sexuality, Volume 1: An Introduction.* Translated by Robert Hurley. 1976. New York: Vintage, 1990.

Frühstück, Sabine. *Playing War: Children and the Paradoxes of Modern Militarism in Japan.* Oakland: University of California Press, 2017.

Fujitani, Takashi. *Race for Empire: Koreans as Japanese and Japanese as Americans during World War II.* Berkeley: University of California Press, 2011.

"Fukuzawa Yukichi." In *Portraits of Modern Japanese Historical Figures.* National Diet Library, Japan. https://www.ndl.go.jp/portrait/e/datas/185/.

Fwu, Bih-Jen, and Hsiou-Huai Wang. "The Social Status of Teachers in Taiwan." *Comparative Education* 38, no. 2 (May 2002): 211–24. http://www.jstor.org/stable/3099785.

Garon, Sheldon M. *Molding Japanese Minds: The State in Everyday Life.* Princeton, NJ: Princeton University Press, 1997.

Gerrard, Teresa, and Alexis Weedon. "Working-Class Women's Education in Huddersfield: A Case Study of the Female Educational Institute Library, 1856–1857." *Information & Culture* 49, no. 2 (2014): 234–64. http://www.jstor.org/stable/43737487.

Goldstein, Joshua S. *War and Gender: How Gender Shapes the War System and Vice Versa.* Cambridge: Cambridge University Press, 2001.

Hansen, Annette Skovsted. "Practicing 'Kokugo': Teachers in Hokkaido and Okinawa Classrooms, 1895–1904." *Journal of Japanese Studies* 40, no. 2 (2014): 329–51.

Hauser, William B. "Women and War: The Japanese Film Image." In *Recreating Japanese Women, 1600–1945*, edited by Gail Lee Bernstein, 296–313. Berkeley: University of California Press, 1991.

Havens, Thomas R. H. "Women and War in Japan, 1937–45." *American Historical Review* 80, no. 4 (1975): 913–34. doi:10.2307/1867444.

Howe, Christopher. "Taiwan in the 20th Century: Model or Victim? Development Problems in a Small Asian Economy." *China Quarterly*, no. 165 (2001): 37–60. http://www.jstor.org/stable/3451105.

Hu, Fang Yu. "The 'Modern Woman' in Colonial Taiwan: The Intellectuals' Construction in *Taiwan minbao*, 1924–1927." Master's thesis, University of Chicago, 2006.

———. "Taiwanese Girls' Education, 1897–1945: Policy and Practice in a Gendered Colonial System." *Eras: Monash University School of Historical Studies Online Journal* 13, no. 1 (December 2011). https://www.monash.edu/__data/assets/pdf_file/0011/1672859/fang-yu-hu-taiwanese-1.pdf.

Huang Ling'e 黃玲娥. "Yan'ge zai Taiwan de fazhan yu bianqian—Touguo yan'ge aihao zhe de diaocha" 「演歌」在台灣的發展與變遷 — 透過「演歌」愛好者的調查 [The development and reception of Japanese enka music in Taiwan through the survey of enka fans]. Master's thesis, Donghai Daxue, 2019. https://hdl.handle.net/11296/wmpkz3.

Huang Zhaotang 黃昭堂. Translated by Huang Yingzhe 黃英哲. *Taiwan zongdufu* 台灣總督府 [The Government-General of Taiwan]. Originally published as *Taiwan sōtokufu* 台湾総督府 [The Government-General of Taiwan] in Tokyo: Kyōikusha, 1981. Chinese-language edition published in Taibei: Ziyou Shidai, 1989.

Hundt, David, and Roland Bleiker. "Colonial Memories in Korea and Japan." In "Reconciliation between China and Japan," special issue, *Asian Perspective* 31 (2007): 61–91. http://www.jstor.org/stable/42704577.

Jin Jungwon 陳姃湲. *Higashi ajia no ryōsai kenbo ron: Tsukurareta dentō* 東アジアの良妻賢母論: 創られた伝統 [The ideology of "Good Wife, Wise Mother" in East Asia: An invented tradition]. Tokyo: Keisō Shobō 2006.

Johnson, Eric J. "Under Ideological Fire: Illustrated Wartime Propaganda for Children." In *Under Fire: Childhood in the Shadow of War*, edited by Elizabeth Goodenough and Andrea Immel, 59–76. Detroit, MI: Wayne State University Press, 2008.

Judge, Joan. "The Ideology of 'Good Wives and Wise Mothers': Meiji Japan and Feminine Modernity in Late-Qing China." In *Sagacious Monks and Bloodthirsty Warriors: Chinese Views of Japan in the Ming-Qing Period*, edited by Joshua A. Fogel, 218–48. Norwalk, CT: East Bridge, 2002.

———. *The Precious Raft of History: The Past, the West, and the Woman Question in China*. Stanford, CA: Stanford University Press, 2022.

Kerber, Linda. "The Republican Mother: Women and the Enlightenment—An American Perspective." *American Quarterly* 28, no. 2 (1976): 187–205. https://doi.org/10.2307/2712349.

Kerr, George. "The Surrender on Formosa, 1945." Chapter 3 of *Formosa Betrayed*, by Kerr. Upland, CA: Taiwan Publishing, 2005. http://www.romanization.com/books/formosabetrayed/chap03.html.

———. "On the Eve of Disaster." Chapter 11 of *Formosa Betrayed*, by Kerr. Upland, CA: Taiwan Publishing, 2005. http://www.romanization.com/books/formosabetrayed/chap11.html.

Kim, Janice C. H. "The Pacific War and Working Women in Late Colonial Korea." *Signs* 33, no. 1 (2007): 81–103. https://doi:10.1086/518392.

Kitamura Kae 北村嘉恵. Translated by Guo Tingyu. "Fantong jiaoyu suo jiuxuezhe zengjia de juti qingkuang: Yi Taiwan zongdu fu de ducu jiuxue ji qi xianshi jichu wei zhongxin" 番童教育所就學者增加的具體情況：以臺灣總督府的督促就學及其現實基礎為中心 [Increase of students at aborigines educational center: Under the supervision and actual foundation of the Office of the Governor-General of Taiwan]. In *Taiwan shi luncong jiaoyu pian—Diguo de xuexiao diyu de xuexiao* 台灣史論叢 教育篇—帝國的學校地域的學校 [Taiwan History Series: Education—The history of modern education in Taiwan under Japanese colonial rule], edited by Xu Peixian 許佩賢, 135–64. Taibei: Taida Chuban Zhongxin, 2020.

Ko Ikujo (Hong, Yuru) 洪郁如. *Kindai Taiwan josei shi: Nihon no shokumin tōchi to "Shinjosei" no tanjō* 近代台湾女性史—日本の植民統治と〈新女性〉の誕生 [The history of modern Taiwanese women: Japanese colonial rule and the birth of the "New Woman"]. Tokyo: Keisō Shobō, 2001.

———. "Shokuminchi Taiwan no 'modangāru' genshō to fasshon no seiji-ka" 植民地台湾の〈モダンガール〉現象とファッションの政治化」 [The "Modern Girl" phenomenon and the politicization of fashion in colonial Taiwan]. In *Modangāru to shokuminchi teki kindai—Higashiajia ni okeru teikoku shihon jendā* モダンガールと植民地的近代—東アジアにおける帝国·資本·ジェンダー [The "Modern Girl" and colonial modernity: Empire, capitalism, and gender in East Asia], edited by Itō Ruri, Sakamoto Hiroko, and Tani Barlow, 261–84. Tokyo: Iwanami Shobō, 2010.

"Kobayashi Jun'ichi Taihoku chō keisatsu i nin-su" 小林準一臺北廳警察醫ニ任ス. *Guojia wenhua jiyi ku* 國家文化記憶庫 [Taiwan Cultural Memory Bank]. Ministry of Culture of Taiwan. Accessed May 1, 2023. https://memory.culture.tw/Home/Detail?Id=00001435066&IndexCode=th.

Komagome Takeshi 駒込武. "Dai ni ji Taiwan kyōikurei ka ni okeru shiritsu gakkō—'Shiritsu chūgakkō kōtō jogakkō setsuritsu ninka hyōjun' seitei ikisatsu" 第二次台湾教育令下における私立学校—私立中学校高等女学校設立認可標準」制定経緯 [Private schools under the Revised Taiwan Educational Ordinance—Establishment of "Private junior high school and high school girls' school establishment approval standard"]. In *Chōsen Taiwan ni okeru shokuminchi shihai no seido kikō seisaku ni kansuru sōgō-teki kenkyū Heisei 13-nendo ~ 15-nendo Kagaku kenkyūhi hojokin kenkyū seika hōkoku-sho* 朝鮮・台湾における植民地支配の制度・機構・政策に関する総合的研究 平成13年度～15年度科学研究費補助金研究成果報告書 (May 2004): 114–45.

———. *Shokuminchi teikoku nihon no bunka tōgō* 植民地帝国日本の文化統合 [Cultural integration of colonies in imperial Japan]. Tokyo: Iwanami Shoten, 1996.

"Kōra Tomi 高良とみ (1896–1993)." Webcat Plus. National Institute of Informatics (of Japan). Accessed May 1, 2023. http://webcatplus.nii.ac.jp/webcatplus/details /creator/35554.html.

Kou, Mei-ling Lai. "Development of Music Education in Taiwan (1895–1995)." *Journal of Historical Research in Music Education* 22, no. 2 (2001): 177–90. http://www.jstor .org/stable/41300442.

Koyama Shizuko 小山静子. *Ryōsai kenbo to iu kihan* 良妻賢母という規範 [The standard called "Good Wife, Wise Mother"]. Tokyo: Keisō Shobō, 1991.

Kushner, Barak. "Nationality and Nostalgia: The Manipulation of Memory in Japan, Taiwan, and China since 1990." *International History Review* 29, no. 4 (December 2007): 793–820. http://www.jstor.org/stable/40110927.

Lee, Teng-hui. "Understanding Taiwan: Bridging the Perception Gap." *Foreign Affairs* 78, no. 6 (1999): 9–14. https://doi.org/10.2307/20049528.

Li Liyong 李力庸, "Riben diguo zhimindi de zhanshi liangshi tongzhi tizhi: Taiwan yu Chaoxian de bijiao yanjiu (1937–1945)" 日本帝國殖民地的戰時糧食統治體制臺灣與朝鮮的比較研究 [Wartime grain control in Japanese colonies: Comparative study between Taiwan and Korea]. *Taiwan shi yanjiu* 臺灣史研究 [Taiwan historical research] 16, no. 2 (2009): 63–104.

Li Xiaofeng 李筱峯. "Zhan hou chuqi Taiwan shehui de wenhua chongtu" 戰後初期台灣社會的文化衝突 [Cultural clash in Taiwanese society during the early postwar era]. In *Taiwan shi lunwen jingxuan xia* 臺灣史論文精選 下 [Selection of essays on Taiwan history, vol. 2], edited by Zhang Yanxian 張炎憲, Li Xiaofeng 李筱峯, and Dai Baocun 戴寶村, 273–302. Taibei: Yushan She Chuban, 1996.

Li Yuanhui 李園會. *Ri ju shiqi Taiwan shifan jiaoyu zhidu* 日據時期臺灣師範教育制度 [Teacher training educational system in Taiwan during the Japanese occupation period]. Taibei: Nan Tian Shuju, 1997.

Lin, Ching-Yuan, and Chun-Hung A. Lin. "Does Higher Education Expansion Reduce Credentialism and Gender Discrimination in Education?" *Social Indicators Research* 109, no. 2 (2012): 279–93. http://www.jstor.org/stable/23325427.

Lin, Chin-ju. "Modern Daughters-in-Law in Colonial Taiwanese Families." *Journal of Family History* 30, no. 2 (April 2005): 191–209. http://jfh.sagepub.com/cgi/content /abstract/30/2/191.

Lin Jiwen 林繼文. *Riben ju Tai moqi zhanzheng dongyuan tixi zhi yanjiu* 日本據台末期戰爭動員體系之研究 [A study of wartime mobilization in Taiwan during the late Japanese occupation period]. Taibei: Daoxiang Chuban She, 1996.

Lin Zhimei 林智美. "Yang Qianhe" 楊千鶴. In *Ri ju yilai Taiwan nu zuojia xiaoshuo xuandu (shang)* 日據以來台灣女作家小說選讀(上) [Selected short fictions by women writers in Taiwan since Japanese occupation, vol. 1], edited by Qiu Guifen 邱貴芬, 65. Taibei: Nü Shu Wenhua Shiye Youxian Gongsi, 2001.

Liu Hengwen 劉恆妏. "Jieyan" 戒嚴 [Martial law]. In *Taiwan dabaike quanshu* 台灣大百科全書 [Encyclopedia of Taiwan]. Last modified September 24, 2009. https://nrch.culture.tw/twpedia.aspx?id=3861.

Liu, Michael Shiyung. *Prescribing Colonization: The Role of Medical Practices and Policies in Japan-Ruled Taiwan, 1895–1945*. Ann Arbor, MI: Association for Asian Studies, 2009.

Lo, Ming-cheng Miriam. *Doctors within Borders: Profession, Ethnicity, and Modernity in Colonial Taiwan*. Berkeley: University of California Press, 2002. ProQuest Ebook Central.

Lorcin, Patricia M. E. *Historicizing Colonial Nostalgia: European Women's Narratives of Algeria and Kenya 1900–Present*. New York: Palgrave Macmillan, 2012. ProQuest Ebook Central.

———. "Imperial Nostalgia; Colonial Nostalgia: Differences of Theory, Similarities of Practice?" In "Nostalgia in Modern France: Bright New Ideas about a Melancholy Subject," special issue, *Historical Reflections/Réflexions Historiques* 39, no. 3 (Winter 2013): 97–111. http://www.jstor.org/stable/42703774.

Lucas, Christopher J. "The Politics of National Development and Education in Taiwan." *Comparative Politics* 14, no. 2 (January 1982): 211–25. http://www.jstor.org/stable/421587.

Luo Mingqing 駱明慶. "Gaopu kaofen shengqu ding'e luqu yu tezhong kaoshi de shengji shaixuan xiaoguo" 高普考分省區定額錄取與特種考試的省籍篩選效果 [The effect of acceptance rate with established quota and special exam with screening by home province in civil service examinations]. *Jingji lunwen congkan* 經濟論文叢刊 [Taiwan economic review] 31, no. 1 (2003): 87–106. http://homepage.ntu.edu.tw/~luohm/selection.pdf.

———. "Jiaoyu chengjiu de shengji yu xinbie chayi" 教育成就的省籍與性別差異 [Educational success: Difference in home province and gender]. *Jingji lunwen congkan* 經濟論文叢刊 [Taiwan economic review] 29, no. 2 (2001): 117–52. http://homepage.ntu.edu.tw/~luohm/attainment.pdf.

———. "Shui shi taida xuesheng?—Xingbie, shengji yu chengxiang chayi" 誰是台大學生?—性別、省籍與城鄉差異 [Who are the students at National Taiwan University? Difference in gender, home province, and city/town]. *Jingji lunwen congkan* 經濟論文叢刊 [Taiwan economic review] 30, no. 1(March 2002): 113–47. http://homepage.ntu.edu.tw/~luohm/NTU.pdf.

Lynch, Daniel C. "Taiwan's Self-Conscious Nation-Building Project." *Asian Survey* 44, no. 4 (2004): 513–33. https://doi.org/10.1525/as.2004.44.4.513.

Mackie, Vera. *Feminism in Modern Japan: Citizenship, Embodiment and Sexuality.* Cambridge: Cambridge University Press, 2003.

Mamiya, Christin J. "Nineteenth-Century French Women, the Home, and the Colonial Vision: Les Sauvages de la Mer Pacifique Wallpaper." *Frontiers: A Journal of Women Studies* 28, no. 1/2 (2007): 100–20. http://www.jstor.org/stable/40071949.

Marshall, Byron K. *Learning to Be Modern: Japanese Political Discourse on Education.* London: Routledge, 1994. https://doi-org.proxy.lib.utc.edu/10.4324/9780429499272.

Marukawa, Tetsushi. Translated by Mieko Okamoto. "Situating Yoshinori Kobayashi's Taiwan ron ('The Taiwan Question') in East Asia." *Postcolonial Studies: Culture, Politics, Economy* 6, no. 2 (2003): 239–44. https://doi:10.1080/13688790308102.

Matsuda, Hiroko. *Liminality of the Japanese Empire: Border Crossings from Okinawa to Colonial Taiwan.* Honolulu: University of Hawai'i Press, 2019. http://www.jstor.org/stable/j.ctvvn7ng.

McNamara, Dennis L. "Comparative Colonial Response: Korea and Taiwan." *Korean Studies*, no. 10 (1986): 54–68. http://www.jstor.org/stable/23718831.

Miller, Lisa. "Register of the George H. Kerr Papers." Online Archive of California. Last updated 2003. https://oac.cdlib.org/findaid/ark:/13030/kt558013kc/entire_text/.

Minault, Gail. *Secluded Scholars: Women's Education and Muslim Social Reform in Colonial India.* Delhi: Oxford University Press, 1998.

Miyake, Yoshiko. "Doubling Expectations: Motherhood and Women's Factory Work under State Management in Japan in the 1930s and 1940s." In *Recreating Japanese Women, 1600–1945*, edited by Gail Lee Bernstein, 267–95. Berkeley: University of California Press, 1991.

Miyazaki, Seiko 宮崎聖子. *Shokuminki Taiwan ni okeru seinendan to chiiki no henyō* 植民地期台湾における青年団と地域の変容 [Youth groups and local changes in Taiwan under Japanese colonial rule]. Tokyo: Ochanomizu Shobō, 2008.

Morris, Andrew D. "Introduction: Living as Left Behind in Postcolonial Taiwan." In *Japanese Taiwan: Colonial Rule and Its Contested Legacy*, edited by Morris, 3–23. London: Bloomsbury Academic, 2016.

Neri, Corrado. "Haunted Island: Reflections on the Japanese Colonial Era in Taiwanese Cinema." In *Japanese Taiwan: Colonial Rule and Its Contested Legacy*, edited by Andrew D. Morris, 171–83. London: Bloomsbury Academic, 2016.

Nolte, Sharon H., and Sally Ann Hastings. "The Meiji State's Policy toward Women, 1890–1910." In *Recreating the Japanese Women, 1600–1945*, edited by Gail Lee Bernstein, 151–74. Berkeley: University of California Press, 1991.

Ossian, Lisa L. *The Forgotten Generation: American Children and World War II.* Columbia: University of Missouri Press, 2011. ProQuest Ebook Central.

Otsubo, Sumiko. "Engendering Eugenics: Feminists and Marriage Restriction Legislation in the 1920s." In *Gendering Modern Japanese History*, edited by Barbara Molony and Kathleen Uno, 225–56. Harvard East Asian Monographs 251. Cambridge, MA: Harvard University Asia Center, 2005.

Ou, Zongzhi 歐宗智. *Zouchu lishi de beiqing: Taiwan xiaoshuo pinglun ji wenxue pinglun ji 62* 走出歷史的悲情—臺灣小說評論集 文學評論集62 [Leaving historical sadness: Critical essays on Taiwanese fiction—Collection of literary critique 62]. Banqiao: Taibei Xian Zhengfu Wenhua Ju Chuban, 2002.

Paterson, Andrew. "The Gospel of Work Does Not Save Souls": Conceptions of Industrial and Agricultural Education for Africans in the Cape Colony, 1890–1930." *History of Education Quarterly* 45, no. 3 (2005): 377–404. http://www.jstor.org/stable /20461986.

Qiu Zuyin 邱祖胤. "Taiwan shouwei nu jizhe Yang Qianhe gaobie zhuan qi rensheng" 台灣首位女記者楊千鶴 告別傳奇人生 [Yang Qianhe: First female journalist of Taiwan bids farewell to a legendary life]. *Zhongguo shibao* [China times], October 28, 2011. https://web.archive.org/web/20111031162657/http://news.chinatimes.com /reading/110513/11201110280053 8.html.

Reddy, William M. *The Making of Romantic Love: Longing and Sexuality in Europe, South Asia, and Japan, 900–1200 CE*. Chicago: University of Chicago Press, 2012. ProQuest Ebook Central.

Rodd, Laurel Rasplica. "Yasano Akiko and the Taisho Debate over the 'New Woman.'" In *Recreating the Japanese Women, 1600–1945*, edited by Gail Lee Bernstein, 175–98. Berkeley: University of California Press, 1991.

Roden, Donald. "Thoughts on the Early Meiji Gentleman." In *Gendering Modern Japanese History*, edited by Barbara Molony and Kathleen Uno, 61–98. Harvard East Asian Monographs 251. Cambridge, MA: Harvard University Asia Center, 2005.

Rogaski, Ruth. *Hygienic Modernity: Meanings of Health and Disease in Treaty-Port China*. Berkeley: University of California Press, 2004.

Said, Edward W. *Orientalism*. 1978. New York: Vintage, 1994.

Segalla, Spencer. *The Moroccan Soul: French Education, Colonial Ethnology, and Muslim Resistance, 1912–1956*. Lincoln: University of Nebraska Press, 2009. ProQuest Ebook Central.

Sejrup, Jens. "Reliving the Past: The Narrative Themes of Repetition and Continuity in Japan-Taiwan News Coverage." In *Japanese Taiwan: Colonial Rule and Its Contested Legacy*, edited by Andrew D. Morris, 185–200. London: Bloomsbury Academic, 2016.

Selden, Mark, and Yoshiko Nozaki. "Japanese Textbook Controversies, Nationalism, and Historical Memory: Intra- and Inter-national Conflicts." *Asia-Pacific Journal—Japan Focus* 7, issue 24, no. 5 (June 2009): 1–25. https://apjjf.org/-Yoshiko-Nozaki—Mark -Selden/3173/article.pdf.

Shen Cuilian 沈翠蓮. *Taiwan xiaoxue shizi peiyu shi* 台灣小學師資培育史 [The history of elementary school teacher-training programs in Taiwan]. Taibei: Wu'nan Tushu Chuban Gufen Youxian Gongsi, 2004.

Shirane, Seiji. *Imperial Gateway: Colonial Taiwan and Japan's Expansion in South China and Southeast Asia, 1895–1945*. Ithaca, NY: Cornell University Press, 2022. http://www.jstor.org/stable/10.7591/j.ctv310vk5n.

Silverberg, Miriam. "The Modern Girl as Militant." In *Recreating the Japanese Women, 1600–1945*, edited by Gail Lee Bernstein, 239–66. Berkeley: University of California Press, 1991.

Smith, W. Donald. "Beyond 'The Bridge on the River Kwai': Labor Mobilization in the Greater East Asia Co-Prosperity Sphere." *International Labor and Working-Class History*, no. 58 (2000): 219–38. http://www.jstor.org/stable/27672681.

Southard, Barbara. *The Women's Movement and Colonial Politics in Bengal: The Quest for Political Rights, Education, and Social Reform Legislation, 1921–1936*. New Delhi: Manohar, 1995.

Su Ruiqiang 蘇瑞鏘. "Baise kongbu" 白色恐怖 [White Terror]. In *Taiwan da baike quanshu* 台灣大百科全書 [Encyclopedia of Taiwan]. Last modified March 21, 2012. https://nrch.culture.tw/twpedia.aspx?id=3864.

Su, Ya-Chen. "Ideological Representations of Taiwan's History: An Analysis of Elementary Social Studies Textbooks, 1978–1995." *Curriculum Inquiry* 37, no. 3 (September 2007): 205–37. http://www.jstor.org/stable/30053219.

Suh, Jiyoung. "The 'New Woman' and the Topography of Modernity in Colonial Korea." *Korean Studies* 37 (2013): 11–43. http://www.jstor.org/stable/24575275.

Sun Manlin 孫曼琳. "Qingting yu jilu—Taiwan zai rishi shiqi xia de Riben tongyao" 傾聽與紀錄-臺灣在日治時期下的日本童謠 [Listening and recording: Japanese nursery rhymes in Taiwan during the Japanese period]. Master's thesis, Guoli Taiwan Shifan Daxue, 2017. https://hdl.handle.net/11296/8wacg5.

Tai, Eika. "*Kokugo* and Colonial Education in Taiwan." *positions* 7, no. 2 (May 1, 1999): 503–40. https://muse.jhu.edu/article/27929.

Taiwan zongdu fu zhiyuan lu xitong. Institute of Taiwan History, Academia Sinica. https://who.ith.sinica.edu.tw/.

Takizawa Kanae 瀧澤佳奈枝. "Shokumin chi Taiwan ni okeru gigei kyōiku—Taihoku dai san kōtō jogakkō o chūshin ni" 植民地台湾における技芸教育—台北第三高等女学校を中心に [Handicrafts instruction in colonial Taiwan: A case study of Taihoku No. 3 Girls' Middle School]. Master's thesis, Danjiang Daxue, 2005. https://hdl.handle.net/11296/n9hwct.

Tanaka, Stefan. *Japan's Orient: Rendering Pasts into History*. Berkeley: University of California Press, 1995.

Taylor, Jean. "Education, Colonialism, and Feminism: An Indonesian Case Study." In *Education and the Colonial Experience*, edited by Philip G. Altbach and Gail P. Kelly, 137–51. New York: Advent, 1991.

Teng, Emma. *Taiwan's Imagined Geography: Chinese Colonial Travel Writing and Pictures, 1683–1895*. Cambridge, MA: Harvard University Asia Center, 2004.

Ts'ai, Hui-yu Caroline. "Total War, Labor Drafts, and Colonial Administration: Wartime

Mobilization in Taiwan (1936–1945)." In *Asian Labor in the Wartime Japanese Empire*, edited by Paul H. Kratoska, 101–26, 365–72. New York: M. E. Sharpe, 2005.

Tsurumi, Patricia E. *Japanese Colonial Education in Taiwan, 1895–1945*. Harvard East Asia Series. Cambridge, MA: Harvard University Press, 1977.

Tsuruta Jun 鶴田純. "1950–60 niandai Riben qu Taiyuge yanjiu" 1950、60年代「日本曲台灣歌」研究 [A study of Taiwanese language versions of Japanese songs during the 1950s and 1960s]. Master's thesis, Guoli Chenggong Daxue, 2008. https://hdl.handle.net/11296/9fyh28.

Uchida, Jun. *Brokers of Empire: Japanese Settler Colonialism in Korea, 1876–1945*. Cambridge, MA: Harvard University Asia Center, 2011.

Ueno Hiroko 植野弘子. "Shokuminchi Taiwan niokeru kōtō jōgakkōsei no 'nihon'—seigatsu bunka no henyō ni kansuru shiron" 植民地台湾における高等女学校生の「日本」—生活文化の変容に関する試論 [The "Japan" of middle school girls in colonial Taiwan—A preliminary discussion of the transformation of their life culture]. In Sengo Taiwan ni okeru nihon: Shokuminchi keiken no renzoku henbō riyō 戦後台湾における〈日本〉：植民地経験の連続・変貌・利用 [The "Japan" in postwar Taiwan: The formation, transformation, and use of colonial experience], edited by Igarashi Masako五十嵐真子 and Mio Yūko 三尾裕子, 121–54. Tokyo: Fūkyō Sha, 2006.

Uno, Kathleen. "Womanhood, War, and Empire: Transmutations of 'Good Wife, Wise Mother' before 1931." In *Gendering Modern Japanese History*, edited by Barbara Molony and Kathleen Uno, 493–519. Harvard East Asian Monographs 251. Cambridge, MA: Harvard University Asia Center, 2005.

———. "Women and Changes in the Household Division of Labor." In *Recreating Japanese Women, 1600–1945*, edited by Gail Lee Bernstein, 17–41. Berkeley: University of California Press, 1991.

Wakewich, Pamela, and Helen Smith. "The Politics of 'Selective' Memory: Re-Visioning Canadian Women's Wartime Work in the Public Record." *Oral History* 34, no. 2 (2006): 56–68. http://www.jstor.org/stable/40179897.

Walder, Dennis. *Postcolonial Nostalgias: Writing, Representation and Memory*. London: Taylor & Francis, 2010. ProQuest Ebook Central.

Walker, Brett L. *The Conquest of Ainu Lands: Ecology and Culture in Japanese Expansion, 1590–1800*. Berkeley: University of California Press, 2001.

Wamagatta, Evanson N. "Changes of Government Policies towards Mission Education in Colonial Kenya and Their Effects on the Missions: The Case of the Gospel Missionary Society." *Journal of Religion in Africa* 38, no. 1 (2008): 3–26. http://www.jstor.org/stable/27594443.

Wang, Hong-zen. "Class Structures and Social Mobility in Taiwan in the Initial Post-War Period." *China Journal*, no. 48 (2002): 55–85. https://doi.org/10.2307/3182441.

Wang Jinque 王錦雀. *Ri zhi shiqi Taiwan gongmin jiaoyu yu gongmin texing* 日治時期

台灣公民教育與公民特性 [Civic education and characteristics of citizens in Taiwan under Japanese rule]. Taibei: Taiwan Guji Shuban Youxian Gongsi, 2005.

Wang, T. Y., and I-Chou Liu. "Contending Identities in Taiwan: Implications for Cross-Strait Relations." *Asian Survey* 44, no. 4 (2004): 568–90. https://doi.org/10.1525/as.2004.44.4.568.

Wang, Tay-sheng. *Legal Reform in Taiwan under Japanese Colonial Rule, 1895–1945: The Reception of Western Law*. Seattle: University of Washington Press, 1999. ProQuest Ebook Central.

Washington, Garrett L. "Editor's Introduction." In *Christianity and the Modern Woman in East Asia*, edited by Washington, 1–13. Leiden, the Netherlands: Brill, 2018. https://doi.org/10.1163/9789004369108.

Weber, Max. *The Protestant Ethic and the Spirit of Capitalism*. Translated by Talcott Parsons. 1930. Reprint, London: Routledge, 2005.

Weinbaum, Alys Eve, Lynn M. Thomas, Priti Ramamurthy, Uta G. Poiger, Madeleine Y. Dong, and Tani E. Barlow. "The Modern Girl as Heuristic Device." In *The Modern Girl around the World: Consumption, Modernity, and Globalization*, edited by Weinbaum, Thomas, Ramamurthy, Poiger, Dong, and Barlow, 1–24. Durham, NC: Duke University Press, 2008. ProQuest Ebook Central.

White, Bob W. "Talk about School: Education and the Colonial Project in French and British Africa (1860–1960)." *Comparative Education* 32, no. 1 (1996): 9–25. http://www.jstor.org/stable/3099598.

Wu Micha 吳密察, Huang Zhiwei 黃智偉, and Lin Xinyi 林欣宜. *Taiwan shi xiao shidian* 台灣史小事典 [Pocket dictionary of Taiwan history]. Taibei: Yuanliu Chuban Shiye Gufen Youxian Gongsi, 2000.

Wu Wenxing 吳文星. "Ri ju shiqi Taiwan de fangzu duanfa yundong" 日據時期臺灣的放足斷髮運動 [Unbound-feet and queue hair-cutting movement in Taiwan under Japanese occupation]. Originally published in *Zhongyang yanjiu yuan minzu xue yanjiu suo zhuankan yizhong zhi shiliu* 中央研究院民族學研究所專刊乙種之十六 [Academia Sinica Institute of Ethnology special issue B, no. 16 (June 1986)]. Reprinted in *Zhongguo funü shi lunwen ji di er ji* 中國婦女史論文第二集 [Collection of essays on the history of Chinese women], edited by Li Youning and Zhang Yufa, 465–510. Taibei: Taiwan Shangwu Yinshu Guan, 1988.

———. *Ri ju shiqi Taiwan shehui lingdao jieji zhi yanjiu* 日據時期臺灣社會領導階級之研究 [Study on Taiwanese elites under Japanese occupation]. Taibei: Wu'nan Shuju, 1992.

———. *Ri ju shiqi Taiwan shifan jiaoyu zhi yanjiu* 日據時期臺灣師範教育之研究 [Research on normal education in Taiwan under Japanese occupation]. *Guoli Taiwan shifan daxue lishi yanjiu suo zhuankan* (8) [National Taiwan Normal University Institute of History research journal]. Taibei: Guoli Taiwan Shifan Daxue Lishi Yanjiu Suo, 1983.

"Wu Zhuoliu 吳濁流." Taiwan da baike quanshu 臺灣大百科全書 [Encyclopedia of Taiwan]. Wenhua Bu (Ministry of Culture of Taiwan). Accessed August 6, 2018. http://nrch.culture.tw/twpedia.aspx?id=2219.

"Wu Zhuoliu 吳濁流." *Taiwan wenxue guan xianshang ziliao pingtai* 台灣文學館線上資料平台 [Taiwan Literature Museum online platform]. National Museum of Taiwan Literature. Accessed June 14, 2023. https://db.nmtl.gov.tw/site4/s6/writerinfo?id=458.

Xu Junya 許俊雅, ed. *Ri zhi sh qi Taiwan xiaoshuo xuandu* 日治時期台灣小說選讀 [Selected short fictions of Taiwan under Japanese rule]. Taibei: Wanjuanlo Tushu Gufen Youxian Gongsi, 2003.

———. *Taiwan wenxue luncong: Cong xiandai dao dangdai* 臺灣文學論叢 從現代到當代 [Essays on Taiwanese literature: From the modern to the contemporary period]. Taibei: Shida Shuyuan Youxian Gongsi, 1997.

Xu Peixian 許佩賢. *Zhimin di Taiwan de jindai xuexiao* 殖民地台灣的近代學校 [Modern schools in colonial Taiwan]. Taibei: Yuanliu Chuban She, 2005.

Xue Huayuan 薛化元. "Donyuan kanluan shiqi linshi tiaokuan" 動員戡亂時期臨時條款 [Temporary provisions during the period of the Communist rebellion]. In *Taiwan da baike quanshu* 台灣大百科全書 [Encyclopedia of Taiwan]. Last modified September 24, 2009. https://nrch.culture.tw/twpedia.aspx?id=3860.

Yang Cui 楊翠. "*Ai de jiejing* dao du" 《愛的結晶》導讀 [Interpretation of 'Beloved']. In *Ri ju yilai Taiwan nu zuojia xiaoshuo xuandu (shang)* 日據以來台灣女作家小說選讀(上) [Selected short fictions by women writers in Taiwan since Japanese occupation, vol. 1], edited by Qiu Guifen 邱貴芬, 60–63. Taibei: Nü Shu Wenhua Shiye Youxian Gongsi, 2001.

———. "Hai de nü'er 'Wu ji mu'—Geming nü doushi, Ye Tao" 海的女兒「烏雞母」– 革命女鬥士葉陶 [Daughter of the sea, "Black Hen"—Ye Tao the Revolutionary Woman Fighter]. In *Ama de gushi* 阿媽的故事 [Grandma's stories], ed. Jiang Wenyu, 36–49. Taibei: Yushan She Chuban, 1995.

———. *Ri ju shiqi Taiwan funü jiefang yundong: Yi Taiwan minbao wei fenxi changyu, 1920–1932* 日據時期臺灣婦女解放運動—以台灣民報為分析場域 1920–1932 [Taiwanese women's liberation movement under Japanese rule: Using Taiwan minbao as site of analysis (1920–1932)]. Taibei: Shibao Wenhua Chuban Qiye Youxian Gongsi, 1993.

Yang, Dominic Meng-Hsuan. *The Great Exodus from China: Trauma, Memory, and Identity in Modern Taiwan*. Cambridge: Cambridge University Press, 2020. https://doi:10.1017/9781108784306.

Yang Yahui 楊雅慧. "Zhan shi tizhi xia de Taiwan funü (1937–1945): Riben zhimin zhengfu de jiaohua yu dongyuan" 戰時體制下的臺灣婦女(1937–1945): 日本殖民政府的教化與動員 [Taiwanese women under wartime policy (1937–1945): The education and mobilization of the Japanese colonial government]. Master's thesis, Guoli Qinghua Daxue, 1993. https://hdl.handle.net/11296/xajk35.

Yasumura Kensuke 安村賢祐. *Nihon tōchi ka no Taiwan to Okinawa shusshin kyōin* 日本統治下の台湾と沖縄出身教員 [Teachers born in Taiwan and Okinawa under Japanese rule]. Minamijo: Yamaneko shuppan, 2012.

"Yoshioka Yayoi 吉岡弥生." *Kindai Nihonjin no Shōzō* 近代日本人の肖像 [Portrait of modern Japanese figures]. National Diet Library Japan. Accessed May 1, 2023. https://www.ndl.go.jp/portrait/datas/6045/.

Young, Louise. *Japan's Total Empire: Manchuria and the Culture of Wartime Imperialism*. Berkeley: University of California Press, 1998.

Yu Chien-ming (You Jianming) 游鑑明. "Ri zhi shiqi Taiwan xuexiao nüzi tiyu de fazhan." 日治時期臺灣學校女子體育的發展 [The development of female physical education in Taiwanese schools under Japanese rule]. *Zhongyang yanjiu yuan jindai shi yanjiu suo jikan* 中央研究院近代史研究所集刊 33 (2000): 1–75.

———. *Ri ju shiqi Taiwan de nüzi jiaoyu* 日據時期臺灣的女子教育 [Women's education in Taiwan under Japanese occupation, 1895–1945]. Taibei: Guoli Taiwan Shifan Daxue Lishi Yanjiu Suo, 1988.

———. "Ri ju shiqi Taiwan de zhiye funü" 日據時期台灣的職業婦女 [Professional Taiwanese women during the Japanese occupation period]. PhD diss., Guoli Taiwan Shifan Daxue, 1995.

Zhang Jingyi 張靜宜. *Zhan shi tizhi xia Taiwan teyong zuowu zengchan zhengce zhi yanjiu (1934–1944)* 戰時體制下臺灣特用作物增產政策之研究 (1934–1944) [The study of the policy on production increase of special crops in wartime Taiwan (1934–1944)]. Gaoxiong: Gaoxiong Fu Wen, 2007.

"Zhang Shuzi 張淑子." *Guojia wenhua jiyi ku* 國家文化記憶庫 [Taiwan Cultural Memory Bank]. Ministry of Culture of Taiwan. Accessed June 13, 2023. https://memory.culture.tw/Home/Detail?Id=606608&IndexCode=Culture_People.

Zhang Subi 張素碧. "Ri ju shiqi Taiwan nüzi jiaoyu yanjiu" 日據時期臺灣女子教育研究 [Research on women's education in Taiwan under Japanese occupation]. In *Zhongguo funü shi lunwen ji di er ji* 中國婦女史論文第二集 [Collection of essays on the history of Chinese women], edited by Li Youning and Zhang Yufa, 256–393. Taibei: Taiwan Shangwu Yinshu Guan, 1988.

Zheng Fengqin 鄭鳳晴. "Ri ju shiqi xin nüxing de zaixian fenxi: Yi meiti jishi yu xiaoshuo chuangzuo wei zhongxin" 日據時期新女性的再現分析：以媒體記事與小說創作為中心 [An analysis of the reproduction of the new woman under Japanese occupation: An examination of news articles and novels]. Master's thesis, Guoli Qinghua Daxue, 2008. https://hdl.handle.net/11296/48nau3.

Zheng Hanyun 鄭涵云. "Zhimin di Taiwan de funü zazhi *Taiwan furen jie* zhi yanjiu (1934–1939)" 殖民地臺灣的婦女雜誌《臺灣婦人界》之研究 (1934–1939) [Research of the women's magazine "Taiwan jujin kai" in colonial Taiwan (1934–1939)]. Master's thesis, Guoli Taiwan Shifan Daxue, 2017. https://hdl.handle.net/11296/w49yn7.

Zheng Xiumei 鄭秀美. "Ri zhi shiqi Taiwan funü laodong qun xiang" 日治時期臺

灣婦女勞動群相 (1895–1937) [Working women during the Japanese colonial rule in Taiwan (1895–1937). Master's thesis, Guoli Chenggong Daxue, 2007. https://hdl .handle.net/11296/cqt397.

Zhu Delan (Shu, Tokuran) 朱德蘭. *Taiwan sōtokufu to ianfu* 台湾総督府と慰安婦 [Office of the Governor-General of Taiwan and "comfort women"]. Tokyo: Akashi Shoten, 2005.

———. *Taiwan wei'anfu* 台灣慰安婦 [Taiwanese "comfort women"]. Taibei: Wunan tushu, 2009.

Zhuang Tianci 莊天賜. *Er ci dazhan xia de Taibei da kongxi* 二次大戰下的台北大空襲 [Major air raids in Taipei during World War II]. Taibei: Taibei Shi Zhengfu Wenhuaju Taibei Er-er-ba Ji'nianguan, 2007.

Zhuo Yiwen 卓意雯. *Qingdai Taiwan funü de shenghuo* 清代臺灣婦女的生活 [Life of Taiwanese women during the Qing dynasty]. Taibei: Zili Wanbao She Wenhua Chuban Bu, 2004.

Ziomek, Kirsten L. *Lost Histories: Recovering the Lives of Japan's Colonial Peoples.* Cambridge, MA: Harvard University Asia Center, 2019.

INDEX

Page numbers in *italics* refer to illustrations.

academic performance, 57, 119, 131, 179

activism: political, 19, 61, 75, 81, 82; women's, 73–74, 75, 76, 133

activities: collective, 117, 130; *dōka*, 74; gender-specific, 92, 110–11, 234n79; patriotic, 130, 131, 136, 203; war-support, 130; women's, 51

admission rates, 103, 192, 193, 206

Agricultural Education for Primary School, 119

agriculture, 28, 54, 98, 100, 137, 144; production, 22, 92, 96, 117, 118, 119, 120, 130; training in, 58, 119, 120, 138, 142; wartime, 118

air raids, 124, 125–26, 127, 128, 129, 131

Akebono (Shu) Primary School, 119, 126

Akiyoshi Otoji, 37, 38

Andō Rikichi, 230n10

anticolonialism, 40, 66–67, 75, 76, 79, 89

anti-foot-binding movement, 45, 110

Aoyama Women's Academy, 74

Arita Otomatsu, 51, 52

assimilation, 3, 45, 103, 104, 106, 107; civilizational, 66; cultural, 5, 54, 92, 95; *dōka* and, 5, 23, 137; French, 11; gendered, 4–11, 12, 14, 18, 59, 80, 88, 92, 93, 101, 130, 131, 137, 174, 196, 199; national, 66. See also *dōka*

Baozhu (in "Beloved Child"), 81, 82, 83

"Be Clean" (lesson), 36, 37

behavior, 33, 192, 196; corporal punishment and, 188; inappropriate, 156, 189; law-abiding, 197; moral/ethical, 200; patriotic, 95

"Beloved Child" (Ye), 81–82

"Better Wife, Wiser Mother" (article), 76

Bhabha, Homi, 4, 5, 45

Bissell, William Cunningham, 172, 173

"black cat," 62, 70, 73; and "good wife, wise mother" compared, 71; "modern girl" and, 72; "new woman" and, 89

Blessed Imelda's School, 228n57. *See also* Seishū (Jinxiu) Girls' Academy

Bren Gun Girl, 99

bride price, 12, 50, 83–84, 146, 158, 162

Bridge to Taiwan, 182, 206

Cai Jintang, 174

Cai Shitian, 38, 220n52

calligraphy, 28, 30, 185, 186, 218n20, 219n30

capitalism, 57, 71, 72, 75, 146; Christianity and, 10; colonial, 137

Chang, Doris, 75, 160

chastity, 78, 109, 156, 157, 190, 204

Chatani, Sayaka, 6, 11, 15, 96, 169

Chatterjee, Partha, 40

Chen Peifeng, 6, 65–66

Chen Peiting, 143, 144

Cheng Tun-jen, 224n100

Chiang Kai-shek, 245n18

childcare centers, 64, 161

child-rearing, 16, 60, 252n132

Chinese Civil War, 175, 195

Chinese Nationalists, 128, 131, 144, 181, 191, 192; colonialism and, 183; control by, 198, 200; corruption and, 20, 180; critique of, 183, 193, 194; discriminatory policies of, 177–78; education and, 178; nostalgia and, 196; rule of, 4, 143, 165, 169, 171, 175–77, 179, 197, 199, 204, 205, 207–10; teacher selection and, 195; 2-28 Incident and, 173–74. *See also* Kuomintang

Ching, Leo, 171, 174, 182, 198–99, 200, 205–6, 208, 250–51n104; on colonial violence, 206; cultural assimilation and, 95; kōminka and, 94; on materialization/assimilation, 96

Chou, Wan-yao, 54, 174, 231n20

Chu, Shui On, 180

civil servants, 150, 179, 180

civil service exams, 179, 246–47n37

civilization, 12, 20, 23, 35, 37, 58; colonial discourse on, 10; concepts of, 5, 6, 9; gendering levels of, 11, 36, 40–46, 48–49; modernization and, 66; nation-empire and, 49

civilizing mission, 7, 11, 23, 43, 58, 64

Classic of Filial Piety, 38

clothing, 44; Han, 32, 49, 103; Japanese, 46, 103; making, 140, 143, 203; Taiwanese, 103, 143; traditional, 42, 221n64; Western, 42, 106, 142, 143

Cold War, 144

colonial authority, 8, 15, 69, 84, 146, 226n22; criticism of, 79

colonial educators, 18, 23, 33, 110; gendered lessons and, 39, 46, 48, 49; "good wife, wise mother" and, 56, 58; love/marriage and, 153

colonialism, 45, 66, 90, 130, 184, 208; educational system and, 167; gender and, 79; Japanese, 19, 58, 62, 70–80, 86, 137, 145, 170–72; scientific, 35; stabilizing, 50; women's status and, 89

colonization, 3, 35, 55, 78, 106, 179; "good wife, wise mother" and, 88; Japanese, 11, 25, 57, 84, 137, 224n100; nation-empire and, 12; war and, 128

"Colorful Taiwanese Culture: Taiwanese Women, The" (series), 55

"comfort women," 97, 232n33

commerce, 28, 58, 137, 138, 145

"Compassionate Daughter" (lesson), 46, 48

Confucianism, 7, 33, 38, 147, 168

consumerism, 68, 70, 71, 73

cooking, 130, 150, 151, 152, 197; lessons, 123, 167

corporal punishment, 168, 170, 187, 195; behavior and, 188

corruption, 20, 176, 180, 207

"Crossing" (lesson), 43

culture, 150, 152, 199, 208, 209, 210; European, 14; Han Chinese, 76; Han Taiwanese, 76, 101; Japanese, 96, 166, 168, 169, 185

curriculum, 145, 180, 187, 253n144; Chinese Nationalist, 200; educational, 119, 137, 197; gendered, 26, 28, 58; Japanese, 2, 187; Sino-Han-centric, 209

customs: Han, 75, 86, 89, 159; Han Taiwanese, 19, 38, 65, 79, 110

Dai Liang, 41, 50, 221n59

Daikei (Daxi) Primary School, 112

"Daily Hygiene at Home" (Mishima), 44

Daitotei (Dadaocheng) Girls' Primary School, 43

Daminghao, (Ta ming pao), 176, 246n30

Dawley, Evan, 6, 15, 208

Daxi, 112, 121

"Delicious Meal I" (lesson), 46, 47

"Delicious Meal II" (lesson), 46, 47

democratization, 4, 198, 201, 208–9, 243n4

Department of Education (Chinese Nationalist government), 192

discrimination, 5, 87, 134, 185; education and, 131, 206; ethnic, 10; impartiality and, 66; institutional, 20, 176, 177; Japanese, 175–84

divorce, 68, 77; women-initiated, 51, 160, 161, 162

dōbun dōshu (same script, same race), 9

"Doctor" (lesson), 33, 35

Dojo (Tucheng) Primary School, 194

dōka, 42, 77, 103, 106–8, 137; achieving, 20, 38, 65, 138, 147; contradiction of, 59; dimension of, 79; education and, 8, 28, 58, 66, 90, 140, 198; gender and, 12, 17, 57–58, 109; goal of, 6; "good wife, wise mother" and, 4, 22, 88; implementing, 23, 45, 135, 186; inequality in, 95; interpretations of, 3; Japanese proficiency and, 56; Japanization and, 11, 18; modernization and, 23, 65, 79; national integration and, 5; nation-empire building and, 6, 10; opposition to, 15; race and, 9; successful, 49, 56, 80, 84, 96, 104; training of, 141. *See also* assimilation

Doll's House, A (Ibsen), 68

"Doll's Illness" (lesson), 33, 34

domesticity, 12, 13, 65, 73, 145, 189

Dower, John, 203

Du Pan Fangge, 148, 163–64

economic development, 54, 133, 144, 182

economic growth, 74, 135, 136, 178, 184

economic interests, 15, 88, 149, 158, 166

education, 3, 13, 26, 61, 132, 145; acceptance of, 62–80, 84, 90; advanced, 50, 219n27; agricultural, 120; childhood, 39, 65, 144; Chinese, 81, 83, 178, 199; Chinese Nationalist, 131, 185; civilized, 23, 43, 50, 65–66, 84; discrimination and, 206; *dōka* and, 58, 66, 90, 140, 198; gendered, 4, 8, 36, 76, 175; "good wife, wise mother" and, 55, 75; hobbies/culture and, 149–50; home, 15–16, 26, 38, 39, 41, 69–70; impact of, 18, 19, 54, 70, 79, 84, 133–34, 136; indigene, 9; Japanese, 3–4, 16, 19, 64, 122–24, 135, 142, 146, 147; lack of, 135, 193; levels of, 198; literacy, 11; modernization and, 45, 50, 62–80, 84, 134; physical, 109, 110, 111, 116; postprimary, 8, 160; postwar, 197; public, 4, 25, 133; responsibility for, 53; segregated, 9, 76, 185, 191; as status symbol, 136, 150; technical, 11; war and, 92, 93, 124; Western-style, 73; women's, 3–4, 19, 24, 57, 66, 67, 71, 76, 79, 88, 145, 169. *See also kokugo* education; primary education; secondary education

Education Ministry (Japan), 8

Educational Association of Taiwan, 219n27

educational opportunities, 28, 67, 134, 135, 167, 183; familial/compassionate, 185

Educational Ordinance Concerning Girls' Middle Schools, 26

Educational Ordinance of Taiwan (1919), 138, 154, 238n12

educational system, 166; colonial, 20, 167; critique of, 201; postwar, 205

Educational System Order (1872), 7

Emperor System, 10, 11

employment, 82, 83, 135, 158; gendered division of, 136; premarital, 70

Enomoto, Miyuki, 142, 218n20, 239n18

enrollment rates, 9, 63, 63, 64, 70, 89; elementary school, 25; gap in, 88–89; primary school, 62–63

ethics, 26, 54, 142, 198, 200, 202; imperial, 4, 21, 28, 148; lessons, 10, 152

INDEX

275

ethnic divisions, 20, 95, 170, 190–91
ethnicity, 2, 11, 16, 77, 93, 179; gender
    and, 80; Japanese, 46, 48; as marker,
    4; Taiwanese, 195; teacher, 78
Examination Yuan, 179, 180
exploitation: labor, 79, 89, 188, 190;
    sexual, 77, 78, 79, 89

Family Instructions of Zhu Xi, 38
Female Auxiliary Units, 98
feminism, 19, 62, 75, 76
First Attached School, 27
First Sino-Japanese War (1894–95), 9,
    25, 68
Food Bureau, 2
foot-binding, 49, 76; eradication of, 44,
    45, 110
"Four Seasons in the Countryside," 110
"Free Love? Is It for 'Good Wives,
    Wise Mothers'?" (*Taiwan nichinichi
    shimpō*), 51
Frühstuck, Sabine, 92–93
Fujin to katei, 43–44, 45, 222n67
Fukuzawa Yukichi, 53

games: competitive, 110, 111; gendered,
    33; marching/singing, 110
Games and Sports, 110
Gao Sumei, 115, 140, 200
Gao Zhuyuan, 160
gender, 3, 8, 16, 76, 78, 124; boundar-
    ies, 155, 170; colonialism and, 79;
    differences, 26, 81; division, 18, 20,
    95, 111, 170, 210; ethnicity and, 80;
    segregation, 132, 134, 135, 154–57, 162,
    168; status, 2, 4
gender roles, 20, 46, 93, 106, 111, 189;
    children and, 92; focus on, 33; Han
    Chinese, 18; Han Taiwanese, 12;
    modernization and, 36; normative, 23;
    reversed, 81

Ginling Women's College, 225n4
Giran (Yilan) Agriculture Vocational
    School, 56
Giran (Yilan) Girls' Primary School, 112
Girls' Attached School, 56, 234n76
Girls' Department (National Language
    School), 27, 154
"Girls' Middle School Students? Maids?"
    (*Taiwan minbao*), 78–79
girls' middle schools, 25, 75, 76, 141, 164,
    192, 194–95; education at, 28; house-
    wife training at, 26; number of, 27
Goldstein, Joshua S., 92
"good husbands, wise fathers," 33,
    54, 58
"Grandmother's Kokugo," 103, 104, 106
Great Learning, 38

hairstyles, 37; traditional, 5, 36, 42,
    221n64; (Manchu) queue, 5, 22, 36, 45,
    76; Western, 42
Hakka language, 57, 106, 148, 165, 180, 191
Han Taiwanese, 49, 57, 76, 94, 107, 165;
    cleanliness and, 36; girls' education
    and, 64; westernization of, 42
Han Taiwanese society, 9, 19, 23, 35, 83,
    90; backwardness of, 12; "good wife,
    wise mother" and, 2, 27; *kokugo* lan-
    guage and, 166
Hana (in "Grandmother's Kokugo"
    lesson), 103
handicrafts (shugei), 26, 27, 64, 141
handiwork (shukō), 28, 119, 137
Hara Takashi, 6
Hasegawa Kiyoshi, 107, 230n10
Havens, Thomas, 230n8
hierarchy: colonial, 18, 80, 184; ethnic, 11,
    17, 23, 59, 191, 210; family, 201; gender,
    11, 17, 18, 20, 23, 53, 59, 62, 79, 80, 89,
    90, 162; sociopolitical, 4
Hiromatsu Yoshiomi, 44

INDEX

276

Hoklo language, 17, 57, 147, 148, 165; learning, 191; names in, 14; speaking, 106, 180

Hokutō (Beitou) Primary School, 108, 113, 114, 115, 118, 119

home economics, 141, 144, 150; agricultural production and, 120; learning, 26, 29, 54, 138, 155; schools, 27, 91, 142

homemaking, 28, 40, 121; skills for, 50, 134, 167; training for, 22, 25–26, 58, 134, 137, 138, 139, 140, 151

Honda Mokichi, 43, 53

Hong Zhimei, 127, 128, 147, 190

"Hope for the Spread of Girls' Education: The Need to Establish Women's Normal Education" (*Taiwan minbao*), 70

Hōrai (Penglai) Girls' Primary School, 141

Hōrai (Penglai) Primary School, 56

Hōrai Society, 206, 251–52n130

household: control of, 54; "good wife, wise mother" and, 54; management, 16; marital, 152, 158; patriarchal, 135; responsibilities, 39; training, 29

housewives, 16, 26; preparing future, 40–41

Howe, Christopher, 248n59

Hsinchu. *See* Shinchiku

Hu Shi, 159

Hu Taiming (in *Orphan of Asia*), 60, 86–88

Huang Jinde, 187

Huiying (in "The Season When the Flowers Blossom"), 84–85

Hunan Women's No. 1 Normal School, 69

hygiene, 6, 87, 198, 220n48; importance of, 36, 37, 44

Ibsen, Henrik, 68

identity, 3, 9, 10, 17, 20, 197; ethnic, 252n138; national, 40, 209; native, 36;

Taiwanese, 101, 106, 173–74, 207, 208, 209, 210

Imperial Rescript on Education (Kyōiku Chokug), 7–8, 10, 38, 39; guidance from, 183; *kokugo* education and, 200; memorization of, 198, 205

imperialism, 5, 6, 93, 174; Euro-Americanism, 40; Japanese, 67, 94, 171, 184; wartime, 84

indigenes, 177, 180, 215n39, 215n40; Taiwanese, 9, 49, 137, 215n41

industrialization, 4, 8, 32, 57, 72, 118

isshi dōjin (impartiality, equal favor), 9

Izawa Shuji, 182, 248n62

Japan Women's College, 234n78

Japanese language, 17, 66, 202; discourse in, 28; proficiency in, 56, 165, 166, 169; purification of, 57; spread of, 38

Japanese spirit, 200, 203, 204; defining, 198–99; "good wife, wise mother" and, 30; *junjō* and, 205

Japaneseness, 7, 48, 49, 94

Japanization, 6, 49, 57, 66, 90, 96; avoiding, 65; *dōka* and, 18; replacing, 54

Jinling University, 61, 225n4

junjō, 203, 204, 205, 251n119

Kaibara Ekken, 24

Kakinuma Fumiaki, 56, 224n92

Kannonyama (Guanyinshan) Primary School, 189

Karyō (Guoling) Primary School, 1

Katō Harumasa, 101, 220n47

Katō Tadatarō, 21, 22

Ke Yuancheng, 41

Keh King-en, 177

Kensei (Jiancheng) Elementary School, 56

Kerr, George, 176

"Kimi ga yo," 106–7

INDEX

277

Kiryū Handicrafts Women's Private School, 239n18
Kito Eiji, 183
KMT. *See* Kuomintang
Knowing Taiwan (Renshi Taiwan), 209
knowledge, 14, 22, 119, 148, 168; high-level, 133–34; Japanese, 140, 168; practical, 137; scientific, 26, 39; transmission of, 32; Western, 140
Ko Ikujo (Hong Yuru), 65, 66, 134, 149, 226n26
Kobayashi Jun'ichi, 53, 224n94
Kobayashi Seizō, 94, 230n10
Kobayashi Yoshinori, 172, 200
kōgyōka (industrialization), 94
kokka (nation), 13–14, 66
kokugo, 5, 30, 59, 107, 202; campaign, 101, 102–3; proficiency in, 103, 108
kokugo education, 54, 177, 199; *dōka* and, 17, 59, 65, 147, 189, 191; gendering modernization in, 27–33, 35–39, 138; "good wife, wise mother" and, 152; hierarchy and, 11; home training and, 134; impartiality and, 183; Japanese language and, 154; mobilizing patriotic thinking through, 101–8; modernization and, 39; pollutants of, 57; romantic love and, 156; success of, 198; Taiwanese children and, 30; Taiwanese identity and, 106
"Kokugo Household," 102, *105*
kokugo language, 106, 166
kokugo no ie, 101, 102, 103, 104–6
"Kokugo no ie," (lesson), 101, 103
kokumin (modern national subjects), 25, 29, 30
Komagome Takeshi, 5
kōminka, 48, 106, 130, 174, 181; campaign of, 101, 102, 107, 108; movement, 94, 103, 179, 181; Taiwan and, 94–100

Kōra Tomi (Kōra Tomiko), 52, 53, 223n88
Koyama Shizuko, 24–26
Kuomintang (KMT), 174, 181, 195, 208

labor: agricultural, 96; child, 100, 189; Christianity and, 10; clerical/administrative, 99; colonial, 39; conscription, 98; construction, 96; domestic, 100, 189; exploitation of, 79, 89, 188, 190; female, 92, 93, 99; gendered, 18, 25, 30, 53–54; household, 2, 30, 64, 146, 189; industrial, 93, 98; manual, 79, 80, 117, 118; military, 96; mobilization of, 93, 118; outdoor, 120; schoolgirl, 116–24; unpaid, 100, 189; wartime, 92, 97, 98, 100
Lai Huazhu, 157, 158, 159
Lan Linlin, 155, 156, 161, 163, 165
Lan Qinhua, 119, 126, 199, 201
Law 63 (1896), 5
Li Piqing, 114, 115, 116, 121, 163, 242n91
Li Que'niang, 1, 2
Liang Qichao, 41, 68
Life Event: Marriage (Hu Shi), 159
Lin, Chin-ju, 242n87
Lin Cairong, 179
Lin Jiao'e, 132, 133, 140, 185–86, 198, 249n77
Lin Meihu, 241n47
Lin Shuangsui, 73, 74
Lin Tiantian, 119, 126, 156, 157, 160, 161, 163; narrative of, 188, 189
Lin Xianyan, 126, 130, 165, 178–79, 198, 203; agriculture and, 117–18; care packages and, 113; colonial policy and, 235n114; *junjō* and, 204; military training for, 108; narrative of, 109, 122; pure heart and, 251n125; sewing and, 121
Lin Yuzhu, 159–60, 241n68

literacy, 137, 147, 153, 163, 164; Chinese, 167; Japanese, 158

Liu, I-Chou, 209

Liu Duan, 151

Long Yingzong, 83–84, 88

Lorcin, Patricia M. E., 172, 174, 185, 244n6

love, romantic, 82, 153, 154, 156, 159, 160

loyalty, 39, 84, 94–95, 122, 130, 131; to emperor, 7, 24; national, 65; proclamation on, 38; showing, 111, 112, 177, 178, 198, 202, 205

Lü Jinwu, 69

Lü Lietong, 189

Lu Xun, 159

Lü Zhunju, 114, 147, 150–51, 197

Lynch, Daniel C., 253n144

MacArthur, Douglas, 250n103

Mackie, Vera, 204

Main Principles for Instructing Sewing and Home Economics in Primary School (manual), 139

(Manchu) queue hairstyle, 5, 22, 36, 45, 76

Mandarin Chinese, 17, 144, 165, 179, 180, 193

manners, 96, 108, 170, 173; cultivating, 196–205; teaching, 41

manufacturing, 98, 100, 140

March First Movement, 67

marriage, 143, 148, 149, 150–51, 152; arranged, 154, 160, 162, 166; early, 12, 83; economic gains and, 136; free-choice, 153, 159, 162, 163, 166, 168; home training and, 147; loveless, 84; marketability, 70; money and, 52; resisting, 61; romance and, 153–67, 168; transition to adulthood and, 85; working after, 65, 161

Marukawa, Tstsushi, 172

Masao (in "Kokugo no ie," lesson), 105

Matsuda, Hiroko, 250n92

Matsuyama Airport, 125

May Fourth Movement, 67

McNamara, Dennis, 248n59

Meiji period, 10, 13, 24, 25, 30, 53, 72; school system, 7

Meiji Primary School: cooking lesson at, 123; sewing lesson at, *121*

Mencius, 147

"Men's Duties and Women's Duties" (lesson), 202

Michio (in "Kokugo no ie," lesson), 101

Mikami Takatoshi, 189

military service: mobilization for, 97; Taiwanese men and, 95–96

military sex slaves ("comfort women"), 97, 232n33

Minato (Gang) Primary School, 114

Mishima Namaroku, 44, 222n70

Miyake, Yoshiko, 93

Miyazaki Naosuke, 56, 57, 225n104

Miyazaki Saiji, 183, 252n133

mobilization, 112, 116, 117, 127, 179, 204; economic, 93; female, 98, 99, 129–30; gendered, 88; labor, 93, 118; military, 93; rural youth, 15; wartime, 18–19, 26, 71, 85, 92–95, 97, 107, 120, 124, 130–32, 142, 146, 167

"modern girl," 52, 89; "black cat" and, 72; "new woman" and, 73

modernity, 7, 20, 139–40, 154, 182; Asian, 76; "good wife, wise mother" and, 48; Indian, 40; markers of, 33, 36

modernization, 6, 43, 48, 54, 58, 93; acceptance of, 49, 80; civilization and, 66; *dōka* and, 23, 65, 84, 90; education and, 62–80; gendering, 27–33, 35–39; hairstyles and, 45; Japanese, 5, 11, 181, 182, 183; success at, 40

Mōkō (Mengjia) Primary School, 21

Monopoly Bureau, 170, 245n17

INDEX

279

"Moon over the Ruined Castle," 110
motherhood, 13, 29, 39, 71
Mother's Love (Honda), 53
"Mountain March," 110

naichi enchō,(extending to the mainland), 6, 10
Naito Hisako, 86–87
Nakamura Masanao, 24
Nanjing Massacre, 184
nanshinka (southern expansion), 94
Naruse Jinzō, 234n78
nation-empire, 24, 43, 46, 71, 79, 93; building, 15, 39, 40, 50, 57, 66; civilization and, 49; colonization and, 12; defending, 122; *dōka* and, 6, 10; "good wife, wise mother" and, 130, 134; home and, 14; Japanese, 133, 139; loyalty to, 58
nation-state, 13, 66, 69, 95, 170, 205; building, 24
"National Anthem Boy," 106
National Eugenics Law, 230n7
National General Mobilization Law (1938), 97
National Language School (Kokugo Gakkō), 1, 27, 56, 154
National School Ordinance (Kokumin Gakkō Rei), 218n19
National Taiwan University, 177
nationalism, 5, 54; anticolonialism and, 40; Chinese, 65, 180; Korean, 73
nationality, 4, 66, 107, 182
neoconservatives, 174, 184, 200
nepotism, 176, 179, 180, 196, 207
Neri, Corrado, 210
New Culture Movement, 2–3, 87, 153, 159, 207; "good wife, wise mother" and, 68–69; women's movement and, 74

New Educational Ordinance of Taiwan (1922), 54, 55, 138, 141
New Imperialism, 4–11, 40
"new woman," 52, 71, 72, 87, 134; "black cat" and, 89; education of, 62, 70; emergence of, 51; "good wife, wise mother" and, 60–61; Korean, 73; "modern girl" and, 73
Nixon Shock (1970–72), 184
Nogi Shizuko (in "Women's Virtue" lesson), 202–3
Nora (in *A Doll's House*), 68, 69
normal schools, 24, 69, 86, 123, 127, 194; education at, 195; establishment of, 191–92
nostalgia: colonial, 19, 20, 170–73, 175–85, 187, 189, 190, 193, 195, 196, 200, 205–8; constructing, 175–84, 187, 188; gendered, 191; postcolonial, 171, 172, 173

Okayama Airport, 125
Okinawans, 191, 233n66
"On the Necessity of Female Learning" (Seosan), 41
Onna daigaku (Kaibara), 24
Opium War (1839–42), 9
oral histories, 16, 130–31, 152, 163, 166
Ordinance of Student Labor (1944), 117
Ordinance of the National Uniform of the Greater Japanese Empire (1940), 114–15
Orphan of Asia (Wu Zhuoliu), 60–61, 76, 86, 87
Othered, 9
Ou Zongzhi, 80
Outline for Education in the Decisive Battle, 126

Pacific War, 107, 117, 125
patriarchy, 62, 75, 90, 135, 160, 162; women and, 81, 89

INDEX

280

Patriotic Higher Handcrafts Women's Academy, 239n18

patriotic songs, 112, 113

patriotic spirits, 113, 130

patriotism, 7, 111, 112, 115, 116, 205; feminine, 121; gendered, 108; Japanese, 96, 121, 130, 131; mobilizing, 101–8

"Peach Boy," 165, 243n97

"Persuading Girls to Attend School" (Ke), 41

political change, 74, 208

political developments, 67, 133

political rights, women's, 19

postal service, 10, 30, 32

"Postal Service" (lesson), 30–31, 31

primary education, 8, 50, 69, 140, 145; colonial, 58, 138; completing, 3, 135, 141, 158; enrollment in, 27; ideal woman and, 24; impact of, 167; motherhood and, 29; receiving, 7; segregation of, 9, 10, 26; years of, 28

Primary School Ethics Textbook, 202

Primary School Ordinance (Kōgakkō Rei), 28, 30, 238n12

Primary School Organization Regulations of Taiwan, 154

primary schools, 1, 2, 30, 141, 145, 149; enrollment rates at, 64; girls' education in, 120; hours of instruction at, 55; indigene, 9, 215n39; number of, 63; Taiwanese, 9, 63, 186, 187, 215n39, 218n19; tuition for, 240n41

propaganda, 99, 109, 125, 126

prostitution, 78, 146, 159, 227n33

public health, 36, 145

Public Service Association of Imperial Subjects (Kōmin Hōkō Kai), 126

pure heart, term, 251n125

purity, 78, 198, 204, 251n125; sexual, 156; spiritual, 203

Qing rule, 63–64, 134, 140–41, 149, 161, 191

Ranyō (Lanyang) Girls' Middle School, 1–2, 149, 155

reading, 28, 30, 96, 105, 137, 219n30

Red Army, 98

Reddy, William M., 153, 160

relationships: colonizer-colonized, 174; extramarital, 161–62; familial, 195; personal, 195; romantic, 158, 168; teacher-student, 77; women-home, 93

Revised Primary School Regulation (1907), 28

ribunjinshin, 199, 251n104

romance, marriage and, 153–67

Romance of the Three Kingdoms, 147, 148

Rosie the Riveter, 99, 100

Russo-Japanese War (1904–5), 9, 72, 120

Said, Edward, 14

"Sayo's Bell" (lesson), 107

schoolgirls: agriculture and, 120; economic exploitation of, 79; mobilization of, 108–16, 116–24; patriotic, 29; roles of, 92; sexual exploitation of, 77, 78, 79

science, 6, 31, 35, 150

"Season When Flowers Blossom, The" (Yang Qianhe), 60, 84

Second Sino-Japanese War (1937–45), 125, 195

secondary education, 26, 53, 54, 117, 141, 145; value of, 150

segregation, 5; educational, 9, 76, 183, 185, 191; ethnic, 8, 10, 60; gender, 17, 27, 64, 132, 134, 154, 155, 156–57, 158, 162, 168; "good wife, wise mother" and, 132; racial, 8, 60

Seira (Xilio) Primary School, 108, 111, 119, 126

INDEX

Seishū (Jinxiu) Girls' Academy, 144, 228n57
Seishū (Jinxiu) Girls' Middle School, 53
Sejrup, Jens, 210
senninbari, 117, 120, 121, 124, 236n131
Seosan Gyodō, 41
sewing, 146, 152, 153, 155, 167, 197; Han/non-Han Taiwanese, 139; lesson, 121; skills in, 136; styles of, 139, 141, 142; textbooks, 140; training for, 26, 28, 13, 132–34, 137–38, 143–44
sexual assault, student-teacher, 77
sexual harassment, 78, 190
Shi Suyun, 141, 144, 155, 162, 239n24
Shimadu Kenpō, 206, 251n129
Shinchiku (Hsinchu), 97, 110, 117, 155, 221n55; bombing of, 15
Shinchiku (Hsinchu) Airport, 125
Shinchiku (Hsinchu) Girls' Middle School, 112, 155
Shinchiku (Hsinchu) Girls' Primary School, 40, 41, 64
Shinchiku (Hsinchu) Station, 155
Shinten Minami (Xindian Nan) Primary School, 119
Shintō, 7, 94
Shizangan spirit, 182, 183
Shuchun (in *Orphan of Asia*), 51, 60, 87, 88
Shulin Elementary School, 194
shūshin (imperial ethics), 200, 201, 202, 203, 205
Silverberg, Miriam, 72
Sinicization, 165, 180, 181
skills: abacus, 167; arithmetic, 148; cooking, 167; cultivating, 196–205; education and, 86; feminine, 121; homemaking, 50, 134, 167; housewife, 152; letter-writing, 131; manual labor,

10, 118; practical, 137, 148, 196; sewing, 167; vocational, 152
social change, 72, 74, 184, 208
social critiques, 80, 173
social expectations, 140, 157, 168, 197
social ills, 171, 200, 202
social networks, 85, 124, 158, 159
social rights, women's, 19
social status, 137, 164, 186
socioeconomic status, 22, 36, 68, 71, 119, 124; *dōka* and, 3; educational/professional opportunities and, 16; examining, 2; gender and, 8; home training and, 153; markers of, 4; reinforcing, 150, 152; term, 238n7; women and, 19, 35
"Steam" (lesson), 31, 32
stereotypes, racial, 10, 45
Student Labor Law (1944), 97, 117
Su, Ya-Chen, 247n55
Suh, Jiyoung, 73
suicide, 83, 84, 160, 164
Sun Moon Lake Electricity Plant, 125
Sun Yat-sen, 180–81
Suying (in "Beloved Child"), 81, 82, 83
Suzuki Uemon, 46
Suzuki Yuzusaburo, 53, 54

Tai, Eika, 5, 184
Taichū (Taichung) Girls' No. 2 Middle School, 108, 118, 122, 126, 178
Taichū (Taichung) Middle School, 163–64, 226n22
Taichung (Taichū), 126, 127, 157, 221n55, 249n87
Taihoku (Taipei), 53, 97, 103, 117, 123, 182
Taihoku (Taipei) Girls' Common Middle School, 44
Taihoku (Taipei) Girls' Middle School, 37

Taihoku (Taipei) Girls' No. 1 Middle School, 123, 201
Taihoku (Taipei) Girls' No. 2 Middle School, 53
Taihoku (Taipei) Girls' No. 3 Middle School, 27, 127, 129, 141, 148, 150, 162
Taihoku (Taipei) Higher Elementary School, 43
Taihoku (Taipei) Prefecture, 106, 218n20
Taihoku Commercial School, 125
Taihoku National Language School, 223n81
Taihoku No. 2 Middle School, 194
Taihoku No. 1 Normal School, 123
Taihoku No. 2 Normal School, 56
Taihoku Normal School (Taihoku Shihan Gakkō), 86
Taihoku Railway Factory, 125
Taihoku Tobacco Factory, 125
Taihoku Women's Higher Academy, 61, 239n18
Taihoku Women's Professional Private School, 239n1
Taikakan (Dakekan) Primary School, 110
Tainan Airport, 125
Tainan Elementary School, 206
Tainan Home Economics Sewing Training School, 239n18
Tainan Home Economics Women's Academy, 239n18
Tainan Prefecture, schools in, 218n20
Tainan Presbyterian Girls' Academy, 228n57
Taipei, 91, 114, 118, 128, 129, 141; bombing of, 125
Taiwan Business School, 83
Taiwan Cultural Association (Taiwan Bunka Yōkai), 67
Taiwan Educational Ordinance (Taiwan Kyōku Rei), 54

Taiwan Farmers' Association, Women's Section of, 81
Taiwan fujinkai, 53, 56, 224n92
Taiwan kyōiku, 29, 38, 43, 50, 69, 219n27
Taiwan kyoikukai zasshi, 29, 41
Taiwan minbao, 64, 67, 68, 69, 70, 74, 76, 77, 78
Taiwan New Literature, 81
Taiwan nichinichi shimpō, 21, 28, 55, 60, 65, 69
Taiwan Political Reconstruction Association, 176
Taiwan Popular Party, 67
Taiwan Primary School Regulation, 202
Taiwan ron (Yoshinori Kobayashi), 172
Taiwan seinen, 67, 69, 74, 146, 227n28
Taiwan Women, Inc., 224n92
Taiwan xin minbao, 67–68
Takagi Heitarō, 40, 41, 221n55
Takao (Kaohsiung), 112, 115, 125
Takao Branch (Women's Patriotic Association), 115
Takao Bridge, 112
Takashi Fujitani, 95, 179
"Taking Medicine" (lesson), 34; described, 32–33
Tamsui, 123, 127, 128, 129, 147
Tamsui Elementary School, 193
Tamsui Girls' Academy, 137, 228n57
Tamsui Middle School, 228n57
Tanahashi Gentarō, 28–29
Tanaka, Stefan, 9
Tanaka Kurō, 237n158, 252n133; article by, 44–45
Tanaka Yujirō, 38, 44
Tang Yanyan, 118, 146, 147
Tansui (Tamsui) Boys' Primary School, 113
Tansui (Tamsui) Elementary School, 113
Tansui (Tamsui) Girls' Academy, 129

INDEX

283

Tansui (Tamsui) Girls' Primary School, 113

Tantō (Taitung) Elementary School, 251n129

teacher-training programs, 70, 86, 191–92, 206, 219n27, 220n52, 248n62

textile industry, 143–44

Third Attached School, 154

Three Principles of the People (Sun), 180–81

Tokyo Women's Higher Normal School, 24, 144, 239n24

Tomiyama Ichirō, 108

Torao (Huwei) Girls' Middle School, 200

"Town with Papaya Trees, The" (Long), 83–84

Tōyama Waketsuyoshi, 182

training: agricultural, 142; bodily/physical, 108; business, 142; educational, 8, 147; female, 109, 130, 146; gendered, 39, 54, 137–39, 154; "good wife, wise mother" and, 22–23, 25, 29, 38–39, 58, 82–83, 124, 133, 134, 136, 137–53, 167–68; home, 134, 141, 147, 153; home-making, 22, 25–26, 58, 134, 137–40, 151; industrial, 142; military, 109, 116, 124; programs, 191, 248n62; self-defense, 109; vocational, 8, 10, 11, 138, 141, 142; wartime, 93, 97

transportation, 32, 98, 125, 145

Tsuruko (in *Orphan of Asia*), 87

tuberculosis, 81, 82, 83

2-28 Incident, 144, 173–74, 175, 209, 245n17, 245n18

Uchida, Jun, 6, 15

Ueda Sumio, 182

Ueno Hiroko, 164

unemployment rates, 176, 178

Uno, Kathleen, 13

urbanization, 6, 71, 118

virtues, 37, 46, 48, 92, 114, 122; children's, 49; Confucianism, 7–8; feminine, 22, 50–51, 52, 108, 109, 137, 141, 166, 168; gender segregation and, 157; moral/ethical, 198, 199; motherly, 93; school-girl, 203, 204, 205; superior, 201

vocational schools, 141, 142, 192

Wakamatsu Primary School, 125

Walder, Dennis, 171, 172

Wang, T. Y., 209

Wang Feimei, 163, 242n90

Wang Lingyi, 241n68

Wang Zhirui, 243n97

Washington, Garrett L., 228n56

Watanabe Yaeko, 182

"Waving the Japanese Flag," 110

Weber, Max, 10

"When Flowers Blossom" (Yang Qianhe), 88

White Terror, 245n18

Wilson, Woodrow, 67

womanhood, 73, 74; "good wife, wise mother" and, 12–13; ideal, 15–16, 17, 22, 23, 38, 50–57, 65, 76, 80–88, 98; modern, 13, 39, 58, 59; republican, 12; wartime, 99

Women's Agriculture School, 239n18

Women's Army Corps, 99

Women's Commerce School, 239n18

Women's Labor Volunteer Corps, 98

women's liberation, 44, 68, 69, 74; campaign for, 134; "good wife, wise mother" and, 73, 89; participation in, 75–76; social reform and, 86

Women's Patriotic Association, 115

women's rights, 76, 89, 159

Women's Section (Taiwan Farmers' Association), 81

women's social rights, 19

"Women's Virtue" lesson, 202–3

Wu Sheng, 194–95, 250n100

Wu Surong, 112, 113, 131; on Japanese spirit, 194; on Japanese teachers, 178, 185; *senninbari* and, 121

Wu Taiming (in *Orphan of Asia*), 61, 62, 76

Wu Wenxing, 45, 186–87, 189, 192

Wu Zhuoliu, 60, 62, 86, 88, 89

Xia Yujia, 157, 246n26, 246n29, 249n87

Xin qingnian, 68

Xinlou Girls' School, 137

Xu Junya, 85–86

Xu Kuidi, 108, 111, 119, 126

Xu Peixian, 54

Xu Xianxian, 91, 148, 157

Yang, Dominic, 252n139

Yang Cui, 75

Yang Jiyin, 41, 221n61

Yang Kui, 81

Yang Qianhe, 60, 61, 62, 84, 85, 88

Yang Yahui, 93

Yasukani Shrine, 171

Yasumura Kensuke, 191

Ye Tao, 81–82, 83, 84, 88

Yilan (Giran), 1, 132, 147, 149, 151, 155

Yilan Provincial Hospital, 2

Ying Xinrui, 108, 113, 116, 118, 119, 122

Yoshimi Sewing Private Academy, 239n18

Young, Louise, 93

Yū (in "Kokugo no ie," lesson), 105

Yu Chien-ming, 74, 134, 234n76

Yūichi (in "Kokugo no ie," lesson), 101, 102, 104–5

yukata, 42, 141

Zeng Chamei, 128

Zeng Jinjin, 158, 159, 241n63

Zeng Qinglian, 161

Zeng Xiuying, 181–82, 187

Zeng Yuanyuan, 185

Zhan Dekun, 106, 107

Zhang Hongchou, 55–56, 225n101

Zhang Shuzi, 50, 51

Zhang Subi, 133, 134

Zhang Taishan, 181–82, 193

Zhang Wojun, 227n28

Zhang Yue'e, 149, 155, 156, 157, 160

Zheng Rongrong, 163, 242n91

Zhou Dengxin, 29

Zhou Lianyu, 122, 170–71, 200

Zhou Yingying, 127, 193, 194, 201

Zhu Qiufeng, 113, 123, 127, 128, 129, 131, 147

TAIWAN AND THE WORLD

Good Wife, Wise Mother: Educating Han Taiwanese under Japanese Rule, 1895–1945, by Fang Yu Hu

Taiwan Lives: A Social and Political History, by Niki J. P. Alsford